The
NIV HARMONY
of the
GOSPELS

with Explanations and Essays

Using the Text of the
NEW INTERNATIONAL VERSION

ROBERT L. THOMAS
EDITOR

STANLEY N. GUNDRY
ASSOCIATE EDITOR

A Revised Edition of the John A. Broadus and
A. T. Robertson Harmony of the Gospels

HarperSanFrancisco
A Division of HarperCollins*Publishers*

NEW INTERNATIONAL VERSION A HARMONY OF THE GOSPELS Copyright © 1988 by Robert L. Thomas and Stanley N. Gundry. All rights reserved. Printed in the United States of America. No part of this book may be used or reproduced in any manner whatsoever without written permission except in the case of brief quotations embodied in critical articles and reviews. For information address HarperCollins Publishers, 10 East 53rd Street, New York, N.Y. 10022.

Library of Congress Cataloging-in-Publication Data

Bible. N.T. Gospels. English. New International. 1988.
    The NIV harmony of the Gospels.

    1. Bible. N.T. Gospels—Harmonies, English.
I. Thomas, Robert L., 1928–   . II. Gundry,
Stanley N., 1937–
BS2553.N48   1987   226'.1   86–43023
ISBN 0–06–063523–1

03 04 05 06 HAD 25 24 23 22

TABLE OF CONTENTS

PREFACE TO THE 1988 REVISION

The roots of this *Harmony* extend deep into the soil of nineteenth-century biblical scholarship. The renowned John A. Broadus began teaching the life of Jesus in 1859. At the suggestion of his colleague A. T. Robertson, in 1893 he published the fruit of these thirty-plus years of instruction. Robertson himself began offering the same course in 1888, and after thirty-four years published his own *Harmony*, which was a revision of Broadus's work. In the meantime Robertson had prepared notes for the end of Broadus's first edition and had published a minor revision of Broadus's work in 1903. This lineage of gospel harmonies has gone through many printings and has been a powerful force in the church of Jesus Christ through the decades of the twentieth century.

One of the reasons for this widespread influence is that Broadus blazed a trail that has been followed by many twentieth-century harmonists. Rather than trying to force an issue and make the feasts into turning points in Christ's ministry, as had his predecessors, he organized Jesus' ministry into well-defined periods according to a gradual progress in three realms: in Jesus' self-manifestation, in the hostility of his enemies, and in the training of the Twelve. This new approach, as Broadus noted in his preface in 1893, facilitated an understanding of "the *inner movements* of the history, towards that long-delayed, but foreseen and inevitable collision, in which, beyond all other instances, the wrath of man was made to praise God."

Robertson built upon Broadus's successful endeavor with his 1922 revision by refining, expanding, and updating the work of his former mentor. It is the purpose of this 1988 revision to build upon Robertson's revision and fine tune the work even more in the light of more than six decades of Christian thought that have passed since the popular revision was first published.

The current work, for one thing, attempts a greater precision in defining the "inner movements" of Jesus' life. This is done through the subdivision of some of the longer sections into smaller, more manageable portions. For convenience, however, Robertson's paragraph numbers have been retained and assigned lowercase suffixes, such as *a, b, c,* to indicate subdivisions. Also, explanatory footnotes of historical and geographical features, of theological and chronological relationships, and of a variety of other matters have been multiplied in this revision. These enable a reader to focus quickly upon major themes in the process of their unfolding.

The Broadus-Robertson proposed divisions of Christ's life have been retained because of their accuracy. Differences in viewpoint about the placement of a few sections, however, are reflected in the footnotes of this revision. In such cases the placement of the text remains the same as is found in Robertson, with the preferences of the revisers indicated by bracketed section titles and Scripture references only. Another difference from Robertson lies in the choice of section titles. In practically all cases a new title that more accurately portrays the substance of the section's content has been assigned.

Perhaps the greatest expansion in our revision lies in the reworking of Robertson's "Notes on Special Points," found at the end of his *Harmony*. Criticism of the gospels and of specific features in them has been the focal point of New Testament scholarship through the middle six decades of this century. Discussion generated by this activity has necessitated a thorough reworking of these, even to the point of isolating new topics to which the essays (no longer "notes") are devoted. A selected reading list appears at the conclusion of each of these twelve essays, so that those interested in pursuing the subjects further have suggested resources.

Another marked difference from the earlier works is the Bible translation employed. In place of the English Revised Version (1881) of Broadus's *Harmony* and Robertson's *Harmony*, the New International Version has been chosen for this revision. This version is a fresh translation into smoothly flowing contemporary English that provides insights into the gospels that have often been veiled from those less familiar with the Old English style of the Revised Version.

Other aspects of this *Harmony* are explained in "Explanation of the *Harmony's* Format and Features," and their resemblance to or difference from Robertson can be observed by those familiar with this time-honored work. Two broad comparisons are worthy of special note here. First, Broadus's column sequence for listing the texts has been followed. From left to right, it is Matthew, Mark, Luke, John. This varies from the order of Robertson, who reversed Matthew and Mark because he thought Mark wrote first and Matthew depended on him. After more than a century of popularity, the theory of Marcan priority is encountering a declining acceptance and, in the opinion of the revisers, has little to commend it in comparison with the more traditional view of Matthean priority. Hence the reversion to Broadus's sequence.

The second comparison lies in eschatological perspective. Occasionally Broadus and Robertson reflected the amillennial or postmillennial temperament of their times. The twentieth century has witnessed a surge of interest in the premillennial interpretation of Scripture. It is the persuasion of the revisers that a consistent grammatical-historical interpretation of the Bible inevitably leads to this latter view. For this reason several of the explanatory footnotes reflect a corresponding difference in perspective from the earlier editions.

Besides the text of the *Harmony*, a number of other features have been incorporated. An outline of the *Harmony*, which follows the probable chronological sequence of Christ's life, follows this Preface. The same outline is woven into the body of the *Harmony*. A glance at this outline reflects when various events occurred in relation to each other. Whenever possible, the geographical location of each event is given in the body of the *Harmony*. The maps at the close of the volume provide a means of identifying these places in relation to the rest of Palestine. The sources of Old Testament quotations have also been included, as have notes clarifying some of the New International Version renderings.

Sections of the *Harmony* that bear a special resemblance to other sections have also been noted in the *Harmony* proper. All section cross-references are listed in the "Table of Section Cross-References" found at the back of the volume. This table also notes what the points of similarity between sections are. The "Tables for Finding Passages in the *Harmony*" facilitates the locating of any passage in the *Harmony* by listing the passages according to chapter and verse sequence. Time lines for the whole Life of Christ, the Ministry of Christ, and Passion Week have also been included for the sake of showing broad chronological relationships.

A harmony of the gospels provides an important means for studying the four gospels at one time. Though it could never completely replace the four gospels studied individually, it is an indispensable tool for gaining a well-rounded overview of Jesus' life in all its facets. The editors have geared this work to provide such an overview for those studying in a college or seminary. Yet a serious student of Scripture studying privately and without a familiarity with New Testament Greek will be able to follow the discussion easily. Detailed and technical issues belonging to more advanced levels of scholarship have not, of course, been included in the work.

In recent years the practice of harmonization has received increasing criticism in some scholarly circles. Even some who are evangelical have wondered about its legitimacy. Needless to say, we make no apologies for this *Harmony*, because we have confidence in the historical accuracy of the events recorded in the gospels. If they are historically accurate, they are in principle harmonizable into a historical sequence that can be read and studied with profit by followers of Jesus Christ. Christianity is a faith that is solidly anchored in history. It requires such an exposition of its historical foundation as is provided by a harmonization of the gospels.

A prolonged exposure to the person of Jesus Christ is inevitable when one studies a harmony of the gospels. Such exposure is bound to enhance appreciation for him. When we appreciate him more, we will serve him more faithfully and glorify him more consistently. May God grant this as the fruit of his servants' labors.

Sun Valley, CA
Grand Rapids, MI

ROBERT L. THOMAS
STANLEY N. GUNDRY

PREFACE TO THE 1922 REVISION

It is now just thirty years since one day his young assistant suggested to Dr. John A. Broadus that he prepare a harmony of the Gospels that should depart from the old plan of following the feasts as the turning points in the life of Jesus. He acted on the hint and led the way that all modern harmonies have followed. The book has gone through a dozen large editions and has become the standard harmony for many thousands of students all over the world. Broadus was concerned to bring out "the *inner movements* of the history, towards that long-delayed, but foreseen and inevitable collision, in which, beyond all other instances, the wrath of man was made to praise God." This he succeeded in doing with marvelous power.

A generation has passed by and it is meet that the work of Broadus should be reviewed in the light of modern synoptic criticism and research into every phase of the life of Christ. So I have made a new analysis that preserves Broadus's real purpose, but with new sections and new notes. The notes at the end of the old volume, written by me for the first edition, have been thoroughly revised and brought up to date. The Old Testament passages referred to in the Gospels are given in the text. The Gospel of Mark appears in the first column, then Matthew, Luke, and John. It is now known that Matthew and Luke made use of Mark for the framework of their Gospels. This change simplifies amazingly the unfolding of the narrative.

There is still dispute concerning the historical worth of the Gospel of John, but the Johannine authorship is not disproved. It still holds the field in my opinion. Dr. C. F. Burney's theory of an Aramaic original is already giving a new turn to Johannine criticism.

A harmony of the Gospels cannot meet every phase of modern criticism. The data are given, as free from bias as circumstances allow, so that all students can use the book and interpret the facts according to their various theories. Numerous historical items call for notes of various kinds that throw light on the passage in question. No effort is made to reconcile all the divergent statements of various details in the different Gospels. The differences challenge the student's interest as much as the correspondences and are natural marks of individual work. The notes and appendices at the end of the volume are meant for students who wish help for historical study of the life of Christ. A harmony cannot

9

give all the aid that one needs, but it is the one essential book for the serious study of the life of Jesus. Students in colleges, theological seminaries, Young Men's Christian Association and Young Women's Christian Association classes, Sunday School teachers and pupils, preachers, all who read the Gospels intelligently must have a modern harmony of the Gospels. One who has never read a harmony will be amazed at the flood of light that flashes from the parallel and progressive records of the life of Jesus Christ.

Broadus began teaching the life of Jesus in 1859 and kept it up till his death in 1895. I began like work in 1888 and have kept on without a break till now. I count it one of the crowning mercies of my life that I have led so many successive classes of young ministers and young women (some five thousand in all) through the study of Christ's life. If only one can pass on to others in all their freshness and power the teachings of Jesus, he cannot fail. There was a time when men hung in wonder upon the words of Jesus, listening with awe and rapture as he spoke. The Figure of Christ fills the world today as never before. Back to Christ the world has come, the Christ of Faith and of Experience, the Jesus of History, the Man of Galilee, the Hope of Today, the Jesus Christ of the Four Gospels in the full blaze of modern critical and historical study.

Louisville, Kentucky   A. T. ROBERTSON.

PREFACE TO THE 1903 REVISION

It has been ten years since Dr. Broadus issued his Harmony, which has already gone through six editions. This has seemed a fitting time to give the book a close revision. Some important changes have been made in the notes at the end of the book. Dr. Broadus' Harmony was the first one to depart from the traditional division of the ministry of Christ by the Passovers rather than by the natural unfolding of the ministry itself. He also introduced an Analytical Outline into the body of the Harmony in italics, made cross references to similar incidents or sayings, had helpful summaries at the beginning of each of the General Divisions (Parts), preserved the marginal notes of the Revised Version, which is the text used, and added at suitable points very valuable footnotes that helped the student to seize the movement of the history. The plan of his Harmony is to give the best helps for historical study. The Gospel material is arranged in the order accepted by the best New Testament scholars, but difficulties at various points are freely recognized and indicated. The student at least has a working basis to start with.

In accordance with this conception of the Harmony some further helps are added in this Revised Edition. An excellent map of Palestine is furnished, the Analytical Outline is put by itself in front as well as preserved in the body of the text, the cross references to similar incidents and sayings are added in a separate appendix, besides being preserved in the text, Dr. Broadus' "Analysis and Peculiarities of the Gospel" is given in an appendix, besides new lists of the Parables, Miracles, Old Testament Quotations, Uncanonical Sayings of Jesus, and a list of the chief Harmonies. References to the sections and pages of the Harmony go with those appendices. There is added, moreover, a full Index of Persons and Places which will be helpful. There is also the usual Synopsis with tables for finding passages. It is believed that this Harmony thus offers peculiar advantages to the student engaged in historical study. Dr. Broadus' work in the volume is the ripe fruit of a lifetime of rich study and reflection by one of the rarest teachers of the New Testament that any age or country has ever seen.

Southern Bapt. Theol. Seminary,   A. T. ROBERTSON.
Louisville, Ky., Jan. 1, 1903.

PREFACE TO THE 1893 EDITION

This work is the fruit of more than thirty years spent in teaching the English New Testament. I first used as a text-book the Harmony of Dr. Ed. Robinson, and for some twenty years past that of Dr. G. W. Clark. Both are valuable works, deserving their wide reputation. But I have become more and more convinced that most harmonists seriously err in laying stress on the division of our Lord's ministry into Passover years. It is quite impossible to determine with any great confidence whether the feast of John 5:1 was a passover, and the two known passovers of John 2:13 and 6:4 have really no important relation to the development of our Lord's ministry. Besides, the length of his ministry, and the dates of his birth and death, cannot be precisely fixed. But cease to labor for an exact chronology, quit regarding the feasts (except the last Passover) as important epochs in his work, and you presently perceive that his ministry divides itself easily into well-defined periods, in each of which you can trace a gradual progress, (a) in our Lord's self-manifestation, (b) in the hostility of his enemies, and (c) in his training of the Twelve Apostles. Thus we become able to follow the inner movements of the history, towards that long-delayed, but foreseen and inevitable collision, in which, beyond all other instances, the wrath of man was made to praise God.

The chief marks of this historical progress in the Life of our Lord I have tried to indicate by brief foot-notes, and other notes in italic letters placed here and there between the sections. Many of these brief notes also touch various points of harmonizing, of chronology, and other matters, so that the reader may quickly get the most important necessary information or help, and move forward. Questions requiring more elaborate discussion have been treated by my colleague, Dr. A. T. Robertson, in longer notes placed at the end of the volume, which in my judgment are remarkably complete and discriminating, and will greatly aid the careful student.

It has seemed best to print the Harmony in the Revised Version, commonly known as the Canterbury, or Anglo-American Revision, which is nowadays given in many lesson helps and commentaries along with the Common or King James translation. In printing this revised text some use has been made of Waddy's Harmony.

Probably most persons look upon a Harmony of the Gospels as useful only to Bible class work or other regular forms of study. But I invite any one who takes pleasure in reading his Bible to try the experiment of reading this Harmony as a connected and complete Life of Christ, moving steadily on through the successive periods, and striving to come ever nearer to him as our Teacher, Exemplar, Redeemer, Lord. It is hoped also that Y.M.C.A. classes, in Colleges and elsewhere, may in many cases like to take up a series of lessons in that great Life, which is the focus of human history, and the centre of Scripture. When Sunday School lessons are taken from any one of the Gospels, it is an important advantage for all teachers, and the more intelligent pupils, to compare every such lesson with the other Gospels as presented in a Harmony; while for regular lessons on the Life of Christ a Harmony is indispensable to thorough treatment. In Theological Seminaries, not merely students who use only the English Bible, but those who study the Gospels in Greek, would be much profited by first making a survey of the Harmony in English. And no minister can afford to prepare a sermon on any text from a Gospel without looking up the parallel passages from other Gospels, and also considering where his text stands in the gradual unfolding of the Saviour's teaching and work.

Southern Bapt. Theol. Seminary,   J.A.B.
Louisville, Ky., June 15, 1893.

AN ANALYTICAL OUTLINE FOR *The NIV HARMONY OF THE GOSPELS*

16

18

Part Nine: The Ministry of Christ in and Around Perea

PRINCIPLES OF DISCIPLESHIP

TEACHING WHILE ON FINAL JOURNEY TO JERUSALEM

Part Ten: The Formal Presentation of Christ to Israel and the Resulting Conflict

TRIUMPHAL ENTRY AND THE FIG TREE

EXPLANATION OF THE *HARMONY*'S FORMAT AND FEATURES

1. THE TEXT OF THE GOSPELS The text of one, two, three, or four gospels, depending on how many describe each episode, is found on each page of the *Harmony*. The gospel text is arranged in columns, and material in each column is placed so as to be adjacent to similar material in other columns. The width of the columns varies in accordance with how many gospels record the events of each section. The order of the gospels, from left to right, is the same as that in the modern editions of the New Testament.

2. SECTION NUMBERS The text of the gospels has been divided into sections and arranged in a probable chronological sequence. Each section has been assigned a number that appears in Arabic numerals at the beginning of each section heading. The numbering system is based on A. T. Robertson's *Harmony*, the 1922 revision of earlier John A. Broadus editions of the *Harmony*. In every case this new edition follows the sequence preferred by A. T. Robertson and assigns the same Arabic numerals to the sections. In some cases, however, Robertson's sections are too long and unwieldy. The editors have subdivided these sections, retained Robertson's section numbers, and added suffix letters to the numbers to indicate the subdivisions. Thus where Robertson simply had a Section 8, this edition has Section 8a, Section 8b, and Section 8c. As a result this edition can be used with other works based on the Robertson numbering system, but the student can deal with smaller units of text, units that more accurately reflect the natural divisions within the texts of the gospels.

3. SECTION TITLES Each section has been assigned a title. The titles are intended to be analytical and descriptive. The editors have not felt bound to use the wording of Robertson's section headings, just as Robertson himself was not bound by the headings in the earlier Broadus editions of the *Harmony*.

4. SECTION CROSS-REFERENCES WITH POINTS OF SIMILARITY Just after some section titles are parenthetical notations begun by the abbreviation *cf.* and followed by other section numbers and a brief description of the point of similarity. These are sections that contain features in some way similar to the section where the cross-reference is in-

dicated. The "Table of Section Cross-References" on pp. 329–32 summarizes the points of similarity between all sections.

5. GEOGRAPHICAL NOTATIONS Below most section titles is a word or phrase set off by dashes, indicating the place where the events of that section took place.

6. SCRIPTURE REFERENCES Just above each column in the *Harmony* are the book name, chapters, and verses. These tell which biblical passage is found in that column.

7. OLD TESTAMENT QUOTATIONS The sources of quotations from the Old Testament are shown in brackets immediately after each quotation. The brackets indicate that these Old Testament references are not part of the NIV text itself, but are inserted into the text by the editors of the *Harmony* and express their own judgment. The perceptive reader will notice that frequently these same Old Testament references are also found in the NIV textual notes collected at the end of each section. The committee that controls the text of the NIV requires that in a work such as this *Harmony*, the textual notes be printed in their entirety, regardless of possible redundancy.

8. NIV TEXT NOTES AND FORMAT FEATURES Superscript italic letters within the text (which follow the words with which they belong) refer to notes from the NIV translators dealing with such matters as alternate translations and uncertainty regarding the original text. Some sources of quotations from the Old Testament are also given in these notes. The NIV text notes are collected at the end of each *Harmony* section. These are related to the NIV text in the section above by book-chapter-verse notations, or by verse only whenever book and chapter are not needed for easy location.

To achieve clarity of style, the NIV translators sometimes supplied words not in the original texts but made necessary by the context. When there is uncertainty about such material, it is enclosed in brackets.

In the NIV prose is printed in paragraph form (rather than in verse divisions), and poetical passages are printed as poetry (that is, with indentations of lines and with separate stanzas). The *Harmony* preserves this format so far as possible, but the required rearrangements of material in a harmony sometimes make it impossible for paragraphs to be preserved as united wholes in one location.

9. EXPLANATORY FOOTNOTES Superscript boldface letters within the text or a heading (which precede the words with which they belong) refer to notes at the foot of the page. The explanatory notes, written by the revising editors, contain information especially helpful in harmonistic and comparative study of the gospels and the life and ministry of Jesus Christ. On occasion the revising editors also use

them to explain how and why they disagree with A. T. Robertson's judgments on parallel passages and chronological sequence. Because this edition is a revision of Robertson's *Harmony* published in 1922, it seemed best to retain Robertson's original arrangement and sequence of gospel materials and to place the revising editors' disagreements in the footnotes.

10. ALTERNATE CHRONOLOGICAL SEQUENCE When the revising editors differ with Robertson regarding chronological sequence, the alternate placement of a passage is indicated in the body of the *Harmony* by the section title and Scripture references enclosed in brackets. The text itself is not reprinted in such instances.

A HARMONY OF THE GOSPELS

PART ONE
A PREVIEW OF WHO JESUS IS

Sec. 1 Luke's purpose in writing a gospel

Luke 1:1–4

[1a]Many have undertaken to draw up an account of the things that have been fulfilled[a] among us, [2]just as they were handed down to us by those who from the first were eyewitnesses and servants of the word. [3]Therefore, since [b]I myself have carefully investigated everything from the beginning, it seemed good also to me to write an orderly account for you, most excellent Theophilus, [4]so that you may know the certainty of the things you have been taught.

[a]1 Or *been surely believed*

Sec. 2 John's prologue: Jesus Christ, the preexistent Word incarnate

John 1:1–18

[1]In the beginning was the Word, and the Word was with God, and the Word was God. [2]He was with God in the beginning. [3]Through him all things were [c]made; without him nothing was made that has been made. [4]In him was life, and that life was the light of men. [5]The light shines in the darkness, but the darkness has not understood[a] it.
[6]There [c]came a man who was sent from God; his name was John. [7]He came as a witness to testify concerning that light, so that through him all men might believe. [8]He himself was not the light; he came only as a witness to the light. [9]The true light that gives light to every man was coming into the world.[b]
[10]He was in the world, and though the world was made through him, the world did not recognize him. [11]He came to that which was his own, but his own did not receive him. [12]Yet to all who received him, to those who believed in his name, he gave the right to become children of God— [13]children born not of natural descent,[c] nor of human decision or a husband's will, but born of God.
[14]The Word [c]became flesh and made his dwelling among us. We have seen his glory, the glory of the One and Only,[d] who came from the Father, full of grace and truth.
[15]John testifies concerning him. He cries out, saying, "This was he of whom I said, 'He who comes after me has surpassed me because he was before me.' "
[16]From the fullness of his grace we have all received one blessing after another.

---

[a](Luke 1:1) Recognizing that other second-generation Christians had already undertaken a similar task, Luke joined them in producing an account of Christ's life. His reason for doing so was apparently inadequacies in the other efforts, at least insofar as they failed to meet Theophilus' need. If Luke had been aware of the works by Matthew or Mark, it is doubtful that he would have viewed either of them in this light. He would not have looked on either as the work of another noneyewitness, nor would he have been likely to imply he could improve on them. His sources therefore are best restricted to oral and written tradition, which has been long ago replaced by the canonical gospels.

[b](Luke 1:3) Luke, probably the only Gentile writer of Scripture (cf. Col. 4:11, 14), is responsible for two books, Luke and Acts. These are the two longest books in the New Testament. From the standpoint of volume, then, Luke is the most prolific New Testament writer, even though Paul and John each wrote more books.

[c]John seems to organize his introduction around four significant happenings, each referred to by a use of the Greek verb *egeneto*: the creation (1:3), the coming of the forerunner John (1:6), the incarnation of Christ (1:14), and the crucifixion of Christ (1:17). These four reflect the progress of the gospel as it moves toward its climax in the passion of Christ.

29

John 1:1–18 (cont'd)

[17]For the law was given through Moses; grace and truth [c]came through Jesus Christ. [18]No one has ever seen God, but God the One and Only,[de] who is at the Father's side, has made him known.

[a]Jn 1:5 Or *darkness, and the darkness has not overcome*   [b]9 Or *This was the true light that gives light to every man who comes into the world*   [c]13 Greek *of bloods*   [d]14,18 Or *the Only Begotten* [e]18 Some manuscripts *but the only* (or *only begotten*) *Son*

[d]Sec. 3   Jesus' legal lineage through Joseph and natural lineage through Mary

Matthew 1:1–17	Luke 3:23b–38
[1]A record of the genealogy of Jesus Christ the son of David, the son of Abraham:	He was the son, so it was thought, of Joseph,

[2]Abraham was the father of Isaac, Isaac the father of Jacob, Jacob the father of Judah and his brothers,
[3]Judah the father of Perez and Zerah, whose mother was Tamar, Perez the father of Hezron, Hezron the father of Ram,
[4]Ram the father of Amminadab, Amminadab the father of Nahshon, Nahshon the father of Salmon,
[5]Salmon the father of Boaz, whose mother was Rahab, Boaz the father of Obed, whose mother was Ruth, Obed the father of Jesse,
[6]and Jesse the father of King David.

David was the father of Solomon, whose mother had been Uriah's wife,
[7]Solomon the father of Rehoboam, Rehoboam the father of Abijah, Abijah the father of Asa,
[8]Asa the father of Jehoshaphat, Jehoshaphat the father of Jehoram, Jehoram the father of Uzziah,
[9]Uzziah the father of Jotham, Jotham the father of Ahaz, Ahaz the father of Hezekiah,
[10]Hezekiah the father of Manasseh, Manasseh the father of Amon, Amon the father of Josiah,
[11]and Josiah the father of Jeconiah[a] and his brothers at the time of the exile to Babylon.

the son of Heli, [24]the son of Matthat, the son of Levi, the son of Melki, the son of Jannai, the son of Joseph, [25]the son of Mattathias, the son of Amos, the son of Nahum, the son of Esli, the son of Naggai, [26]the son of Maath, the son of Mattathias, the son of Semein, the son of Josech, the son of Joda, [27]the son of Joanan, the son of Rhesa, the son of Zerubbabel, the son of Shealtiel, the son of Neri, [28]the son of Melki, the son of Addi, the son of Cosam, the son of Elmadam, the son of Er, [29]the son of Joshua, the son of Eliezer, the son of Jorim, the son of Matthat, the son of Levi, [30]the son of Simeon, the son of Judah, the son of Joseph, the son of Jonam, the son of Eliakim, [31]the son of Melea, the son of Menna, the son of Mattatha, the son of Nathan, the son of David, [32]the son of Jesse, the son of Obed, the son of Boaz, the son of Salmon,[c] the son of Nahshon, [33]the son of Amminadab, the son of Ram,[d] the son of Hezron, the son of Perez, the son of Judah, [34]the son of Jacob, the son of Isaac, the son of Abraham, the son of Terah, the son of Nahor, [35]the son of Serug, the son of Reu, the son of Peleg, the son of Eber,

[d]For discussion of the two genealogies, see essay 9 at the back of this volume (pp. 304–10).

Matthew 1:1–17 (cont'd)

¹²After the exile to Babylon:
Jeconiah was the father of Sheal-
tiel,
Shealtiel the father of Zerubba-
bel,
¹³Zerubbabel the father of Abiud,
Abiud the father of Eliakim,
Eliakim the father of Azor,
¹⁴Azor the father of Zadok,
Zadok the father of Akim,
Akim the father of Eliud,
¹⁵Eliud the father of Eleazar,
Eleazar the father of Matthan,
Matthan the father of Jacob,
¹⁶and Jacob the father of Joseph,
the husband of Mary, of whom
was born Jesus, who is called
Christ.

¹⁷Thus there were fourteen genera-
tions in all from Abraham to David,
fourteen from David to the exile to Babylon, and fourteen from the exile to the
Christ.^b

Luke 3:23b–38 (cont'd)

the son of Shelah, ³⁶the son of Cai-
nan,
the son of Arphaxad, the son of
Shem,
the son of Noah, the son of Lamech,
³⁷the son of Methuselah, the son of
Enoch,
the son of Jared, the son of Mahala-
lel,
the son of Kenan, ³⁸the son of
Enosh,
the son of Seth, the son of Adam,
the son of God.

---

^aMt 1:11 That is, Jehoiachin; also in verse 12   ^b17 Or *Messiah*. "The Christ" (Greek) and "the
Messiah" (Hebrew) both mean "the Anointed One."   ^cLk 3:32 Some early manuscripts *Sala*
^d33 Some manuscripts *Amminadab, the son of Admin, the son of Arni*; other manuscripts vary widely.

PART TWO
THE EARLY YEARS OF JOHN THE BAPTIST

Sec. 4   John's birth foretold to Zechariah
(cf. Secs. 5, 9—foretelling a miraculous birth)
—Jerusalem, in the temple—

Luke 1:5–25

⁵ᵉIn the time of Herod king of Judea there was a priest named Zechariah, who belonged to the priestly division of Abijah; his wife Elizabeth was also a descendant of Aaron. ⁶Both of them were upright in the sight of God, observing all the Lord's commandments and regulations blamelessly. ⁷But they had no children, because Elizabeth was barren; and they were both well along in years.

⁸Once when Zechariah's division was on duty and he was serving as priest before God, ⁹he was ᶠchosen by lot, according to the custom of the priesthood, to go into the temple of the Lord and burn incense. ¹⁰And when the time for the burning of incense came, all the assembled worshipers were praying outside.

¹¹Then an angel of the Lord appeared to him, standing at the right side of the altar of incense. ¹²When Zechariah saw him, he was startled and was gripped with fear. ¹³But the angel said to him: "Do not be afraid, Zechariah; your prayer has been heard. Your wife Elizabeth will bear you a son, and you are to give him the name John. ¹⁴He will be a joy and delight to you, and many will rejoice because of his birth, ¹⁵for he will be great in the sight of the Lord. He is never to take wine or other fermented drink, and he will be filled with the Holy Spirit even from birth. *ᵃ* ¹⁶Many of the people of Israel will he bring back to the Lord their God. ¹⁷And he will go on before the Lord, in the spirit and power of Elijah, to turn the hearts of the fathers to their children [Mal. 4:6] and the disobedient to the wisdom of the righteous—to make ready a people prepared for the Lord."

¹⁸Zechariah asked the angel, "How can I be sure of this? I am an old man and my wife is well along in years."

¹⁹The angel answered, "I am Gabriel. I stand in the presence of God, and I have been sent to speak to you and to tell you this good news. ²⁰And now you will be silent and not able to speak until the day this happens, because you did not believe my words, which will come true at their proper time."

²¹Meanwhile, the people were waiting for Zechariah and wondering why he stayed so long in the temple. ²²When he came out, he could not speak to them. They realized he had seen a vision in the temple, for he kept making signs to them but remained unable to speak.

²³When his time of service was completed, he returned home. ²⁴After this his wife Elizabeth became pregnant and for five months remained in seclusion. ²⁵"The Lord has done this for me," she said. "In these days he has shown his favor and taken away my disgrace among the people."

ᵃLk 1:15 Or *from his mother's womb*

ᵉ(Luke 1:5) At 1:5 Luke departs from the idiomatic, classical Greek writing style found in Luke 1:1–4. His accounts of the early years of John and Christ (Luke 1:5—2:52) are distinctly Hebraistic Greek, probably due to the Aramaic sources on which he depended for that material. Then, too, he knew well the Hebraic style from the Septuagint and from his associations with Paul. Good indications exist that much in these first two chapters of the third gospel came from Mary, the mother of Jesus, or some oral and written tradition traceable to her.

ᶠ(Luke 1:9) Because of the large number of priests like Zechariah, he probably was called on to perform this daily service only once in his life. This obligation of representing Israel on such a rare occasion doubtless weighed heavily on the shoulders of this righteous man.

Sec. 5   Jesus' birth foretold to Mary
(cf. Secs. 4, 9—foretelling a miraculous birth)
—Nazareth—

Luke 1:26–38

[26]In the sixth month, God sent the angel Gabriel to Nazareth, a town in Galilee, [27]to a virgin pledged to be married to a man named Joseph, a descendant of David. The virgin's name was Mary. [28]The angel went to her and said, "Greetings, you who are highly favored! The Lord is with you."

[29]Mary was greatly troubled at his words and wondered what kind of greeting this might be. [30]But the angel said to her, "Do not be afraid, Mary, you have found favor with God. [31]You will be with child and give birth to a son, and you are to give him the name Jesus. [32]He will be great and will be called the Son of the Most High. The Lord God will give him the [g]throne of his father David, [33]and he will reign over the house of Jacob forever; his kingdom will never end."

[34]"How will this be," Mary asked the angel, "since I am a [h]virgin?"

[35]The angel answered, "The Holy Spirit will come upon you, and the power of the Most High will overshadow you. So the holy one to be born will be called[a] the Son of God. [36]Even Elizabeth your relative is going to have a child in her old age, and she who was said to be barren is in her sixth month. [37]For nothing is impossible with God."

[38]"I am the Lord's servant," Mary answered. "May it be to me as you have said." Then the angel left her.

[a]Lk 1:35 Or *So the child to be born will be called holy,*

Sec. 6   Mary's visit to Elizabeth and Elizabeth's song
(cf. Secs. 7, 8b, 13—song because of a miraculous birth)
—Judean hills—

Luke 1:39–45

[39]At that time Mary got ready and hurried to a town in the hill country of Judea, [40]where she entered Zechariah's home and greeted Elizabeth. [41]When Elizabeth heard Mary's greeting, the baby leaped in her womb, and Elizabeth was filled with the Holy Spirit. [42]In a loud voice she exclaimed: "Blessed are you among women, and blessed is the child you will bear! [43]But why am I so favored, that the mother of my Lord should come to me? [44]As soon as the sound of your greeting reached my ears, the baby in my womb leaped for joy. [45]Blessed is she who has believed that what the Lord has said to her will be accomplished!"

[g](Luke 1:32) The language Gabriel uses undoubtedly reflects the strong Old Testament belief in the earthly rule of Israel's Messiah. Just as David, from whom Mary was descended, had a throne located on earth, so will the One whose miraculous birth is promised to Mary. Unlike David's kingdom, however, Jesus' kingdom will be endless (Luke 1:33).

[h](Luke 1:34) Among New Testament writers, only Luke (in this section) and Matthew (Sec. 9) directly teach the virgin birth of Jesus. Galatians 4:4 probably does not refer to this specific teaching. John 1:13 apparently refers to this belief indirectly by using language related to the virgin birth when describing the new birth of Christians. Since earliest times in the history of the church this doctrine has been an integral part of orthodox Christianity.

Sec. 7   Mary's song of joy
            (cf. Secs. 6, 8b, 13—song because of a miraculous birth)
            —*Judean hills*—

Luke 1:46–56

⁴⁶And Mary said:

"ᶦMy soul glorifies the Lord
⁴⁷   and my spirit rejoices in God my Savior,
⁴⁸for he has been mindful
       of the humble state of his servant.
From now on all generations will call me blessed,
⁴⁹   for the Mighty One has done great things for me—
       holy is his name.
⁵⁰His mercy extends to those who fear him,
       from generation to generation [Psalm 103:17].
⁵¹He has performed mighty deeds with his arm;
       he has scattered those who are proud in their inmost thoughts.
⁵²He has brought down rulers from their thrones
       but has lifted up the humble.
⁵³He has filled the hungry with good things [Psalm 107:9]
       but has sent the rich away empty.
⁵⁴He has helped his servant Israel,
       remembering to be merciful
⁵⁵to Abraham and his descendants forever,
       even as he said to our fathers."

⁵⁶Mary stayed with Elizabeth for about three months and then returned home.

Sec. 8a   John's birth
             —*Judean hills*—

Luke 1:57–66

⁵⁷When it was time for Elizabeth to have her baby, she gave birth to a son. ⁵⁸Her neighbors and relatives heard that the Lord had shown her great mercy, and they shared her joy.

⁵⁹On the eighth day they came to circumcise the child, and they were going to name him after his father Zechariah, ⁶⁰but his mother spoke up and said, "No! He is to be called John."

⁶¹They said to her, "There is no one among your relatives who has that name."

⁶²Then they made signs to his father, to find out what he would like to name the child. ⁶³He asked for a writing tablet, and to everyone's astonishment he wrote, "His name is John." ⁶⁴Immediately his mouth was opened and his tongue was loosed, and he began to speak, praising God. ⁶⁵The neighbors were all filled with awe, and throughout the hill country of Judea people were talking about all these things. ⁶⁶Everyone who heard this wondered about it, asking, "What then is this child going to be?" For the Lord's hand was with him.

ᶦ(Luke 1:46) This song has frequently been called "The Magnificat," a title derived from the first word of the Latin translation of it. This "vocal meditation" of Mary recalls the type of literature found in the Old Testament Psalms. Mary describes God's actions with seven past tense (Greek aorist tense) verbs (1:51–54). From the nature of the circumstances, however, it is obvious that these are anticipations of what God would do in the future through the child in her womb. Hence these verbs are probably "prophetic aorists" after the analogy of the Hebrew "prophetic perfect."

Sec. 8b Zechariah's prophetic song
(cf. Secs. 6, 7, 13—song because of a miraculous birth)
—*Judean hills*—

Luke 1:67–79

[67]His father Zechariah was filled with the Holy Spirit and prophesied:

[68]"ʲPraise be to the Lord, the God of Israel,
  because he has come and has redeemed his people.
[69]He has raised up a horn[a] of salvation for us
  in the house of his servant David
[70](as he said through his holy prophets of long ago),
[71]salvation from our enemies
  and from the hand of all who hate us [Psalm 106:10]—
[72]to show mercy to our fathers
  and to remember his holy covenant,
[73] the oath he swore to our father Abraham:
[74]to rescue us from the hand of our enemies,
  and to enable us to serve him without fear
[75] in holiness and righteousness before him all our days.

[76]And you, my child, will be called a prophet of the Most High;
  for you will go on before the Lord to prepare the way for him [Mal. 3:1],
[77]to give his people the knowledge of salvation
  through the forgiveness of their sins,
[78]because of the tender mercy of our God,
  by which the rising sun will come to us from heaven
[79]to shine on those living in darkness
  and in the shadow of death [Isa. 9:1–2],
  to guide our feet into the path of peace."

[a]Lk 1:69 *Horn* here symbolizes strength.

Sec. 8c John's growth and early life
—*Judean desert*—

Luke 1:80

[80]And the child grew and became strong in spirit; and he lived in the desert until he appeared publicly to Israel.

---

[j](Luke 1:68) "Benedictus" is the name often applied to this song because this is the first word of the song in Latin. Here is a literary form modeled after the Old Testament prophecies. Like Mary, Zechariah anticipates the redemption and salvation of his nation Israel from the enemy's oppression (1:68, 71). In line with this hope, he alludes to three prominent covenants (agreements or contracts) God made with his people: the Abrahamic (1:72–74; cf. Gen. 15:12–21; 17:7; Psalm 105:8–9), the Davidic (1:69–71; cf. 1 Sam. 2:10; 2 Sam. 7:8–17; Psalm 89), and the New (1:77; cf. Jer. 31:31–34). Of course, Messiah's political deliverance (1:68–74) is inseparable from a moral preparation of his people (1:75–79). Zechariah's son, the forerunner of Messiah, was commissioned to accomplish this latter task (1:76–79).

PART THREE
THE EARLY YEARS OF JESUS CHRIST

Sec. 9 Circumstances of Jesus' birth explained to Joseph
(cf. Secs. 4, 5—foretelling a miraculous birth)
—Nazareth—

Matthew 1:18–25

[18]This is how the birth of Jesus Christ came about: His mother Mary was pledged to be married to Joseph, but before they came together, she was [k]found to be with child through the Holy Spirit. [19]Because Joseph her husband was a righteous man and did not want to expose her to public disgrace, he had in mind to divorce her quietly.

[20]But after he had considered this, an angel of the Lord appeared to him in a dream and said, "Joseph son of David, do not be afraid to take Mary home as your wife, because what is conceived in her is from the Holy Spirit. [21]She will give birth to a son, and you are to give him the name Jesus,[a] because he will save his people from their sins."

[22]All this took place to fulfill what the Lord had said through the prophet: [23]"The virgin will be with child and will give birth to a son, and they will call him Immanuel"[b] [Isa. 7:14]—which means, "God with us."

[24]When Joseph woke up, he did what the angel of the Lord had commanded him and took Mary home as his wife. [25]But he had no union with her until she gave birth to a son. And he gave him the name Jesus.

[a]Mt 1:21 *Jesus* is the Greek form of *Joshua*, which means *the LORD saves*.   [b]23 Isaiah 7:14

Sec. 10   Birth of Jesus
—Bethlehem—

Luke 2:1–7

[1]In those days Caesar Augustus issued a [l]decree that a census should be taken of the entire Roman world. [2](This was the first census that took place while Quirinius was governor of Syria.) [3]And everyone went to his own town to register.

[4]So Joseph also went up from the town of Nazareth in Galilee to Judea, to Bethlehem the town of David, because he belonged to the house and line of David. [5]He went there to register with Mary, who was pledged to be married to him and was expecting a child. [6]While they were there, the time came for the baby to be born, [7]and she gave birth to her firstborn, a son. She wrapped him in cloths and placed him in a manger, because there was no room for them in the inn.

---

[k](Matt. 1:18) Because Mary probably stayed with Elizabeth until after the birth of John (Luke 1:56), Joseph had not seen her for about four months. By the time of her return her pregnancy was obvious, so that Joseph was forced to do one of two things, either have Mary stoned (Deut. 22:23–27) or divorce her privately. He had already decided on the latter course when the angel came and explained the unique situation. As a righteous man, Joseph had not yet considered what the angel suggested, that is, proceeding with the marriage arrangements. When informed of the nature of the conception, however, he dismissed all thoughts of divorce.

[l](Luke 2:1) Luke, perhaps because of his special attention to Jesus' humanity, is anxious to locate his life in the mainstream of human history. His chronological notations, such as those in 2:1–2, are part of this effort (see essay 11, pp. 315–19 for more discussion of chronology). At one time opponents of biblical infallibility criticized the accuracy of Luke's historical notations in this paragraph, but a careful study of ancient history and archaeological discoveries has overwhelmingly vindicated his reliability. Objections to Luke's accuracy have pertained particularly to the dating of Quirinius' governorship in Syria, but with further research, satisfactory answers to these have surfaced. (For further discussion, see Harold W. Hoehner, *Chronological Aspects of the Life of Christ* [Grand Rapids: Zondervan, 1977], pp. 13–23.)

Sec. 11　Praise of the angels and witness of the shepherds
—*Fields near Bethlehem*—

Luke 2:8–20

[8]And there were shepherds living out in the fields nearby, keeping watch over their flocks at night. [9]An angel of the Lord appeared to them, and the glory of the Lord shone around them, and they were terrified. [10]But the angel said to them, "Do not be afraid. I bring you good news of great joy that will be for all the people. [11]Today in the town of David a Savior has been born to you; he is Christ[a] the Lord. [12]This will be a sign to you: You will find a baby wrapped in cloths and lying in a manger."
[13]Suddenly a great company of the heavenly host appeared with the angel, praising God and saying,

[14]"Glory to God in the highest,
　and on earth peace to men on whom his favor rests."

[15]When the angels had left them and gone into heaven, the shepherds said to one another, "Let's go to Bethlehem and see this thing that has happened, which the Lord has told us about."
[16]So they hurried off and found Mary and Joseph, and the baby, who was lying in the manger. [17]When they had seen him, they spread the word concerning what had been told them about this child, [18]and all who heard it were amazed at what the shepherds said to them. [19]But [m]Mary treasured up all these things and pondered them in her heart. [20]The shepherds returned, glorifying and praising God for all the things they had heard and seen, which were just as they had been told.

[a]Lk 2:11 Or *Messiah*. "The Christ" (Greek) and "the Messiah" (Hebrew) both mean "the Anointed One"; also in verse 26.

Sec. 12　Circumcision of Jesus
—*Bethlehem*—

Luke 2:21

[21]On the eighth day, when it was time to circumcise him, he was named Jesus, the name the angel had given him before he had been conceived.

Sec. 13　Jesus presented in the temple with the homage of Simeon and Anna (cf. Secs. 6, 7, 8b—song because of miraculous birth)
—*Jerusalem*—

Luke 2:22–38

[22]When the time of their purification according to the Law of Moses had been completed, Joseph and Mary took him to Jerusalem to present him to the Lord [23](as it is written in the Law of the Lord, "Every firstborn male is to be consecrated to the Lord"[a]) [Exod. 13:2,12], [24]and to offer a sacrifice in keeping with what is said in the Law of the Lord: "a pair of doves or two young pigeons"[b] [Lev. 5:11; 12:8].
[25]Now there was a man in Jerusalem called Simeon, who was righteous and devout. He was waiting for the consolation of Israel, and the Holy Spirit was upon him. [26]It had been revealed to him by the Holy Spirit that he would not die before he had seen the Lord's Christ. [27]Moved by the Spirit, he went into the temple courts.

[m]Luke 2:19 is one of the strong indications that Mary, the mother of Jesus, was a principal source of Luke's information found in the early chapters of his gospel.

Luke 2:22–38 (cont'd)

When the parents brought in the child Jesus to do for him what the custom of the Law required, [28]Simeon took him in his arms and praised God, saying:

[29]"Sovereign Lord, as you have promised,
    you now dismiss[c] your servant in peace.
[30]For my eyes have seen your salvation,
[31]   which you have prepared in the sight of all people,
[32]a light for revelation to the Gentiles [Isa. 42:6; 49:6],
    and for glory to your people Israel."

[33]The child's father and mother marveled at what was said about him. [34]Then Simeon blessed them and said to Mary, his mother: "This child is destined to cause the falling and rising of many in Israel, and to be a sign that will be spoken against, [35]so that the thoughts of many hearts will be revealed. And a sword will pierce your own soul too."

[36]There was also a prophetess, Anna, the daughter of Phanuel, of the tribe of Asher. She was very old; she had lived with her husband seven years after her marriage, [37]and then was a widow until she was eighty-four.[d] She never left the temple but worshiped night and day, fasting and praying. [38]Coming up to them at that very moment, she gave thanks to God and spoke about the child to all who were looking forward to the redemption of Jerusalem.

[a]Lk 2:23 Exodus 13:2,12   [b]24 Lev. 12:8   [c]29 Or promised, / now dismiss   [d]37 Or widow for eighty-four years

[**Return to Nazareth**

°Luke 2:39]

Sec. 14   Visit of the Magi
    —*Jerusalem and Bethlehem*—

Matthew 2:1–12

[1]After Jesus was born in Bethlehem in Judea, during the time of King [p]Herod, Magi[a] from the east came to Jerusalem [2]and asked, "Where is the one who has been born king of the Jews? We saw his star in the east[b] and have come to worship him."
[3]When King Herod heard this he was disturbed, and all Jerusalem with him. [4]When he had called together all the people's chief priests and teachers of the law,

[n](Luke 2:29) The song of Simeon, often referred to as the *Nunc Dimittis* (the first two words of the Latin translation), portrays the expectation of Israel's Messianic deliverance by yet another of the godly remnant. For other songs see Sections 7 and 8b.

[o] (Luke 2:39) See Section 16 for the text of Luke 2:39. Whether this return to Nazareth came before or after the events of Matthew 2:1–18 (Secs. 14–15) is not easily determined. Plummer suggests the family returned immediately to Bethlehem because the parents thought it most appropriate to rear the Son of David in the city of David (Alfred Plummer, *A Critical and Exegetical Commentary on the Gospel According to Luke*, International Critical Commentary on the Holy Scriptures of the Old and New Testaments [NY: Scribners, 1896], pp. 73–74). If this is true, the return of Luke 2:39 came after the visit of the magi and the flight into Egypt (Matt. 2:1–18), as A. T. Robertson placed it in his *Harmony* and as is the sequence represented by the placement of the text of Luke 2:39 in this revision of his *Harmony*. The sequence preferred by the revisers of this *Harmony*, however, has the family returning directly to Nazareth from Jerusalem, as the wording of Luke 2:39 is most easily interpreted. Their purpose was to fetch as many of their personal belongings as possible and move their home to Bethlehem, which they did. Matthew 2, then, finds them in their own home (Matt. 2:11) some time after they have been back to Nazareth (Luke 2:39). That they had already transported their household goods to Bethlehem is seen from Joseph's initial plan to return to Bethlehem, not Nazareth, from Egypt (Matt. 2:21–22) (William F. Arndt, *The Gospel According to Luke* [St. Louis: Concordia, 1956], pp. 97–98).

[p](Matt. 2:1) This Herod (Herod the Great) ruled Palestine for the Roman government from 37 B.C. to 4 B.C. He considered himself to be "king of the Jews." The question asked by the Magi aggravated his already insane jealousy to the point of committing another of his characteristic atrocities. The murder of the infants (Matt. 2:16, Sec. 15) was his attempt to rid himself of another rival to the throne. The number slain, however, was not as large as some have supposed. In a village the size of Bethlehem probably not more than twenty babies were involved in this *Massacre of the Innocents*, as it has been traditionally called.

Matthew 2:1–12 (cont'd)

he asked them where the Christ[c] was to be born. [5]"In Bethlehem in Judea," they replied, "for this is what the prophet has written:

[6]" 'But you, Bethlehem, in the land of Judah,
  are by no means least among the rulers of Judah;
for out of you will come a ruler
  who will be the shepherd of my people Israel'[d]" [Mic. 5:2].

[7]Then Herod called the Magi secretly and found out from them the exact time the star had appeared. [8]He sent them to Bethlehem and said, "Go and make a careful search for the child. As soon as you find him, report to me, so that I too may go and worship him."

[9]After they had heard the king, they went on their way, and the star they had seen in the east[e] went ahead of them until it stopped over the place where the child was. [10]When they saw the star, they were overjoyed. [11]On coming to the house, they saw the child with his mother Mary, and they bowed down and worshiped him. Then they opened their treasures and presented him with gifts of gold and of incense and of myrrh. [12]And having been warned in a dream not to go back to Herod, they returned to their country by another route.

[a]Mt 2:1 Traditionally Wise Men   [b]2 Or *star when it rose*   [c]4 Or *Messiah*   [d]6 Micah 5:2   [e]9 Or *seen when it rose*

Sec. 15   Escape into Egypt and murder of boys in Bethlehem
—*Bethlehem and Egypt*—

Matthew 2:13–18

[13]When they had gone, an angel of the Lord appeared to Joseph in a dream. "Get up," he said, "take the child and his mother and escape to Egypt. Stay there until I tell you, for Herod is going to search for the child to kill him."

[14]So he got up, took the child and his mother during the night and left for Egypt, [15]where he stayed until the death of Herod. And so was fulfilled what the Lord had said through the prophet: "Out of Egypt I called my son"[a] [Hos. 11:1].

[16]When Herod realized that he had been outwitted by the Magi, he was furious, and he gave orders to kill all the boys in Bethlehem and its vicinity who were two years old and under, in accordance with the time he had learned from the Magi. [17]Then what was said through the prophet Jeremiah was fulfilled:

[18]"A voice is heard in Ramah,
  weeping and great mourning,
Rachel weeping for her children
  and refusing to be comforted,
because they are no more"[b] [Jer. 31:15].

[a]Mt 2:15 Hosea 11:1   [b]18 Jer. 31:15

Sec. 16   Return to Nazareth
—*Egypt and Nazareth*—

Matthew 2:19–23   [q]Luke 2:39

[19]After Herod died, an angel of the Lord appeared in a dream to Joseph in Egypt [20]and said, "Get up, take the child and his mother and go to the land of Israel, for those who were trying to take the child's life are dead."

[q](Luke 2:39) See note o, pg. 38.

Matthew 2:19–23 (cont'd)

²¹So he got up, took the child and his mother and went to the land of Israel. ²²But when he heard that Archelaus was reigning in Judea in place of his father Herod, he was afraid to go there. Having been warned in a dream, he withdrew to the district of Galilee, ²³and he went and lived in a town called Nazareth. So was fulfilled what was said through the ʳprophets: "He will be called a Nazarene."

Luke 2:39 (cont'd)

³⁹When Joseph and Mary had done everything required by the Law of the Lord, they returned to Galilee to their own town of Nazareth.

Sec. 17 Growth and early life of Jesus
—Nazareth—

Luke 2:40

⁴⁰And the child ˢgrew and became strong; he was filled with wisdom, and the grace of God was upon him.

Sec. 18 Jesus' first Passover in Jerusalem
—Jerusalem—

Luke 2:41–50

⁴¹Every year his parents went to Jerusalem for the Feast of the Passover. ⁴²When he was twelve years old, they went up to the Feast, according to the custom. ⁴³After the Feast was over, while his parents were returning home, the boy Jesus stayed behind in Jerusalem, but they were unaware of it. ⁴⁴Thinking he was in their company, they traveled on for a day. Then they began looking for him among their relatives and friends. ⁴⁵When they did not find him, they went back to Jerusalem to look for him. ⁴⁶After three days they found him in the temple courts, sitting among the teachers, listening to them and asking them questions. ⁴⁷Everyone who heard him was amazed at his understanding and his answers. ⁴⁸When his parents saw him, they were astonished. His mother said to him, "Son, why have you treated us like this? Your father and I have been anxiously searching for you."
⁴⁹"Why were you searching for me?" he asked. "Didn't you know I had to be in my Father's house?" ⁵⁰But they did not understand what he was saying to them.

ʳ(Matt. 2:23) No Old Testament prophecy can be singled out as the source of this statement. Probably the reference is to a number of prophecies that together anticipated the low estate and rejection of Messiah (cf. Psalms 22:6–8, 13; 69:8, 20, 21; Isa. 11:1; 49:7; 53:2, 5, 8; Dan. 9:26). Of particular prominence is Isaiah 11:1, where the Hebrew word for "branch" (*neser*) is built around the same consonants as "Nazarene."
ˢ(Luke 2:40) Luke's attention to Jesus' humanity is perhaps nowhere more clearly seen than in this statement. His was a development along the same line as his cousin John (cf. Luke 1:80, Sec. 8c). Yet the two were not exactly the same, because in Jesus for the first time a human being was developing under ideal conditions, unimpeded by hereditary or acquired defects. See also Luke 2:52 (Sec. 19).
ᵗ(Luke 2:49) These are the first recorded words of Jesus. When he referred to God as "my Father," he was probably responding to his mother's words, "Your father and I." His deity as the one and only Son of God and his virgin birth lay behind his statement (cf. Luke 10:21–22, Sec. 102b).

Sec. 19   Jesus' growth to adulthood
—Nazareth—

Luke 2:51–52

[51]Then he went down to Nazareth with them and was obedient to them. But his mother treasured all these things in her heart. [52]And Jesus ᵘgrew in wisdom and stature, and in favor with God and men.

ᵘ(Luke 2:52) As Luke 2:40 summarizes Jesus' boyhood until age twelve, Luke 2:52 furnishes a summary of his growth toward manhood, that is, the approximately eighteen years until he was about thirty (cf. Luke 3:23, Sec. 24). We have no detailed information about this latter period, beyond the statement of this verse. Some general data about the eighteen years can be assumed, however. Jesus grew up as the oldest of the children in a rather large family (cf. Mark 6:3, Sec. 69). Joseph supported the family through carpentry in which Jesus assisted. Joseph apparently died during the period before Jesus' public appearance and, by implications in the gospels and from early church Fathers, we can presume Jesus became the provider for his mother and younger brothers and sisters (Mark 6:3). He therefore seemingly continued to work at carpentry until the beginning of his public ministry. His frequent mention of articles of furniture, houses, plows, yokes, and the like in his teaching reflects an intimate acquaintance with items built by carpenters.

PART FOUR
THE PUBLIC MINISTRY OF JOHN THE BAPTIST

Sec. 20   His ministry launched
—Judean desert—

Mark 1:1	Luke 3:1–2
[1]The beginning of the gospel about Jesus Christ, the Son of God. [a]	[1]In the fifteenth year of the reign of [v]Tiberius Caesar—when Pontius Pilate was governor of Judea, Herod tetrarch of Galilee, his brother Philip tetrarch of Iturea and Traconitis, and Lysanias tetrarch of Abilene— [2]during the high priesthood of Annas and Caiaphas, the word of God came to John son of Zechariah in the desert.

[a]Mk 1:1 Some manuscripts do not have *the Son of God.*

Sec. 21   His person, proclamation, and baptism
(cf. Sec. 26—a voice in the desert)
—Judean desert and the country around the Jordan River—

Matthew 3:1–6	Mark 1:2–6	Luke 3:3–6
[1]In those days John the Baptist came, [w]preaching in the Desert of Judea [2]and saying, "Repent, for the kingdom of heaven is near." [3]This is he who was spoken of through the prophet Isaiah:	[2]It is written in Isaiah the prophet:	[3]He went into all the country around the Jordan, [w]preaching a baptism of repentance for the forgiveness of sins. [4]As is written in the book of the words of Isaiah the prophet:
"A voice of one calling in the desert, 'Prepare the way for the Lord, make straight paths for him' " [a] [Isa. 40:3].	"I will send my messenger ahead of you, who will prepare your way" [b] [Mal. 3:1]— [3]"a voice of one calling in the desert, 'Prepare the way for the Lord, make straight paths for him' " [a] [Isa. 40:3].	"A voice of one calling in the desert, 'Prepare the way for the Lord, make straight paths for him. [5]Every valley shall be filled in, every mountain and hill made low.
[4]John's clothes were made of camel's hair, and he had a leather belt	[4]And so John came, baptizing in the desert region and preaching a baptism of repentance for the for-	

---

[v](Luke 3:1) See essay 11, "Chronology of the Life of Christ" (pp. 315–19). In fixing the date of John's ministry, Luke lists five political leaders and two religious leaders. They are, in order, the Roman emperor, rulers of the three divisions of the "kingdom of the Jews," the ruler of the territory just to the north of the Jewish territory, and the father-son combination that presided over worship in Jerusalem for so many years. The Lysanias mentioned comes later than the Lysanias who was king of Abila until 36 B.C. An archaeological discovery at Abila has confirmed that there was a later Lysanias who was tetrarch during the reign of Tiberius (A.D. 14–37).

[w](Matt. 3:1; Luke 3:3) The mission of John was comparable to that of an Oriental courier who preceded his monarch to proclaim the king's coming and the need for citizens to prepare the roads for his arrival. John's preparation, however, was in matters pertaining to moral behavior and outlook. To receive the kingdom promised them by the Old Testament prophets, Israel's people needed to repent. John's baptism then identified the remnant that had achieved such moral preparation.

Matthew 3:1–6 (cont'd)	Mark 1:2–6 (cont'd)	Luke 3:3–6 (cont'd)
around his waist. His food was locusts and wild honey. [5]People went out to him from Jerusalem and all Judea and the whole region of the Jordan. [6]Confessing their sins, they were baptized by him in the Jordan River.	giveness of sins. [5]The whole Judean countryside and all the people of Jerusalem went out to him. Confessing their sins, they were baptized by him in the Jordan River. [6]John wore clothing made of camel's hair, with a leather belt around his waist, and he ate locusts and wild honey.	The crooked roads shall become straight, the rough ways smooth. [6]And all mankind will see God's salvation' "[c] [Isa. 40:3–5].

[a]Mt 3:3; Mk 1:3   [b]Mk 1:2 Mal. 3:1   [c]Lk 3:6 Isaiah 40:3-5

Sec. 22   His messages to the Pharisees, Sadducees, crowds, tax collectors, and soldiers
—Judean desert and the country around the Jordan River—

Matthew 3:7–10	Luke 3:7–14
[7]But when he saw many of the Pharisees and Sadducees coming to where he was baptizing, he said to them: "You brood of vipers! Who warned you to flee from the [x]coming wrath? [8]Produce fruit in keeping with repentance. [9]And do not think you can say to yourselves, 'We have Abraham as our father.' I tell you that out of these stones God can raise up children for Abraham. [10]The ax is already at the root of the trees, and every tree that does not produce good fruit will be cut down and thrown into the fire.	[7]John said to the crowds coming out to be baptized by him, "You brood of vipers! Who warned you to flee from the [x]coming wrath? [8]Produce fruit in keeping with repentance. And do not begin to say to yourselves, 'We have Abraham as our father.' For I tell you that out of these stones God can raise up children for Abraham. [9]The ax is already at the root of the trees, and every tree that does not produce good fruit will be cut down and thrown into the fire." [10]"What should we do then?" the crowd asked. [11]John answered, "The man with two tunics should share with him who has none, and the one who has food should do the same." [12]Tax collectors also came to be baptized. "Teacher," they asked, "what should we do?" [13]"Don't collect any more than you are required to," he told them. [14]Then some soldiers asked him, "And what should we do?" He replied, "Don't extort money and don't accuse people falsely—be content with your pay."

[x](Matt. 3:7; Luke 3:7) The well-known "coming wrath" will immediately precede Christ's second advent. The Old Testament fixes this time at the beginning of "the day of the Lord," and makes it a prelude to Messiah's reign (Isa. 3:16–24; 13:9–11; Jer. 30:7; Ezek. 38–39; Amos 5:18–19; Zeph. 1:14–18; cf. Matt. 24:21; 1 Thess. 1:10, 5:9; Rev. 6:16–17). Messiah's first coming to die for sin was not in John's mind at this moment. His theme for those not yet morally prepared was the threat of coming judgment. Being a member of the covenant nation was not synonymous with enjoying the benefits of the covenants, as so many Jews thought. Personal moral preparation was also necessary.

Sec. 23 His description of the Christ
(cf. Sec. 26—preparatory nature of John's ministry)
—Country around the Jordan River—

Matthew 3:11–12	Mark 1:7–8	Luke 3:15–18
[11]"I baptize you with[a] water for repentance. [y]But after me will come one who is more powerful than I, whose sandals I am not fit to carry. He will baptize you with the Holy Spirit and with fire.	[7]And this was his message: "After me will come one more powerful than I, the thongs of whose sandals I am not worthy to stoop down and untie. [8]I baptize you with[a] water, [y]but he will baptize you with the Holy Spirit."	[15]The people were waiting expectantly and were all wondering in their hearts if John might possibly be the Christ.[b] [16]John answered them all, "I baptize you with[a] water. [y]But one more powerful than I will come, the thongs of whose sandals I am not worthy to untie. He will baptize you with the Holy Spirit and with fire. [17]His winnowing fork is in his hand to clear his threshing floor and to gather the wheat into his barn, but he will burn up the chaff with unquenchable fire." [18]And with many other words John exhorted the people and preached the good news to them.
[12]His winnowing fork is in his hand, and he will clear his threshing floor, gathering his wheat into the barn and burning up the chaff with unquenchable fire."		

^aMt 3:11; Mk 1:8; Lk 3:16 Or *in*   ^bLk 3:15 Or *Messiah*

ʸ(Matt. 3:11; Mark 1:8; Luke 3:16) In contrasting Christ's baptism with the Holy Spirit and his own baptism with water, John had in mind the promised coming of the Holy Spirit in accord with such prophecies as Joel 2:28–29.

PART FIVE
THE END OF JOHN'S MINISTRY AND THE BEGINNING
OF CHRIST'S PUBLIC MINISTRY

Sec. 24 Jesus' baptism by John
(cf. Sec. 27—Spirit's descent on Jesus)
(cf. Sec. 85—identification of the Son by the Father)
—ᶻBethany on the east side of the Jordan River—

Matthew 3:13–17	Mark 1:9–11	Luke 3:21–23a
¹³ᵃThen Jesus came from Galilee to the Jordan to be baptized by John. ¹⁴But John tried to deter him, saying, "I need to be baptized by you, and do you come to me?" ¹⁵Jesus replied, "Let it be so now; it is proper for us to do this to fulfill all righteousness." Then John consented.		
¹⁶As soon as Jesus was ᵇbaptized, he went up out of the water. At that moment heaven was opened, and he saw the Spirit of God descending like a dove and lighting on him. ¹⁷And a voice from heaven said, "This is my Son, whom I love; with him I am well pleased."	⁹At that time Jesus came from Nazareth in Galilee and was ᵇbaptized by John in the Jordan. ¹⁰As Jesus was coming up out of the water, he saw heaven being torn open and the Spirit descending on him like a dove. ¹¹And a voice came from heaven: "You are my Son, whom I love; with you I am well pleased."	²¹When all the people were being baptized, Jesus was ᵇbaptized too. And as he was praying, heaven was opened ²²and the Holy Spirit descended on him in bodily form like a dove. And a voice came from heaven: "You are my Son, whom I love; with you I am well pleased." ²³Now Jesus himself was about thirty years old when he began his ministry.

first use of Spirit [handwritten annotation]

ᶻSee John 1:28 (Sec. 26).

ᵃ(Matt. 3:13) Jesus' first Passover following his baptism (John 2:13–22, Sec. 31) came in April, of course. Calculating the amount of time occupied by the events between his baptism and Passover leads to the probable conclusion that he was baptized in the summer or spring of the previous year.

ᵇ(Matt. 3:16; Mark 1:9; Luke 3:21) The baptism of Jesus was a significant event for several reasons:
1. His baptism was different from the baptism of others because he had not sinned and did not need to repent.
2. By it he became publicly identified with the group whom John recognized as morally prepared for the kingdom.
3. It is recognized by other New Testament sources as the formal beginning of Christ's public ministry (Acts 1:21–22; 10:37–38).

45

Sec. 25   Jesus' temptation in the desert
—Judean desert—

Matthew 4:1–11	Mark 1:12–13	Luke 4:1–13

[1]Then Jesus was led by the Spirit into the desert to be tempted by the devil. [2c]After fasting forty days and forty nights, he was hungry. [3]The tempter came to him and said, "If you are the Son of God, tell these stones to become bread."

[4]Jesus answered, "It is written: 'Man does not live on bread alone, but on every word that comes from the mouth of God'[a]" [Deut. 8:3].

[5]Then the devil took him to the holy city and had him stand on the highest point of the temple. [6]"If you are the Son of God," he said, "throw yourself down. For it is written:

" 'He will command his
      angels concerning
      you,
and they will lift you
      up in their hands,
so that you will not
      strike your foot
      against a stone'[b]"
[Psalm 91:11–12].

[7]Jesus answered him, "It is also written: 'Do not put the Lord your God to the test'[c]" [Deut. 6:16].

[8]Again, the devil took him to a very high mountain and showed him all the kingdoms of the world and their splendor. [9]"All this I will give you," he said, "if you will bow down and worship me."

[10]Jesus said to him, "Away from me, Satan!

[12]At once the Spirit sent him out into the desert, [13]and he was in the desert forty days, being tempted by Satan. He was with the wild animals,

[1]Jesus, full of the Holy Spirit, returned from the Jordan and was led by the Spirit in the desert, [2]where for forty days he was tempted by the devil. He ate nothing during those days, and at the end of them he was hungry.

[3]The devil said to him, "If you are the Son of God, tell this stone to become bread."

[4]Jesus answered, "It is written: 'Man does not live on bread alone'[a]" [Deut. 8:3].

[5]The devil led him up to a high place and showed him in an instant all the kingdoms of the world. [6]And he said to him, "I will give you all their authority and splendor, for it has been given to me, and I can give it to anyone I want to. [7]So if you worship me, it will all be yours."

[8]Jesus answered, "It is written: 'Worship the Lord your God and serve him only'[d]" [Deut. 6:13].

[9]The devil led him to Jerusalem and had him stand on the highest point of the temple. "If you are the Son of God," he said, "throw yourself down from here. [10]For it is written:

" 'He will command his
      angels concerning
      you
to guard you
      carefully;

---

[c](Matt 4:2) The three temptations in the paragraph came at the close of the forty days, when Jesus was most vulnerable. The sequence of temptations in Matthew is preferred over that in Luke (cf. "then," Matt. 4:5). Jesus' victorious encounter with the devil places him in contrast with Adam (Gen. 3) and the Israelites in the desert. He drew each of his responses to the devil from Deuteronomy, which recounts the desert experiences. Failure in the desert has now become triumph in the desert. Now Christians have a basis for confidence in overcoming temptation through Jesus' sympathetic help (Heb. 2:18; 4:14–16).

Matthew 4:1–11 (cont'd)	Mark 1:12–13 (cont'd)	Luke 4:1–13 (cont'd)
For it is written: 'Worship the Lord your God, and serve him only'ᵈ" [Deut. 6:13].		¹¹they will lift you up in their hands, so that you will not strike your foot against a stone'ᵇ" [Psalm 91:11–12].
		¹²Jesus answered, "It says: 'Do not put the Lord your God to the test'ᶜ" [Deut. 6:16].
¹¹Then the devil left him, and angels came and attended him.	and angels attended him.	¹³When the devil had finished all this tempting, he left him until an opportune time.

ᵃMt 4:4; Lk 4:4 Deut. 8:3   ᵇMt 4:6; Lk 4:11 Psalm 91:11,12   ᶜMt 4:7; Lk 4:12 Deut. 6:16
ᵈMt 4:10; Lk 4:8 Deut. 6:13

Sec. 26   John's testimony about himself to the priests and Levites (cf. Sec. 21—a voice in the desert) (cf. Sec. 23—preparatory nature of John's ministry)

Day 1

—ᵈ*Bethany on the east side of the Jordan River*—

John 1:19–28

¹⁹Now this was John's testimony when the Jews of Jerusalem sent priests and Levites to ask him who he was. ²⁰He did not fail to confess, but confessed freely, "I am not the Christ.ᵃ"

²¹They asked him, "Then who are you? Are you Elijah?"
He said, "I am not."
"Are you the Prophet?"
He answered, "ᵉNo."

²²Finally they said, "Who are you? Give us an answer to take back to those who sent us. What do you say about yourself?"

²³John replied in the words of Isaiah the prophet, "I am the voice of one calling in the desert, 'Make straight the way for the Lord' "ᵇ [Isa. 40:3].

²⁴Now some Pharisees who had been sent ²⁵questioned him, "Why then do you baptize if you are not the Christ, nor Elijah, nor the Prophet?"

²⁶"I baptize withᶜ water," John replied, "but among you stands one you do not know. ²⁷He is the one who comes after me, the thongs of whose sandals I am not worthy to untie."

²⁸This all happened at Bethany on the other side of the Jordan, where John was baptizing.

ᵃJn 1:20 Or *Messiah.* "The Christ" (Greek) and "the Messiah" (Hebrew) both mean "the Anointed One"; also in verse 25.   ᵇ23 Isaiah 40:3   ᶜ26 Or *in;* also in verses 31 and 33

ᵈThis Bethany is to be distinguished from the Bethany near Jerusalem (Sec. 104; cf. also Secs. 105–110).

ᵉ(John 1:21) John's relationship to Malachi's prophecy about Elijah (Mal. 4:5–6) is difficult to determine in light of his response to this question. Perhaps the key is found in the condition "if you are willing to accept it" (Matt. 11:14, Sec. 57). At any rate, John was certainly unaware that he was fulfilling the prophecy, if he was.

Sec. 27   John's testimony to Jesus as the Son of God
(cf. Sec. 24—Spirit's descent on Jesus)

Day 2

—*Bethany on the east side of the Jordan River*—

John 1:29–34

[29]The next day John saw Jesus coming toward him and said, "[f]Look, the Lamb of God, who takes away the sin of the world! [30]This is the one I meant when I said, 'A man who comes after me has surpassed me because he was before me.' [31]I myself did not know him, but the reason I came baptizing with water was that he might be revealed to Israel."

[32]Then John gave this testimony: "I saw the Spirit come down from heaven as a dove and remain on him. [33]I would not have known him, except that the one who sent me to baptize with water told me, 'The man on whom you see the Spirit come down and remain is he who will baptize with the Holy Spirit.' [34]I have seen and I testify that this is the Son of God."

Sec. 28   Jesus' first [g]followers
(cf. Secs. 41, 47a—calling disciples)

Day 3

—*Bethany on the east side of the Jordan River, and Galilee*—

John 1:35–51

[35]The next day John was there again with two of his disciples. [36]When he saw Jesus passing by, he said, "Look, the Lamb of God!"

[37]When the two disciples heard him say this, they followed Jesus. [38]Turning around, Jesus saw them following and asked, "What do you want?"

They said, "Rabbi" (which means Teacher), "where are you staying?"

[39]"Come," he replied, "and you will see."

So they went and saw where he was staying, and spent that day with him. It was about the tenth hour.

[40]Andrew, Simon Peter's brother, was one of the two who heard what John had said and who had followed Jesus. [41]The first thing Andrew did was to find his brother Simon and tell him, "We have found the Messiah" (that is, the Christ). [42]And he brought him to Jesus.

Jesus looked at him and said, "You are Simon son of John. You will be called Cephas" (which, when translated, is Peter[a]).

[43]The next day Jesus decided to leave for Galilee. Finding Philip, he said to him, "Follow me."

[44]Philip, like Andrew and Peter, was from the town of Bethsaida. [45]Philip found [h]Nathanael and told him, "We have found the one Moses wrote about in the Law, and about whom the prophets also wrote—Jesus of Nazareth, the son of Joseph."

[46]"Nazareth! Can anything good come from there?" Nathanael asked.

"Come and see," said Philip.

---

[f](John 1:29) John was a student of the Old Testament, particularly of Isaiah's prophecy (cf. Sec. 21 with Isa. 40:3–5). It is no surprise, therefore, that he focuses on Messiah's soteriological work ("Look, the Lamb of God," cf. Isa. 53:6–7) as well as his eschatological ("The kingdom of heaven is near," Matt. 3:2, Sec. 21). John did not completely comprehend how the two ministries would combine (Matt. 11:2–3, Sec. 57; cf. 1 Pet. 1:10–11). Even those closest to Christ did not see, until after his resurrection, why he must die.

[g]These followers were won through a variety of means: the first two were won by the testimony of John (v. 36); Simon Peter by the testimony of one of these two, namely, Andrew (vv. 40–42); Philip by the invitation of Jesus (v. 43); and Nathanael by the testimony of Philip (vv. 46–47). Each seems to have acknowledged Jesus' Messiahship (vv. 41, 45, 49) on the basis of John's testimony (vv. 29, 34, 36). Yet they did not become his permanent followers at this point, because at least two of them returned to their occupation as fishermen. See Section 41 and note f.

[h](John 1:45) If Nathanael became one of the Twelve, he should probably be identified with Bartholomew in the lists found in the synoptic gospels and Acts. It cannot be concluded dogmatically, however, that he was one of this select group.

John 1:35–51 (cont'd)

[47]When Jesus saw Nathanael approaching, he said of him, "Here is a true Israelite, in whom there is nothing false."

[48]"How do you know me?" Nathanael asked.

Jesus answered, "I saw you while you were still under the fig tree before Philip called you."

[49]Then Nathanael declared, "Rabbi, you are the Son of God; you are the King of Israel."

[50]Jesus said, "You believe[b] because I told you I saw you under the fig tree. You shall see greater things than that." [51]He then added, "I tell you[c] the truth, you[c] shall see heaven open, and the angels of God ascending and descending on the [i]Son of Man."

[a]Jn 1:42 Both *Cephas* (Aramaic) and *Peter* (Greek) mean rock.   [b]50 Or *Do you believe . . . ?*
[c]51 The Greek is plural.

Sec. 29   Jesus' first miracle: water becomes wine
—*Cana in Galilee*—

John 2:1–11

[1][j]On the third day a wedding took place at Cana in Galilee. Jesus' mother was there, [2]and Jesus and his disciples had also been invited to the wedding. [3]When the wine was gone, Jesus' [k]mother said to him, "They have no more wine."

[4]"Dear woman, why do you involve me?" Jesus replied. "My time has not yet come."

[5]His mother said to the servants, "Do whatever he tells you."

[6]Nearby stood six stone water jars, the kind used by the Jews for ceremonial washing, each holding from twenty to thirty gallons.[a]

[7]Jesus said to the servants, "Fill the jars with water"; so they filled them to the brim.

[8]Then he told them, "Now draw some out and take it to the master of the banquet."

They did so, [9]and the master of the banquet tasted the water that had been turned into wine. He did not realize where it had come from, though the servants who had drawn the water knew. Then he called the bridegroom aside [10]and said, "Everyone brings out the choice wine first and then the cheaper wine after the guests have had too much to drink; but you have saved the best till now."

[11]This, the first of his miraculous signs, Jesus performed at Cana in Galilee. He thus revealed his glory, and his disciples put their faith in him.

[a]Jn 2:6 Greek *two to three metretes* (probably about 75 to 115 liters)

---

[i](John 1:51) "The Son of Man" was a frequent self-designation adopted by the Lord. Its source was Daniel 7:13–14. The nature of the title both alluded to his Messiahship and veiled it. Listeners probably read into the title as much as they apprehended of Jesus and no more. Its scope of meaning is broad, including overtones of deity, undertones of humanity, and redemption of lost man, among other connotations.

[j](John 2:1) "On the third day" marks the conclusion of a week about which we have a rather full account. Beginning with 1:19–28 as the first day, we have then the second day in vv. 29–34, the third in vv. 35–43, the fourth in vv. 43–51, and the seventh in 2:1–11.

[k](John 2:3) Jesus' mother showed the same lack of understanding as John the Baptist and Peter did later on (Matt. 11:2–3, Sec. 57; 16:22, Sec. 83). Though they were right as to the fact of his Messiahship, they were wrong as to the time and manner of its glorious manifestation (John 2:4). Jesus did perform a miracle to meet the need, but in a manner that revealed his identity to only a few (John 2:9, 11).

Sec. 30   Jesus' first stay in Capernaum with his relatives and early disciples
—Capernaum—

John 2:12

[12]After this he went down to Capernaum with his mother and brothers and his disciples. There they stayed for a few days.

Sec. 31   [1]First cleansing of the temple at the Passover
(cf. Sec. 129b—cleansing the temple)
—Jerusalem—

John 2:13–22

[13]When it was almost time for the Jewish [m]Passover, Jesus went up to Jerusalem. [14]In the temple courts he found men selling cattle, sheep and doves, and others sitting at tables exchanging money. [15]So he made a whip out of cords, and drove all from the temple area, both sheep and cattle; he scattered the coins of the money changers and overturned their tables. [16]To those who sold doves he said, "Get these out of here! How dare you turn my Father's house into a market!"

[17]His disciples remembered that it is written: "Zeal for your house will consume me"[a] [Psalm 69:9].

[18]Then the Jews demanded of him, "What miraculous sign can you show us to prove your authority to do all this?"

[19]Jesus answered them, "Destroy this temple, and I will raise it again in three days."

[20]The Jews replied, "It has taken [n]forty-six years to build this temple, and you are going to raise it in three days?" [21]But the temple he had spoken of was his body. [22]After he was raised from the dead, his disciples recalled what he had said. Then they believed the Scripture and the words that Jesus had spoken.

[a]Jn 2:17 Psalm 69:9

Sec. 32a   Early response to Jesus' miracles
—Jerusalem—

John 2:23–25

[23]Now while he was in Jerusalem at the Passover Feast, many people saw the miraculous signs he was doing and believed in his name.[a] [24]But Jesus would not entrust himself to them, for he knew all men. [25]He did not need man's testimony about man, for he [o]knew what was in a man.

[a]Jn 2:23 Or and believed in him

---

[1]This cleansing of the temple should be kept distinct from the one at the close of the Lord's ministry (cf. Sec. 129b). The differences in wording and setting, along with John's chronological placement of it, verify that the two narratives refer to two different events. Three years between the two is more than ample for the practice of buying and selling to have arisen again on the temple premises, especially in light of the avaricious tendencies of the Jewish leaders.

[m](John 2:13) This is the first of four Passovers that provide a chronological framework for Jesus' public ministry. See essay 11, "Chronology of the Life of Christ" (pp. 315–19).

[n](John 2:20) Forty-six years is to be reckoned from either the initiation of Herod's rebuilding project in 20/19 B.C., or from completion of the work on the sanctuary (naos) proper in 18/17 B.C. See essay 11, "Chronology of the Life of Christ" (pp. 315–19).

[o](John 2:25) Jesus, being God as well as man, was omniscient. His awareness of human depravity revealed the basically selfish reasons of those attracted to him at this point. The moral preparation of these prospective subjects was not yet sufficient for their participation in the kingdom of which he and John the Baptist spoke.

Sec. 32b   Nicodemus' interview with Jesus
—*Jerusalem*—

John 3:1–21

[1]Now there was a man of the Pharisees named Nicodemus, a member of the Jewish ruling council. [2]He came to Jesus at night and said, "Rabbi, we know you are a teacher who has come from God. For no one could perform the miraculous signs you are doing if God were not with him."

[3]In reply Jesus declared, "I tell you the truth, no one can see the kingdom of God unless he is [p]born again.[a]"

[4]"How can a man be born when he is old?" Nicodemus asked. "Surely he cannot enter a second time into his mother's womb to be born!"

[5]Jesus answered, "I tell you the truth, no one can enter the kingdom of God unless he is born of water and the Spirit. [6]Flesh gives birth to flesh, but the Spirit[b] gives birth to spirit. [7]You should not be surprised at my saying, 'You[c] must be born again.' [8]The wind blows wherever it pleases. You hear its sound, but you cannot tell where it comes from or where it is going. So it is with everyone born of the Spirit."

[9]"How can this be?" Nicodemus asked.

[10]"You are Israel's teacher," said Jesus, "and do you not understand these things? [11]I tell you the truth, we speak of what we know, and we testify to what we have seen, but still you people do not accept our testimony. [12]I have spoken to you of earthly things and you do not believe; how then will you believe if I speak of heavenly things? [13]No one has ever gone into heaven except the one who came from heaven—the Son of Man.[d] [14]Just as Moses lifted up the snake in the desert, so the Son of Man must be lifted up, [15]that everyone who believes in him may have eternal life.[e]

[16]"[q]For God so loved the world that he gave his one and only Son,[f] that whoever believes in him shall not perish but have eternal life. [17]For God did not send his Son into the world to condemn the world, but to save the world through him. [18]Whoever believes in him is not condemned, but whoever does not believe stands condemned already because he has not believed in the name of God's one and only Son.[g] [19]This is the verdict: Light has come into the world, but men loved darkness instead of light because their deeds were evil. [20]Everyone who does evil hates the light, and will not come into the light for fear that his deeds will be exposed. [21]But whoever lives by the truth comes into the light, so that it may be seen plainly that what he has done has been done through God."[h]

[a]3 Or *born from above; also in verse 7*   [b]6 Or *but spirit*   [c]7 The Greek is plural.   [d]13 Some manuscripts *Man, who is in heaven*   [e]15 Or *believes may have eternal life in him*   [f]16 Or *his only begotten Son*   [g]18 Or *God's only begotten Son*   [h]21 Some interpreters end the quotation after verse 15.

Sec. 33   John superseded by Jesus
—*Aenon near Salim*—

John 3:22–36

[22][r]After this, Jesus and his disciples went out into the Judean countryside, where he spent some time with them, and baptized. [23]Now John also was baptizing at Aenon near Salim, because there was plenty of water, and people were constantly

[p](John 3:3) Being born again is not specifically mentioned in the Old Testament. The ideas closest to it are those of a new heart and a special activity of the Spirit in conjunction with the inauguration of the New Covenant and Israel's Kingdom (Jer. 31:31–34; Ezek. 36:26–27; Joel 2:28–32).

[q](John 3:16) John the apostle is noted for his reflective sections in this gospel, and John 3:16–21 may be one of them. It seems a more natural assumption, however, to view these verses as continuing the Lord's teaching already in progress.

[r](John 3:22) Suggestions that relocate John 3:22–30 after 2:12 or after 3:36 are not well-founded. No convincing reason for doing this has been forthcoming. Besides, John 3:31 does not follow smoothly after 3:21.

John 3:22–36 (cont'd)

coming to be baptized. [24](This was before John was put in prison.) [25]An argument developed between some of John's disciples and a certain Jew[a] over the matter of ceremonial washing. [26]They came to John and said to him, "Rabbi, that man who was with you on the other side of the Jordan—the one you testified about—well, he is baptizing, and everyone is going to him."

[27]To this John replied, "A man can receive only what is given him from heaven. [28]You yourselves can testify that I said, 'I am not the Christ[b] but am sent ahead of him.' [29]The bride belongs to the bridegroom. The friend who attends the bridegroom waits and listens for him, and is full of joy when he hears the bridegroom's voice. That joy is mine, and it is now complete. [30]He must become greater; I must become less.

[31]"sThe one who comes from above is above all; the one who is from the earth belongs to the earth, and speaks as one from the earth. The one who comes from heaven is above all. [32]He testifies to what he has seen and heard, but no one accepts his testimony. [33]The man who has accepted it has certified that God is truthful. [34]For the one whom God has sent speaks the words of God, for God[c] gives the Spirit without limit. [35]The Father loves the Son and has placed everything in his hands. [36]Whoever believes in the Son has eternal life, but whoever rejects the Son will not see life, for God's wrath remains on him."[d]

[a]Jn 3:25 *Some manuscripts and certain Jews*   [b]28 *Or Messiah*   [c]34 *Greek he*   [d]36 *Some interpreters end the quotation after verse 30.*

Sec. 34   Jesus' departure from Judea
(cf. Sec. 71b—John's imprisonment)
—*From Judea, through Samaria, to Galilee*—

John 4:1–4

[1]The Pharisees heard that Jesus was gaining and baptizing more disciples than John, [2]although in fact it was not Jesus who baptized, but his disciples. [3]When the Lord learned of this, he left Judea and went back once more to Galilee.
[4]Now he had to go through Samaria.

Luke 3:19–20

[19]But when John rebuked Herod the tetrarch because of Herodias, his brother's wife, and all the other evil things he had done, [20]Herod added this to them all: He locked John up in prison.

Matthew 4:12	Mark 1:14a	Luke 4:14a
[12]When Jesus heard that John had been put in prison, he returned to Galilee.	[14]After John was put in prison, Jesus went into Galilee,	[14]Jesus returned to Galilee in the power of the Spirit,

s(John 3:31) John 3:31–36 may be a continuation of John the Baptist's speech, the words of Jesus, or reflections of the apostle John. The second possibility is unlikely without relocating some verses. The third possibility is a characteristic of this writer, but comes too much by surprise. The more natural flow is obtained by taking this as a continuation of the Baptist's words.

tJesus had two obvious reasons for leaving Judea to go to Galilee at this time: potential opposition from the Pharisees (John 4:1–3) and the imprisonment of John the Baptist (Matt. 4:12; Mark 1:14a; Luke 4:14a). According to Luke, Herod imprisoned John because of being rebuked by John for taking his brother's wife, and also because, according to the secular historian Josephus, Herod feared a revolution led by John.

Sec. 35a   Discussion with a Samaritan woman
—*Sychar in Samaria*—

John 4:5–26

[5]So he came to a town in ᵘSamaria called Sychar, near the plot of ground Jacob had given to his son Joseph. [6]Jacob's well was there, and Jesus, tired as he was from the journey, sat down by the well. It was about the sixth hour.
[7]When a Samaritan woman came to draw water, Jesus said to her, "Will you give me a drink?" [8](His disciples had gone into the town to buy food.)
[9]The Samaritan woman said to him, "You are a Jew and I am a Samaritan woman. How can you ask me for a drink?" (For Jews do not associate with Samaritans.ᵃ)
[10]Jesus answered her, "If you knew the gift of God and who it is that asks you for a drink, you would have asked him and he would have given you living water."
[11]"Sir," the woman said, "you have nothing to draw with and the well is deep. Where can you get this living water? [12]Are you greater than our father Jacob, who gave us the well and drank from it himself, as did also his sons and his flocks and herds?"
[13]Jesus answered, "Everyone who drinks this water will be thirsty again, [14]but whoever drinks the water I give him will never thirst. Indeed, the water I give him will become in him a spring of water welling up to eternal life."
[15]The woman said to him, "Sir, give me this water so that I won't get thirsty and have to keep coming here to draw water."
[16]He told her, "Go, call your husband and come back."
[17]"I have no husband," she replied.
Jesus said to her, "You are right when you say you have no husband. [18]The fact is, you have had five husbands, and the man you now have is not your husband. What you have just said is quite true."
[19]"Sir," the woman said, "I can see that you are a prophet. [20]Our fathers worshiped on this mountain, but you Jews claim that the place where we must worship is in Jerusalem."
[21]Jesus declared, "Believe me, woman, a time is coming when you will worship the Father neither on this mountain nor in Jerusalem. [22]You Samaritans worship what you do not know; we worship what we do know, for salvation is from the – Jews. [23]Yet a time is coming and has now come when the true worshipers will worship the Father in spirit and truth, for they are the kind of worshipers the Father seeks. [24]God is spirit, and his worshipers must worship in spirit and in truth."
[25]The woman said, "I know that Messiah" (called Christ) "is coming. When he comes, he will explain everything to us."
[26]Then Jesus declared, "ᵛI who speak to you am he."

ᵃJn 4:9 Or *do not use dishes Samaritans have used*

Sec. 35b   Challenge of a spiritual harvest
—*Sychar in Samaria*—

John 4:27–38

[27]Just then his disciples returned and were ʷsurprised to find him talking with a woman. But no one asked, "What do you want?" or "Why are you talking with her?"

ᵘ(John 4:5) Among the gospel writers only Luke and John devote special attention to Samaria and Samaritans. Both are especially conscious of how Christ met the needs of non-Jews, because both gospels were composed with readers of Gentile background in view.

ᵛ(John 4:26) This was Jesus' only open declaration of his Messiahship until his trial. See Mark 14:62, Section 155.

ʷ(John 4:27) The disciples' surprise arose from Jesus' unconventional conduct. Rabbis would not have carried on a conversation with a woman, because they regarded women as inferior in every way. Yet the disciples did not question the action because they had already been with Jesus long enough to know he did not always conform to conventional rabbinic behavior.

John 4:27–38 (cont'd)

[28]Then, leaving her water jar, the woman went back to the town and said to the people, [29]"Come, see a man who told me everything I ever did. Could this be the Christ[a]?" [30]They came out of the town and made their way toward him.

[31]Meanwhile his disciples urged him, "Rabbi, eat something."

[32]But he said to them, "I have food to eat that you know nothing about."

[33]Then his disciples said to each other, "Could someone have brought him food?"

[34]"My food," said Jesus, "is to do the will of him who sent me and to finish his work. [35]Do you not say, 'Four months more and then the harvest'? I tell you, open your eyes and look at the fields! They are ripe for harvest. [36]Even now the reaper draws his wages, even now he harvests the crop for eternal life, so that the sower and the reaper may be glad together. [37]Thus the saying 'One sows and another reaps' is true. [38]I sent you to reap what you have not worked for. Others have done the hard work, and you have reaped the benefits of their labor."

[a]Jn 4:29 Or Messiah

Sec. 35c   Evangelization of Sychar
—*Sychar in Samaria*—

John 4:39–42

[39]Many of the Samaritans from that town believed in him because of the woman's testimony, "He told me everything I ever did." [40]So when the Samaritans came to him, they urged him to stay with them, and he stayed two days. [41]And because of his words many more became believers.

[42]They said to the woman, "We no longer believe just because of what you said; now we have heard for ourselves, and we know that this man really is the [x]Savior of the world."

Sec. 36   Arrival in Galilee
(cf. Secs. 37, 39, 69—no honor at home)
—*From Samaria to Galilee*—

John 4:43–45

[43]After the two days he left for Galilee. [44](Now Jesus himself had pointed out that a prophet has no honor in [y]his own country.) [45]When he arrived in Galilee, the Galileans welcomed him. They had seen all that he had done in Jerusalem at the Passover Feast, for they also had been there.

---

[x](John 4:42) Recording the salvation of the Samaritans is John's way of showing his predominantly Gentile readership that salvation in Christ is for all people regardless of race.

[y](John 4:44) "His own country" must be Galilee, not Judea as some have understood. Galilee is the meaning of the expression in the synoptic gospels. A reference to Judea at this point would not fit unless this departure were placed before Jesus' time in Samaria.

PART SIX
THE ²MINISTRY OF CHRIST IN GALILEE
OPPOSITION AT HOME AND A NEW HEADQUARTERS

Sec. 37 Nature of the ªGalilean ministry
(cf. Secs. 36, 39, 69—no honor at home)
—Galilee—

Matthew 4:17	Mark 1:14b–15	Luke 4:14b–15
¹⁷From that time on Jesus began to preach, "Repent, for the kingdom of heaven is near."	proclaiming the good news of God. ¹⁵"The ᵇtime has come," he said. "The kingdom of God is near. Repent and believe the good news!"	and news about him spread through the whole countryside. ¹⁵He taught in their synagogues, and everyone praised him.

Sec. 38 Child at Capernaum healed by Jesus while at Cana
(cf. Sec. 55—healing at a distance)
—Cana in Galilee—

John 4:46–54

⁴⁶Once more he visited Cana in Galilee, where he had turned the water into wine. And there was a certain royal official whose son lay sick at Capernaum. ⁴⁷When this man heard that Jesus had arrived in Galilee from Judea, he went to him and begged him to come and heal his son, who was close to death.

⁴⁸"ᶜUnless you people see miraculous signs and wonders," Jesus told him, "you will never believe."

⁴⁹The royal official said, "Sir, come down before my child dies."

⁵⁰Jesus replied, "You may go. Your son will live."

The man took Jesus at his word and departed. ⁵¹While he was still on the way, his servants met him with the news that his boy was living. ⁵²When he inquired as to the time when his son got better, they said to him, "The fever left him yesterday at the seventh hour."

⁵³Then the father realized that this was the exact time at which Jesus had said to him, "Your son will live." So he and all his household believed.

⁵⁴This was the second miraculous sign that Jesus performed, having come from Judea to Galilee.

ᶻFor a discussion of the length of this Galilean ministry, see essay 11, "Chronology of the Life of Christ" (pp. 315–19).

ªMatthew, Mark, and Luke devote much space to the period spent in Galilee. Early stages of the period were marked by increasing popularity, which reached its peak probably at about the time of the Sermon on the Mount. A rising opposition, beginning with a series of Sabbath controversies with Jewish leaders, is also perceived. This culminated in the first public rejection of Jesus by these leaders. At that point, toward the end of the period, Jesus inaugurated his parabolic teaching ministry so that he might reveal truth to those with receptive hearts while hiding it from the unreceptive.

ᵇ(Mark 1:15) The timing of God's programs in history is a major theme of biblical teaching. The first (Gal. 4:4) and second (Acts 1:7; 3:19–21) comings of Christ are foundational to God's schedule for world history.

ᶜ(John 4:48) Jesus was not rebuking the royal official but lamenting over what was a typical attitude of the Galileans. The official was different in that he believed solely on the basis of Jesus' word (John 4:50).

Sec. 39   Ministry and rejection at Nazareth
          (cf. Secs. 36, 37, 69—no honor at home)
          —Nazareth—

Luke 4:16–31a

[16]He went to Nazareth, [d]where he had been brought up, and on the Sabbath day he went into the synagogue, as was his custom. And he stood up to read. [17]The scroll of the prophet Isaiah was handed to him. Unrolling it, he found the place where it is written:

[18]"The Spirit of the Lord is on me,
    because he has anointed me
    to preach good news to the poor.
He has sent me to proclaim freedom for the prisoners
    and recovery of sight for the blind,
    to release the oppressed,
[19]   to proclaim the year of the Lord's favor"[a] [Isa. 61:1–2].

[20]Then he rolled up the scroll, gave it back to the attendant and sat down. The eyes of everyone in the synagogue were fastened on him, [21]and he began by saying to them, "Today this scripture is fulfilled in your hearing."

[22]All spoke well of him and were amazed at the gracious words that came from his lips. "Isn't this Joseph's son?" they asked.

[23]Jesus said to them, "Surely you will quote this proverb to me: 'Physician, heal yourself! Do here in your hometown what we have heard that you did in Capernaum.' "

[24]"I tell you the truth," he continued, "no prophet is accepted in his hometown. [25]I assure you that there were many widows in Israel in Elijah's time, when the sky was shut for three and a half years and there was a severe famine throughout the land. [26]Yet Elijah was not sent to any of them, but to a widow in Zarephath in the region of Sidon. [27]And there were many in Israel with leprosy[b] in the time of Elisha the prophet, yet not one of them was cleansed—only Naaman the Syrian."

[28]All the people in the synagogue were furious when they heard this. [29]They got up, drove him out of the town, and took him to the brow of the hill on which the town was built, in order to throw him down the cliff. [30]But he walked right through the crowd and went on his way.

[31]Then he went down to Capernaum, a town in Galilee,

[a]Lk 4:19 Isaiah 61:1,2   [b]27 The Greek word was used for various diseases affecting the skin—not necessarily leprosy.

Sec. 40   Move to Capernaum
          —Capernaum—

Matthew 4:13–16

[13]Leaving Nazareth, he went and [e]lived in Capernaum, which was by the lake in the area of Zebulun and Naphtali— [14]to fulfill what was said through the prophet Isaiah:

---

[d](Luke 4:16) This statement implies that Nazareth had ceased to be Jesus' home already. It had been his boyhood custom to attend the synagogue services in that town. He retained the habit after reaching manhood.

[e](Matt. 4:13) Capernaum became Jesus' new home after his unfriendly reception at Nazareth. It had by New Testament times grown into a city, having a tax office (Matt. 9:9, Sec. 47a) and a garrison for Roman soldiers (Matt. 8:9, Sec. 55). Jesus had earlier visited Capernaum (John 2:12, Sec. 30). Here a little later he will encounter Peter and Andrew, who had apparently not gone with him to Nazareth, and James and John, the sons of Zebedee (Matt. 4:18–22; Mark 1:16–20, Sec. 41). He would preach in this city's synagogue, which had been built by the good centurion (Luke 7:5, Sec. 55) and of which Jairus was an official (Mark 5:22. Sec. 67). Jesus' famous message on the bread of life was delivered here (John 6:59, Sec. 76a). It is no wonder that Matthew calls Capernaum Jesus' "own town" (Matt. 9:1, Sec. 46).

Matthew 4:13–16 (cont'd)

15"Land of Zebulun and land of Naphtali,
the way to the sea, along the Jordan,
Galilee of the Gentiles—
16the people living in darkness
have seen a great light;
on those living in the land of the shadow of death
a light has dawned"[a] [Isa. 9:1–2].

[a]Mt 4:16 Isaiah 9:1,2

DISCIPLES CALLED AND MINISTRY THROUGHOUT GALILEE

Sec. 41 Call of the four
(cf. Secs. 28, 47a—calling disciples)
—*By the Sea of Galilee, near Capernaum*—

Matthew 4:18–22	Mark 1:16–20	[f]Luke 5:1–11
18As Jesus was walking beside the Sea of Galilee, he saw two brothers, Simon called Peter and his brother Andrew. They were casting a net into the lake, for they were fishermen. 19"Come, follow me," Jesus said, "and I will make you fishers of men." 20At once they left their nets and followed him. 21Going on from there, he saw two other brothers, James son of Zebedee and his brother John. They were in a boat with their father Zebedee, preparing their nets. Jesus called them, 22and immediately they left the boat	16As Jesus walked beside the Sea of Galilee, he saw Simon and his brother Andrew casting a net into the lake, for they were fishermen. 17"Come, follow me," Jesus said, "and I will make you fishers of men." 18At once they left their nets and followed him. 19When he had gone a little farther, he saw James son of Zebedee and his brother John in a boat, preparing their nets. 20Without delay he called them, and they left their father Zebedee in the boat with the hired men and followed him.	1One day as Jesus was standing by the Lake of Gennesaret,[a] with the people crowding around him and listening to the word of God, 2he saw at the water's edge two boats, left there by the fishermen, who were washing their nets. 3He got into one of the boats, the one belonging to Simon, and asked him to put out a little from shore. Then he sat down and taught the people from the boat. 4When he had finished speaking, he said to Simon, "Put out into deep

---

[f](Luke 5:1–11) If, as tradition says, John the son of Zebedee was one of the two unnamed disciples at Bethany (John 1:35, Sec. 28), three of these four fishermen had already followed Jesus for a time without having a specific call. This, then, was their first explicit call to follow Jesus and perhaps their only one, if A. T. Robertson is correct in seeing Luke 5:1–11 as parallel to the accounts of Matt. 4:18–22 and Mark 1:16–20, a parallelism indicated by the placement of the text of Luke 5:1–11 above. The revisers of this *Harmony*, however, prefer another option. Subsequent to this first call by Jesus, these four fishermen responded by resuming their association with Jesus only temporarily, after which they returned to their original vocation of fishing. This latter option is preferred because features of Luke 5:1–11 are sufficiently distinct from this paragraph to indicate another call later on. The sequence of the account is one difference, but not the only one. Other differences are that Simon and Andrew were not fishing from a boat in Matthew and Mark, but they were in Luke. In Matthew and Mark Jesus did not enter a boat as he did in Luke. Luke records a great catch of fish, but Matthew and Mark say nothing about one. Hence it appears that the two brothers went back to their fishing trade after the tour of Section 44. After responding to the second call of Luke 5:1–11, they seem to have remained with Jesus permanently. Following his crucifixion, however, they did return to fishing once again (Sec. 180).

Matthew 4:18–22 (cont'd)

and their father and followed him.

Luke 5:1–11 (cont'd)

water, and let down[b] the nets for a catch."

[5]Simon answered, "Master, we've worked hard all night and haven't caught anything. But because you say so, I will let down the nets."

[6]When they had done so, they caught such a large number of fish that their nets began to break. [7]So they signaled their partners in the other boat to come and help them, and they came and filled both boats so full that they began to sink.

[8]When Simon Peter saw this, he fell at Jesus' knees and said, "Go away from me, Lord; I am a sinful man!" [9]For he and all his companions were astonished at the catch of fish they had taken, [10]and so were James and John, the sons of Zebedee, Simon's partners.

Then Jesus said to Simon, "Don't be afraid; from now on you will catch men." [11]So they pulled their boats up on shore, left everything and followed him.

[a]Lk 5:1 That is, Sea of Galilee   [b]4 The Greek verb is plural.

Sec. 42   Teaching in the synagogue of [g]Capernaum authenticated by healing a demoniac
—Capernaum, in the synagogue—

Mark 1:21–28

[21]They went to Capernaum, and when the Sabbath came, Jesus went into the synagogue and began to teach. [22]The people were amazed at his teaching, because he taught them as one who had authority, not as the teachers of the law.

Luke 4:31b–37

and on the Sabbath began to teach the people. [32]They were amazed at his teaching, because his message had authority.

[33]In the synagogue there was a man possessed by a demon, an evil[b] spirit.

[g]Two aspects of Jesus' reception at Capernaum stand out. First, the citizens received him warmly, which was the very opposite of what had happened at Nazareth. Second, Jesus was not criticized for performing a deed such as this on the Sabbath as he was so frequently later on (Secs. 49a, 50, 51). Apparently Jewish leadership in Jerusalem had not yet become alarmed to the point of sending representatives to Galilee to oppose him.

Mark 1:21–28 (cont'd)

Luke 4:31b–37 (cont'd)

²³Just then a man in their synagogue who was possessed by an evil^a spirit cried out, ²⁴"What do you want with us, Jesus of Nazareth? Have you come to destroy us? I know who you are—the Holy One of God!"
²⁵"^hBe quiet!" said Jesus sternly. "Come out of him!" ²⁶The evil spirit shook the man violently and came out of him with a shriek.
²⁷The people were all so amazed that they asked each other, "What is this? A new teaching—and with authority! He even gives orders to evil spirits and they obey him." ²⁸News about him spread quickly over the whole region of Galilee.

He cried out at the top of his voice, ³⁴"Ha! What do you want with us, Jesus of Nazareth? Have you come to destroy us? I know who you are—the Holy One of God!"

³⁵"^hBe quiet!" Jesus said sternly. "Come out of him!" Then the demon threw the man down before them all and came out without injuring him.
³⁶All the people were amazed and said to each other, "What is this teaching? With authority and power he gives orders to evil spirits and they come out!" ³⁷And the news about him spread throughout the surrounding area.

^aMk 1:23 Greek *unclean*; also in verses 26 and 27   ^bLk 4:33 Greek *unclean*; also in verse 36

Sec. 43   Peter's mother-in-law and others healed
—*Capernaum, in Peter's home*—

Matthew 8:14–17

Mark 1:29–34

Luke 4:38–41

¹⁴When Jesus came into Peter's house, he saw Peter's mother-in-law lying in bed with a fever. ¹⁵He ⁱtouched her hand and the fever left her, and she got up and began to wait on him.

²⁹As soon as they left the synagogue, they went with James and John to the home of Simon and Andrew. ³⁰Simon's mother-in-law was in bed with a fever, and they told Jesus about her. ³¹So he ⁱwent to her, took her hand and helped her up. The fever left her and she began to wait on them.

³⁸Jesus left the synagogue and went to the home of Simon. Now Simon's mother-in-law was suffering from a high fever, and they asked Jesus to help her. ³⁹So he bent over her and ⁱrebuked the fever, and it left her. She got up at once and began to wait on them.

¹⁶When evening came, many who were demon-possessed were brought to him, and he drove out the spirits with a word and healed all the sick. ¹⁷This was to fulfill what was spoken through the prophet Isaiah:

"He took up our
    infirmities

³²That evening after sunset the people brought to Jesus all the sick and demon-possessed. ³³The whole town gathered at the door, ³⁴and Jesus healed many who had various diseases. He also drove out many demons,

⁴⁰When the sun was setting, the people brought to Jesus all who had various kinds of sickness, and laying his hands on each one, he healed them. ⁴¹Moreover, demons came out of many people, shouting, "You are the Son of God!" But he re-

^h(Mark 1:25; Luke 4:35) It was altogether inappropriate that Jesus' Messiahship should be proclaimed by representatives of the evil one. Had he allowed this by not silencing the demons, he would have given grounds for a charge brought against him later by the Pharisees, that of being Satan's ally (Matt. 12:24; Mark 3:22, Sec. 61). Compare also Mark 1:34; Luke 4:41, Section 43.

ⁱ(Matt. 8:15; Mark 1:31; Luke 4:39) The emphases and backgrounds of the synoptic writers differed. Matthew in describing Messiah the King notes that he merely "touched her hand and the fever left her." Mark describes Messiah the Servant from a slightly different perspective: "He went to her, took her hand and helped her up." Luke the physician, after giving a more professional description of the sickness, pictures Messiah the Man as simply rebuking the fever. Luke alone tells how in the subsequent healings Jesus laid "his hands on each one" (4:40), indicating his deep concern for his fellow human beings as individuals.

^j(Matt. 4:23–25) The general type of the description in Matt. 4:24–25 reflects the summary nature of

Matthew 8:14–17	Mark 1:29–34 (cont'd)	Luke 4:38–41 (cont'd)
and carried our diseases"[a] [Isa. 53:4].	but he would not let the demons speak because they knew who he was.	buked them and would not allow them to speak, because they knew he was the Christ.[b]

[a]Mt 8:17 Isaiah 53:4   [b]Lk 4:41 Or *Messiah*

Sec. 44   Tour of Galilee with Simon and others
—Galilee—

[j]Matthew 4:23–25	Mark 1:35–39	Luke 4:42–44
	[35]Very early in the morning, while it was still dark, Jesus got up, left the house and went off to a solitary place, where he prayed. [36]Simon and his companions went to look for him, [37]and when they found him, they exclaimed: "Everyone is looking for you!"	[42]At daybreak Jesus went out to a solitary place. The people were looking for him and when they came to where he was, they tried to keep him from leaving them. [43]But he said, "I must preach the good news of the kingdom of God to the other towns also, because that is why I was sent."
	[38]Jesus replied, "Let us go somewhere else—to the nearby villages—so I can preach there also. That is why I have come."	
[23]Jesus went throughout Galilee, [k]teaching in their synagogues, preaching the good news of the kingdom, and healing every disease and sickness among the people. [24]News about him spread all over Syria, and people brought to him all who were ill with various diseases, those suffering severe pain, the demon-possessed, those having seizures, and the paralyzed, and he healed them. [25]Large crowds from Galilee, the Decapolis,[a] Jerusalem, Judea and the region across the Jordan followed him.	[39]So he traveled throughout Galilee, preaching in their synagogues and driving out demons.	[44]And he kept on preaching in the synagogues of Judea.[b]

[a]Mt 4:25 That is, the Ten Cities   [b]Lk 4:44 Or *the land of the Jews*; some manuscripts *Galilee*

---

the verses. They describe a long period of Jesus' Galilean ministry. Consequently they could just as accurately be included as part of Section 52, just before the appointment of the Twelve and the Sermon on the Mount, as here in Section 44. Matthew chose to use such a summary early in his gospel because in his topical arrangement of the incidents of Jesus' life, he incorporated the Sermon on the Mount at a relatively early stage in the gospel.

    [k](Matt. 4:23) The threefold thrust of Jesus' ministry is reflected here: He taught in Jewish synagogues, he proclaimed the kingdom of God, and he healed diseases and sicknesses in certification of the authority of his teaching and preaching.

[Second call of the four
ᶦLuke 5:1–11]

Sec. 45　Cleansing of a man with leprosy, followed by much publicity
—In one of the cities by the Sea of Galilee—

Matthew 8:2–4	Mark 1:40–45	Luke 5:12–16
²A man with leprosyᵃ came and knelt before him and said, "Lord, if you are willing, you can make me clean." ³Jesus reached out his hand and touched the man. "I am willing," he said. "Be clean!" Immediately he was curedᵇ of his leprosy.	⁴⁰A man with leprosyᵃ came to him and begged him on his knees, "If you are willing, you can make me clean." ⁴¹Filled with compassion, Jesus reached out his hand and touched the man. "I am willing," he said. "Be clean!" ⁴²Immediately the leprosy left him and he was cured.	¹²While Jesus was in one of the towns, a man came along who was covered with leprosy.ᵃ When he saw Jesus, he fell with his face to the ground and begged him, "Lord, if you are willing, you can make me clean." ¹³Jesus reached out his hand and touched the man. "I am willing," he said. "Be clean!" And immediately the leprosy left him.
⁴Then Jesus said to him, "ᵐSee that you don't tell anyone. But go, show yourself to the priest and offer the gift Moses commanded, as a testimony to them."	⁴³Jesus sent him away at once with a strong warning: ⁴⁴"ᵐSee that you don't tell this to anyone. But go, show yourself to the priest and offer the sacrifices that Moses commanded for your cleansing, as a testimony to them." ⁴⁵Instead he went out and began to talk freely, spreading the news. As a result, Jesus could no longer enter a town openly but stayed outside in lonely places. Yet the people still came to him from everywhere.	¹⁴Then Jesus ordered him, "Don't ᵐtell anyone, but go, show yourself to the priest and offer the sacrifices that Moses commanded for your cleansing, as a testimony to them." ¹⁵Yet the news about him spread all the more, so that crowds of people came to hear him and to be healed of their sicknesses. ¹⁶But Jesus often withdrew to lonely places and prayed.

ᵃ*Mt 8:2; Mk 1:40; Lk 5:12* The Greek word was used for various diseases affecting the skin—not necessarily leprosy.　ᵇ*Mt 8:3* Greek *made clean*

ᶦ(Luke 5:1–11) See note f, Section 41.

ᵐ(Matt. 8:4; Mark 1:44; Luke 5:14) The proper course would have been for the priests to verify the cleansing and announce to the nation the arrival of Messiah. Whether the cleansed leper complied with this instruction is doubtful in light of his disobedience in telling others besides the priests. Even if he had complied, the willingness of the priests to acknowledge Jesus' Messiahship is not established, as reflected in the Sadducees' attitude toward him later on.

Sec. 46 Forgiving and healing of a paralytic
—*Capernaum*—

Matthew 9:1–8	Mark 2:1–12	Luke 5:17–26

[1]Jesus stepped into a boat, crossed over and came to his own town.

[2]Some men brought to him a paralytic, lying on a mat.

When Jesus saw their faith, he said to the paralytic, "Take heart, son; your sins are forgiven." [3]At this, some of the teachers of the law said to themselves, "This fellow is blaspheming!"

[4]Knowing their thoughts, Jesus said, "Why do you entertain evil thoughts in your hearts? [5]Which is easier: to say, 'Your sins are forgiven,' or to say, 'Get up and walk'? [6]But so that you may know that the Son of Man has authority on earth to forgive sins. . . ." Then he said to the paralytic, "Get up, take your mat and go home." [7]And the man got up and went home.

[1]A few days later, when Jesus again entered Capernaum, the people heard that he had come home. [2]So many gathered that there was no room left, not even outside the door, and he preached the word to them. [3]Some men came, bringing to him a paralytic, carried by four of them. [4]Since they could not get him to Jesus because of the crowd, they made an opening in the roof above Jesus and, after digging through it, lowered the mat the paralyzed man was lying on. [5]When Jesus saw their faith, he said to the paralytic, "Son, your sins are forgiven."

[6]Now some teachers of the law were sitting there, thinking to themselves, [7]"Why does this fellow talk like that? He's blaspheming! Who can forgive sins but God alone?" [8]Immediately Jesus knew in his spirit that this was what they were thinking in their hearts, and he said to them, "Why are you thinking these things? [9]Which is easier: to say to the paralytic, 'Your sins are forgiven,' or to say, 'Get up, take your mat and walk'? [10]But that you may know that the Son of Man has authority on earth to forgive sins. . . ." He said to the paralytic, [11]"I tell you, get up, take your mat and go home." [12]He got up, took his mat and walked

[17]One day as he was teaching, [n]Pharisees and teachers of the law, who had come from every village of Galilee and from Judea and Jerusalem, were sitting there. And the power of the Lord was present for him to heal the sick. [18]Some men came carrying a paralytic on a mat and tried to take him into the house to lay him before Jesus. [19]When they could not find a way to do this because of the crowd, they went up on the roof and lowered him on his mat through the tiles into the middle of the crowd, right in front of Jesus. [20]When Jesus saw their faith, he said, "Friend, your sins are forgiven." [21]The Pharisees and the teachers of the law began thinking to themselves, "Who is this fellow who speaks blasphemy? Who can forgive sins but God alone?" [22]Jesus knew what they were thinking and asked, "Why are you thinking these things in your hearts? [23]Which is easier: to say, 'Your sins are forgiven,' or to say, 'Get up and walk'? [24]But that you may know that the Son of Man has authority on earth to forgive sins. . . ." He said to the paralyzed man, "I tell you, get up, take your mat and go home." [25]Immediately he stood up in front of them, took what he had been lying on and went home

[n](Luke 5:17) This is the first mention of the Pharisees in Luke's gospel. This is also the first time that opposition to Jesus from religious leaders appeared in Galilee. It began earlier in Jerusalem because of jealousy (John 4:1–4, Sec. 34), and representatives soon came from Judea to continue their campaign against him. The recent tour of Galilee (Sec. 44) had created wider interest, and therefore the Jewish leaders felt a need to investigate and thwart, if necessary, this new public figure.

Matthew 9:1–8 (cont'd)	Mark 2:1–12 (cont'd)	Luke 5:17–26 (cont'd)
[8]When the crowd saw this, they were filled with awe; and they praised God, who had given such authority to men.	out in full view of them all. This amazed everyone and they praised God, saying, "We have never seen anything like this!"	praising God. [26]Everyone was amazed and gave praise to God. They were filled with awe and said, "We have seen remarkable things today."

Sec. 47a   Call of Matthew
(cf. Secs. 28, 41—calling disciples)
—Capernaum—

Matthew 9:9	Mark 2:13–14	Luke 5:27–28
	[13]Once again Jesus went out beside the lake. A large crowd came to him, and he began to teach them. [14]As he walked along, he saw Levi son of Alphaeus sitting at the °tax collector's booth. "Follow me," Jesus told him, and Levi got up and followed him.	[27]After this, Jesus went out and saw a tax collector by the name of Levi
[9]As Jesus went on from there, he saw a man named Matthew sitting at the °tax collector's booth. "Follow me," he told him, and Matthew got up and followed him.		sitting at his °tax booth. "Follow me," Jesus said to him, [28]and Levi got up, left everything and followed him.

Sec. 47b   Banquet at Matthew's house
—Capernaum—

Matthew 9:10–13	Mark 2:15–17	Luke 5:29–32
[10]While Jesus was having dinner at Matthew's house, many tax collectors and "sinners" came and ate with him and his disciples. [11]When the Pharisees saw this, they asked his disciples, "Why does your teacher eat with tax collectors and 'sinners'?" [12]On hearing this, Jesus said, "It is not the healthy	[15]While Jesus was having dinner at Levi's house, many tax collectors and "sinners" were eating with him and his disciples, for there were many who followed him. [16]When the teachers of the law who were Pharisees saw him eating with the "sinners" and tax collectors, they asked his disciples: "Why does he eat	[29]Then Levi held a ᵖgreat banquet for Jesus at his house, and a large crowd of tax collectors and others were eating with them. [30]But the Pharisees and the teachers of the law who belonged to their sect complained to his disciples, "Why do you eat and drink with tax collectors and 'sinners'?" [31]Jesus answered them,

°(Matt. 9:9; Mark 2:14; Luke 5:27) Tax collectors such as Matthew (also called Levi) estimated the worth of merchants' goods that were in transit and collected taxes on them for the Roman government. Matthew apparently dealt with the shipping trade on the Sea of Galilee (cf. Mark 2:13). Vague tariff rates allowed the tax collector to levy higher fees so as to increase his own profit. Whether Matthew was among the dishonest majority of his occupation is not known, but merely belonging to a class that had been excommunicated by fellow Jews was enough to make him despised. His cooperation with the Romans further alienated him from his countrymen. Jesus went against the theocratic notions of the teachers of the law and Pharisees by calling a person with this background. Matthew responded and left his occupation, never to return to it ("everything," Luke 5:28; cf. Luke 5:11, Sec. 41).

ᵖ(Luke 5:29) Matthew's willingness to use his wealth to evangelize his friends is reflected in the size of the reception he hosted. Jesus' participation with despised tax collectors and sinners marked a departure from customary Jewish procedure and demonstrated his concern for those who were spiritually sick and would admit it. For those who felt themselves righteous, but were actually unrighteous, he could do nothing.

Matthew 9:10–13 (cont'd)	Mark 2:15–17 (cont'd)	Luke 5:29–32 (cont'd)
who need a doctor, but the sick. [13]But go and learn what this means: 'I desire mercy, not sacrifice'[a] [Hos. 6:6]. For I have not come to call the righteous, but sinners."	with tax collectors and 'sinners'?" [17]On hearing this, Jesus said to them, "It is not the healthy who need a doctor, but the sick. I have not come to call the righteous, but sinners."	"It is not the healthy who need a doctor, but the sick. [32]I have not come to call the righteous, but sinners to repentance."

ᵃMt 9:13 Hosea 6:6

Sec. 48   Jesus defends his disciples for [q]feasting instead of fasting with three parables
—*Capernaum*—

Matthew 9:14–17	Mark 2:18–22	Luke 5:33–39
[14]Then John's disciples came and asked him, "How is it that we and the Pharisees fast, but your disciples do not fast?"	[18]Now John's disciples and the Pharisees were fasting. Some people came and asked Jesus, "How is it that John's disciples and the disciples of the Pharisees are fasting, but yours are not?"	[33]They said to him, "John's disciples often fast and pray, and so do the disciples of the Pharisees, but yours go on eating and drinking."
[15]Jesus answered, "How can the guests of the bridegroom mourn while he is with them? The time will come when the bridegroom will be taken from them; then they will fast. [16]"No one sews a patch of unshrunk cloth on an old garment, for the patch will pull away from the garment, making the tear worse. [17]Neither do men pour new wine into old wineskins. If they do, the skins will burst, the wine will run out and the wineskins will be ruined. No, they pour new wine into new wineskins, and both are preserved."	[19]Jesus answered, "How can the guests of the bridegroom fast while he is with them? They cannot, so long as they have him with them. [20]But the time will come when the bridegroom will be taken from them, and on that day they will fast. [21]"No one sews a patch of unshrunk cloth on an old garment. If he does, the new piece will pull away from the old, making the tear worse. [22]And no one pours new wine into old wineskins. If he does, the wine will burst the skins, and both the wine and the wineskins	[34]Jesus answered, "Can you make the guests of the bridegroom fast while he is with them? [35]But the time will come when the bridegroom will be taken from them; in those days they will fast." [36]He told them this [r]parable: "No one tears a patch from a new garment and sews it on an old one. If he does, he will have torn the new garment, and the patch from the new will not match the old. [37]And no one pours new wine into old wineskins. If he does, the new wine

[q]Changed conditions arise when Messiah comes. John the Baptist had indicated this (cf. Sec. 33), but had not dealt specifically with the issue of feasting versus fasting.
[r](Luke 5:36) By *parable* Luke means "illustration." A more technical sense of *parable* later on marks a major change in the Lord's teaching technique (cf. Sec. 64a–64k). In this latter sense a parable is designed to hide the truth from unbelievers while revealing truth to believers. The former aspect is not in evidence here.

Mark 2:18–22 (cont'd)   Luke 5:33–39 (cont'd)

will be ruined. No, he pours new wine into new wineskins."

will burst the skins, the wine will run out and the wineskins will be ruined. [38]No, new wine must be poured into new wineskins. [39]And no one after drinking old wine wants the new, for he says, 'The old is better.' "

SABBATH CONTROVERSIES
AND WITHDRAWALS
(cf. Secs. 100c, 110, 114—Sabbath controversies)

Sec. 49a   Jesus heals an invalid on the Sabbath
—*Jerusalem*—

John 5:1–9

[1]Some time later, Jesus went up to Jerusalem for a [s]feast of the Jews. [2]Now there is in Jerusalem near the Sheep Gate a pool, which in Aramaic is called Bethesda[a] and which is surrounded by five covered colonnades. [3]Here a great number of disabled people used to lie—the blind, the lame, the paralyzed.[b] [5]One who was there had been an invalid for thirty-eight years. [6]When Jesus saw him lying there and learned that he had been in this condition for a long time, he asked him, "Do you want to get well?"

[7]"Sir," the invalid replied, "I have no one to help me into the pool when the water is stirred. While I am trying to get in, someone else goes down ahead of me."

[8]Then Jesus said to him, "Get up! Pick up your mat and walk." [9]At once the man was cured; he picked up his mat and walked.

The day on which this took place was a Sabbath,

[a]Jn 5:2 Some manuscripts *Bethzatha*; other manuscripts *Bethsaida*   [b]3 Some less important manuscripts *paralyzed—and they waited for the moving of the waters.* [4]*From time to time an angel of the Lord would come down and stir up the waters. The first one into the pool after each such disturbance would be cured of whatever disease he had.*

Sec. 49b   Effort to kill Jesus for breaking the Sabbath and saying he was equal with God
—*Jerusalem*—

John 5:10–18

[10]and so the Jews said to the man who had been healed, "It is the [t]Sabbath; the law forbids you to carry your mat."

[11]But he replied, "The man who made me well said to me, 'Pick up your mat and walk.' "

[12]So they asked him, "Who is this fellow who told you to pick it up and walk?"

[13]The man who was healed had no idea who it was, for Jesus had slipped away into the crowd that was there.

[14]Later Jesus found him at the temple and said to him, "See, you are well again. Stop sinning or something worse may happen to you." [15]The man went away and told the Jews that it was Jesus who had made him well.

[16]So, because Jesus was doing these things on the Sabbath, the Jews persecuted him. [17]Jesus said to them, "My Father is always at his work to this very day, and I, too, am working." [18]For this reason the Jews tried all the harder to kill him; not only was he breaking the Sabbath, but he was even calling God his own Father, making himself equal with God.

[s](John 5:1) The two most probable identifications of this feast are Passover and Tabernacles. Of the two, the latter seems the better choice for reasons given in essay 11, "Chronology of the Life of Christ" (pp. 315–19).

[t](John 5:10) On no other subject did the religious leaders differ with the Lord more frequently than that of the Sabbath. This is the first of three controversies that came in rather rapid succession (cf. Secs. 50, 51). The rabbis had listed thirty-nine principal works that were forbidden on the Sabbath, one group of which included ordinary house chores. Carrying a pallet violated this. A year and a half of ministry still remained, and already the Jerusalem authorities were ready to kill him (John 5:18). This animosity spread very quickly to Galilee (cf. Mark 3:6, Sec. 51).

Sec. 49c Discourse demonstrating the Son's ᵘequality with the Father
—Jerusalem—

John 5:19–47

¹⁹Jesus gave them this answer: "I tell you the truth, the Son can do nothing by himself; he can do only what he sees his Father doing, because whatever the Father does the Son also does. ²⁰For the Father loves the Son and shows him all he does. Yes, to your amazement he will show him even greater things than these. ²¹For just as the Father raises the dead and gives them life, even so the Son gives life to whom he is pleased to give it. ²²Moreover, the Father judges no one, but has entrusted all judgment to the Son, ²³that all may honor the Son just as they honor the Father. He who does not honor the Son does not honor the Father, who sent him.

²⁴"I tell you the truth, whoever hears my word and believes him who sent me has eternal life and will not be condemned; he has crossed over from death to life. ²⁵I tell you the truth, a time is coming and has now come when the dead will hear the voice of the Son of God and those who hear will live. ²⁶For as the Father has life in himself, so he has granted the Son to have life in himself. ²⁷And he has given him authority to judge because he is the Son of Man.

²⁸"Do not be amazed at this, for a time is coming when all who are in their graves will hear his voice ²⁹and come out—those who have done good will rise to live, and those who have done evil will rise to be condemned. ³⁰By myself I can do nothing; I judge only as I hear, and my judgment is just, for I seek not to please myself but him who sent me.

³¹"If I testify about myself, my testimony is not valid. ³²There is another who testifies in my favor, and I know that his testimony about me is valid.

³³"You have sent to John and he has testified to the truth. ³⁴Not that I accept human testimony; but I mention it that you may be saved. ³⁵John was a lamp that burned and gave light, and you chose for a time to enjoy his light.

³⁶"I have testimony weightier than that of John. For the very work that the Father has given me to finish, and which I am doing, testifies that the Father has sent me. ³⁷And the Father who sent me has himself testified concerning me. You have never heard his voice nor seen his form, ³⁸nor does his word dwell in you, for you do not believe the one he sent. ³⁹You diligently studyᵃ the Scriptures because you think that by them you possess eternal life. These are the Scriptures that testify about me, ⁴⁰yet you refuse to come to me to have life.

⁴¹"I do not accept praise from men, ⁴²but I know you. I know that you do not have the love of God in your hearts. ⁴³I have come in my Father's name, and you do not accept me; but if someone else comes in his own name, you will accept him. ⁴⁴How can you believe if you accept praise from one another, yet make no effort to obtain the praise that comes from the only Godᵇ?

⁴⁵"But do not think I will accuse you before the Father. Your accuser is Moses, on whom your hopes are set. ⁴⁶If you believed Moses, you would believe me, for he wrote about me. ⁴⁷But since you do not believe what he wrote, how are you going to believe what I say?"

ᵃJn 5:39 Or *Study diligently* (the imperative)   ᵇ44 Some early manuscripts *the Only One*

Sec. 50 Controversy over disciples' picking grain on the Sabbath
—Perhaps in Galilee—

Matthew 12:1–8	Mark 2:23–28	Luke 6:1–5
¹At that time Jesus went through the grainfields on the Sabbath. His disciples	²³One Sabbath Jesus was going through the grainfields, and as his dis-	¹One ᵛSabbath Jesus was going through the grainfields, and his disci-

ᵘThis discourse takes its cue from and accepts the accuracy of the statement by the Jews in John 5:18 (Sec. 49b): "he was even calling God his own Father, making himself equal with God."

ᵛ(Luke 6:1) 'Picking' and 'rubbing' were, according to rabbinic tradition, tantamount to reaping, threshing, winnowing, and preparing food. Jesus' disciples thus were labeled Sabbath breakers.

Matthew 12:1–8 (cont'd)	Mark 2:23–28 (cont'd)	Luke 6:1–5 (cont'd)
were hungry and began to pick some heads of grain and eat them. ²When the Pharisees saw this, they said to him, "Look! Your disciples are doing what is unlawful on the Sabbath."	ciples walked along, they began to pick some heads of grain. ²⁴The Pharisees said to him, "Look, why are they doing what is unlawful on the Sabbath?"	ples began to pick some heads of grain, rub them in their hands and eat the kernels. ²Some of the Pharisees asked, "Why are you doing what is unlawful on the Sabbath?"
³He answered, "ʷHaven't you read what David did when he and his companions were hungry? ⁴He entered the house of God, and he and his companions ate the consecrated bread— which was not lawful for them to do, but only for the priests. ⁵Or haven't you read in the Law that on the Sabbath the priests in the temple desecrate the day and yet are innocent? ⁶I tell you that one ᵃ greater than the temple is here. ⁷If you had known what these words mean, 'I desire mercy, not sacrifice'ᵇ [Hos. 6:6], you would not have condemned the innocent. ⁸For the Son of Man is Lord of the Sabbath."	²⁵He answered, "Have you never read what David did when he and his companions were hungry and in need? ²⁶In the days of Abiathar the high priest, he entered the house of God and ate the consecrated bread, which is lawful only for priests to eat. And he also gave some to his companions." ²⁷Then he said to them, "The Sabbath was made for man, not man for the Sabbath. ²⁸So the Son of Man is Lord even of the Sabbath."	³Jesus answered them, "Have you never read what David did when he and his companions were hungry? ⁴He entered the house of God, and taking the consecrated bread, he ate what is lawful only for priests to eat. And he also gave some to his companions." ⁵Then Jesus said to them, "The Son of Man is Lord of the Sabbath."

ᵃMt 12:6 Or *something;* also in verses 41 and 42   ᵇ7 Hosea 6:6

Sec. 51   Healing of a man's shriveled hand on the Sabbath
    —*In a synagogue in Galilee*—

Matthew 12:9–14	Mark 3:1–6	Luke 6:6–11
⁹Going on from that place, he went into their synagogue, ¹⁰and a man with a shriveled hand was there. Looking for a reason to accuse Jesus, they asked him, "Is it lawful to heal on the Sabbath?"	¹Another time he went into the ˣsynagogue, and a man with a shriveled hand was there. ²Some of them were looking for a reason to accuse Jesus, so	⁶On another Sabbath he went into the synagogue and was teaching, and a man was there whose right hand was shriveled. ⁷The Pharisees and the teachers of the law were looking for a reason to ac-

ʷ(Matt. 12:3) Jesus' fivefold rebuttal to the accusation is given in Matthew: (1) the example of David (12:3–4), (2) the teaching of the Law (12:5), (3) the prophetic anticipation of someone greater than the temple (12:6; cf. Mark 2:27), and (5) Messiah's lordship over the Sabbath (12:8).

ˣ(Mark 3:1) That this synagogue was in Galilee is demonstrated by Mark's association of the event with the Sea of Galilee immediately afterward (Mark 3:7, Sec. 52).

Matthew 12:9–14 (cont'd)	Mark 3:1–6 (cont'd)	Luke 6:6–11 (cont'd)

[11]He said to them, "If any of you has a sheep and it falls into a pit on the Sabbath, will you not take hold of it and lift it out? [12]How much more valuable is a man than a sheep!

Therefore it is lawful to do good on the Sabbath." [13]Then he said to the man, "Stretch out your hand." So he stretched it out and it was completely restored, just as sound as the other. [14]But the Pharisees went out and plotted how they might kill Jesus.

they watched him closely to see if he would heal him on the Sabbath. [3]Jesus said to the man with the shriveled hand, "Stand up in front of everyone."

[4]Then Jesus asked them, "Which is lawful on the Sabbath: to do good or to do evil, to save life or to kill?" But they remained silent.

[5]He looked around at them in anger and, deeply distressed at their stubborn hearts, said to the man, "Stretch out your hand." He stretched it out, and his hand was completely restored. [6]Then the Pharisees went out and began to plot with the Herodians how they might kill Jesus.

cuse Jesus, so they watched him closely to see if he would heal on the Sabbath. [8]But Jesus knew what they were thinking and said to the man with the shriveled hand, "[y]Get up and stand in front of everyone." So he got up and stood there.

[9]Then Jesus said to them, "I ask you, which is lawful on the Sabbath: to do good or to do evil, to save life or to destroy it?"

[10]He looked around at them all, and then said to the man, "Stretch out your hand." He did so, and his hand was completely restored. [11]But they were furious and began to discuss with one another what they might do to Jesus.

Sec. 52 Withdrawal to the Sea of Galilee with large crowds from many places
—*Sea of Galilee*—

Matthew 12:15–21	Mark 3:7–12

[15]Aware of this, Jesus withdrew from that place. Many followed him, and he healed all their sick,

[z][Matthew 4:25]

[7]Jesus withdrew with his disciples to the lake, and a [a]large crowd from Galilee followed. [8]When they heard all he was doing, many people came to him from Judea, Jerusalem, Idumea, and the regions across the Jordan and around Tyre and Sidon. [9]Because of the crowd he told his disciples to have a small boat ready for him, to keep the people from crowding him. [10]For he had healed many, so that those with diseases were pushing forward to touch him. [11]Whenever the evil[b] spirits saw him, they fell down before him and cried out, "You are the Son of God." [12]But he gave them strict orders not to tell who he was.

[16]warning them not to tell who he was. [17]This was to fulfill what was spoken through the prophet Isaiah:

[18]"Here is my servant whom I have
    chosen,

---

[y](Luke 6:8) Jesus' intent to make this an occasion for a theological confrontation is evidenced in his words, "Get up and stand in front of everyone" (Luke 6:8). This Sabbath healing received maximum publicity.

[z](Matt. 4:25) For the text of Matthew 4:25, see Section 44 and note j associated with that section.

[a](Mark 3:7) A widespread interest in Jesus had now developed. Distant as well as nearby regions were represented in these large crowds.

Matthew 12:15–21 (cont'd)

the one I love, in whom I delight;
I will put my Spirit on him,
    and he will proclaim justice to the
        nations.
[19]He will not quarrel or cry out;
    no one will hear his voice in the
        streets.
[20]A bruised reed he will not break,
    and a smoldering wick he will not
        snuff out,
    till he leads justice to victory.
[21]   In his name the nations will put
        their hope"[a] [Isa. 42:1–4].

[a]Mt 12:21 Isaiah 42:1–4 [b]Mk 3:11 Greek unclean; also in verse 30

APPOINTMENT OF THE TWELVE AND SERMON ON THE MOUNT

Sec. 53   Twelve apostles chosen
(cf. Sec. 70b, Acts 1:13—twelve apostles listed)
—A mountain near the Sea of Galilee—

Mark 3:13–19

[13]Jesus went up on a mountainside and called to him those he wanted, and they came to him. [14]He appointed twelve—designating them apostles[a]—that they might be with him and that he might send them out to preach [15]and to have authority to drive out demons. [16]These are the twelve he appointed: [b]Simon (to whom he gave the name Peter); [17]James son of Zebedee and his brother John (to them he gave the name Boanerges, which means Sons of Thunder); [18]Andrew, Philip, Bartholomew, Matthew, Thomas, James son of Alphaeus, Thaddaeus, Simon the Zealot [19]and Judas Iscariot, who betrayed him.

Luke 6:12–16

[12]One of those days Jesus went out to a mountainside to pray, and spent the night praying to God. [13]When morning came, he called his disciples to him and chose twelve of them, whom he also designated apostles:

[14b]Simon (whom he named Peter), his brother Andrew, James, John, Philip, Bartholomew, [15]Matthew, Thomas, James son of Alphaeus, Simon who was called the Zealot, [16]Judas son of James, and Judas Iscariot, who became a traitor.

[a]Mk 3:14 Some manuscripts do not have designating them apostles.

Sec. 54a   Setting of the sermon
—A level place on the mountain—

Matthew 5:1–2

[1]Now when he saw the crowds, he went up on a [c]mountainside and sat down. His disciples came to him, [2]and he began to teach them, saying:

Luke 6:17–19

[17]He went down with them and stood on a [c]level place. A large crowd of his disciples was there and a great number of people from all over Judea, from Jeru-

[b](Mark 3:16; Luke 6:14) Two other lists of the Twelve are given, in Matthew 10:2–4 (Sec. 70b) and Acts 1:13. By noting that Thaddaeus is another name for Judas the brother of James, the lists are seen to agree with one another except in sequence. Simon Peter is first in all four lists, however. All were Galileans except Judas Iscariot, who was a Judean.
    [c](Matt. 5:1; Luke 6:17) Though some have suggested that the Sermon on the Mount consists of

Luke 6:12–16 (cont'd)

salem, and from the coast of Tyre and
Sidon, [18]who had come to hear him and
to be healed of their diseases. Those
troubled by evil[a] spirits were cured,
[19]and the people all tried to touch him,
because power was coming from him
and healing them all.

[a]Lk 6:18 Greek *unclean*

Sec. 54b   [d]**Blessings of those who inherit the kingdom and woes to those who do not**

Matthew 5:3–12	Luke 6:20–26

Matthew 5:3–12

[3]"Blessed are the poor in spirit,
for theirs is the kingdom of heaven.
[4]Blessed are those who mourn,
for they will be comforted.
[5]Blessed are the meek,
for they will inherit the earth.
[6]Blessed are those who hunger and
thirst for righteousness,
for they will be filled.
[7]Blessed are the merciful,
for they will be shown mercy.
[8]Blessed are the pure in heart,
for they will see God.
[9]Blessed are the peacemakers,
for they will be called sons of God.
[10]Blessed are those who are persecuted
because of righteousness,
for theirs is the kingdom of heaven.

[11]"Blessed are you when people insult you, persecute you and falsely say
all kinds of evil against you because of
me. [12]Rejoice and be glad, because great
is your reward in heaven, for in the
same way they persecuted the prophets
who were before you.

Luke 6:20–26

[20]Looking at his disciples, he said:
"Blessed are you who are poor,
for yours is the kingdom of God.
[21]Blessed are you who hunger now,
for you will be satisfied.
Blessed are you who weep now,
for you will laugh.
[22]Blessed are you when men hate you,
when they exclude you and insult
you
and reject your name as evil,
because of the Son of Man.

[23]"Rejoice in that day and leap for joy,
because great is your reward in heaven.
For that is how their fathers treated the
prophets.

---

teachings given at different times, evidence is convincing that it was delivered on a single occasion, as
Matthew and Luke describe it. That the two gospels contain the same sermon is also well taken. Similarities
between the two are too numerous to allow for two different sermons. Jesus delivered this sermon from
a level place on the side of a mountain. It was addressed to his disciples (Matt. 5:1–2; Luke 6:20), but the
multitude was not excluded from the benefit of his words (Matt. 7:28, Sec. 54i; Luke 6:19; 7:1, Sec. 55).
The sermon was probably much longer than the combined accounts that are preserved. Because each writer
has recorded things that the other does not, and because differing details in some of the sayings indicate
that Jesus repeated himself by varying his wording, there probably was other matter not included in either
gospel account.
    [d]Each beatitude is associated with an Old Testament promise to those who will participate in the
future kingdom. By this means Jesus informed his listeners as to what kingdom he was discussing.

Luke 6:20–26 (cont'd)

24"But woe to you who are rich,
    for you have already received your
      comfort.
25Woe to you who are well fed now,
    for you will go hungry.
Woe to you who laugh now,
    for you will mourn and weep.
26Woe to you when all men speak well
    of you,
    for that is how their fathers treated
      the false prophets.

Sec. 54c   Responsibility while awaiting the kingdom
(cf. Secs. 64b, 106—lighting a lamp)
(cf. Secs. 91, 115—salt of the earth)

Matthew 5:13–16

13"You are the salt of the earth. But if the salt loses its saltiness, how can it be made salty again? It is no longer good for anything, except to be thrown out and trampled by men.
14"You are the light of the world. A city on a hill cannot be hidden. 15Neither do people light a lamp and put it under a bowl. Instead they put it on its stand, and it gives light to everyone in the house. 16In the same way, let your light shine before men, that they may see your good deeds and praise your Father in heaven.

Sec. 54d   Law, righteousness, and the kingdom
(cf. Sec. 117b—permanence of the law)

Matthew 5:17–20

17"Do not think that I have come to ᵉabolish the Law or the Prophets; I have not come to abolish them but to fulfill them. 18I tell you the truth, until heaven and earth disappear, not the smallest letter, not the least stroke of a pen, will by any means disappear from the Law until everything is accomplished. 19Anyone who breaks one of the least of these commandments and teaches others to do the same will be called least in the kingdom of heaven, but whoever practices and teaches these commands will be called great in the kingdom of heaven. 20For I tell you that unless your righteousness surpasses that of the Pharisees and the teachers of the law, you will certainly not enter the kingdom of heaven.

ᵉ(Matt. 5:17) Far from breaking with Old Testament teachings, Jesus came to bring them to fruition by contrasting the true intent of the law with the common rabbinic interpretations of his day. The key verse of the sermon, therefore, is Matthew 5:20. The righteousness of the teachers of the law and Pharisees was not adequate to gain entrance into the kingdom because it dealt only with external behavior. Qualifications for entering this promised kingdom are what Jesus outlines in this discourse (cf. Matt. 7:21, Sec. 54h).

Sec. 54e   **Six ᵍcontrasts in interpreting the law**
           (cf. Sec. 91—loss of hand or eye)
           (cf. Sec. 108e—reconciliation)
           (cf. Secs. 117b, 122—divorce and remarriage)
           (cf. Sec. 137a—taking an oath)

Matthew 5:21–48

[21]"You have heard that it was said to the people long ago, 'Do not murder[a] [Exod. 20:13; Deut. 5:17], and anyone who murders will be subject to judgment.' [22]But I tell you that anyone who is angry with his brother[b] will be subject to judgment. Again, anyone who says to his brother, 'Raca,[c]' is answerable to the Sanhedrin. But anyone who says, 'You fool!' will be in danger of the fire of hell.

[23]"Therefore, if you are offering your gift at the altar and there remember that your brother has something against you, [24]leave your gift there in front of the altar. First go and be reconciled to your brother; then come and offer your gift.

[25]"Settle matters quickly with your adversary who is taking you to court. Do it while you are still with him on the way, or he may hand you over to the judge, and the judge may hand you over to the officer, and you may be thrown into prison. [26]I tell you the truth, you will not get out until you have paid the last penny.[d]

[27]"You have heard that it was said, 'Do not commit adultery'[e] [Exod. 20:14; Deut. 5:18]. [28]But I tell you that anyone who looks at a woman lustfully has already committed adultery with her in his heart. [29]If your right eye causes you to sin, gouge it out and throw it away. It is better for you to lose one part of your body than for your whole body to be thrown into hell. [30]And if your right hand causes you to sin, cut it off and throw it away. It is better for you to lose one part of your body than for your whole body to go into hell.

[31]"It has been said, 'Anyone who divorces his wife must give her a certificate of divorce'[f] [Deut. 24:1,3]. [32]But I tell you that anyone who divorces his wife, except for marital unfaithfulness, causes her to become an adulteress, and anyone who marries the divorced woman commits adultery.

[33]"Again, you have heard that it was said to the people long ago, 'Do not break your oath, but keep the oaths you have made to the Lord' [Lev. 19:12; Num. 30:2; Deut. 23:21]. [34]But I tell you, Do not swear at all: either by heaven, for it is God's throne; [35]or by the earth, for it is his footstool; or by Jerusalem, for it is the city of the Great King [Psalm 48:2]. [36]And do not swear by your head, for you cannot make even one hair white or black. [37]Simply let your 'Yes' be 'Yes,' and your 'No,' 'No'; anything beyond this comes from the evil one.

[38]"You have heard that it was said, 'Eye for eye, and tooth for tooth'[g] [Exod. 21:24; Lev. 24:20; Deut. 19:21]. [39]But I tell you, Do not resist an evil person. If someone strikes you on the right cheek, turn to him the other also. [40]And if someone wants to sue you and take your tunic, let him have your cloak as well. [41]If someone forces you to go one mile, go with him two miles. [42]Give to the one who asks you, and do not turn away from the one who wants to borrow from you.

[43]"You have heard that it was said, 'Love your neighbor[h] [Lev. 19:18] and hate your enemy.' [44]But I tell you: Love your enemies[i] and pray for those who persecute you, [45]that you may be sons of your Father in heaven. He causes his sun to rise on the evil and the good, and sends rain on the righteous and the unrighteous.

Luke 6:27–30, 32–36

[27]"But I tell you who hear me: Love your enemies, do good to those who hate you, [28]bless those who curse you, pray for those who mistreat you. [29]If someone strikes you on one cheek, turn to him the other also. If someone takes your cloak, do not stop him from taking your tunic. [30]Give to everyone who asks

---

[f]Sections 54e–54g deal with the inward conditioning God requires, in contrast with the mere outward conformity with which the teachers of the law and Pharisees were content.

[g]The six contrasts are in vv. 21–22, 27–28, 31–32, 33–35, 38–39, and 43–44. In each case the interpretation of the Jewish tradition is given first, then that of Jesus. Tradition concentrated on outward tangible acts, but Jesus showed that the Law was intended to regulate motives as well. In this regard the teachings of the scribes (teachers of the law) were deficient.

Matthew 5:21–48 (cont'd)

⁴⁶If you love those who love you, what reward will you get? Are not even the tax collectors doing that? ⁴⁷And if you greet only your brothers, what are you doing more than others? Do not even pagans do that?

⁴⁸Be perfect, therefore, as your heavenly Father is perfect.

Luke 6:27–30, 32–36 (cont'd)

you, and if anyone takes what belongs to you, do not demand it back. ³²"If you love those who love you, what credit is that to you? Even 'sinners' love those who love them. ³³And if you do good to those who are good to you, what credit is that to you? Even 'sinners' do that. ³⁴And if you lend to those from whom you expect repayment, what credit is that to you? Even 'sinners' lend to 'sinners,' expecting to be repaid in full. ³⁵But love your enemies, do good to them, and lend to them without expecting to get anything back. Then your reward will be great, and you will be sons of the Most High, because he is kind to the ungrateful and wicked. ³⁶Be merciful, just as your Father is merciful.

ᵃMt 5:21 Exodus 20:13   ᵇ22 Some manuscripts brother *without cause*   ᶜ22 An Aramaic term of contempt   ᵈ26 Greek *kodrantes*   ᵉ27 Exodus 20:14   ᶠ31 Deut. 24:1   ᵍ38 Exodus 21:24; Lev. 24:20; Deut. 19:21   ʰ43 Lev. 19:18   ⁱ44 Some late manuscripts *enemies, bless those who curse you, do good to those who hate you*

Sec. 54f   Three hypocritical ʰ"acts of righteousness" to be avoided
   (cf. Sec. 105—the disciple's prayer)
   (cf. Sec. 121—unhypocritical prayer)
   (cf. Sec. 131—forgiveness of others and forgiveness by God)

Matthew 6:1–18

¹"Be careful not to do your 'acts of righteousness' before men, to be seen by them. If you do, you will have no reward from your Father in heaven.
²"So when you give to the needy, do not announce it with trumpets, as the hypocrites do in the synagogues and on the streets, to be honored by men. I tell you the truth, they have received their reward in full. ³But when you give to the needy, do not let your left hand know what your right hand is doing, ⁴so that your giving may be in secret. Then your Father, who sees what is done in secret, will reward you.
⁵"And when you pray, do not be like the hypocrites, for they love to pray standing in the synagogues and on the street corners to be seen by men. I tell you the truth, they have received their reward in full. ⁶But when you pray, go into your room, close the door and pray to your Father, who is unseen. Then your Father, who sees what is done in secret, will reward you. ⁷And when you pray, do not keep on babbling like pagans, for they think they will be heard because of their many words. ⁸Do not be like them, for your Father knows what you need before you ask him.
⁹"This, then, is how you should pray:

   " 'Our Father in heaven,
   hallowed be your name,
   ¹⁰your kingdom come,
   your will be done

ʰThe three "acts of righteousness" specified are giving alms (6:2–4), prayer (6:5–15), and fasting (6:16–18). The Pharisees did these for the sake of human recognition and for this reason forfeited all prospects of divine reward.

Matthew 6:1–18 (cont'd)

on earth as it is in heaven.
11Give us today our daily bread.
12Forgive us our debts,
    as we also have forgiven our debtors.
13And lead us not into temptation,
    but deliver us from the evil one.ᵃ'

14For if you forgive men when they sin against you, your heavenly Father will also forgive you. 15But if you do not forgive men their sins, your Father will not forgive your sins.
    16"When you fast, do not look somber as the hypocrites do, for they disfigure their faces to show men they are fasting. I tell you the truth, they have received their reward in full. 17But when you fast, put oil on your head and wash your face, 18so that it will not be obvious to men that you are fasting, but only to your Father, who is unseen; and your Father, who sees what is done in secret, will reward you.

ᵃMt 6:13 Or *from evil*; some late manuscripts *one*, / *for yours is the kingdom and the power and the glory forever. Amen.*

Sec. 54g   **Three prohibitions against avarice, harsh judgment, and unwise exposure of sacred things**
            (cf. Sec. 64b—measuring out)
            (cf. Secs. 64b, 108b—anxieties of life)
            (cf. Secs. 70b, 145, 150b—followers not above the leader)
            (cf. Sec. 106—lamp of the body)
            (cf. Sec. 108a—value of birds)
            (cf. Sec. 108b—danger of riches)
            (cf. Sec. 117a—impossibility of being a slave to two masters)

Matthew 6:19–7:6

19"Do not store up for yourselves treasures on earth, where moth and rust destroy, and where thieves break in and steal. 20But store up for yourselves treasures in heaven, where moth and rust do not destroy, and where thieves do not break in and steal. 21For where your treasure is, there your heart will be also.
    22"The eye is the lamp of the body. If your eyes are good, your whole body will be full of light. 23But if your eyes are bad, your whole body will be full of darkness. If then the light within you is darkness, how great is that darkness!
    24"No one can serve two masters. Either he will hate the one and love the other, or he will be devoted to the one and despise the other. You cannot serve both God and Money.
    25"Therefore I tell you, do not worry about your life, what you will eat or drink; or about your body, what you will wear. Is not life more important than food, and the body more important than clothes? 26Look at the birds of the air; they do not sow or reap or store away in barns, and yet your heavenly Father feeds them. Are you not much more valuable than they? 27Who of you by worrying can add a single hour to his lifeᵃ?
    28"And why do you worry about clothes? See how the lilies of the field grow. They do not labor or spin. 29Yet I tell you that not even Solomon in all his splendor was dressed like one of these. 30If that is how God clothes the grass of the field, which is here today and tomorrow is thrown into the fire, will he not much more clothe you, O you of little faith? 31So do not worry, saying, 'What shall we eat?' or 'What shall we drink?' or 'What shall we wear?' 32For the pagans run after all these things, and your heavenly Father knows that you need them. 33But seek first his kingdom and his righteousness, and all these things will be given to you as well. 34Therefore do not worry about tomorrow, for tomorrow will worry about itself. Each day has enough trouble of its own.

Matthew 6:19– 7:6 (cont'd)

¹"Do not judge, or you too will be judged.

²For in the same way you judge others, you will be judged, and with the measure you use, it will be measured to you.

³"Why do you look at the speck of sawdust in your brother's eye and pay no attention to the plank in your own eye? ⁴How can you say to your brother, 'Let me take the speck out of your eye,' when all the time there is a plank in your own eye? ⁵You hypocrite, first take the plank out of your own eye, and then you will see clearly to remove the speck from your brother's eye.

⁶"Do not give dogs what is sacred; do not throw your pearls to pigs. If you do, they may trample them under their feet, and then turn and tear you to pieces.

ᵃMt 6:27 Or *single cubit to his height*

Luke 6:37–42

³⁷"Do not judge, and you will not be judged. Do not condemn, and you will not be condemned. Forgive, and you will be forgiven. ³⁸Give, and it will be given to you. A good measure, pressed down, shaken together and running over, will be poured into your lap. For with the measure you use, it will be measured to you."

³⁹He also told them this parable: "Can a blind man lead a blind man? Will they not both fall into a pit? ⁴⁰ⁱA student is not above his teacher, but everyone who is fully trained will be like his teacher. ⁴¹"Why do you look at the speck of sawdust in your brother's eye and pay no attention to the plank in your own eye? ⁴²How can you say to your brother, 'Brother, let me take the speck out of your eye,' when you yourself fail to see the plank in your own eye? You hypocrite, first take the plank out of your eye, and then you will see clearly to remove the speck from your brother's eye.

Sec. 54h Application and conclusion
(cf. Sec. 61—recognition by fruit)
(cf. Sec. 105—ask, seek, knock)
(cf. Sec. 113a—narrow entrance)

Matthew 7:7–27

⁷"Ask and it will be given to you; seek and you will find; knock and the door will be opened to you. ⁸For everyone who asks receives; he who seeks finds; and to him who knocks, the door will be opened.

⁹"Which of you, if his son asks for bread, will give him a stone? ¹⁰Or if he asks for a fish, will give him a snake? ¹¹If you, then, though you are evil, know how to give good gifts to your children, how much more will your Father in heaven give good gifts to those who ask

Luke 6:31, 43–49

ⁱ(Luke 6:40) The first part of Luke 6:40 is one of the frequent sayings of Christ. In the present context it means the student or disciple of the Pharisees will be blind like his teachers. In Matthew 10:24 (Sec. 70b) it means that Jesus' disciples can expect no better treatment than he received. On another occasion, in John 15:20 (Sec. 150b), a slightly different wording conveys a similar meaning. In John 13:16 (Sec. 145) the saying urges the disciples to follow Christ's example of humility. Also, the essence of this proverb lies behind Luke 22:27 (Sec. 144).

Matthew 7:7–27 (cont'd)

him! ¹²So in everything, do to others what you would have them do to you, for this sums up the Law and the Prophets.

¹³"Enter through the narrow gate. For wide is the gate and broad is the road that leads to ʲdestruction, and many enter through it. ¹⁴But small is the gate and narrow the road that leads to ʲlife, and only a few find it.

¹⁵"Watch out for false prophets. They come to you in sheep's clothing, but inwardly they are ferocious wolves. ¹⁶By their fruit you will recognize them. Do people pick grapes from thornbushes, or figs from thistles? ¹⁷Likewise every good tree bears good fruit, but a bad tree bears bad fruit. ¹⁸A good tree cannot bear bad fruit, and a bad tree cannot bear good fruit. ¹⁹Every tree that does not bear good fruit is cut down and thrown into the fire. ²⁰Thus, by their fruit you will recognize them.

²¹"Not everyone who says to me, 'Lord, Lord,' will enter the ʲkingdom of heaven, but only he who does the will of my Father who is in heaven. ²²Many will say to me on that day, 'Lord, Lord, did we not prophesy in your name, and in your name drive out demons and perform many miracles?' ²³Then I will tell them plainly, 'I never knew you. ʲAway from me, you evildoers!' [Psalm 6:8].

²⁴"Therefore everyone who hears these words of mine and puts them into practice is like a wise man who built his house on the rock. ²⁵The rain came down, the streams rose, and the winds blew and beat against that house; yet it did not fall, because it had its foundation on the rock. ²⁶But everyone who hears these words of mine and does not put them into practice is like a foolish man who built his house on sand. ²⁷The rain came down, the streams rose, and the winds blew and beat against that house, and it fell with a great crash."

Luke 6:31, 43–49 (cont'd)

³¹Do to others as you would have them do to you.

⁴³"No good tree bears bad fruit, nor does a bad tree bear good fruit. ⁴⁴Each tree is recognized by its own fruit. People do not pick figs from thornbushes, or grapes from briers. ⁴⁵The good man brings good things out of the good stored up in his heart, and the evil man brings evil things out of the evil stored up in his heart. For out of the overflow of his heart his mouth speaks.

⁴⁶"Why do you call me, 'Lord, Lord,' and do not do what I say?

⁴⁷I will show you what he is like who comes to me and hears my words and puts them into practice. ⁴⁸He is like a man building a house, who dug down deep and laid the foundation on rock. When a flood came, the torrent struck that house but could not shake it, because it was well built. ⁴⁹But the one who hears my words and does not put them into practice is like a man who built a house on the ground without a foundation. The moment the torrent struck that house, it collapsed and its destruction was complete."

ʲ(Matt. 7:13–14, 21, 23) In Jesus' teachings, to find life was equivalent to entering the kingdom, and to meet with destruction was equated with exclusion from it. One's relationship to the anticipated kingdom was thus of crucial importance.

Sec. 54i   Reaction of the crowds

Matthew 7:28–8:1

[28]When Jesus had finished saying these things, the crowds were amazed at his teaching, [29]because he taught as one who had authority, and not as their teachers of the law.

[1]When he came down from the mountainside, large crowds followed him.

GROWING FAME AND EMPHASIS ON REPENTANCE

Sec. 55   A centurion's faith and the healing of his servant
(cf. Sec. 38—healing at a distance)
—*Capernaum*—

Matthew 8:5–13

[5]When Jesus had entered Capernaum, a centurion came to him, asking for help. [6]"Lord," he said, "my servant lies at home paralyzed and in terrible suffering."

[7]Jesus said to him, "I will go and heal him."

[8]The centurion replied, "Lord, I do not deserve to have you come under my roof. But just say the word, and my servant will be healed.

[9]For I myself am a man under authority, with soldiers under me. I tell this one, 'Go,' and he goes; and that one, 'Come,' and he comes. I say to my servant, 'Do this,' and he does it."

[10]When Jesus heard this, he was astonished and said to those following him, "I tell you the truth, I have not found anyone in [k]Israel with such great faith. [11]I say to you that many will come from the east and the west, and will take their places at the feast with Abraham, Isaac and Jacob in the kingdom of heaven. [12]But the subjects of the kingdom will be thrown outside, into the dark-

Luke 7:1–10

[1]When Jesus had finished saying all this in the hearing of the people, he entered Capernaum. [2]There a centurion's servant, whom his master valued highly, was sick and about to die. [3]The centurion heard of Jesus and sent some elders of the Jews to him, asking him to come and heal his servant. [4]When they came to Jesus, they pleaded earnestly with him, "This man deserves to have you do this, [5]because he loves our nation and has built our synagogue." [6]So Jesus went with them.

He was not far from the house when the centurion sent friends to say to him: "Lord, don't trouble yourself, for I do not deserve to have you come under my roof. [7]That is why I did not even consider myself worthy to come to you. But say the word, and my servant will be healed. [8]For I myself am a man under authority, with soldiers under me. I tell this one, 'Go,' and he goes; and that one, 'Come,' and he comes. I say to my servant, 'Do this,' and he does it."

[9]When Jesus heard this, he was amazed at him, and turning to the crowd following him, he said, "I tell you, I have not found such great faith even in [k]Israel."

---

[k](Matt. 8:10; Luke 7:9) Jesus' dealings with a non-Jewish person such as this centurion were striking in view of his avowed purpose of limiting his ministry to the lost sheep of the house of Israel (cf. Matt. 15:24, Sec. 78). The immediate beneficiaries of his ministry, the Jews, would do well to learn from this Gentile.

Matthew 8:5–13 (cont'd)	Luke 7:1–10 (cont'd)
ness, where there will be weeping and gnashing of teeth." [13]Then Jesus said to the centurion, "Go! It will be done just as you believed it would." And his servant was healed at that very hour.	[10]Then the men who had been sent returned to the house and found the servant well.

Sec. 56   A widow's son raised at Nain
—*Nain*—

Luke 7:11–17

[11]Soon afterward, Jesus went to a town called Nain, and his disciples and a large crowd went along with him. [12]As he approached the town gate, a dead person was being carried out—the only son of his mother, and she was a widow. And a large crowd from the town was with her. [13]When the Lord saw her, his heart went out to her and he said, "Don't cry."

[14]Then he went up and touched the coffin, and those carrying it stood still. He said, "Young man, I say to you, get up!" [15]The dead man [l]sat up and began to talk, and Jesus gave him back to his mother.

[16]They were all filled with awe and praised God. "A great prophet has appeared among us," they said. "God has come to help his people." [17]This news about Jesus spread throughout Judea[a] and the surrounding country.

     [a]Lk 7:17 Or *the land of the Jews*

Sec. 57   John the Baptist's relationship to the kingdom
—*Galilee*—

Matthew 11:2–19	Luke 7:18–35
[2]When John heard in prison what Christ was doing, he sent his disciples [3]to ask him, "[m]Are you the [n]one who was to come, or should we expect someone else?"	[18]John's disciples told him about all these things. Calling two of them, [19]he sent them to the Lord to ask, "[m]Are you the [n]one who was to come, or should we expect someone else?" [20]When the men came to Jesus, they said, "John the Baptist sent us to you to ask, 'Are you the one who was to come, or should we expect someone else?'" [21]At that very time Jesus cured many who had diseases, sicknesses and evil spirits, and gave sight to many who were blind. [22]So he replied to the messengers, "Go back and report to John what you have seen and heard: The
[4]Jesus replied, "Go back and report to John what you hear and see: [5]The blind	blind receive sight, the lame walk, those

     [l](Luke 7:15) Jesus is known to have raised dead persons on other occasions (cf. Sec. 67, 118b). Luke 7:22 (Sec. 57) implies that he did so at times that are not specifically described.

     [m](Matt. 11:3; Luke 7:19) Some have accused John of a faltering faith at this point. This seems unjust. His question was probably prompted rather by impatience with his own personal plight that grew out of an inability to grasp why the death of Christ had to precede his kingly rule. Prior to the crucifixion no one understood this sequence of events.

     [n](Matt. 11:3; Luke 7:19) "The one who was to come," or more literally, "the coming one," was a well-known designation of Israel's Messiah. The title describes him in a manner that views his coming as certain.

Matthew 11:2–19 (cont'd)

receive sight, the lame walk, those who have leprosy[a] are cured, the deaf hear, the dead are raised, and the good news is preached to the poor [Isa. 35:5–6; 61:1]. [6]Blessed is the man who does not fall away on account of me."

[7]As John's disciples were leaving, Jesus began to speak to the crowd about John: "What did you go out into the desert to see? A reed swayed by the wind? [8]If not, what did you go out to see? A man dressed in fine clothes? No, those who wear fine clothes are in kings' palaces. [9]Then what did you go out to see? A prophet? Yes, I tell you, and more than a prophet. [10]This is the one about whom it is written:

" 'I will send my messenger ahead of you,
who will prepare your way before you'[b] [Mal. 3:1].

[11]I tell you the truth: Among those born of women there has not risen anyone [o]greater than John the Baptist; yet he who is least in the kingdom of heaven is greater than he. [12]From the days of John the Baptist until now, the kingdom of heaven has been forcefully advancing, and forceful men lay hold of it. [13]For all the Prophets and the Law prophesied until John. [14]And if you are willing to accept it, he is the Elijah who was to come. [15]He who has ears, let him hear.

[16]"To what can I compare this generation? They are like children sitting in the marketplaces and calling out to others:

[17]" 'We played the flute for you,
and you did not dance;
we sang a dirge,
and you did not mourn.'

[18]For John came neither eating nor drinking, and they say, 'He has a de-

Luke 7:18–35 (cont'd)

who have leprosy[a] are cured, the deaf hear, the dead are raised, and the good news is preached to the poor [Isa. 35:5–6; 61:1]. [23]Blessed is the man who does not fall away on account of me."

[24]After John's messengers left, Jesus began to speak to the crowd about John: "What did you go out into the desert to see? A reed swayed by the wind? [25]If not, what did you go out to see? A man dressed in fine clothes? No, those who wear expensive clothes and indulge in luxury are in palaces. [26]But what did you go out to see? A prophet? Yes, I tell you, and more than a prophet. [27]This is the one about whom it is written:

" 'I will send my messenger ahead of you,
who will prepare your way before you'[b] [Mal. 3:1].

[28]I tell you, among those born of women there is no one [o]greater than John; yet the one who is least in the kingdom of God is greater than he."

[29](All the people, even the tax collectors, when they heard Jesus' words, acknowledged that God's way was right, because they had been baptized by John. [30]But the Pharisees and experts in the law rejected God's purpose for themselves, because they had not been baptized by John.)

[31]"To what, then, can I compare the people of this generation? What are they like? [32]They are like children sitting in the marketplace and calling out to each other:

" 'We played the flute for you,
and you did not dance;
we sang a dirge,
and you did not cry.'

[33]For John the Baptist came neither eating bread nor drinking wine, and you

---

[o](Matt. 11:11; Luke 7:28) John was greater than those of the past because of his proximity to Messiah. Yet those in the kingdom will be greater than John because they will be even closer to him.

Matthew 11:2–19 (cont'd)

Luke 7:18–35 (cont'd)

say, 'He has a demon.' [34]The Son of Man
mon.' [19]The Son of Man came eating and
drinking, and they say, 'Here is a glutton and a drunkard, a friend of tax collectors and "sinners." ' But wisdom is
proved right by her actions."

came eating and drinking, and you say,
'Here is a glutton and a drunkard, a
friend of tax collectors and "sinners." '
[35]But wisdom is proved right by all her
children."

[a]Mt 11:5; Lk 7:22 The Greek word was used for various diseases affecting the skin—not necessarily
leprosy.   [b]Mt 11:10; Lk 7:27 Mal. 3:1

Sec. 58   Woes upon Korazin and Bethsaida for failure to repent
(cf. Sec. 102a—woes to cities)
—Galilee—

Matthew 11:20–30

[20]Then Jesus [p]began to denounce the cities in which most of his miracles had
been performed, because they did not repent. [21]"Woe to you, Korazin! Woe to you,
Bethsaida! If the miracles that were performed in you had been performed in Tyre
and Sidon, they would have repented long ago in sackcloth and ashes. [22]But I tell
you, it will be more bearable for Tyre and Sidon on the day of judgment than for
you. [23]And you, Capernaum, will you be lifted up to the skies? No, you will go
down to the depths.[a] If the miracles that were performed in you had been performed in Sodom, it would have remained to this day. [24]But I tell you that it will be
more bearable for Sodom on the day of judgment than for you."

[25]At that time Jesus said, "I praise you, Father, Lord of heaven and earth, because
you have hidden these things from the wise and learned, and revealed them to little
children. [26]Yes, Father, for this was your good pleasure.

[27]"All things have been committed to me by my Father. No one knows the Son
except the Father, and no one knows the Father except the Son and those to whom
the Son chooses to reveal him.

[28]"Come to me, all you who are weary and [q]burdened, and I will give you rest.
[29]Take my yoke upon you and learn from me, for I am gentle and humble in heart,
and you will find rest for your souls [Jer. 6:16]. [30]For my yoke is easy and my burden
is light."

[a]Mt 11:23 Greek *Hades*

Sec. 59   Christ's feet anointed by a sinful but contrite woman
(cf. Sec. 141—anointing with perfume)
—Galilee, in the house of Simon the Pharisee—

Luke 7:36–50

[36]Now one of the [r]Pharisees invited Jesus to have dinner with him, so he went to
the Pharisee's house and reclined at the table. [37]When a [s]woman who had lived a
sinful life in that town learned that Jesus was eating at the Pharisee's house, she

[p](Matt. 11:20) Another beginning in the ministry of Christ is noted here: his announcement of
retribution against those who refused to repent in response to both John the Baptist and himself. The Lord's
language became more severe at this point. For other beginnings, see Matthew 4:17, Section 37 and
Matthew 16:21, Section 83.
    [q](Matt. 11:28) The heavy load was probably that imposed by the teachers of the law and Pharisees
in their manmade traditions (Matt. 23:4, Sec. 137a).
    [r](Luke 7:36) The rupture between Jesus and the Pharisees was far advanced by now, but was not
complete. Simon seemed to be one who had not as yet decided with whom to side. He believed Jesus to
be a prophet (7:39), but his love for him was meager compared with that of the sinful woman.
    [s](Luke 3:37) This woman should be distinguished from Mary of Bethany, who at a later time also
anointed the Lord's feet (cf. Secs. 118a, 141).

Luke 7:36–50 (cont'd)

brought an alabaster jar of perfume, [38]and as she stood behind him at his feet weeping, she began to wet his feet with her tears. Then she wiped them with her hair, kissed them and poured perfume on them.

[39]When the Pharisee who had invited him saw this, he said to himself, "If this man were a prophet, he would know who is touching him and what kind of woman she is—that she is a sinner."

[40]Jesus answered him, "Simon, I have something to tell you."

"Tell me, teacher," he said.

[41]"Two men owed money to a certain moneylender. One owed him five hundred denarii,[a] and the other fifty. [42]Neither of them had the money to pay him back, so he canceled the debts of both. Now which of them will love him more?"

[43]Simon replied, "I suppose the one who had the bigger debt canceled."

"You have judged correctly," Jesus said.

[44]Then he turned toward the woman and said to Simon, "Do you see this woman? I came into your house. You did not give me any water for my feet, but she wet my feet with her tears and wiped them with her hair. [45]You did not give me a kiss, but this woman, from the time I entered, has not stopped kissing my feet. [46]You did not put oil on my head, but she has poured perfume on my feet. [47]Therefore, I tell you, her many sins have been forgiven—for she loved much. But he who has been forgiven little loves little."

[48]Then Jesus said to her, "Your sins are forgiven."

[49]The other guests began to say among themselves, "Who is this who even forgives sins?"

[50]Jesus said to the woman, "Your faith has saved you; go in peace."

[a]Lk 7:41 A denarius was a coin worth about a day's wages.

FIRST PUBLIC REJECTION BY JEWISH LEADERS

Sec. 60   A tour with the Twelve and other followers
       —Galilee—

Luke 8:1–3

[1]After this, Jesus traveled about from one town and village to another, proclaiming the good news of the kingdom of God. The Twelve were with him, [2]and also some [t]women who had been cured of evil spirits and diseases: Mary (called Magdalene) from whom seven demons had come out; [3]Joanna the wife of Cuza, the manager of Herod's household; Susanna; and many others. These women were helping to support them out of their own means.

[t](Luke 8:2) It was not unusual for first-century Jewish women to contribute large sums of money to support rabbis. The additional incentive for these to give, however, was the spiritual and physical help they had received from Jesus. This tour, which included female followers and the Twelve, is mentioned only by Luke, who gives special prominence to women in his gospel.

Sec. 61   Blasphemous accusation by the teachers of the law and Pharisees
(cf. Sec. 54h—recognition by fruit)
(cf. Secs. 68, 106—casting out demons, and blasphemous statements)
(cf. Secs. 91, 106—casting out demons, being for and against)
(cf. Sec. 108a—blasphemous statements)
—Galilee—

Matthew 12:22–37

Mark 3:20–30

²⁰Then Jesus entered a house, and again a crowd gathered, so that he and his disciples were not even able to eat. ²¹When his family heard about this, they went to take charge of him, for they said, "He is out of his mind."

²²Then they brought him a demon-possessed man who was blind and mute, and Jesus healed him, so that he could both talk and see. ²³All the people were astonished and said, "ᵘCould this be the Son of David?"

²⁴But when the Pharisees heard this, they said, "It is only by Beelzebub,ᵃ the prince of demons, that this fellow drives out demons."

²²And the teachers of the law who came down from Jerusalem said, "He is possessed by Beelzebubᵇ! By the prince of demons he is driving out demons."

²⁵Jesus knew their thoughts and said to them, "Every kingdom divided against itself will be ruined, and every city or household divided against itself will not stand. ²⁶If Satan drives out Satan, he is divided against himself. How then can his kingdom stand? ²⁷And if I drive out demons by Beelzebub, by whom do your people drive them out? So then, they will be your judges. ²⁸But if I drive out demons by the Spirit of God, then the ᵛkingdom of God has come upon you.

²³So Jesus called them and spoke to them in parables: "How can Satan drive out Satan? ²⁴If a kingdom is divided against itself, that kingdom cannot stand. ²⁵If a house is divided against itself, that house cannot stand. ²⁶And if Satan opposes himself and is divided, he cannot stand; his end has come.

²⁹"Or again, how can anyone enter a strong man's house and carry off his possessions unless he first ties up the strong man? Then he can rob his house. ³⁰"He who is not with me is against me, and he who does not gather with me scatters. ³¹And so I tell you, every sin and blasphemy will be forgiven men, but the blasphemy against the Spirit will not be forgiven. ³²Anyone who

²⁷In fact, no one can enter a strong man's house and carry off his possessions unless he first ties up the strong man. Then he can rob his house. ²⁸I tell you the truth, all the sins and blasphemies of men will be forgiven them. ²⁹But whoever blasphemes against the Holy Spirit will never be forgiven; he is guilty of an ʷeternal sin."

ᵘ(Matt. 12:23) This question forced the first public showdown in the growing rift between Jesus and the Jewish authorities. Son of David was a much used title for Messiah. So the antagonistic representatives of Jewish leadership in Jerusalem (Mark 3:22) were forced to speak out strongly against this identification of Jesus. So tense was the confrontation that Jesus' own family wondered about his sanity (Mark 3:21). This encounter was a major turning point in Jesus' ministry.

ᵛ(Matt. 12:28) The arrival of the kingdom of God coincided with the arrival of the King. Yet the unfavorable response of Israel retarded the full realization of all the Old Testament prophecies about it. Without doubt Jesus also spoke of a future kingdom, when all expectations would be brought to fruition (cf. Matt. 25:31, Sec. 139g).

ʷThe unforgivable (Matt. 12:32) or eternal (Mark 3:29) sin bore a special relationship to the unusual circumstances of that day. The leaders of Israel publicly demonstrated their deliberate and final rejection of the Holy Spirit's clear attestation to the incarnate Messiah. Such definitive circumstances are not found elsewhere.

Matthew 12:22–37 (cont'd)

speaks a word against the Son of Man will be forgiven, but anyone who speaks against the Holy Spirit will ʷnot be forgiven, either in this age or in the age to come.
³³"Make a tree good and its fruit will be good, or make a tree bad and its fruit will be bad, for a tree is recognized by its fruit. ³⁴You brood of vipers, how can you who are evil say anything good? For out of the overflow of the heart the mouth speaks. ³⁵The good man brings good things out of the good stored up in him, and the evil man brings evil things out of the evil stored up in him. ³⁶But I tell you that men will have to give account on the day of judgment for every careless word they have spoken. ³⁷For by your words you will be acquitted, and by your words you will be condemned."

Mark 3:20–30 (cont'd)

³⁰He said this because they were saying, "He has an evil spirit."

ᵃMt 12:24 Greek *Beezeboul* or *Beelzeboul*; also in verse 27   ᵇMk 3:22 Greek *Beezeboul* or *Beelzeboul*

Sec. 62   Request for a sign refused
(cf. Secs. 80, 106—request for a sign)
—*Galilee*—

Matthew 12:38–45

³⁸Then some of the Pharisees and teachers of the law said to him, "Teacher, we want to see a miraculous sign from you."
³⁹He answered, "A wicked and adulterous generation asks for a miraculous sign! But none will be given it except the sign of the prophet Jonah. ⁴⁰For as Jonah was three days and three nights in the belly of a huge fish [Jonah 1:17], so the Son of Man will be three days and three nights in the heart of the earth. ⁴¹The men of Nineveh will stand up at the judgment with this generation and condemn it; for they repented at the preaching of Jonah, and now oneᵃ greater than Jonah is here. ⁴²The Queen of the South will rise at the judgment with this generation and condemn it; for she came from the ends of the earth to listen to Solomon's wisdom, and now one greater than Solomon is here.
⁴³"When an evilᵇ spirit comes out of a man, it goes through arid places seeking rest and does not find it. ⁴⁴Then it says, 'I will return to the house I left.' When it arrives, it finds the house unoccupied, swept clean and put in order. ⁴⁵Then it goes and takes with it seven other spirits more wicked than itself, and they go in and live there. And the final condition of that man is ˣworse than the first. That is how it will be with this wicked generation."

ᵃMt 12:41 Or *something*; also in verse 42   ᵇ43 Greek *unclean*

ˣ(Matt. 12:45) Because of the rejection (Sec. 61), this generation of Israelites had become worse than Nineveh, worse than the Queen of Sheba, and even worse than their own former condition. Their leaders' public rejection, in committing the unforgivable sin, dashed any hopes this generation might have had of receiving the kingdom's blessings.

Sec. 63   Announcement of new spiritual kinship
—Galilee—

Matthew 12:46–50	Mark 3:31–35	Luke 8:19–21
[46]While Jesus was still talking to the crowd, his [y]mother and brothers stood outside, wanting to speak to him. [47]Someone told him, "Your mother and brothers are standing outside, wanting to speak to you." [a] [48]He replied to him, "Who is my mother, and who are my brothers?" [49]Pointing to his disciples, he said, "Here are my mother and my brothers. [50]For whoever does the will of my Father in heaven is my brother and sister and mother."	[31]Then Jesus' [y]mother and brothers arrived. Standing outside, they sent someone in to call him. [32]A crowd was sitting around him, and they told him, "Your mother and brothers are outside looking for you." [33]"Who are my mother and my brothers?" he asked. [34]Then he looked at those seated in a circle around him and said, "Here are my mother and my brothers! [35]Whoever does God's will is my brother and sister and mother."	[19]Now Jesus' [y]mother and brothers came to see him, but they were not able to get near him because of the crowd. [20]Someone told him, "Your mother and brothers are standing outside, wanting to see you." [21]He replied, "My mother and brothers are those who hear God's word and put it into practice."

[a]Mt 12:47 Some manuscripts do not have verse 47.

SECRETS ABOUT THE KINGDOM GIVEN IN PARABLES
—To the crowds by the sea—

Sec. 64a   The setting of the parables

Matthew 13:1–3a	Mark 4:1–2	Luke 8:4
[1]That same [z]day Jesus went out of the house and sat by the lake. [2]Such large crowds gathered around him that he got into a boat and sat in it, while all the people stood on the shore. [3]Then he told them many things in parables, saying:	[1]Again Jesus began to teach by the lake. The crowd that gathered around him was so large that he got into a boat and sat it out on the lake, while all the people were along the shore at the water's edge. [2]He taught them many things by parables, and in his teaching said:	[4]While a large crowd was gathering and people were coming to Jesus from town after town, he told this parable:

---

[y](Matt. 12:46; Mark 3:31; Luke 8:19) Though quite sincere in trying to help him, Jesus' family came with a suspicion that he had lost his sanity. Mary had already evidenced her impatience (John 2:3, Sec. 29), and his brothers were critical of him (John 7:3–5, Sec. 94). They wanted him to give up this course of opposition to their religious leaders. Knowing his family's motives, Jesus seized the occasion to declare the primacy of spiritual relationships over physical. What a fitting lesson just after his own people had severed themselves from him by accusing him of an alliance with Satan.

[z](Matt. 13:1) These parables were spoken later on the same day as the landmark events of Sections 61–63. They exhibited a new phase of the Lord's teaching. As a teaching tool, parables enabled him to continue instructing his disciples without giving his enemies unnecessary opportunities to catch him in his words (Matt. 13:13 and parallels in Sec. 64b). They also provided him with a means of revealing kingdom characteristics not previously described (Matt. 13:11, 17; Mark 4:11; Luke 8:10). These features depicted a new dimension of the kingdom in light of the confrontation earlier in the day (Sec. 61). The parables do not invalidate earlier teachings about Christ's reign, but add to them.

Sec. 64b The parable of the soils
(cf. Secs. 54c, 106—lighting a lamp)
(cf. Sec. 54g—measuring out)
(cf. Secs. 54g, 108b—anxieties of life)
(cf. Sec. 71a—deadened hearts and blinded eyes)

Matthew 13:3b–23	Mark 4:3–25	Luke 8:5–18
"A farmer went out to sow his seed. ⁴As he was scattering the seed, some fell along the path, and the birds came and ate it up. ⁵Some fell on rocky places, where it did not have much soil. It sprang up quickly, because the soil was shallow. ⁶But when the sun came up, the plants were scorched, and they withered because they had no root. ⁷Other seed fell among thorns, which grew up and choked the plants.	³"Listen! A farmer went out to sow his seed. ⁴As he was scattering the seed, some fell along the path, and the birds came and ate it up. ⁵Some fell on rocky places, where it did not have much soil. It sprang up quickly, because the soil was shallow. ⁶But when the sun came up, the plants were scorched, and they withered because they had no root. ⁷Other seed fell among thorns, which grew up and choked the plants, so that they did not bear grain. ⁸Still other	⁵"A farmer went out to sow his seed. As he was scattering the seed, some fell along the path; it was trampled on, and the birds of the air ate it up. ⁶Some fell on rock, and when it came up, the plants withered because they had no moisture. ⁷Other seed fell among thorns, which grew up with it and choked the plants.
⁸Still other seed fell on good soil, where it produced a crop—a hundred, sixty or thirty times what was sown. ⁹He who has ears, let him hear."	seed fell on good soil. It came up, grew and produced a crop, multiplying thirty, sixty, or even a hundred times." ⁹Then Jesus said, "He who has ears to hear, let him hear."	⁸Still other seed fell on good soil. It came up and yielded a crop, a hundred times more than was sown." When he said this, he called out, "He who has ears to hear, let him hear."
¹⁰The disciples came to him and asked, "Why do you speak to the people in parables?" ¹¹He replied, "The knowledge of the secrets of the kingdom of heaven has been given to you, but not to them. ¹²Whoever has will be given more, and he will have an abundance. Whoever does not have, even what he has will be taken from him. ¹³This is why I speak to them in parables:	¹⁰When he was alone, the Twelve and the others around him asked him about the parables. ¹¹He told them, "The secret of the kingdom of God has been given to you. But to those on the outside everything is said in parables	⁹His disciples asked him what this parable meant. ¹⁰He said, "The knowledge of the secrets of the kingdom of God has been given to you, but to others I speak in parables, so that,
	¹²ªso that,	
"Though seeing, they do not see; though hearing, they do not hear or understand.	" 'they may be ever seeing but never perceiving, and ever hearing but never	" 'though seeing, they may not see; though hearing, they may not understand' ᵇ [Isa. 6:9].

ª(Mark 4:12) The conclusion that Jesus' desire to hide truth from outsiders was prompted by events earlier in the day is very inviting. Whom could he have more in mind than those who, a few hours before, had refused to acknowledge his obvious divine credentials (cf. Sec. 61)?

Matthew 13:3b–23 (cont'd)	Mark 4:3–25 (cont'd)	Luke 8:5–18 (cont'd)

14In them is fulfilled the prophecy of Isaiah:

" 'You will be ever
    hearing but never
    understanding;
you will be ever
    seeing but never
    perceiving.
15For this people's heart
    has become
    calloused;
they hardly hear with
    their ears,
and they have closed
    their eyes.
Otherwise they might
    see with their eyes,
hear with their ears,
understand with their
    hearts
and turn, and I would
    heal them'[a] [Isa.
    6:9–10].

16But blessed are your eyes because they see, and your ears because they hear. 17For I tell you the truth, many prophets and righteous men longed to see what you see but did not see it, and to hear what you hear but did not hear it.

18"Listen then to what the parable of the sower means: 19When anyone hears the message about the kingdom and does not understand it, the evil one comes and snatches away what was sown in his heart. This is the seed sown along the path. 20The one who received the seed that fell on rocky places is the man who hears the word and at once receives it with joy. 21But since he has no root, he lasts only a short time. When trouble or persecution comes because of the word, he quickly falls away. 22The one who received the seed that fell among the thorns is the

understanding;
otherwise they might
turn and be
forgiven!'[b] " [Isa.
6:9–10].

13Then Jesus said to them, "Don't you understand this parable? How then will you understand any parable? 14The farmer sows the word. 15Some people are like seed along the path, where the word is sown. As soon as they hear it, Satan comes and takes away the word that was sown in them. 16Others, like seed sown on rocky places, hear the word and at once receive it with joy. 17But since they have no root, they last only a short time. When trouble or persecution comes because of the word, they quickly fall away. 18Still others, like seed sown among thorns,

11"This is the meaning of the parable: The seed is the word of God. 12Those along the path are the ones who hear, and then the devil comes and takes away the word from their hearts, so that they may not believe and be saved. 13Those on the rock are the ones who receive the word with joy when they hear it, but they have no root. They believe for a while, but in the time of testing they fall away. 14The seed that fell among thorns stands for those who hear, but as they go on their way they are choked by life's worries,

Matthew 13:3b–23 (cont'd)   Mark 4:3–25 (cont'd)   Luke 8:5–18 (cont'd)

man who hears the word, but the worries of this life and the deceitfulness of wealth choke it, making it unfruitful. ²³But the one who received the seed that fell on good soil is the man who hears the word and understands it. He produces a crop, yielding a hundred, sixty or thirty times what was sown."

hear the word; ¹⁹but the worries of this life, the deceitfulness of wealth and the desires for other things come in and choke the word, making it unfruitful. ²⁰Others, like seed sown on good soil, hear the word, accept it, and produce a crop—thirty, sixty or even a hundred times what was sown."

²¹He said to them, "Do you bring in a lamp to put it under a bowl or a bed? Instead, don't you put it on its stand? ²²For whatever is hidden is meant to be disclosed, and whatever is concealed is meant to be brought out into the open. ²³If anyone has ears to hear, let him hear."

²⁴"Consider carefully what you hear," he continued. "With the measure you use, it will be measured to you—and even more. ²⁵Whoever has will be given more; whoever does not have, even what he has will be taken from him."

riches and pleasures, and they do not mature. ¹⁵But the seed on good soil stands for those with a noble and good heart, who hear the word, retain it, and by persevering produce a crop.

¹⁶"No one lights a lamp and hides it in a jar or puts it under a bed. Instead, he puts it on a stand, so that those who come in can see the light. ¹⁷For there is nothing hidden that will not be disclosed, and nothing concealed that will not be known or brought out into the open. ¹⁸Therefore consider carefully how you listen. Whoever has will be given more; whoever does not have, even what he thinks he has will be taken from him."

ᵃMt 13:15; Mk 4:12 Isaiah 6:9,10   ᵇLk 8:10 Isaiah 6:9

Sec. 64c   The ᵇparable of the seed's spontaneous growth

Mark 4:26–29

²⁶He also said, "This is what the kingdom of God is like. A man scatters seed on the ground. ²⁷Night and day, whether he sleeps or gets up, the seed sprouts and grows, though he does not know how. ²⁸All by itself the soil produces grain—first the stalk, then the head, then the full kernel in the head. ²⁹As soon as the grain is ripe, he puts the sickle to it, because the harvest has come."

Sec. 64d   The parable of the weeds

Matthew 13:24–30

²⁴Jesus told them another parable: "The kingdom of heaven is like a man who sowed good seed in his field. ²⁵But while everyone was sleeping, his enemy came

---

ᵇThe first four parables (Secs. 64b–64e) are taken from the agricultural realm. This Marcan parable seems appropriately placed before the parable of the weeds (Sec. 64d) rather than after it, because it describes the activity of the Word in cases where it falls on "good soil." The weeds illustrate the opposite case (cf. Sec. 64g).

Matthew 13:24–30 (cont'd)

and sowed weeds among the wheat, and went away. [26]When the wheat sprouted and formed heads, then the weeds also appeared.

[27]"The owner's servants came to him and said, 'Sir, didn't you sow good seed in your field? Where then did the weeds come from?'

[28]" 'An enemy did this,' he replied.

"The servants asked him, 'Do you want us to go and pull them up?'

[29]" 'No,' he answered, 'because while you are pulling the weeds, you may root up the wheat with them. [30]Let both grow together until the harvest. At that time I will tell the harvesters: First collect the weeds and tie them in bundles to be burned; then gather the wheat and bring it into my barn.' "

Sec. 64e   The parable of the mustard tree
(cf. Sec. 110—mustard tree)

Matthew 13:31–32	Mark 4:30–32
[31]He told them another parable: "The kingdom of heaven is like a mustard seed, which a man took and planted in his field. [32]Though it is the [c]smallest of all your seeds, yet when it grows, it is the largest of garden plants and becomes a tree, so that the birds of the air come and perch in its branches" [Psalm 104:12; Ezek. 17:23; 31:6; Dan. 4:12].	[30]Again he said, "What shall we say the kingdom of God is like, or what parable shall we use to describe it? [31]It is like a mustard seed, which is the [c]smallest seed you plant in the ground. [32]Yet when planted, it grows and becomes the largest of all garden plants, with such big branches that the birds of the air can perch in its shade" [Psalm 104:12; Ezek. 17:23; 31:6; Dan. 4:12].

Sec. 64f   The parable of the leavened loaf
(cf. Sec. 110—leaven)

Matthew 13:33–35	Mark 4:33–34
[33]He told them still another parable: "The kingdom of heaven is like yeast that a woman took and mixed into a large amount[a] of flour until it worked all through the dough."	
[34]Jesus spoke all these things to the crowd in [d]parables; he did not say anything to them without using a parable. [35]So was fulfilled what was spoken through the prophet:	[33]With many similar [d]parables Jesus spoke the word to them, as much as they could understand. [34]He did not say anything to them without using a parable. But when he was alone with his own disciples, he explained everything.

"I will open my mouth in parables,
  I will utter things hidden since the
     creation of the world"[b] [Psalm
     78:2].

[a]Mt 13:33 Greek three satas (probably about 1/2 bushel or 22 liters)   [b]35 Psalm 78:2

---

[c](Matt. 13:32; Mark 4:31) It is wrong to construe this as a statement of absolute scientific fact and thereby impute error to Jesus or the gospel writers. To illustrate another feature of the kingdom, Jesus was simply resorting to a generally acknowledged characteristic of Palestinian agriculture in that day. That seeds smaller than the mustard seed are known in other times and places is no obstacle to biblical inerrancy. In the circumstances in which it was used, Jesus' statement was completely accurate.

[d](Matt. 13:34; Mark 4:33) Jesus' extensive use of this new pedagogical device suggests that other parables not recorded in this series of Sections 64a–64k were also spoken on this significant day.

—To the disciples in the house—

Sec. 64g   The parable of the weeds explained

Matthew 13:36–43

[36]Then he left the crowd and went into the house. His disciples came to him and said, "[e]Explain to us the parable of the weeds in the field."

[37]He answered, "The one who sowed the good seed is the Son of Man. [38]The field is the world, and the good seed stands for the sons of the kingdom. The weeds are the sons of the evil one, [39]and the enemy who sows them is the devil. The harvest is the end of the age, and the harvesters are angels.

[40]"As the weeds are pulled up and burned in the fire, so it will be at the end of the age. [41]The Son of Man will send out his angels, and they will weed out of his kingdom everything that causes sin and all who do evil. [42]They will throw them into the fiery furnace, where there will be weeping and gnashing of teeth. [43]Then the righteous will shine like the sun [Dan. 12:3] in the kingdom of their Father. He who has ears, let him hear.

Sec. 64h   The parable of the hidden treasure

Matthew 13:44

[44]"The kingdom of heaven is like treasure hidden in a field. When a man found it, he hid it again, and then in his joy went and sold all he had and bought that field.

Sec. 64i   The parable of the valuable pearl

Matthew 13:45–46

[45]"Again, the kingdom of heaven is like a merchant looking for fine pearls. [46]When he found one of great value, he went away and sold everything he had and bought it.

Sec. 64j   The parable of the net

Matthew 13:47–50

[47]"Once again, the kingdom of heaven is like a net that was let down into the lake and caught all kinds of fish. [48]When it was full, the fishermen pulled it up on the shore. Then they sat down and collected the good fish in baskets, but threw the bad away. [49]This is how it will be at the end of the age. The angels will come and separate the wicked from the righteous [50]and throw them into the fiery furnace, where there will be weeping and gnashing of teeth.

---

[e](Matt. 13:36) A reason for the disciples' asking about this particular parable lay in their inability to reconcile a long delay for gradual ripening of wheat and weeds with earlier teachings of John (Matt. 3:2, Sec. 21; Matt. 3:10–12, Secs. 22, 23) and Jesus (Matt. 4:17, Sec. 37) about the impending judgment and kingdom to follow. Reconciliation of these apparently contradictory teachings probably relates to the new character of Jesus' discussion about the kingdom that began earlier that day (see note for Matt. 13:1, Sec. 64a).

[f]Though quite similar to the parable of the weeds (Matt. 13:24–30, Sec. 64d) and its explanation (Matt. 13:36–43, Sec. 64g), this parable concentrates on the end of the age, and the earlier one gives more details about the period prior to the end.

Sec. 64k   The parable of the house owner

Matthew 13:51–53

[51]"Have you understood all these things?" Jesus asked.

"Yes," they replied.

[52]He said to them, "Therefore every teacher of the law who has been instructed about the kingdom of heaven is like the owner of a house who ᵍbrings out of his storeroom new treasures as well as old."

[53]When Jesus had finished these parables, he moved on from there.

CONTINUING OPPOSITION

Sec. 65   Crossing the lake and calming the storm
—On the Sea of Galilee—

Matthew 8:18, 23–27	Mark 4:35–41	Luke 8:22–25
[18]When Jesus saw the crowd around him, he gave orders to cross to the other side of the lake. [23]Then he got into the boat and his disciples followed him. [24]Without warning, a furious storm came up on the lake, so that the waves swept over the boat. But Jesus was ʰsleeping.	[35]That day when evening came, he said to his disciples, "Let us go over to the other side." [36]Leaving the crowd behind, they took him along, just as he was, in the boat. There were also other boats with him. [37]A furious squall came up, and the waves broke over the boat, so that it was nearly swamped. [38]Jesus was in the stern, sleeping on a cushion. The disciples	[22]One day Jesus said to his disciples, "Let's go over to the other side of the lake." So they got into a boat and set out. [23]As they sailed, he fell asleep. A squall came down on the lake, so that the boat was being swamped, and they were in great danger.
[25]The disciples went and woke him, saying, "Lord, save us! We're going to drown!" [26]He replied, "You of little faith, why are you so afraid?" Then he got up and rebuked the winds and the waves, and it was completely ⁱcalm.	woke him and said to him, "Teacher, don't you care if we drown?" [39]He got up, rebuked the wind and said to the waves, "Quiet! Be still!" Then the wind died down and it was completely ⁱcalm. [40]He said to his disciples, "Why are you so afraid? Do you still have no faith?"	[24]The disciples went and woke him, saying, "Master, Master, we're going to drown!" He got up and rebuked the wind and the raging waters; the storm subsided, and all was ⁱcalm. [25]"Where is your faith?" he asked his disciples. In fear and amazement
[27]The men were amazed and asked, "ʲWhat kind of man is this? Even the winds and the waves obey him!"	[41]They were terrified and asked each other, "ʲWho is this? Even the wind and the waves obey him!"	they asked one another, "ʲWho is this? He commands even the winds and the water, and they obey him."

ᵍ(Matt. 13:52) This parable points up the necessity of understanding these new parabolic teachings properly and, on the basis of such understanding, disseminating them along with previously given teachings about the kingdom.

ʰ(Matt. 8:24) It is no wonder that Jesus slept soundly after the taxing day he had been through (Secs. 61–64k).

ⁱ(Matt. 8:26; Mark 4:39; Luke 8:24) Here is a double miracle, the cessation of the wind and the immediate calming of the water. Ordinarily the waters would remain rough for a time after the wind stopped, but not this time.

ʲ(Matt. 8:27; Mark 4:41; Luke 8:25) Though privileged to be insiders in regard to the mysteries of the

Sec. 66   Healing the Gerasene demoniacs and resultant opposition
—Gerasa—

Matthew 8:28–34	Mark 5:1–20	Luke 8:26–39
[28]When he arrived at the other side in the region of the Gadarenes,[a] [k]two demon-possessed men coming from the tombs met him. They were so violent that no one could pass that way.	[1]They went across the lake to the region of the Gerasenes.[b] [2]When Jesus got out of the boat, a [k]man with an evil[c] spirit came from the tombs to meet him. [3]This man lived in the tombs, and no one could bind him any more, not even with a chain. [4]For he had often been chained hand and foot, but he tore the chains apart and broke the irons on his feet. No one was strong enough to subdue him. [5]Night and day among the tombs and in the hills he would cry out and cut himself with stones.	[26]They sailed to the region of the Gerasenes,[e] which is across the lake from Galilee. [27]When Jesus stepped ashore, he was met by a [k]demon-possessed man from the town. For a long time this man had not worn clothes or lived in a house, but had lived in the tombs.
[29]"What do you want with us, Son of God?" they shouted. "Have you come here to torture us before the appointed time?"	[6]When he saw Jesus from a distance, he ran and fell on his knees in front of him. [7]He shouted at the top of his voice, "What do you want with me, Jesus, Son of the Most High God? Swear to God that you won't torture me!" [8]For Jesus had said to him, "Come out of this man, you evil spirit!" [9]Then Jesus asked him, "What is your name?" "My name is Legion," he replied, "for we are many." [10]And he begged Jesus again and again not to send them out of the area.	[28]When he saw Jesus, he cried out and fell at his feet, shouting at the top of his voice, "What do you want with me, Jesus, Son of the Most High God? I beg you, don't torture me!" [29]For Jesus had commanded the evil[f] spirit to come out of the man. Many times it had seized him, and though he was chained hand and foot and kept under guard, he had broken his chains and had been driven by the demon into solitary places. [30]Jesus asked him, "What is your name?" "Legion," he replied, because many demons had gone into him. [31]And

kingdom, it is evident that the disciples still needed much strengthening in conviction about the identity of the king. Some of them had begun learning early (Sec. 28), but the process was slow.

[k](Matt. 8:28; Mark 5:2; Luke 8:27) Apparently there were two demon-possessed men, but Mark and Luke single out the one who was leader.

Matthew 8:28–34 (cont'd)   Mark 5:1–20 (cont'd)   Luke 8:26–39 (cont'd)

they begged him repeatedly not to order them to go into the Abyss.

[30]Some distance from them a large herd of [l]pigs was feeding. [31]The demons begged Jesus, "If you drive us out, send us into the herd of pigs." [32]He said to them, "Go!" So they came out and went into the pigs, and the whole herd rushed down the steep bank into the lake and died in the water. [33]Those tending the pigs ran off, went into the town and reported all this, including what had happened to the demon-possessed men. [34]Then the whole town went out to meet Jesus.

[11]A large herd of [l]pigs was feeding on the nearby hillside. [12]The demons begged Jesus, "Send us among the pigs; allow us to go into them." [13]He gave them permission, and the evil spirits came out and went into the pigs. The herd, about two thousand in number, rushed down the steep bank into the lake and were drowned. [14]Those tending the pigs ran off and reported this in the town and countryside, and the people went out to see what had happened. [15]When they came to Jesus, they saw the man who had been possessed by the legion of demons, sitting there, dressed and in his right mind; and they were afraid. [16]Those who had seen it told the people what had happened to the demon-possessed man— and told about the pigs as well. [17]Then the people began to plead with Jesus to leave their region.

[32]A large herd of [l]pigs was feeding there on the hillside. The demons begged Jesus to let them go into them, and he gave them permission. [33]When the demons came out of the man, they went into the pigs, and the herd rushed down the steep bank into the lake and was drowned. [34]When those tending the pigs saw what had happened, they ran off and reported this in the town and countryside, [35]and the people went out to see what had happened. When they came to Jesus, they found the man from whom the demons had gone out, sitting at Jesus' feet, dressed and in his right mind; and they were afraid. [36]Those who had seen it told the people how the demon-possessed man had been cured. [37]Then all the people of the region of the Gerasenes asked Jesus to leave them, because they were overcome with fear. So he got into the boat and left.

And when they saw him, they pleaded with him to leave their region.

[18]As Jesus was getting into the boat, the man who had been demon-possessed begged to go with him. [19]Jesus did not let him, but said, "Go home to your family and [m]tell them how much the Lord has done for you, and how he has had mercy on you." [20]So the man went away and began to

[38]The man from whom the demons had gone out begged to go with him, but Jesus sent him away, saying, [39]"Return home and [m]tell how much God has done for you." So the man went away and told all over town how much Jesus had done for him.

---

[l](Matt. 8:30; Mark 5:11; Luke 8:32) The presence of pigs in this predominantly Gentile area of Decapolis is not surprising. Pigs were, however, unclean animals to the Jews.

[m](Mark 5:19; Luke 8:39) Whereas Jesus for various reasons forbade others to speak about their cures, the situation in half-heathen Perea where this miracle was performed was different. Political repercussions from Jewish opponents were nonexistent here. Furthermore, there were no other missionaries to the area.

Mark 5:1–20 (cont'd)

tell in the Decapolis[d] how
much Jesus had done for
him. And all the people
were amazed.

[a]Mt 8:28 Some manuscripts *Gergesenes*; others *Gerasenes*   [b]Mk 5:1 Some manuscripts
Gadarenes; other manuscripts *Gergesenes*   [c]2 Greek *unclean*; also in verses 8 and 13   [d]20 That is, the
Ten Cities   [e]Lk 8:26 Some manuscripts *Gadarenes*; other manuscripts *Gergesenes*; also in verse 37
[f]29 Greek *unclean*

Sec. 67   Return to Galilee, healing of woman who touched Jesus' garment, and raising of Jairus' daughter
—*Galilee, by the lake*—

Matthew 9:18–26	Mark 5:21–43	Luke 8:40–56
	[21]When Jesus had again crossed over by boat to the other side of the lake, a large crowd gathered around him while he was by the lake. [22]Then one of the synagogue rulers, named Jairus, came there. Seeing Jesus, he fell at his feet [23]and [o]pleaded earnestly with him, "My little daughter is dying. Please come and put your hands on her so that she will be healed and live."	[40]Now when Jesus returned, a crowd welcomed him, for they were all expecting him. [41]Then a man named Jairus, a ruler of the synagogue, came and fell at Jesus' feet, [o]pleading with him to come to his house [42]because his only daughter, a girl of about twelve, was dying.
[18n]While he was saying this, a ruler came and knelt before him and [o]said, "My daughter has just died. But come and put your hand on her, and she will live." [19]Jesus got up and went with him, and so did his disciples. [20]Just then a woman who had been subject to bleeding for twelve years	[24]So Jesus went with him. A large crowd followed and pressed around him. [25]And a woman was there who had been subject to bleeding for twelve years. [26]She had [p]suffered a great deal under the care of many doctors and had spent all she had, yet instead of getting better she grew worse. [27]When she heard about Jesus, she	As Jesus was on his way, the crowds almost crushed him. [43]And a woman was there who had been subject to bleeding for twelve years,[a] but [p]no one could heal her.
came up behind him and touched the edge of his cloak. [21]She said to herself, "If I only touch his cloak, I will be healed."	came up behind him in the crowd and touched his cloak, [28]because she thought, "If I just touch his clothes, I will be	[44]She came up behind him and touched the edge of his cloak, and immediately her bleeding stopped.

[n](Matt. 9:18) At times this introductory phrase has been taken to indicate chronological sequence between Matthew 9:14–17 (Sec. 48) and 9:18–26. Even though plausible, this sequence would intolerably disrupt the order of Mark and Luke. Besides, this portion of Matthew's gospel is not chronologically arranged. As A. T. Robertson indicates, this sequence is more probable.

[o](Matt. 9:18; Mark 5:23; Luke 8:41) Because Jesus had established his headquarters at Capernaum (cf. Sec. 40), it is quite probable that Jairus had had previous contact with him. As a synagogue leader in the city, he probably knew about the healing of the royal official's child (cf. Sec. 38) and of the centurion's servant (cf. Sec. 55). These furnished ample incentive for him to seek Jesus' help.

[p](Mark 5:26; Luke 8:43) Luke the physician is more sympathetic to the efforts of those of his own profession than is Mark.

Matthew 9:18–26 (cont'd)	Mark 5:21–43 (cont'd)	Luke 8:40–56 (cont'd)

healed." [29]Immediately her bleeding stopped and she felt in her body that she was freed from her suffering.

[30]At once Jesus realized that power had gone out from him. He turned around in the crowd and asked, "Who touched my clothes?"

[31]"You see the people crowding against you," his disciples answered, "and yet you can ask, 'Who touched me?'"

[32]But Jesus kept looking around to see who had done it. [33]Then the woman, knowing what had happened to her, came and fell at his feet and, trembling with fear, told him the whole truth. [34]He said to her, "Daughter, your faith has healed you. Go in peace and be freed from your suffering."

[45]"Who touched me?" Jesus asked.

When they all denied it, Peter said, "Master, the people are crowding and pressing against you."

[46]But Jesus said, "Someone touched me; I know that power has gone out from me."

[47]Then the woman, seeing that she could not go unnoticed, came trembling and fell at his feet. In the presence of all the people, she told why she had touched him and how she had been instantly healed. [48]Then he said to her, "Daughter, your faith has healed you. Go in peace."

[22]Jesus turned and saw her. "Take heart, daughter," he said, "your faith has healed you." And the woman was healed from that moment.

[35]While Jesus was still speaking, some men came from the house of Jairus, the synagogue ruler. "Your daughter is dead," they said. "Why bother the teacher any more?"

[36]Ignoring what they said, Jesus told the synagogue ruler, "Don't be afraid; just believe."

[37]He did not let anyone follow him except Peter, James and John the brother of James. [38]When they came to the home of the synagogue ruler, Jesus saw a commotion, with people crying and wailing loudly. [39]He went in and said to them,

[49]While Jesus was still speaking, someone came from the house of Jairus, the synagogue ruler. "Your daughter is dead," he said. "Don't bother the teacher any more."

[50]Hearing this, Jesus said to Jairus, "Don't be afraid; just believe, and she will be healed."

[51]When he arrived at the house of Jairus, he did not let anyone go in with him except Peter, John and James, and the child's father and mother. [52]Meanwhile, all the peo-

Matthew 9:18–26 (cont'd)   Mark 5:21–43 (cont'd)   Luke 8:40–56 (cont'd)

ple were wailing and mourning for her. "Stop wailing," Jesus said. "She is not dead but asleep."

[23]When Jesus entered the ruler's house and saw the flute players and the noisy crowd, [24]he said, "Go away. The girl is not dead but asleep." But they laughed at him.

"Why all this commotion and wailing? The child is not dead but asleep." [40]But they laughed at him.

[53]They laughed at him, knowing that she was dead.

After he put them all out, he took the child's father and mother and the disciples who were with him, and went in where the child was. [41]He took [25]After her by the hand and said the crowd had been to her, "Talitha koum!" put outside, he went in (which means, "Little and took the girl by the girl, I say to you, get up!"). hand, and she got up. [42]Immediately the girl stood up and walked around (she was twelve years old). At this they were completely astonished. [43]He gave strict orders [q]not to let anyone know about this, and told [26]News of this spread them to give her something to eat.

[54]But he took her by the hand and said, "My child, get up!" [55]Her spirit returned, and at once she stood up. Then Jesus told them to give her something to eat.

[56]Her parents were astonished, but he ordered them [q]not to tell anyone what had happened.

through all that region.

[a]Lk 8:43 Many manuscripts *years, and she had spent all she had on doctors*

Sec. 68   Three miracles of healing and another blasphemous accusation
       (cf. Secs. 61, 106—casting out demons, and blasphemous statements)
       (cf. Sec. 126—healing the blind)
       —Galilee—

Matthew 9:27–34

[27]As Jesus went on from there, two blind men followed him, calling out, "Have mercy on us, Son of David!"

[28]When he had gone indoors, the blind men came to him, and he asked them, "Do you believe that I am able to do this?"

"Yes, Lord," they replied.

[29]Then he touched their eyes and said, "According to your faith will it be done to you"; [30]and their sight was restored. Jesus warned them sternly, "See that [r]no one knows about this." [31]But they went out and spread the news about him all over that region.

---

[q](Mark 5:43; Luke 8:56) The manner in which the girl was raised from the dead was to be kept from unbelieving and scornful mourners (Mark 5:40; Luke 8:53) and reserved for those who responded to his invitation to believe (Mark 5:36; Luke 8:50). The scene of the incident was Capernaum, where earlier (perhaps the same day) his ministry had changed its complexion because of "an eternal sin" (Mark 3:29, Sec. 61). Now he is quite careful as to whom he gives the gospel.

[r](Matt. 9:30) The prohibition intended to silence the healed blind man was prompted by the antagonistic atmosphere that prevailed in Galilee against Jesus. Wrong implications derived from his miraculous deeds furnished an opportunity for further blasphemy against the Holy Spirit (cf. Matt. 9:34; cf. Sec. 61). No further sign was to be given the rejectors (Matt. 12:39, Sec. 62).

Matthew 9:27–34 (cont'd)

[32]While they were going out, a man who was demon-possessed and could not talk was brought to Jesus. [33]And when the demon was driven out, the man who had been mute spoke. The crowd was amazed and said, "Nothing like this has ever been seen in Israel."

[34]But the Pharisees said, "It is by the prince of demons that he drives out demons."

Sec. 69   Final visit to unbelieving Nazareth
(cf. Secs. 36, 37, 39—no honor at home)
—Nazareth—

Matthew 13:54–58	Mark 6:1–6a
[54]Coming to his hometown, he began teaching the people in their synagogue, and they were amazed. "Where did this man get this wisdom and these miraculous powers?" they asked.	[1]Jesus left there and went to his hometown, accompanied by his disciples. [2]When the Sabbath came, he began to teach in the synagogue, and many who heard him were amazed. "Where did this man get these things?" they asked. "What's this wisdom that has been given him, that he even does miracles! [3]Isn't this the carpenter? Isn't this Mary's son and the brother of James, Joseph,[a] Judas and Simon? Aren't his sisters here with us?" And they took offense at him.
[55]"Isn't this the carpenter's son? Isn't his mother's name Mary, and aren't his brothers James, Joseph, Simon and Judas? [56]Aren't all his sisters with us? Where then did this man get all these things?" [57]And they took offense at him. But Jesus said to them, "Only in his hometown and in his own house is a prophet without honor." [58]And he did not do many miracles there because of their [s]lack of faith.	[4]Jesus said to them, "Only in his hometown, among his relatives and in his own house is a prophet without honor." [5]He could not do any miracles there, except lay his hands on a few sick people and heal them. [6]And he was amazed at their [s]lack of faith.

[a]Mk 6:3 Greek *Joses*, a variant of *Joseph*

FINAL GALILEAN CAMPAIGN

Sec. 70a   Shortage of workers
(cf. Secs. 70b, 102a—workers dispatched)
—Itineration in Galilee—

Matthew 9:35–38	Mark 6:6b
[35]Jesus went through all the towns and villages, teaching in their synagogues, preaching the good news of the kingdom and healing every disease and sickness. [36]When he saw the crowds, he had compassion on them, because they	Then Jesus went around teaching from village to village.

---

[s](Matt. 13:58; Mark 6:6a) This visit to Nazareth came about a year after the citizens of the town had attempted to murder Jesus (Luke 4:29, Sec. 39). As their earlier treatment stood in contrast to the belief of the Samaritans (Sec. 35c) and the royal official (Sec. 38), so now their unbelief is in marked contrast to the faith of those who benefited from Jesus' ministry in Capernaum (Secs. 67, 68).

Matthew 9:35–38 (cont'd)

were harassed and helpless, like ᵗsheep without a shepherd. ³⁷Then he said to his disciples, "The harvest is plentiful but the workers are few. ³⁸Ask the Lord of the harvest, therefore, to send out workers into his harvest field."

Sec. 70b   Commissioning of the Twelve
(cf. Sec. 53, Acts 1:13—twelve apostles listed)
(cf. Secs. 54g, 108a—value of birds)
(cf. Secs. 54g, 145, 150b—followers not above the leader)
(cf. Secs. 70a, 102a—workers dispatched)
(cf. Secs. 83, 115—cost of discipleship)
(cf. Sec. 91—a cup of water)
(cf. Sec. 108a—confession before others)
(cf. Secs. 108d, 139b—divided households)
—*Galilee*—

Matthew 10:1–42	Mark 6:7–11	Luke 9:1–5
¹He called his twelve disciples to him and gave them authority to drive out evil*ᵃ* spirits and to heal every disease and sickness.	⁷Calling the Twelve to him, he sent them out two by two and gave them authority over evil*ᵃ* spirits.	¹When Jesus had called the Twelve together, he gave them power and authority to drive out all demons and to cure diseases, ²and he sent them out to preach the kingdom of God and to heal the sick.
²These are the names of the twelve apostles: first, Simon (who is called Peter) and his brother Andrew; James son of Zebedee, and his brother John; ³Philip and Bartholomew; Thomas and Matthew the tax collector; James son of Alphaeus, and Thaddaeus; ⁴Simon the Zealot and Judas Iscariot, who betrayed him.		
⁵These twelve Jesus sent out with the following instructions: "ᵘDo not go among the Gentiles or enter any town of the Samaritans. ⁶Go rather to the lost sheep of Israel. ⁷As you go, preach this message: 'The kingdom of		

ᵗ(Matt. 9:36) The "sheep" are identified more fully in Matt. 10:6 as "the lost sheep of Israel." To evangelize this people more thoroughly was his compassionate objective at this point. Every person had a right to hear the good news about the kingdom, even though the leadership had already turned its back on the King (cf. Sec. 61).

ᵘ(Matt. 10:5) Jesus at this point continued restricting his outreach—and that of his disciples—to the people to whom the kingdom had been promised. A broadened responsibility was not outlined until his rejection by this people became more general as reflected in the crucifixion. Then the disciples were told to go to all nations (cf. Sec. 181).

Matthew 10:1–42 (cont'd)   Mark 6:7–11 (cont'd)   Luke 9:1–5 (cont'd)

heaven is near.' [8]Heal the sick, raise the dead, cleanse those who have leprosy,[b] drive out demons. Freely you have received, freely give. [9]Do not take along any gold or silver or copper in your belts; [10]take no bag for the journey, or extra tunic, or sandals or a staff; for the worker is worth his keep.

[11]"Whatever town or village you enter, search for some worthy person there and stay at his house until you leave. [12]As you enter the home, give it your greeting. [13]If the home is deserving, let your peace rest on it; if it is not, let your peace return to you. [14]If anyone will not welcome you or listen to your words, shake the dust off your feet when you leave that home or town. [15]I tell you the truth, it will be more bearable for Sodom and Gomorrah on the day of judgment than for that town. [16]I am sending you out like sheep among wolves. Therefore be as shrewd as snakes and as innocent as doves.

[8]These were his instructions: "Take nothing for the journey except a staff—no bread, no bag, no money in your belts. [9]Wear sandals but not an extra tunic. [10]Whenever you enter a house, stay there until you leave that town.

[11]And if any place will not welcome you or listen to you, shake the dust off your feet when you leave, as a testimony against them."

[3]He told them: "Take nothing for the journey— no staff, no bag, no bread, no money, no extra tunic. [4]Whatever house you enter, stay there until you leave that town.

[5]If people do not welcome you, shake the dust off your feet when you leave their town, as a testimony against them."

[17]"Be on your guard against men; they will hand you over to the local councils and flog you in their synagogues. [18]On my account you will be brought before governors and kings as witnesses to them and to the Gentiles. [19]But when they arrest you, do not worry about what to say or how to say it. At that time you will be given what to say, [20]for it will not be you speaking, but the Spirit of your Father speaking through you.

[21]"Brother will betray brother to death, and a father his child; children will rebel against their parents and have them put to death. [22]All men will hate you because of me, but he who stands firm to the end will be saved. [23]When you are persecuted in one place, flee to another. I tell you the truth, you will not finish going through the cities of Israel before the Son of Man comes.

[24]"A student is not above his teacher, nor a servant above his master. [25]It is enough for the student to be like his teacher, and the servant like his master. [v]If the head of the house has been called Beelzebub,[c] how much more the members of his household!

[26]"So do not be afraid of them. There is nothing concealed that will not be disclosed, or hidden that will not be made known. [27]What I tell you in the dark,

---

[v](Matt. 10:25) Jesus apparently did not expect widespread repentance to result from this mission. In the bulk of the discourse (e.g., Matt. 10:14–39) he anticipated an unfavorable reception of the Twelve. This anticipation was based on earlier treatment of himself (cf. Sec. 61).

Matthew 10:1–42 (cont'd)

speak in the daylight; what is whispered in your ear, proclaim from the roofs. [28]Do not be afraid of those who kill the body but cannot kill the soul. Rather, be afraid of the One who can destroy both soul and body in hell. [29]Are not two sparrows sold for a penny[d]? Yet not one of them will fall to the ground apart from the will of your Father. [30]And even the very hairs of your head are all numbered. [31]So don't be afraid; you are worth more than many sparrows.

[32]"Whoever acknowledges me before men, I will also acknowledge him before my Father in heaven. [33]But whoever disowns me before men, I will disown him before my Father in heaven.

[34]"Do not suppose that I have come to bring peace to the earth. I did not come to bring peace, but a sword. [35]For I have come to turn

" 'a man against his father,
   a daughter against her mother,
   a daughter-in-law against her mother-in-law—
[36]   a man's enemies will be the members of his own household'[e] [Mic. 7:6].

[37]"Anyone who loves his father or mother more than me is not worthy of me; anyone who loves his son or daughter more than me is not worthy of me; [38]and anyone who does not take his cross and follow me is not worthy of me. [39]Whoever finds his life will lose it, and whoever loses his life for my sake will find it.

[40]"He who receives you receives me, and he who receives me receives the one who sent me. [41]Anyone who receives a prophet because he is a prophet will receive a prophet's reward, and anyone who receives a righteous man because he is a righteous man will receive a righteous man's reward. [42]And if anyone gives even a cup of cold water to one of these little ones because he is my disciple, I tell you the truth, he will certainly not lose his reward."

[a]Mt 10:1; Mk 6:7 Greek *unclean*   [b]Mt 10:8 The Greek word was used for various diseases affecting the skin—not necessarily leprosy.   [c]25 Greek *Beezeboul* or *Beelzeboul*   [d]29 Greek *an assarion*   [e]36 Micah 7:6

Sec. 70c   [w]Workers sent out
—Itineration in Galilee—

Matthew 11:1	Mark 6:12–13	Luke 9:6
[1]After Jesus had finished instructing his twelve disciples, he went on from there to teach and preach in the towns of Galilee.[a]	[12]They went out and preached that people should repent. [13]They drove out many demons and anointed many sick people with oil and healed them.	[6]So they set out and went from village to village, preaching the gospel and healing people everywhere.

[a]1 Greek *in their towns*

Sec. 71a   Antipas' mistaken identification of Jesus

Matthew 14:1–2	Mark 6:14–16	Luke 9:7–9
[1]At that time Herod the tetrarch [x]heard the reports about Jesus, [2]and he said	[14]King Herod [x]heard about this, for Jesus' name had become well known.	[7]Now Herod the tetrarch [x]heard about all that was going on. And he

[w]See Section 72a for Mark's and Luke's reports about the return of the workers after their mission.
[x](Matt. 14:1; Mark 6:14; Luke 9:7) The multiplied outreach of Jesus' ministry through the Twelve (Secs. 70b, 70c) was what brought him increased fame. Herod Antipas, whose domain included Galilee and Perea, was now forced to give him attention.

Matthew 14:1–2 (cont'd)	Mark 6:14–16 (cont'd)	Luke 9:7–9 (cont'd)
to his attendants, "This is John the Baptist; he has risen from the dead! That is why miraculous powers are at work in him."	Some were saying,[a] "John the Baptist has been raised from the dead, and that is why miraculous powers are at work in him." [15]Others said, "He is Elijah." And still others claimed, "He is a prophet, like one of the prophets of long ago." [16]But when Herod heard this, he said, "John, the man I beheaded, has been raised from the dead!"	was perplexed, because some were saying that John had been raised from the dead, [8]others that Elijah had appeared, and still others that one of the prophets of long ago had come back to life. [9]But Herod said, "I beheaded John. Who, then, is this I hear such things about?" And he tried to see him.

[a]Mk6:14 Some early manuscripts *He was saying*

Sec. 71b [y]Earlier imprisonment and beheading of John the Baptist (cf. Sec. 34—John's imprisonment)
—Probably Tiberias—

Matthew 14:3–12	Mark 6:17–29
[3]Now Herod had arrested John and bound him and put him in prison because of Herodias, his brother Philip's wife, [4]for John had been saying to him: "It is not lawful for you to have her." [5]Herod wanted to kill John, but he was afraid of the people, because they considered him a prophet.	[17]For Herod himself had given orders to have John arrested, and he had him bound and put in prison. He did this because of Herodias, his brother Philip's wife, whom he had married. [18]For John had been saying to Herod, "It is not lawful for you to have your brother's wife." [19]So Herodias nursed a grudge against John and wanted to kill him. But she was not able to, [20]because Herod feared John and protected him, knowing him to be a righteous and holy man. When Herod heard John, he was greatly puzzled[a]; yet he liked to listen to him.
[6]On Herod's birthday the daughter of Herodias danced for them and pleased Herod so much [7]that he promised with an oath to give her whatever she asked.	[21]Finally the opportune time came. On his birthday Herod gave a banquet for his high officials and military commanders and the leading men of Galilee. [22]When the daughter of Herodias came in and danced, she pleased Herod and his dinner guests. The king said to the girl, "Ask me for anything you want, and I'll give it to you." [23]And he promised her with an oath, "Whatever you ask I will give you, up to half my kingdom."

[y]This section is a historical flashback given as background to the execution of John, which occurred at this point in the chronology. John's imprisonment had begun about a year and a half earlier, at the time Jesus began his Galilean ministry (cf. Sec. 34).

Matthew 14:3–12 (cont'd)

Mark 6:17–29 (cont'd)

[24]She went out and said to her mother, "What shall I ask for?"

"The head of John the Baptist," she answered.

[25]At once the girl hurried in to the king with the request: "I want you to give me right now the head of John the Baptist on a platter."

[8]Prompted by her mother, she said, "Give me here on a platter the head of John the Baptist." [9]The king was distressed, but because of his oaths and his dinner guests, he ordered that her request be granted [10]and had John beheaded in the prison. [11]His head was brought in on a platter and given to the girl, who carried it to her mother. [12]John's disciples came and took his body and buried it. Then they went and told Jesus.

[26]The king was greatly distressed, but because of his oaths and his dinner guests, he did not want to refuse her. [27]So he immediately sent an executioner with orders to bring John's head. The man went, beheaded John in the prison, [28]and brought back his head on a platter. He presented it to the girl, and she gave it to her mother. [29]On hearing of this, John's disciples came and took his body and laid it in a tomb.

[a]Mk6:20 Some early manuscripts *he did many things*

PART SEVEN

THE MINISTRY OF CHRIST AROUND GALILEE
LESSON ON THE BREAD OF LIFE

Sec. 72a Return of the workers
—Galilee—

Mark 6:30	Luke 9:10a
[30]The apostles gathered around Jesus and reported to him all they had done and taught.	[10]When the apostles returned, they reported to Jesus what they had done.

Sec. 72b Withdrawal from Galilee
—From Galilee to ᶻBethsaida, near Julias—

Matthew 14:13–14	Mark 6:31–34	Luke 9:10b–11	John 6:1–3
	[31]Then, because so many people were coming and going that they did not even have a chance to eat, he said to them, "ᵇCome with me by yourselves to a quiet place and get some rest."		
[13]When Jesus heard what had happened, he ᵃwithdrew by boat	[32]So they went away by themselves in a boat to a solitary place.	Then he took them with him and they ᵃwithdrew by themselves to a	[1]Some time after this, Jesus crossed to the far shore of

---

ᶻApparently two communities were named Bethsaida. That of Luke 9:10 should be identified with Bethsaida near Julias on the northeast side of the Sea of Galilee. In Mark 6:45 (Sec. 73) the name designates a village on the western shore, near Capernaum.

ᵃ(Matt. 14:13; Luke 9:10) At this point in his ministry, Jesus' relationship with the crowds changed. Prior to this he had made it a point for the most part to go to them, though there were exceptions (e.g., Sec. 65). The following months were especially characterized by his withdrawal from them. In addition to this section, see Sections 73, 78, 79a, and 81a. Five factors have merit in accounting for these withdrawals:

> 1. The jealousy of Herod Antipas (cf. Matt. 14:13 with Mark 6:30, Sec. 72a). Apparently the arrival of John's disciples with the news of his burial coincided with the return of the Twelve from their preaching tour of Galilee, which was part of Herod's domain. Jesus left the area to avoid any further retaliatory steps by Herod because of the widespread publicity resulting from the tour of the Twelve.
> 2. The misguided zeal of followers who sought to force Jesus to accept the throne of Israel prematurely (cf. John 6:15, Sec. 73). Jesus avoided such a confrontation and its probable unfortunate aftereffects.
> 3. The hostility of Jewish leaders (cf. Mark 7:1–23, Sec. 77). Opposition from those in high places had surfaced as the Galilean ministry progressed, but now it had developed to the point that further ministry in Galilee had to be curtailed radically.
> 4. The disciples' need for rest after their grueling tours (cf. Mark 6:31). Departure from the hot shores of the Sea of Galilee to the cooler mountain areas afforded an opportunity for this.
> 5. The opportunity for more personalized instruction of the disciples (cf. Secs. 72b–95, where the disciples were either in the role of recipients of instruction or were profiting in a special way from Jesus' dealing with others). Their ministries throughout Galilee had probably created many questions. The Lord thus gave them a different kind of opportunity to learn about and from him.

ᵇ(Mark 6:31) This point marks a shift from a predominantly public ministry to a predominantly private one. Other transitions may be observed in progress at this point: an emphasis on the King replaced an emphasis on the kingdom; instruction was preparatory for a period of his absence in lieu of his presence;

Matthew 14:13–14 (cont'd)	Mark 6:31–34 (cont'd)	Luke 9:10b–11 (cont'd)	John 6:1–3 (cont'd)
privately to a solitary place. Hearing of this, the crowds followed him on foot from the towns. ¹⁴When Jesus landed and saw a large crowd, he had compassion on them and healed their sick.	³³But many who saw them leaving recognized them and ran on foot from all the towns and got there ahead of them. ³⁴When Jesus landed and saw a large crowd, he had compassion on them, because they were like sheep without a shepherd. So he began teaching them many things.	town called Bethsaida, ¹¹but the crowds learned about it and followed him. He welcomed them and spoke to them about the kingdom of God, and healed those who needed healing.	the Sea of Galilee (that is, the Sea of Tiberias), ²and a great crowd of people followed him because they saw the miraculous signs he had performed on the sick. ³Then Jesus went up on a mountainside and sat down with his disciples.

Sec. 72c   Feeding the five thousand
(cf. Secs. 79b, 81a—feeding the crowds)
—Bethsaida—

Matthew 14:15–21	Mark 6:35–44	Luke 9:12–17	John 6:4–13
¹⁵As evening approached, the ᶜdisciples came to him and said, "This is a remote place, and it's already getting late. Send the crowds away, so they can go to the villages and buy themselves some food." ¹⁶Jesus replied, "They do not need to go away. You give them something to eat."	³⁵By this time it was late in the day, so his ᶜdisciples came to him. "This is a remote place," they said, "and it's already very late. ³⁶Send the people away so they can go to the surrounding countryside and villages and buy themselves something to eat." ³⁷But he answered, "You give them something to eat." They said to him, "That would take ᵈeight months of a man's wagesᵃ! Are we to go and	¹²Late in the afternoon the ᶜTwelve came to him and said, "Send the crowd away so they can go to the surrounding villages and countryside and find food and lodging, because we are in a remote place here." ¹³He replied, "You give them something to eat."	⁴The Jewish Passover Feast was near. ⁵When Jesus looked up and saw a great crowd coming toward him, he said to ᶜPhilip, "Where shall we buy bread for these people to eat?" ⁶He asked this only to test him, for he already had in mind

and, with the exception of intermittent visits to Galilee, he limited his ministry to outside that area from this point on.

ᶜ(Matt. 14:15; Mark 6:35; Luke 9:12; John 6:5) The prominence of the disciples thoughout this episode underscores the importance of the learning experience for them. They learned something about their teacher's power they had not realized before (cf. John 6:12–13). Their doubt (Mark 6:37; John 6:7–8) needed to be replaced by confidence in him.

ᵈ(Mark 6:37; John 6:7) "Eight months of a man's wages" or two hundred denarii. Though not a large amount of money this was probably more than the disciples had in their treasury. Even if they had possessed this much, it would not have been enough.

Matthew 14:15–21 (cont'd)	Mark 6:35–44 (cont'd)	Luke 9:12–17 (cont'd)	John 6:4–13 (cont'd)
	spend that much on bread and give it to them to eat?" 38"How many loaves do you have?" he asked. "Go and see."		what he was going to do. 7Philip answered him, "dEight months' wages b would not buy enough bread for each one to have a bite!" 8Another of his disciples, Andrew, Simon Peter's brother, spoke up,
17"We have here only five loaves of bread and two fish," they answered. 18"Bring them here to me," he said. 19And he directed the people to sit down on the grass. Taking the five loaves and the two fish and looking up to heaven, he gave thanks and broke the loaves.Then he gave them to the disciples, and the disciples gave them to the people. 20They all ate and were satisfied, and the disciples picked up twelve basketfuls of broken pieces that were left over. 21The number of those who ate was about ⁿfive thousand men, besides women and children.	When they found out, they said, "Five—and two fish." 39Then Jesus directed them to have all the people sit down in groups on the green grass. 40So they sat down in groups of hundreds and fifties. 41Taking the five loaves and the two fish and looking up to heaven, he gave thanks and broke the loaves. Then he gave them to his disciples to set before the people. He also divided the two fish among them all. 42They all ate and were satisfied, 43and the disciples picked up twelve basketfuls of broken pieces of bread and fish. 44The number of the men who had eaten was ⁿfive thousand.	They answered, "We have only five loaves of bread and two fish—unless we go and buy food for all this crowd." 14(About ⁿfive thousand men were there.) But he said to his disciples, "Have them sit down in groups of about fifty each." 15The disciples did so, and everybody sat down. 16Taking the five loaves and the two fish and looking up to heaven, he gave thanks and broke them. Then he gave them to the disciples to set before the people. 17They all ate and were satisfied, and the disciples picked up twelve basketfuls of broken pieces that were left over.	9"Here is a boy with five small barley loaves and two small fish, but how far will they go among so many?" 10Jesus said, "Have the people sit down." There was plenty of grass in that place, and the men sat down, about ⁿfive thousand of them. 11Jesus then took the loaves, gave thanks, and distributed to those who were seated as much as they wanted. He did the same with the fish. 12When they had all had enough to eat, he said to his disciples, "Gather the pieces that are left over. Let nothing be wasted." 13So they gathered them and filled twelve baskets with the pieces of the five barley loaves left over by those who had eaten.

aMk 14:37 Greek *take two hundred denarii*   bJn 6:7 Greek *two hundred denarii*

ⁿ(Matt. 14:21; Mark 6:44; Luke 9:14; John 6:10) The presence of five thousand men strongly implies an equal number of women and at least an equal number of children. The hungry crowd that was fed probably totaled in excess of fifteen thousand.

Sec. 73   A premature attempt to make Jesus king blocked
—Alone on a mountain—

Matthew 14:22–23	Mark 6:45–46	John 6:14–15
[22]Immediately Jesus made the disciples get into the boat and go on ahead of him to the other side, while he dismissed the crowd. [23]After he had dismissed them, he went up on a mountainside by himself to pray. When evening came, he was there alone,	[45]Immediately Jesus made his disciples get into the boat and go on ahead of him to Bethsaida, while he dismissed the crowd. [46]After leaving them, he went up on a mountainside to pray.	[14]After the people saw the miraculous sign that Jesus did, they began to say, "Surely this is the Prophet who is to come into the world." [15]Jesus, knowing that they intended to come and make him king by force, [f]withdrew again to a mountain by himself.

Sec. 74   Walking on the water during a storm on the lake
—On the Sea of Galilee—

Matthew 14:24–33	Mark 6:47–52	John 6:16–21
[24]but the boat was already a considerable distance[a] from land, buffeted by the waves because the wind was against it. [25]During the [g]fourth watch of the night Jesus went out to them, walking on the lake. [26]When the disciples saw him walking on the lake, they were terrified. "It's a ghost," they said, and cried out in fear. [27]But Jesus immediately said to them: "Take courage! It is I. Don't be afraid." [28]"Lord, if it's you," Peter replied, "tell me to come to you on the water." [29]"Come," he said. Then Peter got down out of the boat, walked on the water and came to-	[47]When evening came, the boat was in the middle of the lake, and he was alone on land. [48]He saw the disciples straining at the oars, because the wind was against them. About the [g]fourth watch of the night he went out to them, walking on the lake. He was about to pass by them, [49]but when they saw him walking on the lake, they thought he was a ghost. They cried out, [50]because they all saw him and were terrified. Immediately he spoke to them and said, "Take courage! It is I. Don't be afraid."	[16]When evening came, his disciples went down to the lake, [17]where they got into a boat and set off across the lake for Capernaum. By now it was dark, and Jesus had not yet joined them. [18]A strong wind was blowing and the waters grew rough. [19]When they had rowed three or three and a half miles,[b] they saw Jesus approaching the boat, walking on the water; and they were terrified. [20]But he said to them, "It is I; don't be afraid."

---

[f](John 6:15) Once again Jesus refused to accede to popular demand (cf. John 2:23, Sec. 32a). He did not deny that he would eventually be King over earthly subjects, but he was unwilling to assume an active rule until his subjects met the moral prerequisites for entering the kind of kingdom that he came to institute (cf. Sermon on the Mount, Secs. 54a–54i). Their recent rejection of him in Galilee, as well as their selfish motives on the present occasion, were ample proof that they were not ready for his kingdom.

[g](Matt. 14:25; Mark 6:48) Between nine and twelve hours must have elapsed since Jesus left the disciples. He had left them at about 6:00 p.m. ("evening," Mark 6:47) and rejoined them between 3:00 a.m. and 6:00 a.m. the next morning ("the fourth watch"). All this time they were fighting the storm, and he was praying.

Matthew 14:24–33 (cont'd)	Mark 6:47–52 (cont'd)	John 6:16–21 (cont'd)

ward Jesus. [30]But when he saw the wind, he was afraid and, beginning to sink, cried out, "Lord, save me!"

[31]Immediately Jesus reached out his hand and caught him. "You of little faith," he said, "why did you doubt?"

[32]And when they climbed into the boat, the wind died down. [33]Then those who were in the boat worshiped him, saying, "Truly you are the [i]Son of God."

[51]Then he climbed into the boat with them, and the [h]wind died down. They were completely amazed, [52]for they had not understood about the loaves; their hearts were hardened.

[21]Then they were willing to take him into the boat, and [h]immediately the boat reached the shore where they were heading.

[a]Mt 14:24 Greek *many stadia*   [b]Jn 6:19 Greek *rowed twenty-five or thirty stadia* (about 5 or 6 kilometers)

Sec. 75 Healings at Gennesaret
—[i]Gennesaret—

Matthew 14:34–36	Mark 6:53–56

[34]When they had crossed over, they landed at [k]Gennesaret. [35]And when the men of that place recognized Jesus, they sent word to all the surrounding country.

People brought all their sick to him [36]and begged him to let the sick just touch the edge of his cloak, and all who touched him were healed.

[53]When they had crossed over, they landed at [k]Gennesaret and anchored there. [54]As soon as they got out of the boat, people recognized Jesus. [55]They ran throughout that whole region and carried the sick on mats to wherever they heard he was. [56]And wherever he went—into villages, towns or countryside—they placed the sick in the marketplaces. They begged him to let them touch even the edge of his cloak, and all who touched him were healed.

Sec. 76a Discourse on the true bread of life
—Capernaum—

John 6:22–59

[22]The next day the crowd that had stayed on the opposite shore of the lake realized that only one boat had been there, and that Jesus had not entered it with his disciples, but that they had gone away alone. [23]Then some boats from Tiberias

h(Mark 6:51; John 6:21) A twofold miracle occurred: the immediate cessation of the wind and the immediate arrival of the boat at its destination.

i(Matt. 14:33) Through this experience the disciples advanced one more step in their appreciation of Jesus' person. The double miracle brought them to acknowledge Jesus to be "such a person as the Son of God" (the Greek text has no definite article). It was to be a while yet before they would confess him to be "the Son of the living God," however, (cf. Matt. 16:16, Sec. 82).

jGennesaret was near Capernaum and Bethsaida. Compare Mark 6:53 with John 6:17, Section 74, and Mark 6:45, Section 73.

k(Matt. 14:34; Mark 6:53) Located on the west coast of the Sea of Galilee, Gennesaret was a fertile plain just south of Capernaum. During this brief visit to Galilee, those who had so recently been party to rejecting him as Messiah (Secs. 61, 68) were still willing to accept benefit from the miracles that proved his Messiahship.

John 6:22–59 (cont'd)

landed near the place where the people had eaten the bread after the Lord had given thanks. [24]Once the crowd realized that neither Jesus nor his disciples were there, they got into the boats and went to Capernaum in search of Jesus.
[25]When they found him on the other side of the lake, they asked him, "Rabbi, when did you get here?"
[26]Jesus answered, "I tell you the truth, you are looking for me, not because you saw miraculous signs but because [l]you ate the loaves and had your fill. [27]Do not work for food that spoils, but for food that endures to eternal life, which the Son of Man will give you. On him God the Father has placed his seal of approval."
[28]Then they asked him, "What must we do to do the works God requires?"
[29]Jesus answered, "The work of God is this: [m]to believe in the one he has sent."
[30]So they asked him, "What miraculous sign then will you give that we may see it and believe you? What will you do? [31]Our forefathers ate the manna in the desert; as it is written: 'He gave them bread from heaven to eat'[a]" [Exod. 16:4,15; Neh. 9:15; Psalm 78:24; 105:40].
[32]Jesus said to them, "I tell you the truth, it is not Moses who has given you the bread from heaven, but it is my Father who gives you the true bread from heaven. [33]For the bread of God is he who comes down from heaven and gives life to the world."
[34]"Sir," they said, "from now on give us this bread."
[35]Then Jesus declared, "[n]I am the bread of life. He who comes to me will never go hungry, and he who believes in me will never be thirsty. [36]But as I told you, you have seen me and still you do not believe. [37]All that the Father gives me will come to me, and whoever comes to me I will never drive away. [38]For I have come down from heaven not to do my will but to do the will of him who sent me. [39]And this is the will of him who sent me, that I shall lose none of all that he has given me, but raise them up at the last day. [40]For my Father's will is that everyone who looks to the Son and believes in him shall have eternal life, and I will raise him up at the last day."
[41]At this the Jews began to grumble about him because he said, "I am the bread that came down from heaven." [42]They said, "Is this not Jesus, the son of Joseph, whose father and mother we know? How can he now say, 'I came down from heaven'?"
[43]"Stop grumbling among yourselves," Jesus answered. [44]"No one can come to me unless the Father who sent me draws him, and I will raise him up at the last day. [45]It is written in the Prophets: 'They will all be taught by God'[b] [Isa. 54:13]. Everyone who listens to the Father and learns from him comes to me. [46]No one has seen the Father except the one who is from God; only he has seen the Father. [47]I tell you the truth, he who believes has everlasting life. [48]I am the bread of life. [49]Your forefathers ate the manna in the desert, yet they died. [50]But here is the bread that comes down from heaven, which a man may eat and not die. [51]I am the living bread that came down from heaven. If anyone eats of this bread, he will live forever. This bread is my flesh, which I will give for the life of the world."
[52]Then the Jews began to argue sharply among themselves, "How can this man give us his flesh to eat?"
[53]Jesus said to them, "I tell you the truth, unless you eat the flesh of the Son of Man and drink his blood, you have no life in you. [54]Whoever eats my flesh and drinks my blood has eternal life, and I will raise him up at the last day. [55]For my flesh is real food and my blood is real drink. [56]Whoever eats my flesh and drinks my blood remains in me, and I in him. [57]Just as the living Father sent me and I live

---

[l](John 6:26) The same selfish motive (cf. Sec. 73) was evident in those who had eaten the loaves and fish on the other side of the sea. They were quite ready for the benefits associated with the kingdom, but not so ready to comply with its moral responsibilities.
[m](John 6:29) "The food which perishes" (John 6:27) represents the externalities, which Israelites of the day thought all important. Jesus constantly sought to correct their misguided efforts. Inward conditioning including faith in him, not outward conformity, was the crying need of the hour.
[n](John 6:35) The "I am" phrases of John's gospel have far-reaching significance. Here as elsewhere it is probably traceable back to Exodus 3:14 and the name of God heard by Moses from the burning bush. This is the first of seven such sayings in John's gospel (cf. 8:12; 10:7, 9; 10:11, 14; 11:25; 14:6; 15:1, 5).

John 6:22–59 (cont'd)

because of the Father, so the one who feeds on me will live because of me. [58]This is the bread that came down from heaven. Your forefathers ate manna and died, but he who feeds on this bread will live forever." [59]He said this while teaching in the synagogue in Capernaum.

[a]Jn 6:31 Exodus 16:4; Neh. 9:15; Psalm 78:24,25   [b]45 Isaiah 54:13

Sec. 76b   Defection among the disciples
(cf. Sec. 82—confessions of Jesus' identity)
—*Capernaum*—

John 6:60–71

[60]On hearing it, many of his disciples said, "This is a hard teaching. Who can accept it?"

[61]Aware that his disciples were grumbling about this, Jesus said to them, "Does this offend you? [62]What if you see the Son of Man ascend to where he was before! [63]The Spirit gives life; the flesh counts for nothing. The words I have spoken to you are spirit[a] and they are life. [64]Yet there are some of you who do not believe." For Jesus had known from the beginning which of them did not believe and who would betray him. [65]He went on to say, "This is why I told you that no one can come to me unless the Father has enabled him."

[66]From this time many of his °disciples turned back and no longer followed him.

[67]"You do not want to leave too, do you?" Jesus asked the Twelve.

[68]Simon Peter answered him, "Lord, to whom shall we go? You have the words of eternal life. [69]We believe and know that you are Pthe Holy One of God."

[70]Then Jesus replied, "Have I not chosen you, the Twelve? Yet one of you is a devil!" [71](He meant Judas, the son of Simon Iscariot, who, though one of the Twelve, was later to betray him.)

[a]Jn 6:63 Or *Spirit*

LESSON ON THE LEAVEN OF THE PHARISEES, SADDUCEES, AND HERODIANS

Sec. 77   Conflict over the tradition of ceremonial uncleanness
—*Galilee, perhaps Capernaum*—

Matthew 15:1–3a, 7–9, 3b–6, 10–20	Mark 7:1–23	John 7:1
[1]Then some qPharisees and teachers of the law came to Jesus from Jerusalem	[1]The qPharisees and some of the teachers of the law who had come from Jerusalem gathered	[1]After this, Jesus went around in Galilee, purposely staying away from Judea because the Jews

°(John 6:66) The strong emphasis on inner response as the only proper basis for external behavior was more than most listeners could bear (John 6:60). As a result, many would-be disciples no longer followed him. John 6:66 marks a turning point in the use of *disciple* in John's gospel. From this point on, it is found in the more restricted sense of *genuine disciple.*

P(John 6:69) Peter and his fellow disciples at this point reached the threshold of what Jesus was teaching them during this period. Their confession was stronger than the previous one (Matt. 14:33, Sec. 74) but not yet as specific as it would be (Matt. 16:16, Sec. 82). "The Holy One of God" was none other than the One whom God anointed to be King (Psalm 16:10; 71:22; 78:41; 89:18; Isa. 1:4). In spite of public rejection of him, the disciples were growing into a full appreciation of his person.

q(Matt. 15:1; Mark 7:1) These represented the official leadership in Jerusalem. Unable to trap Jesus on the issue of Sabbath observance earlier (cf. Secs. 49a, 50, 51), they now have come to Galilee to raise another issue, the tradition of the elders about hand washing before eating.

Matthew 15:1–3a, 7–9, 3b–6, 10–20 (cont'd)	Mark 7:1–23 (cont'd)	John 7:1 (cont'd)
	around Jesus and ²saw some of his disciples eating food with hands that were "unclean," that is, unwashed. ³(The Pharisees and all the Jews do not eat unless they give their hands a ʳceremonial washing, holding to the tradition of the elders. ⁴When they come from the marketplace they do not eat unless they wash. And they observe many other traditions, such as the washing of cups, pitchers and kettles.ʃ)	there were waiting to take his life.
and asked, ²"Why do your disciples break the tradition of the elders? They don't wash their hands before they eat!"	⁵So the Pharisees and teachers of the law asked Jesus, "Why don't your disciples live according to the tradition of the elders instead of eating their food with 'unclean' hands?"	
³Jesus replied, ⁷You hypocrites! Isaiah was right when he prophesied about you:	⁶He replied, "Isaiah was right when he prophesied about you hypocrites; as it is written:	
⁸" 'These people honor me with their lips, but their hearts are far from me. ⁹They worship me in vain; their teachings are but rules taught by men'ᵈ" [Isa. 29:13.	" 'These people honor me with their lips, but their hearts are far from me. ⁷They worship me in vain; their teachings are but rules taught by men'ᵈ [Isa. 29:13].	
	⁸You have let go of the commands of God and are holding on to the traditions of men."	
"And why do you break the command of God for the sake of your tradition? ⁴For God said, 'Honor your father and mother'ᵃ [Exod. 20:12; Deut. 5:16]	⁹And he said to them: "You have a fine way of setting aside the commands of God in order to observeᵍ your own traditions! ¹⁰For Moses said, 'Honor your father and your mother'ᵃ [Exod. 20:12; Deut. 5:16], and,	

ʳ(Mark 7:3) The exact requirement of the tradition is not completely clear. The Greek expression is literally *with the fist*. Suggestions of the specific meaning have included washing carefully (or diligently), washing by turning a clenched fist around in the hollow of the other hand, washing up to the elbow (or wrist), washing with a handful of water, and washing by rubbing the hand dry with the fist. From evidence available, the most probable solution is washing with a handful of water.

Matthew 15:1–3a, 7–9,
3b–6, 10–20 (cont'd)

Mark 7:1–23 (cont'd)

and 'Anyone who curses his father or mother must be put to death'[b] [Exod. 21:17; Lev. 20:9]. [5s]But you say that if a man says to his father or mother, 'Whatever help you might otherwise have received from me is a gift devoted to God,' [6]he is not to 'honor his father[c]' with it. Thus you nullify the word of God for the sake of your tradition.

[10]Jesus called the crowd to him and said, "Listen and understand. [11]What goes into a man's mouth does not make him 'unclean,' but what comes out of his mouth, that is what makes him 'unclean.' "

[12]Then the disciples came to him and asked, "Do you know that the Pharisees were offended when they heard this?"

[13]He replied, "Every plant that my heavenly Father has not planted will be pulled up by the roots. [14]Leave them; they are blind guides.[e] If a blind man leads a blind man, both will fall into a pit."

[15]Peter said, "Explain the parable to us."

[16]"Are you still so dull?" Jesus asked them. [17]"Don't you see that whatever enters the mouth goes into the stomach and then out of the body? [18]But the things that come out of the mouth come from the

'Anyone who curses his father or mother must be put to death'[b] [Exod. 21:17; Lev. 20:9]. [11s]But you say that if a man says to his father or mother: 'Whatever help you might otherwise have received from me is Corban' (that is, a gift devoted to God), [12]then you no longer let him do anything for his father or mother. [13]Thus you nullify the word of God by your tradition that you have handed down. And you do many things like that."

[14]Again Jesus called the crowd to him and said, "Listen to me, everyone, and understand this. [15]Nothing outside a man can make him 'unclean' by going into him. Rather, it is what comes out of a man that makes him 'unclean.'[h]"

[17]After he had left the crowd and entered the house, his disciples asked him about this parable. [18]"Are you so dull?" he asked. "Don't you see that nothing that enters a man from the outside can make him 'unclean'? [19]For it doesn't go into his heart but into his stomach, and then out of his body." (In

---

[s](Matt. 15:5; Mark 7:11) Here is a specific tradition favored by the teachers of the law and the Pharisees. By following this custom they in effect nullified God's commandment about honoring their parents. Their tradition with its emphasis on externalities was diametrically opposed to Jesus' emphasis on the inner character (Matt. 15:11; Mark 7:15). He labored to make this point clear, especially to his disciples (Matt. 15:12–20; Mark 7:17–23).

Matthew 15:1–3a, 7–9,
3b–6, 10–20 (cont'd)

Mark 7:1–23 (cont'd)

heart, and these make a man 'unclean.'

saying this, Jesus declared all foods "clean.")
[20]He went on: "What comes out of a man is what makes him 'unclean.' [21]For from within, out of men's hearts, come evil thoughts, sexual immorality, theft, murder, adultery, [22]greed, malice, deceit, lewdness, envy, slander, arrogance and folly. [23]All these evils come from inside and make a man 'unclean.' "

[19]For out of the heart come evil thoughts, murder, adultery, sexual immorality, theft, false testimony, slander. [20]These are what make a man 'unclean'; but eating with unwashed hands does not make him 'unclean.' "

[a]Mt 15:4,10 Exodus 20:12; Deut. 5:16 *father or his mother* [d]9,6,7 Isaiah 29:13 [b]4,10 Exodus 21:17; Lev. 20:9 [c]6 Some manuscripts [e]14 Some manuscripts *guides of the blind* [f]Mk 7:4 Some early manuscripts *pitchers, kettles and dining couches* [g]9 Some manuscripts *set up* [h]15 Some early manuscripts 'unclean.' [i]16If anyone has ears to hear, let him hear.

Sec. 78   Ministry to a believing Greek woman in Tyre and Sidon
—The vicinity of Tyre and Sidon—

Matthew 15:21–28

Mark 7:24–30

[21]Leaving that place, Jesus withdrew to the region of Tyre and Sidon. [22]A Canaanite woman from that vicinity came to him, crying out, "Lord, Son of David, have mercy on me! My daughter is suffering terribly from demon-possession."
[23]Jesus did not answer a word. So his disciples came to him and urged him, "Send her away, for she keeps crying out after us."
[24]He answered, "I was sent [t]only to the lost sheep of Israel."
[25]The woman came and knelt before him. "Lord, help me!" she said.
[26]He replied, "It is not right to take the children's bread and toss it to their dogs."
[27]"Yes, Lord," she said, "but even the dogs eat the crumbs that fall from their masters' table."
[28]Then Jesus answered, "Woman, you have great faith! Your request is granted." And her daughter was healed from that very hour.

[24]Jesus left that place and went to the vicinity of Tyre.[a] He entered a house and did not want anyone to know it; yet he could not keep his presence secret. [25]In fact, as soon as she heard about him, a woman whose little daughter was possessed by an evil[b] spirit came and fell at his feet. [26]The woman was a Greek, born in Syrian Phoenicia. She begged Jesus to drive the demon out of her daughter.

[27]"First let the children eat all they want," he told her, "for it is not right to take the children's bread and toss it to their dogs."
[28]"Yes, Lord," she replied, "but even the dogs under the table eat the children's crumbs."
[29]Then he told her, "For such a reply, you may go; the demon has left your daughter."
[30]She went home and found her child lying on the bed, and the demon gone.

[a]Mk 7:24 Many early manuscripts *Tyre and Sidon* [b]25 Greek *unclean*

[t](Matt. 15:24) The continuing exclusive character of Jesus' mission (cf. Matt. 10:5–6, Sec. 70b) is nowhere more clearly seen than here. Retreating from his Pharisaic enemies into Gentile territory (Matt. 15:21; Mark 7:24), he at first ignored this woman's request completely (Matt. 15:23). Because she was not of Israel, she had no basis for asking a favor. After she acknowledged that Gentiles receive blessing only indirectly when God blesses Israel, however, Jesus commended her perception and faith and granted her request (Matt. 15:27–28; Mark 7:29–30).

Sec. 79a   Healings in Decapolis
—From Tyre to the region of the Decapolis near the Sea of Galilee—

Matthew 15:29–31	Mark 7:31–37
[29]Jesus left there and went along the Sea of Galilee. Then he went up on a mountainside and sat down.	[31]Then Jesus left the vicinity of Tyre and [u]went through Sidon, down to the Sea of Galilee and into the region of the Decapolis.[a] [32]There some people brought to him a man who was deaf and could hardly talk, and they begged him to place his hand on the man. [33]After he took him aside, away from the crowd, Jesus put his fingers into the man's ears. Then he spit and touched the man's tongue. [34]He looked up to heaven and with a deep sigh said to him, "Ephphatha!" (which means, "Be opened!"). [35]At this, the man's ears were opened, his tongue was loosened and he began to speak plainly.
[30]Great crowds came to him, bringing the lame, the blind, the crippled, the mute and many others, and laid them at his feet; and he healed them. [31]The people were amazed when they saw the mute speaking, the crippled made well, the lame walking and the blind seeing. And they praised the God of Israel.	[36]Jesus [v]commanded them not to tell anyone. But the more he did so, the more they kept talking about it. [37]People were overwhelmed with amazement. "He has done everything well," they said. "He even makes the deaf hear and the mute speak."

[a]Mk 7:31 That is, the Ten Cities

Sec. 79b   Feeding the four thousand in Decapolis (cf. Secs. 72c, 81a—feeding the crowds)
—The region of Decapolis—

Matthew 15:32–38	Mark 8:1–9a
	[1]During those days another large crowd gathered. Since they had nothing to eat, Jesus called his disciples to him and said, [2]"I have compassion for these people; they have already been with me three days and have nothing to eat. [3]If I send them home hungry, they will collapse on the way, because some of them have come a long distance."
[32]Jesus called his disciples to him and said, "I have compassion for these people; they have already been with me three days and have nothing to eat. I do not want to send them away hungry, or they may collapse on the way."	
[33]His disciples answered, "[w]Where could we get enough bread in this remote place to feed such a crowd?"	[4]His disciples answered, "But [w]where in this remote place can anyone get enough bread to feed them?"

---

[u](Mark 7:31) The long, circuitous route followed by Jesus as he traveled from the Mediterranean coast to the eastern shore of the Sea of Galilee was probably designed to guard his privacy with the disciples. This took him back to the area where he had healed two Gerasene demoniacs (Sec. 66).

[v](Mark 7:36) The difference between this instruction to keep silent and the earlier one to spread the news widely (Mark 5:19, Sec. 66) is great. Earlier, Jesus was still reaching out to the multitudes, but now more publicity would have impeded his special training of the Twelve. When performing the healing, he even made special effort to avoid the multitude's attention (Mark 7:33).

[w](Matt. 15:33; Mark 8:4) That the disciples would forget the feeding of the five thousand just a short time before (Sec. 72c) appears inexplicable. Perhaps they misinterpreted Jesus' strong rebuke of the previous crowds' selfishness (John 6:26–27, Sec. 76a) and thought he would not perform such a miracle again. To correct the misimpression, Jesus again miraculously fed a multitude. Patiently he dealt with the Twelve to prove his identity to them and to show that nothing was inherently wrong with such a miracle.

Matthew 15:32–38 (cont'd)

[34]"How many loaves do you have?" Jesus asked.

"Seven," they replied, "and a few small fish."

[35]He told the crowd to sit down on the ground. [36]Then he took the seven loaves and the fish, and when he had given thanks, he broke them and gave them to the disciples, and they in turn to the people.

[37]They all ate and were satisfied. Afterward the disciples picked up seven basketfuls of broken pieces that were left over. [38]The number of those who ate was four thousand, besides women and children.

Mark 8:1–9a (cont'd)

[5]"How many loaves do you have?" Jesus asked.

"Seven," they replied.

[6]He told the crowd to sit down on the ground. When he had taken the seven loaves and given thanks, he broke them and gave them to his disciples to set before the people, and they did so. [7]They had a few small fish as well; he gave thanks for them also and told the disciples to distribute them. [8]The people ate and were satisfied. Afterward the disciples picked up seven basketfuls of broken pieces that were left over. [9]About four thousand men were present.

Sec. 80 Return to Galilee and encounter with the Pharisees and Sadducees (cf. Secs. 62, 106—request for a sign)
—From the Decapolis to Magadan (Dalmanutha)—

Matthew 15:39–16:4

[39]After Jesus had sent the crowd away, he got into the boat and went to the vicinity of [x]Magadan.

[1]The Pharisees and Sadducees came to Jesus and tested him by asking him to show them a [y]sign from heaven.

[2]He replied,[a] "When evening comes, you say, 'It will be fair weather, for the sky is red,' [3]and in the morning, 'Today it will be stormy, for the sky is red and overcast.' You know how to interpret the appearance of the sky, but you cannot interpret the signs of the times. [4]A wicked and adulterous generation looks for a miraculous sign, but none will be given it except the sign of Jonah." Jesus then left them and went away.

Mark 8:9b–12

And having sent them away, [10]he got into the boat with his disciples and went to the region of [x]Dalmanutha.

[11]The Pharisees came and began to question Jesus. To test him, they asked him for a sign from heaven.

[12]He sighed deeply and said, "Why does this generation ask for a miraculous sign? I tell you the truth, no sign will be given to it."

[a]Mt 15:2 Some early manuscripts do not have the rest of verse 2 and all of verse 3.

[x](Matt. 15:39; Mark 8:10) Magadan and Dalmanutha are either two names for the same area or two areas located in the vicinity of each other.

[y](Matt. 16:1) No sooner had Jesus set foot in Galilee again than his enemies were upon him. They asked for a sign, perhaps along the line of what God had done for Moses (Exod. 16:15), Joshua (Josh. 10:13), Samuel (1 Sam. 12:18), Elijah (1 Kings 18:38), and Isaiah (2 Kings 20:11; Isa. 38:8). Jesus stood firm on his previous response, however (Matt. 16:4; Mark 8:12; cf. Matt. 12:39, Sec. 62). For the first time the Sadducees joined the Pharisees in attacking him. Both parties were willing to forget their differences because of their common animosity toward him.

Sec. 81a   Warning about the error of the Pharisees, Sadducees, and Herodians
(cf. Secs. 72c, 79b—feeding the crowds)
(cf. Sec. 108a—the leaven of hypocrisy)
—Crossing to the east side of the Sea of Galilee—

Matthew 16:5–12

⁵When they went across the lake, the disciples forgot to take bread. ⁶"Be careful," Jesus said to them. "Be on your guard against the ᶻyeast of the Pharisees and Sadducees."

⁷They discussed this among themselves and said, "It is because we didn't bring any bread."

⁸Aware of their discussion, Jesus asked, "You of little faith, why are you talking among yourselves about having no bread? ⁹Do you still not understand? Don't you remember the five loaves for the five thousand, and how many basketfuls you gathered? ¹⁰Or the seven loaves for the four thousand, and how many basketfuls you gathered? ¹¹How is it you don't understand that I was not talking to you about bread? But be on your guard against the yeast of the Pharisees and Sadducees." ¹²Then they understood that he was not telling them to guard against the yeast used in bread, but against the teaching of the Pharisees and Sadducees.

Mark 8:13–21

¹³Then he left them, got back into the boat and crossed to the other side.

¹⁴The disciples had forgotten to bring bread, except for one loaf they had with them in the boat. ¹⁵"Be careful," Jesus warned them. "Watch out for the ᶻyeast of the Pharisees and that of Herod."

¹⁶They discussed this with one another and said, "It is because we have no bread."

¹⁷Aware of their discussion, Jesus asked them: "Why are you talking about having no bread? Do you still not see or understand? Are your hearts hardened? ¹⁸Do you have eyes but fail to see, and ears but fail to hear? [Ezek. 12:2]. And don't you remember? ¹⁹When I broke the five loaves for the five thousand, how many basketfuls of pieces did you pick up?"

"Twelve," they replied.

²⁰"And when I broke the seven loaves for the four thousand, how many basketfuls of pieces did you pick up?"

They answered, "Seven."

²¹He said to them, "Do you still not understand?"

Sec. 81b   Healing a blind man at Bethsaida
—Bethsaida, near Julias—

Mark 8:22–26

²²They came to Bethsaida, and some people brought a blind man and begged Jesus to touch him. ²³He took the blind man by the hand and led him outside the village. When he had spit on the man's eyes and put his hands on him, Jesus asked, "Do you see anything?"

²⁴He looked up and said, "I see people; they look like trees walking around."

²⁵Once more Jesus put his hands on the man's eyes. Then his eyes were opened,

---

ᶻ(Matt. 16:6; Mark 8:15) In the Law, yeast was regarded as symbolic of impurity (Exod. 34:25; Lev. 2:11). Jesus expected his disciples to understand this connotation (Matt. 16:11; Mark 8:17, 21). His recent miracles with the five thousand and the four thousand showed he need not be concerned over a lack of bread (cf. Secs. 72c, 79b). His recent explanation about the true source of defilement should have been fresh in the disciples' minds (cf. Sec. 77). Just a moment of reflection would have shown them that he was talking about spiritual defilement. The Pharisees, the Sadducees, and the Herodians all had distorted ideas about the kingdom. The Pharisees would have molded it to conform to the tradition of the elders. By rationalizations the Sadducees explained away Old Testament predictions about it. The Herodians saw some member of Herod's family as the promised king. By ridding themselves of false concepts, the Twelve were readied for the true picture of Messiah that was about to surface (cf. Sec. 82).

Mark 18:22–26 (cont'd)

his sight [a]was restored, and he saw everything clearly. [26]Jesus sent him home, saying, "Don't go into the village.[a]"

[a]Mk 18:26 Some manuscripts *Don't go and tell anyone in the village*

LESSON OF MESSIAHSHIP LEARNED AND CONFIRMED

Sec. 82   Peter's identification of Jesus as the Christ and first prophecy of the church
(cf. Sec. 76b—confessions of Jesus' identity)
—*The region of Caesarea Philippi*—

Matthew 16:13–20	Mark 8:27–30	Luke 9:18–21
[13]When Jesus came to the region of [b]Caesarea Philippi, he asked his disciples, "Who do people say the Son of Man is?" [14]They replied, "Some say John the Baptist; others say Elijah; and still others, Jeremiah or one of the prophets." [15]"But what about you?" he asked. "[c]Who do you say I am?" [16]Simon Peter answered, "[d]You are the Christ,[a] the Son of the living God." [17]Jesus replied, "Blessed are you, Simon son of Jonah, for this was not revealed to you by man, but by my Father in heaven. [18]And I tell you	[27]Jesus and his disciples went on to the villages around [c]Caesarea Philippi. On the way he asked them, "Who do people say I am?" [28]They replied, "Some say John the Baptist; others say Elijah; and still others, one of the prophets." [29]"But what about you?" he asked. "[c]Who do you say I am?" Peter answered, "You are the Christ.[f]"	[18]Once when Jesus was praying in private and his disciples were with him, he asked them, "Who do the crowds say I am?" [19]They replied, "Some say John the Baptist; others say Elijah; and still others, that one of the prophets of long ago has come back to life." [20]"But what about you?" he asked. "[c]Who do you say I am?" Peter answered, "The Christ[g] of God."

[a](Mark 8:25) This is one of two miracles that are recorded by Mark alone (cf. Sec. 79a). From each, one might infer that Christ had difficulty in effecting the cure. In each case Jesus made a point of performing the deed privately (Mark 8:23) and avoiding publicity after the healing (Mark 8:26). This case in Bethsaida, occurring as it did in two stages, is the only instance of a gradual cure by Jesus (Mark 8:24–25). Perhaps the Twelve needed to learn that not every miracle would be instantaneous. In some cases the victory of divine power over sin and sickness would be gradual.

[b](Matt. 16:13; Mark 8:27) Herod Philip was tetrarch in this territory. Compared with his half-brothers Archelaus and Antipas, Philip was a just ruler. He had no reason to be suspicious of Jesus as Antipas was (cf. Sec. 72b, note a). Jesus probably remained with his disciples in this region where the inhabitants were predominantly Gentile and where little occasion would arise for Jewish opposition or large crowds.

[c](Matt. 16:15; Mark 8:29; Luke 9:20) Jesus saw the time was right to solicit a specific identification of himself. This is the objective toward which he had been moving since leaving Galilee several months earlier (Sec. 72b). Practically every activity was designed to lead his disciples to a conviction about his person. It now remained for them to disclose their conclusion in answer to his question.

[d](Matt. 16:16) Matthew retains the fullest record of Peter's reply. The Messiahship and deity of Jesus were not completely new concepts to the Twelve (Matt. 14:33, Sec. 74; John 1:41, 49, Sec. 28), but now Peter and the rest, on the basis of what they had seen and heard, could with strong conviction verify his identity as such. The truth thus elicited from Peter was foundational to the further instruction Jesus was to give his immediate followers.

Matthew 16:13–20 (cont'd)	Mark 8:27–30 (cont'd)	Luke 9:18–21 (cont'd)
that you are Peter,[b] and on this rock I will build my [e]church, and the gates of Hades[c] will not overcome it.[d] [19]I will give you the keys of the kingdom of heaven; whatever you bind on earth will be[e] bound in heaven, and whatever you loose on earth will be[e] loosed in heaven." [20]Then he warned his disciples [f]not to tell anyone that he was the Christ.	[30]Jesus warned them [f]not to tell anyone about him.	[21]Jesus strictly warned them [f]not to tell this to anyone.

[a]Mt 16:16 Or *Messiah*; also in verse 20 [b]18 *Peter means rock.* [c]18 Or *hell* [d]18 Or *not prove stronger than it* [e]19 Or *have been* [f]Mk 8:29 Or *Messiah.* "The Christ" (Greek) and "the Messiah" (Hebrew) both mean "the Anointed One." [g]Lk 9:20 Or *Messiah*

Sec. 83 First direct prediction of the rejection, crucifixion, and resurrection
(cf. Secs. 70b, 115—cost of discipleship)
(cf. Secs. 85, 86, 88, 125a—prophecies of death and resurrection)
(cf. Sec. 130a—loving and hating life)
—*Near Caesarea Philippi*—

Matthew 16:21–26	Mark 8:31–37	Luke 9:22–25
[21]From that time on Jesus [g]began to explain to his disciples that he must go to Jerusalem and suffer many things at the hands of the elders, chief priests and teachers of the law, and that he must be killed and on the third day be raised to life. [22]Peter took him aside and began to rebuke him. "Never, Lord!" he said. "This shall never happen to you!"	[31]He then [g]began to teach them that the Son of Man must suffer many things and be rejected by the elders, chief priests and teachers of the law, and that he must be killed and after three days rise again. [32]He spoke plainly about this, and Peter took him aside and began to rebuke him. [33]But when Jesus turned and looked at his disciples, he rebuked Pe-	[22]And he said, "[g]The Son of Man must suffer many things and be rejected by the elders, chief priests and teachers of the law, and he must be killed and on the third day be raised to life."

[e](Matt. 16:18) This was the first disclosure of a new work that Jesus was to undertake. It was made to a group that would constitute the nucleus of that body which he called the church. This inner circle of disciples at this point began to hear of a subject which they were slow to understand, but which was eventually to become the dominant interest of their lives.

[f](Matt. 16:20; Mark 8:30; Luke 9:21) Jesus' Messiahship and deity, though foundational for the church, were not to be broadcast widely. Israel's leadership had by now forfeited its opportunity for a positive response by refusal to acknowledge his credentials (cf. Sec. 61). The populace had exhibited a similar unwillingness to submit to moral requirements in connection with an earthly reign of Messiah (cf. Sec. 73). It was inappropriate to approach them further on these issues until the time for an open declaration of his identity before the Jewish authorities in Jerusalem (cf. Matt. 26:63–64, Sec. 155).

[g](Matt. 16:21; Mark 8:31; Luke 9:22) Coming immediately after Peter's confession, this prophecy was apparently triggered by the confession. If it had come any earlier, the Twelve would have been unable to receive it without being shaken in their conviction about him. This is Jesus' first open prediction of the events that were now about one year away, though earlier he had referred to them in veiled terminology (cf. John 2:19, Sec. 31). Peter was unwilling to accept such a revelation because he was now so certain about Jesus' Messiahship (Matt. 16:22; Mark 8:32). His misguided zeal drew the same rebuke the Lord used with Satan after the temptation (Matt. 4:10, Sec. 25).

Matthew 16:21–26 (cont'd)	Mark 8:31–37 (cont'd)	Luke 9:22–25 (cont'd)
²³Jesus turned and said to Peter, "Get behind me, Satan! You are a stumbling block to me; you do not have in mind the things of God, but the things of men." ²⁴Then Jesus said to his disciples, "ʰIf anyone would come after me, he must deny himself and take up his cross and follow me. ²⁵For whoever wants to save his lifeᵃ will lose it, but whoever loses his life for me will find it. ²⁶What good will it be for a man if he gains the whole world, yet forfeits his soul? Or what can a man give in exchange for his soul?	ter. "Get behind me, Satan!" he said. "You do not have in mind the things of God, but the things of men." ³⁴Then he called the crowd to him along with his disciples and said: "ʰIf anyone would come after me, he must deny himself and take up his cross and follow me. ³⁵For whoever wants to save his lifeᵇ will lose it, but whoever loses his life for me and for the gospel will save it. ³⁶What good is it for a man to gain the whole world, yet forfeit his soul? ³⁷Or what can a man give in exchange for his soul?	²³Then he said to them all: "ʰIf anyone would come after me, he must deny himself and take up his cross daily and follow me. ²⁴For whoever wants to save his life will lose it, but whoever loses his life for me will save it. ²⁵What good is it for a man to gain the whole world, and yet lose or forfeit his very self?

ᵃMt 16:25 The Greek word means either *life* or *soul*; also in verse 26.   ᵇMk 8:35 The Greek word means either *life* or *soul*; also in verse 36.

Sec. 84   Coming of the Son of Man and judgment
—Near Caesarea Philippi—

Matthew 16:27–28	Mark 8:38–9:1	Luke 9:26–27
²⁷For the Son of Man is going to come in his Father's glory with his angels, and then he will reward each person according to what he has done [Psalm 62:12; Prov. 24:12]. ²⁸I tell you the truth, some who are standing here will not taste death before they see the Son of Man coming in his ⁱkingdom."	³⁸If anyone is ashamed of me and my words in this adulterous and sinful generation, the Son of Man will be ashamed of him when he comes in his Father's glory with the holy angels." ¹And he said to them, "I tell you the truth, some who are standing here will not taste death before they see the ⁱkingdom of God come with power."	²⁶If anyone is ashamed of me and my words, the Son of Man will be ashamed of him when he comes in his glory and in the glory of the Father and of the holy angels. ²⁷I tell you the truth, some who are standing here will not taste death before they see the ⁱkingdom of God."

ʰ(Matt. 16:24; Mark 8:34; Luke 9:23) After the multitude joined the disciples, Jesus extended the scope of the predicted suffering to anyone who desired to be his follower. The necessity of this was axiomatic in the teachings of Jesus (cf. Matt. 16:25; Mark 8:35; Luke 9:24 with Matt. 10:39, Sec. 70b; Luke 17:33, Sec. 120b; John 12:25, Sec. 130a), and formed a basis for Peter's first epistle many years later (1 Pet. 2:20–21).

ⁱ(Matt. 16:28; Mark 9:1; Luke 9:27) Reference to the judgment of faithfulness at the time of the Son of Man's coming occasioned mention of the kingdom. This coming of the Son and his kingdom has been variously identified with Christ's resurrection and ascension, the day of Pentecost, the spread of Christianity, Christ's second advent, or the destruction of Jerusalem in A.D. 70; yet the only interpretation that satisfies the facts of history and the conditions of the context is to understand a reference to the transfiguration scene that immediately followed (Sec. 85). Here a foretaste of the Son's coming with his kingdom was granted to three of the listeners during their normal lifetime.

Sec. 85   Transfiguration of Jesus
(cf. Sec. 24—identification of the Son by the Father)
(cf. Secs. 83, 86, 88, 125a—prophecies of death and resurrection)
—ʲHigh mountain, perhaps Mount Hermon—

2ⁿᵈ time — personally God authentic19 Jesus

Matthew 17:1–8	Mark 9:2–8	Luke 9:28–36a
¹After ᵏsix days Jesus took with him Peter, James and John the brother of James, and led them up a high mountain by themselves. ²There he was transfigured before them. His face shone like the sun, and his clothes became as white as the light. ³Just then there appeared before them Moses and Elijah, talking with Jesus.	²After ᵏsix days Jesus took Peter, James and John with him and led them up a high mountain, where they were all alone. There he was transfigured before them. ³His clothes became dazzling white, whiter than anyone in the world could bleach them. ⁴And there appeared before them Elijah and Moses, who were talking with Jesus.	²⁸ᵏAbout eight days after Jesus said this, he took Peter, John and James with him and went up onto a mountain to pray. ²⁹As he was praying, the appearance of his face changed, and his clothes became as bright as a flash of lightning. ³⁰Two men, Moses and Elijah, ³¹appeared in glorious splendor, talking with Jesus. They spoke about his ˡdeparture, which he was about to bring to fulfillment at Jerusalem. ³²Peter and his companions were very sleepy, but when they became fully awake, they saw his glory and the two men standing with him. ³³As the men were leaving Jesus, Peter said
⁴Peter said to Jesus, "Lord, it is good for us to be here. If you wish, I will put up three shelters—one for you, one for Moses and one for Elijah." ⁵While he was still speaking, a bright cloud enveloped them, and a voice from the cloud said, "This is my Son, whom I love; with him I am well pleased. Listen to him!" ⁶When the disciples	⁵Peter said to Jesus, "Rabbi, it is good for us to be here. Let us put up three shelters—one for you, one for Moses and one for Elijah." ⁶(He did not know what to say, they were so frightened.) ⁷Then a cloud appeared and enveloped them, and a voice came from the cloud: "This is my Son, whom I love. Listen to him!"	to him, "Master, it is good for us to be here. Let us put up three shelters—one for you, one for Moses and one for Elijah." (He did not know what he was saying.) ³⁴While he was speaking, a cloud appeared and enveloped them, and they were afraid as they entered the cloud. ³⁵A voice came from the cloud, saying, "This is my Son,

---

ʲThe exact location of the mount of transfiguration is unknown. Traditionally it has been identified with Mount Tabor, which rises from the Plain of Esdraelon. But that is too far removed from Caesarea Philippi and Capernaum to be a likely site. Furthermore, it is unlikely that Jesus and his disciples would have gone up a mountain where heathen worship had been carried on. Others have suggested one of several hills near Capernaum. But none of these seems to be high enough to qualify as the "high mountain" spoken of by Matthew and Mark. Mount Hermon does answer to this description and has the advantage of being near Caesarea Philippi, where Jesus had recently been.

ᵏ(Matt. 17:1; Mark 9:2; Luke 9:28) Luke's "about eight days" is an approximate figure for the six days of Matthew and Mark. Within a one-week period came Peter's confession, the first prophecy of the church, the first prophecy of crucifixion and resurrection, and now this confirmatory revelation of the King and his kingdom. The disciples probably wondered how the church and Messiah's predicted incarceration and death would affect the unfulfilled prophecies of his coming kingdom. The transfiguration reassured them that these prophecies would still receive a literal fulfillment. For Peter, at least, this was true (2 Pet. 1:16–19).

ˡ(Luke 9:31) Only Luke discloses the subject of conversation among Moses and Elijah and Jesus. "Departure" probably refers to Jesus' death. In this detail, Luke's interest in Jesus' humanity surfaces once again.

Matthew 17:1–8 (cont'd)	Mark 9:2–8 (cont'd)	Luke 9:28–36a (cont'd)
heard this, they fell face-down to the ground, terrified. [7]But Jesus came and touched them. "Get up," he said. "Don't be afraid." [8]When they looked up, they saw no one except Jesus.	[8]Suddenly, when they looked around, they no longer saw anyone with them except Jesus.	whom I have chosen; listen to him." [36]When the voice had spoken, they found that Jesus was alone.

Sec. 86   Discussion of resurrection, Elijah, and John the Baptist (cf. Secs. 83, 85, 88, 125a—prophecies of death and resurrection)
—*Coming down the mountain*—

Matthew 17:9–13	Mark 9:9–13	Luke 9:36b
[9]As they were coming down the mountain, Jesus instructed them, "Don't tell anyone what you have seen, [m]until the Son of Man has been raised from the dead."	[9]As they were coming down the mountain, Jesus gave them orders not to tell anyone what they had seen [m]until the Son of Man had risen from the dead. [10]They kept the matter to themselves, discussing what "rising from the dead" meant.	The disciples kept this to themselves, and told no one at that time what they had seen.
[10]The disciples asked him, "Why then do the teachers of the law say that Elijah must come first?" [11]Jesus replied, "To be sure, Elijah comes and will restore all things. [12]But I tell you, Elijah has already come, and they did not recognize him, but have done to him everything they wished. In the same way the Son of Man is going to suffer at their hands." [13]Then the disciples understood that he was talking to them about [n]John the Baptist.	[11]And they asked him, "Why do the teachers of the law say that Elijah must come first?" [12]Jesus replied, "To be sure, Elijah does come first, and restores all things. Why then is it written that the Son of Man must suffer much and be rejected? [13]But I tell you, Elijah has come, and they have done to him everything they wished, just as it is written about him."	

[m](Matt. 17:9; Mark 9:9) The time limit placed on the silence is probably a key to seeing why the silence was enjoined. As Mark 9:10 shows, the disciples did not yet understand what it meant for the Son of Man to rise from the dead and would not until they witnessed it. Only after the Son's resurrection could they adequately comprehend the real significance of the transfiguration experience (cf. 2 Pet. 1:16–19).

[n](Matt. 17:13) John the Baptist is here identified with Elijah, but earlier John denied such an identification (John 1:21, see note e, Sec. 26). In what sense he fulfilled the prophecy about Elijah (Mal. 4:5–6) is hard to discern. The fulfillment seemed to be contingent on Israel's reception of him and Messiah (Matt. 11:14–15, Sec. 57). Their rejection of the Baptist and Messiah (Matt. 17:12; Mark 9:13) apparently nullified the potential fulfillment.

LESSONS OF RESPONSIBILITY TO OTHERS

Sec. 87   Healing of demoniac boy and unbelief rebuked
—Near the mount of transfiguration—

Matthew 17:14–20   Mark 9:14–29   Luke 9:37–43a

[14] When they came to the other disciples, they saw a large crowd around them and the teachers of the law arguing with them. [15] As soon as all the people saw Jesus, they were overwhelmed with wonder and ran to greet him.

[14] When they came to the crowd, a man approached Jesus and knelt before him. [15] "Lord, have mercy on my son," he said. "He has seizures and is suffering greatly. He often falls into the fire or into the water. [16] I brought him to your disciples, but they could not heal him."

[16] "What are you arguing with them about?" he asked.

[17] A man in the crowd answered, "Teacher, I brought you my son, who is possessed by a spirit that has robbed him of speech. [18] Whenever it seizes him, it throws him to the ground. He foams at the mouth, gnashes his teeth and becomes rigid. I asked your disciples to drive out the spirit, but they could not."

[37] The next day, when they came down from the mountain, a large crowd met him. [38] A man in the crowd called out, "Teacher, I beg you to look at my son, for he is my only child. [39] A spirit seizes him and he suddenly screams; it throws him into convulsions so that he foams at the mouth. It scarcely ever leaves him and is destroying him. [40] I begged your disciples to drive it out, but they could not."

[17] "O unbelieving and perverse generation," Jesus replied, "how long shall I stay with you? How long shall I put up with you? Bring the boy here to me."

[19] "O unbelieving generation," Jesus replied, "how long shall I stay with you? How long shall I put up with you? Bring the boy to me."

[20] So they brought him. When the spirit saw Jesus, it immediately threw the boy into a convulsion. He fell to the ground and rolled around, foaming at the mouth.

[21] Jesus asked the boy's father, "How long has he been like this?"

"From childhood," he answered. [22] "It has often thrown him into fire or

[41] "O unbelieving and perverse generation," Jesus replied, "how long shall I stay with you and put up with you? Bring your son here."

[42] Even while the boy was coming, the demon threw him to the ground in a convulsion. But Jesus rebuked the evil[b] spirit, healed the boy and gave him back to his father. [43] And they were all amazed at the greatness of God.

---

[o] (Matt. 17:17; Mark 9:19; Luke 9:41) This is the only known occasion when Jesus' sensitivity showed itself in the form of momentary impatience with his environment. Coming as a response to the father, the expression probably indicates a connection between the man and the teachers of the law (Mark 9:14). These may have used the man and his son to gather evidence against the nine disciples and, therefore, also against Jesus. The antagonism of the Lord's enemies surfaced once again and was met with this sharp rebuke. Such strong language could hardly be a reprimand of the nine for their inability to perform the miracle, because they did have faith, though it was quite small (cf. Matt. 17:20).

Matthew 17:14–20 (cont'd)	Mark 9:14–29 (cont'd)
	water to kill him. But if you can do anything, take pity on us and help us." [23]"'If you can'?" said Jesus. "Everything is possible for him who believes." [24]Immediately the boy's father exclaimed, "I do believe; help me overcome my unbelief!" [25]When Jesus saw that a
[18]Jesus rebuked the demon, and it came out of the boy, and he was healed from that moment.	crowd was running to the scene, he rebuked the evil[b] spirit. "You deaf and mute spirit," he said, "I command you, come out of him and never enter him again." [26]The spirit shrieked, convulsed him violently and came out. The boy looked so much like a corpse that many said, "He's dead." [27]But Jesus took him by the hand and lifted him to his feet, and he stood up.
[19]Then the disciples came to Jesus in private and asked, "Why couldn't we drive it out?" [20]He replied, "Because you have so little faith. I tell you the truth, if you have faith as small as a mustard seed, you can say to this mountain, 'Move from here to there' and it will move. Nothing will be impossible for you.[a]"	[28]After Jesus had gone indoors, his disciples asked him privately, "Why couldn't we drive it out?" [29]He replied, "This kind can come out only by prayer.[c]"

[a]Mt 17:20 Some manuscripts *you.* [21]*But this kind does not go out except by prayer and fasting.* [b]Mk 9:25; Lk 9:42 Greek *unclean* [c]Mk 9:29 Some manuscripts *prayer and fasting*

Sec. 88   Second prediction of Jesus' death and resurrection (cf. Secs. 83, 85, 86, 125a—prophecies of death and resurrection)
—*Itineration in Galilee*—

Matthew 17:22–23	Mark 9:30–32	Luke 9:43b–45
	[30]They left that place and passed [p]through Gali-	

[p](Mark 9:30) From the area of Caesarea Philippi and northeast Palestine, Jesus at this point began the journey that would take him through Galilee and Perea to Judea and Jerusalem, where his crucifixion and resurrection would take place about six months later.

Matthew 17:22–23 (cont'd)	Mark 9:30–32 (cont'd)	Luke 9:43b–45 (cont'd)
[22]When they came together in Galilee, he said to them, "The Son of Man is going to be betrayed into the hands of men. [23]They will kill him, and on the third day he will be raised to life." And the disciples were filled with grief.	lee. Jesus did not want anyone to know where they were, [31]because he was teaching his disciples. He said to them, "The Son of Man is going to be betrayed into the hands of men. They will kill him, and after three days he will rise." [32]But they did not understand what he meant and were afraid to ask him about it.	While everyone was marveling at all that Jesus did, he said to his disciples, [44]"Listen carefully to what I am about to tell you: The Son of Man is going to be betrayed into the hands of men." [45]But they did not understand what this meant. It was hidden from them, so that they did not grasp it, and they were afraid to ask him about it.

Sec. 89   Payment of the temple tax
—*Capernaum*—

Matthew 17:24–27

[24]After Jesus and his disciples arrived in Capernaum, the collectors of the two-drachma tax came to Peter and asked, "Doesn't your teacher pay the temple tax[a]?"
[25]"Yes, he does," he replied.

When Peter came into the house, Jesus was the first to speak. "What do you think, Simon?" he asked. "From whom do the kings of the earth collect [q]duty and taxes —from their own sons or from others?"

[26]"From others," Peter answered.

"Then the sons are exempt," Jesus said to him. [27]"But so that we may not offend them, go to the lake and throw out your line. Take the first fish you catch; open its mouth and you will find a four-drachma coin. Take it and give it to them for my tax and yours."

[a]Mt 17:24 Greek *the two drachmas*

Sec. 90   Rivalry over greatness in the kingdom
(cf. Sec. 123—example of little children)
(cf. Sec. 145—to receive the Son is to receive the Father)
—*Capernaum*—

Matthew 18:1–5	Mark 9:33–37	Luke 9:46–48
[1]At that time the disciples came to Jesus and asked, "[r]Who is the greatest in the kingdom of heaven?"	[33]They came to Capernaum. When he was in the house, he asked them, "What were you arguing about on the road?" [34]But	[46]An argument started among the disciples as to [r]which of them would be the greatest.

---

[q](Matt. 17:25) Matthew, himself a former tax collector, demonstrates special interest in this episode, though his former occupation involved collecting taxes for the Roman government, not for the temple. The tax here sought was to provide sacrificial victims for temple worship. The regular time for paying this tax was the spring, but it was now early autumn. The Lord and his disciples had been out of the area at the normal time, so the collectors made a special point of approaching them, either to make up the deficit in their quota or to seek yet another avenue for building a case against Jesus.

[r](Matt. 18:1; Mark 9:34; Luke 9:46) In a culture where precedence and rank were the norm, the disciples quite naturally fell into the same mold. The recent choice of those to be with Jesus on the mount of transfiguration (Sec. 85) and the prominence of Peter among them (Secs. 82, 89) gave special occasion for such a discussion at this time. Greatness "in the kingdom of heaven" probably came up also because, with Jerusalem as their destination, a "kingdom fever" had begun to develop (cf. Luke 19:11, Sec. 127b).

Matthew 18:1–5 (cont'd)	Mark 9:33–37 (cont'd)	Luke 9:46–48 (cont'd)
	they kept quiet because on the way they had argued about 'who was the greatest. ³⁵Sitting down, Jesus called the Twelve and said, "If anyone wants to be first, he must be the very last, and the servant of all."	
²He called a little child and had him stand among them. ³And he said: "I tell you the truth, unless you change and become like little children, you will never enter the kingdom of heaven. ⁴Therefore, whoever humbles himself like this child is the greatest in the kingdom of heaven. ⁵"And whoever welcomes a little child like this in my name welcomes me.	³⁶He took a little child and had him stand among them. Taking him in his arms, he said to them,	⁴⁷Jesus, knowing their thoughts, took a little child and had him stand beside him.
	³⁷"Whoever welcomes one of these little children in my name welcomes me; and whoever welcomes me does not welcome me but the one who sent me."	⁴⁸Then he said to them, "Whoever welcomes this little child in my name welcomes me; and whoever welcomes me welcomes the one who sent me. For he who is least among you all—he is the greatest."

Sec. 91   Warning against causing believers to sin
      (cf. Secs. 54c, 115—salt of the earth)
      (cf. Sec. 54e—loss of hand or eye)
      (cf. Secs. 61, 106—casting out demons, being for and against)
      (cf. Sec. 70b—a cup of water)
      (cf. Sec. 116—the one lost sheep)
      (cf. Sec. 117c—warning against causing to sin)
    —Capernaum—

Matthew 18:6–14	Mark 9:38–50	Luke 9:49–50
	³⁸"Teacher," said John, "we saw a man driving out demons in your name and ˢwe told him to stop, because he was not one of us." ³⁹"Do not stop him," Jesus said. "No one who does a miracle in my name can in the next moment say anything bad	⁴⁹"Master," said John, "we saw a man driving out demons in your name and ˢwe tried to stop him, because he is not one of us." ⁵⁰"Do not stop him," Jesus said, "for whoever is not against you is for you."

In response, Jesus indicated that humility was not only the condition of greatness (Matt. 18:4), but also a condition for even entering the kingdom (Matt. 18:3).
    ˢ(Mark 9:38; Luke 9:49) Just as Peter had misunderstood God's program earlier (Sec. 83), so John did on this occasion. Later the third honored disciple, James, would do the same (Sec. 125b). Each misunderstanding followed shortly after a prediction of Jesus' passion and resurrection.

Matthew 18:6–14 (cont'd)   Mark 9:38–50 (cont'd)

about me, [40t]for whoever is not against us is for us. [41]I tell you the truth, anyone who gives you a cup of water in my name because you belong to Christ will certainly not lose his reward.

[6]But if anyone causes one of these little ones who believe in me to sin, it would be better for him to have a large millstone hung around his neck and to be drowned in the depths of the sea.

[42]"And if anyone causes one of these little ones who believe in me to sin, it would be better for him to be thrown into the sea with a large millstone tied around his neck.

[7]"Woe to the world because of the things that cause people to sin! Such things must come, but woe to the man through whom they come! [8]If your [u]hand or your [u]foot causes you to sin cut it off and throw it away. It is better for you to enter life maimed or crippled than to have two hands or two feet and be thrown into eternal fire. [9]And if your [u]eye causes you to sin, gouge it out and throw it away. It is better for you to enter life with one eye than to have two eyes and be thrown into the fire of hell.

[43]If your [u]hand causes you to sin, cut it off. It is better for you to enter life maimed than with two hands to go into hell, where the fire never goes out.[b] [45]And if your [u]foot causes you to sin, cut it off. It is better for you to enter life crippled than to have two feet and be thrown into hell.[c] [47]And if your [u]eye causes you to sin, pluck it out. It is better for you to enter the kingdom of God with one eye than to have two eyes and be thrown into hell, [48]where

[10]"See that you do not look down on one of these little ones. For I tell you that their angels in heaven always see the face of my Father in heaven.[a]

" 'their worm does not die,
and the fire is not quenched'[d] [Isa. 66:24].

[49]Everyone will be salted with fire.

---

[t](Mark 9:40) This statement appears to contradict Matthew 12:30 (Sec. 61), but actually it complements it. Matthew 12:30 speaks of the relation of a man's inner life to Christ, and Mark 9:40 refers to his outward conduct. One who is not a declared enemy may be regarded as a friend; especially in this case, where he invokes the name of Christ.

[u](Matt. 18:8–9; Mark 9:43, 45, 47) According to Palestinian custom, Jews did not refer to the abstract sinful act but to the concrete member of the body by which it was liable to be committed. This was thus not a call to self-mutilation but to a refusal to place the body at the disposal of selfish pleasures (cf. Rom. 12:1).

Matthew 18:6–14 (cont'd)   Mark 9:38–50 (cont'd)

50"ᵛSalt is good, but if it loses its saltiness, how can you make it salty again? Have salt in yourselves, and be at peace with each other."

12"What do you think? If a man owns a hundred sheep, and one of them wanders away, will he not leave the ninety-nine on the hills and go to look for the one that wandered off? 13And if he finds it, I tell you the truth, he is happier about that one sheep than about the ninety-nine that did not wander off. 14In the same way your Father in heaven is not willing that any of these little ones should be lost.

ᵃMt 18:10 Some manuscripts heaven. 11The Son of Man came to save what was lost.
ᵇMk 9:43 Some manuscripts out, 44where / " 'their worm does not die, / and the fire is not quenched.'
ᶜ45 Some manuscripts hell, 46where / " 'their worm does not die, / and the fire is not quenched.'
ᵈ48 Isaiah 66:24

Sec. 92   Treatment and forgiveness of a sinning brother
—Capernaum—

Matthew 18:15–35

15"If your brother sins against you,ᵃ go and show him his fault, just between the two of you. If he listens to you, you have won your brother over. 16But if he will not listen, take one or two others along, so that 'every matter may be established by the testimony of two or three witnesses'ᵇ [Deut. 19:15]. 17If he refuses to listen to them, tell it to the church; and if he refuses to listen even to the church, treat him as you would a pagan or a tax collector.

18"I tell you the truth, whatever you bind on earth will beᶜ bound in heaven, and whatever you loose on earth will beᶜ loosed in heaven.

19"Again, I tell you that if two of you on earth agree about anything you ask for, it will be done for you by my Father in heaven. 20For where two or three come together in my name, there am I with them."

21Then Peter came to Jesus and asked, "Lord, how many times shall I forgive my brother when he sins against me? Up to ʷseven times?"

22Jesus answered, "I tell you, not seven times, but seventy-seven times.ᵈ

23"Therefore, the kingdom of heaven is like a king who wanted to settle accounts with his servants. 24As he began the settlement, a man who owed him ten thousand talentsᵉ was brought to him. 25Since he was not able to pay, the master ordered that he and his wife and his children and all that he had be sold to repay the debt.

ᵛ(Mark 9:50) "The salt of the covenant" (Lev. 2:13) provided for purification and preservation of the sacrifice. As long as the disciples remained pure by not wrangling among themselves over greatness (Sec. 90), they could preserve the world from judgment. The salt of the illustration was salt from the Dead Sea, which, unlike processed salt, contained impurities that could make it lose its saltiness (cf. Matt. 5:13, Sec. 54c).
ʷ(Matt. 18:21) By suggesting seven acts of forgiveness Peter thought he was being quite generous, because the rabbis required only three. Jesus' response was to require unlimited forgiveness. The Greek expression in verse 22 can be either seventy times seven or seventy-seven, but the effect of either is the same: a number so large as to be, for all practical purposes, limitless.

Matthew 18:15–35 (cont'd)

²⁶"The servant fell on his knees before him. 'Be patient with me,' he begged, 'and I will pay back everything.' ²⁷The servant's master took pity on him, canceled the debt and let him go.

²⁸"But when that servant went out, he found one of his fellow servants who owed him a hundred denarii.ᶠ He grabbed him and began to choke him. ˣ'Pay back what you owe me!' he demanded.

²⁹"His fellow servant fell to his knees and begged him, 'Be patient with me, and I will pay you back.'

³⁰"But he refused. Instead, he went off and had the man thrown into prison until he could pay the debt. ³¹When the other servants saw what had happened, they were greatly distressed and went and told their master everything that had happened.

³²"Then the master called the servant in. 'You wicked servant,' he said, 'I canceled all that debt of yours because you begged me to. ³³Shouldn't you have had mercy on your fellow servant just as I had on you?' ³⁴In anger his master turned him over to the jailers to be tortured, until he should pay back all he owed.

³⁵"This is how my heavenly Father will treat each of you unless you forgive your brother from your heart."

ᵃMt 18:15 Some manuscripts do not have *against you.*   ᵇ16 Deut. 19:15   ᶜ18 Or *have been*
ᵈ22 Or *seventy times seven*   ᵉ24 That is, millions of dollars   ᶠ28 That is, a few dollars

JOURNEY TO JERUSALEM FOR THE FEAST OF TABERNACLES

Sec. 93   Complete commitment required of followers
—On the road—

ʸMatthew 8:19–22	ʸLuke 9:57–62
¹⁹Then a teacher of the law came to him and said, "Teacher, I will follow you wherever you go."	⁵⁷As they were walking along the road, a man said to him, "I will follow you wherever you go."
²⁰Jesus replied, "Foxes have holes and birds of the air have nests, but the Son of Man has no place to lay his head."	⁵⁸Jesus replied, "Foxes have holes and birds of the air have nests, but the Son of Man has no place to lay his head."
²¹Another disciple said to him, "Lord, first let me go and bury my father."	⁵⁹He said to another man, "Follow me."
²²But Jesus told him, "Follow me, and ᶻlet the dead bury their own dead."	But the man replied, "Lord, first let me go and bury my father."
	⁶⁰Jesus said to him, "ᶻLet the dead bury their own dead, but you go and proclaim the kingdom of God."
	⁶¹Still another said, "I will follow

ˣ(Matt. 18:28) For a disciple to refuse unlimited forgiveness is like this slave's refusal to forgive a debt of $18 (the amount here) after he himself had been forgiven one of more than $10 million (v. 24).

ʸ(Matt. 8:19–22; Luke 9:57–62) The placement of this double account follows the order of A. T. Robertson's *Harmony.* It is the opinion of the revisers of this *Harmony,* however, that the chronological sequence is more accurately recaptured by placing these two passages after Section 95. This is the way they are arranged in Luke's gospel (i.e., Luke 9:51–56 precedes Luke 9:57–62), and Luke 9:57 notes that the group was on a journey whose beginning has already been indicated in Luke 9:51. There is no reason to depart from Luke's order here.

ᶻ(Matt.8:22; Luke 9:60) The son wished to complete the burial rites for his father, who had just died, or else to observe the customary thirty-day mourning period. But the call to discipleship had to be accepted when issued, or it would be lost. As for his dead father, there were enough who were still spiritually dead to handle the burial.

Luke 9:57–62 (cont'd)

you, Lord; but first let me go back and say good-by to my family."
[62]Jesus replied, "No one who puts his hand to the plow and looks back is fit for service in the kingdom of God."

Sec. 94   Ridicule by Jesus' half-brothers
—Galilee—

John 7:2–9

[2]But when the Jewish Feast of Tabernacles was near, [3]Jesus' brothers said to him, "You ought to leave here and go to Judea, so that your disciples may see the miracles you do. [4]No one who wants to become a public figure acts in secret. Since you are doing these things, [a]show yourself to the world." [5]For even his own brothers did not believe in him.
[6]Therefore Jesus told them, "The right time for me has not yet come; for you any time is right. [7]The world cannot hate you, but it hates me because I testify that what it does is evil. [8]You go to the Feast. I am not yet[a] going up to this Feast, because for me the right time has not yet come." [9]Having said this, he stayed in Galilee.

[a]*Jn 7:8* Some early manuscripts do not have *yet.*

Sec. 95   Journey through Samaria
—Start of journey to Jerusalem—

Luke 9:51–56

[51]As the time approached for him to be taken up to heaven, Jesus [b]resolutely set out for Jerusalem. [52]And he sent messengers on ahead, who went into a Samaritan village to get things ready for him; [53]but the people there did not welcome him, because he was heading for [c]Jerusalem. [54]When the disciples James

John 7:10

[10]However, after his brothers had left for the Feast, he went also, not publicly, but in secret.

---

[a](John 7:4) After the past six months of relative obscurity, the Lord's brothers prodded him to make a dramatic appearance at the impending Feast of Tabernacles in Jerusalem. In their unbelieving state they mockingly asked for a kind of Messianic manifestation that would have been quite untimely in the working out of God's purpose (v. 8).

[b](Luke 9:51) This verse marks the beginning of Luke's so-called "travel account" (Luke 9:51–19:28). Luke has been accused of incorporating chronological and geographical inaccuracies into this account in light of his use of "resolutely set out" in this verse. The words have been taken to indicate the start of a single journey to Jerusalem (Luke 19:28, Sec. 127b), which was to culminate in Jesus' crucifixion, resurrection, and ascension. Luke's critics note that the writer takes Jesus to the vicinity of Jerusalem (Luke 13:22, Sec. 113a) and then takes him all the way back to Galilee, where the journey began (Luke 17:11, Sec. 120a). A number of such alleged inconsistencies have been cited. Yet these criticisms rest on a misconception of what it meant that Jesus "resolutely set out for Jerusalem" (literally, "set his face to go to Jerusalem"). It simply means that Jesus shifted his attention from the task just completed, the training of the Twelve, to the next major challenge on his agenda, his crucifixion in Jerusalem. Such a redirection of his energies does not exclude from this phase of his ministry other visits to Jerusalem besides the last one. Jesus' movements during this period are clarified by noting the chronological and geographical information in the parallel account of John's gospel. John indicates three visits to Jerusalem: for the Feast of Tabernacles (John 7:2, Sec. 94, and John 7:11, Sec. 96a), for the Feast of Dedication (John 10:22, Sec. 111), and for the Passover (John 12:1, Sec. 128a). Luke's account is easily harmonized with this data and his accuracy is thus vindicated.

[c](Luke 9:53) To go to Jerusalem to worship was a repudiation of the Samaritan temple on Mount Gerizim. In return for animosity, James and John wanted to perform a miracle like Elijah, whom they had recently seen (Sec. 85), and destroy the unreceptive (Luke 9:54; cf. 2 Kings 1:10, 12). The two "sons of thunder" probably identified this refusal by the Samaritans with the opposition Jesus had predicted for this Jerusalem visit.

Luke 9:51–56 (cont'd)

and John saw this, they asked, "Lord, do
you want us to call fire down from heav-
en to destroy them[a]?" [55]But Jesus
turned and rebuked them, [56]and[b] they
went to another village.

[a]Lk 9:54 Some manuscripts them, even as Elijah did [b]55,56 Some manuscripts them. And he
said, "You do not know what kind of spirit you are of, for the Son of Man did not come to destroy
men's lives, but to save them." [56]And

[Complete commitment required of followers

—On the road—

[d]Matt. 8:19–22   [d]Luke 9:57–62]

---

[d](Matt. 8:19–22; Luke 9:57–62) See note y, Section 93.

PART EIGHT
THE LATER JUDEAN MINISTRY OF CHRIST
MINISTRY BEGINNING AT THE FEAST
OF TABERNACLES

Sec. 96a   Mixed reaction to Jesus' teaching and miracles
—Jerusalem, in the temple—

John 7:11–31

[11]Now at the ᵉFeast the Jews were watching for him and asking, "Where is that man?"

[12]Among the crowds there was widespread whispering about him. Some said, "He is a good man."

Others replied, "No, he deceives the people." [13]But no one would say anything publicly about him for fear of the ᶠJews.

[14]Not until halfway through the Feast did Jesus go up to the temple courts and begin to teach. [15]The Jews were amazed and asked, "ᵍHow did this man get such learning without having studied?"

[16]Jesus answered, "My teaching is not my own. It comes from him who sent me. [17]If anyone chooses to do God's will, he will find out whether my teaching comes from God or whether I speak on my own. [18]He who speaks on his own does so to gain honor for himself, but he who works for the honor of the one who sent him is a man of truth; there is nothing false about him. [19]Has not Moses given you the law? Yet not one of you keeps the law. Why are you trying to kill me?"

[20]"You are demon-possessed," the crowd answered. "Who is trying to kill you?"

[21]Jesus said to them, "I did one miracle, and you are all astonished. [22]Yet, because Moses gave you circumcision (though actually it did not come from Moses, but from the patriarchs), you circumcise a child on the Sabbath. [23]Now if a child can be circumcised on the Sabbath so that the law of Moses may not be broken, why are you angry with me for healing the whole man on the Sabbath? [24]Stop judging by mere appearances, and make a right judgment."

[25]At that point some of the people of Jerusalem began to ask, "Isn't this the man they are trying to kill? [26]Here he is, speaking publicly, and they are not saying a word to him. Have the authorities really concluded that he is the Christ ᵃ? [27]But we know where this man is from; when the Christ comes, no one will know where he is from."

[28]Then Jesus, still teaching in the temple courts, cried out, "Yes, you know me, and you know where I am from. I am not here on my own, but he who sent me is true. You do not know him, [29]but I know him because I am from him and he sent me."

[30]At this they tried to seize him, but no one laid a hand on him, because his time

---

ᵉ(John 7:11) This is the Feast of Tabernacles. At this point Jesus returned to Jerusalem, the home ground of his strongest enemies. The inevitable result was strong controversy, which dominated the period from beginning to end. The Feast of Dedication marked the conclusion of this period of three months (John 10:22, Sec. 111). By then decisions had been reached regarding the controversial issues, and there remained only the carrying out of the decision to separate Messiah from his people.

ᶠ(John 7:13) In John 7–8 (Secs. 96a–99b), designations of Jesus' enemies include "the Jews" (7:11, 13, 15, 35; 8:22, 48, 52, 57), "the Pharisees" (7:32, 47; 8:13), and "the chief priests and the Pharisees" (7:32, 45). Those who are friendly or mildly friendly to him are called "the crowd" (or "people" or "mob") (7:12, 20, 31–32, 40–41, 43, 49), "Nicodemus" (7:50), and many who "put their faith in him" (8:30). Those who are as yet undecided are "the crowds" (7:12–13), "the people of Jerusalem" (7:25), "temple guards" (7:32, 45), and "the Jews who had believed him" (8:31). In the rapid movement of the narrative the following mixed reactions are recorded: vague inquiries (7:11), debates (7:12, 40–43), fear (7:13, 30, 44), wonder (7:15, 46), perplexity (7:25–27), sincere belief (7:31; 8:30), open hostility (7:32), unfriendly criticism (7:23–27; 8:48–53), and selfish belief (8:33–44).

ᵍ(John 7:15) Two specific issues dominated the discussion: the source of Jesus' authority (7:15–24) and possible identification of him as the Messiah (7:25–31).

130

John 7:11–31 (cont'd)

had not yet come. ³¹Still, many in the crowd put their faith in him. They said, "When the Christ comes, will he do more miraculous signs than this man?"

ᵃJn 7:26 Or *Messiah*; also in verses 27, 31, 41 and 42

Sec. 96b   Frustrated attempt to arrest Jesus
—*Jerusalem*—

John 7:32–52

³²The Pharisees heard the crowd whispering such things about him. Then the chief priests and the Pharisees sent temple guards to arrest him.

³³Jesus said, "I am with you for only a short time, and then I go to the one who sent me. ³⁴You will look for me, but you will not find me; and where I am, you cannot come."

³⁵The Jews said to one another, "Where does this man intend to go that we cannot find him? Will he go where our people live scattered among the Greeks, and teach the Greeks? ³⁶What did he mean when he said, 'You will look for me, but you will not find me,' and 'Where I am, you cannot come'?"

³⁷On the last and greatest day of the Feast, Jesus stood and said in a loud voice, "If anyone is thirsty, let him come to me and ʰdrink. ³⁸Whoever believes in me, asᵃ the Scripture has said, streams of living water will flow from within him." ³⁹By this he meant the Spirit, whom those who believed in him were later to receive. Up to that time the Spirit had not been given, since Jesus had not yet been glorified.

⁴⁰On hearing his words, some of the people said, "Surely this man is the Prophet."

⁴¹Others said, "He is the Christ."

Still others asked, "How can the Christ come from Galilee? ⁴²Does not the Scripture say that the Christ will come from David's familyᵇ and from Bethlehem, the town where David lived?" ⁴³Thus the people were divided because of Jesus. ⁴⁴Some wanted to seize him, but no one laid a hand on him.

⁴⁵Finally the temple guards went back to the chief priests and Pharisees, who asked them, "Why didn't you bring him in?"

⁴⁶"No one ever spoke the way this man does," the guards declared.

⁴⁷"You mean he has deceived you also?" the Pharisees retorted. ⁴⁸"Has any of the rulers or of the Pharisees believed in him? ⁴⁹No! But this mob that knows nothing of the law—there is a curse on them."

⁵⁰Nicodemus, who had gone to Jesus earlier and who was one of their own number, asked, ⁵¹"Does our law condemn anyone without first hearing him to find out what he is doing?"

⁵²They replied, "Are you from Galilee, too? Look into it, and you will find that a prophetᶜ does not come out of Galilee."

ᵃJn 7:37,38 Or / *If anyone is thirsty, let him come to me.* / *And let him drink,* ³⁸*who believes in me.* / *As*   ᵇ42 Greek *seed*   ᶜ52 Two early manuscripts *the Prophet*

ʰ(John 7:37) The Feast of Tabernacles included a daily libation of water to commemorate the miraculous supply of water in the wilderness after Israel departed from Egypt. At the same time, it pointed forward to what the prophets saw as the future blessing of the nation (Ezek. 47:1, 12; Joel 3:18). Jesus claimed ability to fulfill this promise, and the parenthetical interpretation of John 7:39 identifies the fulfillment with the provision of the Holy Spirit following Jesus' glorification.

Sec. 97   Jesus' forgiveness of a woman caught in adultery
—*Jerusalem, in the temple*—

i[John 7:53–8:11]

[⁵³Then each went to his own home.
¹But Jesus went to the Mount of Olives. ²At dawn he appeared again in the temple courts, where all the people gathered around him, and he sat down to teach them. ³The teachers of the law and the Pharisees brought in a woman caught in adultery. They made her stand before the group ⁴and said to Jesus, "Teacher, this woman was caught in the act of adultery. ⁵In the Law Moses commanded us to stone such women. Now what do you say?" ⁶They were using this question as a trap, in order to have a basis for accusing him.

But Jesus bent down and started to write on the ground with his finger. ⁷When they kept on questioning him, he straightened up and said to them, "If any one of you is without sin, let him be the first to throw a stone at her." ⁸Again he stooped down and wrote on the ground.

⁹At this, those who heard began to go away one at a time, the older ones first, until only Jesus was left, with the woman still standing there. ¹⁰Jesus straightened up and asked her, "Woman, where are they? Has no one condemned you?"

¹¹"No one, sir," she said.

"Then neither do I condemn you," Jesus declared. "Go now and leave your life of sin."]

Sec. 98   Conflict over Jesus' claim to be the light of the world
—*Jerusalem, in the temple*—

John 8:12–20

¹²When Jesus spoke again to the people, he said, "I am the ʲlight of the world. Whoever follows me will never walk in darkness, but will have the light of life."

¹³The Pharisees challenged him, "Here you are, appearing as your own witness; your testimony is not valid."

¹⁴Jesus answered, "Even if I testify on my own behalf, my testimony is valid, for I know where I came from and where I am going. But you have no idea where I come from or where I am going. ¹⁵You judge by human standards; I pass judgment on no one. ¹⁶But if I do judge, my decisions are right, because I am not alone. I stand with the Father, who sent me. ¹⁷In your own Law it is written that the testimony of two men is valid. ¹⁸I am one who testifies for myself; my other witness is the Father, who sent me."

¹⁹Then they asked him, "Where is your father?"

"You do not know me or my Father," Jesus replied. "If you knew me, you would know my Father also." ²⁰He spoke these words while teaching in the temple area near the ᵏplace where the offerings were put. Yet no one seized him, because his time had not yet come.

ⁱThis section probably records a historic incident in the life of Christ, but one preserved by Christian tradition and not by the writer of this gospel. Evidence from more reliable textual sources denies this incident a place in John's gospel. Therefore it is impossible to discover the correct chronological placement of this encounter.

ʲ(John 8:12) Some have suggested that "light" drew attention to the pillar of fire in the wilderness (see note h, Sec. 96b). Though an indirect reference to this is probable, the preferable understanding is an allusion to the golden candelabrum that was lit on the first night of the Feast of Tabernacles. This light source in turn was commemorative of the Shekinah that guided the Israelites through the wilderness.

ᵏ(John 8:20) "Where the offerings were put" must be a reference to that part of the court of the women in which thirteen trumpet-shaped collection boxes were located (cf. Mark 12:41, 43 and Luke 21:1, Sec. 138). This court was a gathering place for both sexes, and teaching was permitted there. Interestingly, it was quite near the meeting hall of the Sanhedrin, the official council of Judaism that was determined to dispose of Jesus.

Sec. 99a   Jesus' relationship to God the Father
—*Jerusalem, in the temple*—

John 8:21–30

[21]Once more Jesus said to them, "I am going away, and you will look for me, and you will die in your sin. Where I go, you cannot come."

[22]This made the Jews ask, "Will he kill himself? Is that why he says, 'Where I go, you cannot come'?"

[23]But he continued, "You are from below; I am from above. You are of this world; I am not of this world. [24]I told you that you would die in your sins; [l]if you do not believe that I am the one I claim to be,[a] you will indeed die in your sins."

[25]"Who are you?" they asked.

"Just what I have been claiming all along," Jesus replied. [26]"I have much to say in judgment of you. But he who sent me is reliable, and what I have heard from him I tell the world."

[27]They did not understand that he was telling them about his Father. [28]So Jesus said, "When you have lifted up the Son of Man, then you will know that I am the one I claim to be, and that I do nothing on my own but speak just what the Father has taught me. [29]The one who sent me is with me; he has not left me alone, for I always do what pleases him." [30]Even as he spoke, many put their faith in him.

[a]Jn 8:24 Or *I am he*; also in verse 28

Sec. 99b   Jesus' relationship to Abraham and attempted stoning
—*Jerusalem, in the temple*—

John 8:31–59

[31]To the Jews who had [m]believed him, Jesus said, "If you hold to my teaching, you are really my disciples. [32]Then you will know the truth, and the truth will set you free."

[33]They answered him, "[n]We are Abraham's descendants[a] and have never been slaves of anyone. How can you say that we shall be set free?"

[34]Jesus replied, "I tell you the truth, everyone who sins is a slave to sin. [35]Now a slave has no permanent place in the family, but a son belongs to it forever. [36]So if the Son sets you free, you will be free indeed. [37]I know you are Abraham's descendants. Yet you are ready to kill me, because you have no room for my word. [38]I am telling you what I have seen in the Father's presence, and you do what you have heard from your father.[b]"

[39]"Abraham is our father," they answered.

"If you were Abraham's children," said Jesus, "then you would[c] do the things Abraham did. [40]As it is, you are determined to kill me, a man who has told you the truth that I heard from God. Abraham did not do such things. [41]You are doing the things your own father does."

"We are not illegitimate children," they protested. "The only Father we have is God himself."

[42]Jesus said to them, "If God were your Father, you would love me, for I came from God and now am here. I have not come on my own; but he sent me. [43]Why is my language not clear to you? Because you are unable to hear what I say. [44]You belong to your father, the devil, and you want to carry out your father's desire. He

[l](John 8:24) Jesus' challenge to believe in himself as Messiah is met with a positive response by "many" (John 8:30). Whether these were opponents, neutral bystanders, or both is not disclosed.

[m](John 8:31) The Greek construction is such as to distinguish this group from the sincere believers of John 8:30. "Believed him" does not carry the same connotation of commitment as "put their faith in him." The words of this section are therefore addressed to those who see the plausibility of his messianic claims but are unwilling to comply with the ethical demands accompanying them.

[n](John 8:33) This is the first of several declarations in the section that portray the animosity of Judaism toward Jesus and his teachings. Here the Jews claimed inheritance of freedom through Abraham so as to contradict Jesus' promise of freedom only if they abide in his word. Their other claims and accusations are found in verses 39, 41, 48, 53, 57.

John 8:31–59 (cont'd)

was a murderer from the beginning, not holding to the truth, for there is no truth in him. When he lies, he speaks his native language, for he is a liar and the father of lies. [45]Yet because I tell the truth, you do not believe me! [46]Can any of you prove me guilty of sin? If I am telling the truth, why don't you believe me? [47]He who belongs to God hears what God says. The reason you do not hear is that you do not belong to God."

[48]The Jews answered him, "Aren't we right in saying that you are a Samaritan and demon-possessed?"

[49]"I am not possessed by a demon," said Jesus, "but I honor my Father and you dishonor me. [50]I am not seeking glory for myself; but there is one who seeks it, and he is the judge. [51]I tell you the truth, if anyone keeps my word, he will never see death."

[52]At this the Jews exclaimed, "Now we know that you are demon-possessed! Abraham died and so did the prophets, yet you say that if anyone keeps your word, he will never taste death. [53]Are you greater than our father Abraham? He died, and so did the prophets. Who do you think you are?"

[54]Jesus replied, "If I glorify myself, my glory means nothing. My Father, whom you claim as your God, is the one who glorifies me. [55]Though you do not know him, I know him. If I said I did not, I would be a liar like you, but I do know him and keep his word. [56]Your father Abraham rejoiced at the thought of seeing my day; he saw it and was glad."

[57]"You are not yet fifty years old," the Jews said to him, "and you have seen Abraham!"

[58]"I tell you the truth," Jesus answered, "before Abraham was born, I am!" [59]At this, they picked up stones to stone him, but Jesus hid himself, slipping away from the temple grounds.

[a]Jn 8:33 Greek *seed*; also in verse 37   [b]38 Or *presence. Therefore do what you have heard from the Father.*   [c]39 Some early manuscripts *"If you are Abraham's children," said Jesus, "then*

Sec. 100a   Healing of a man born blind
—Jerusalem—

[o]John 9:1–7

[1]As he went along, he saw a man blind from birth. [2]His disciples asked him, "Rabbi, who sinned, this man or his parents, that he was born blind?"

[3]"Neither this man nor his parents sinned," said Jesus, "but this happened so that the work of God might be displayed in his life. [4]As long as it is day, we must do the work of him who sent me. Night is coming, when no one can work. [5]While I am in the world, I am the light of the world."

[6]Having said this, he spit on the ground, made some mud with the saliva, and put it on the man's eyes. [7]"Go," he told him, "wash in the Pool of Siloam" (this word means Sent). So the man went and washed, and came home seeing.

[o](John 9:1–7) The sequence of A. T. Robertson's *Harmony* is followed in the placement of this section and of the next six sections (i.e., Secs. 100a–e and Secs. 101a–b). This assumes that John 9:1–10:21 took place on the same day as the events of John 8:31–59 (Sec. 99b) at the Feast of Tabernacles. The revisers of Robertson's *Harmony* believe, however, that the happenings of John 9:1–10:21 more probably came at the Feast of Dedication, approximately three months later. The following are reasons for such a conclusion:
1. The Jews would hardly have sought to stone Jesus (John 8:59) on the Sabbath (John 9:14, Sec. 100c).
2. Elapsed time is required after the attempted stoning (John 8:59) to allow antagonism to die down before another public encounter such as that in John 9:1–10:21.
3. "Then" in John 10:22 (Sec. 111) shows the events prior to 10:22 to be part of Jesus' attendance at the Feast of Dedication.
4. The subject of discussion in 9:1–10:21 (sheep) has most affinity with 10:22–29.
5. The tone of 9:1–10:21 is markedly different from the turmoil and debate that dominated the Feast of Tabernacles. In the later section during the Feast of Dedication, Jewish listeners had become confirmed in their rejection, and Jesus turned his attention to those outside Israel.
If these are valid, Sections 100a–e and Sections 101a–b belong between Sections 110 and 111.

Sec. 100b   Response of the blind man's neighbors
—*Jerusalem*—

John 9:8–12

⁸His neighbors and those who had formerly seen him begging asked, "Isn't this the same man who used to sit and beg?" ⁹Some claimed that he was.

Others said, "No, he only looks like him."

But he himself insisted, "I am the man."

¹⁰"How then were your eyes opened?" they demanded.

¹¹He replied, "The ᵖman they call Jesus made some mud and put it on my eyes. He told me to go to Siloam and wash. So I went and washed, and then I could see."

¹²"Where is this man?" they asked him.

"I don't know," he said.

Sec. 100c   Examination and excommunication of the blind man by the Pharisees
(cf. Secs. 49a–51, 110, 114—Sabbath controversies)
—*Jerusalem*—

John 9:13–34

¹³They brought to the Pharisees the man who had been blind. ¹⁴Now the day on which Jesus had made the mud and opened the man's eyes was a Sabbath. ¹⁵Therefore the Pharisees also asked him how he had received his sight. "He put mud on my eyes," the man replied, "and I washed, and now I see."

¹⁶Some of the Pharisees said, "ᵠThis man is not from God, for he does not keep the Sabbath."

But others asked, "How can a sinner do such miraculous signs?" So they were divided.

¹⁷Finally they turned again to the blind man, "What have you to say about him? It was your eyes he opened."

The man replied, "He is a prophet."

¹⁸The Jews still did not believe that he had been blind and had received his sight until they sent for the man's parents. ¹⁹"Is this your son?" they asked. "Is this the one you say was born blind? How is it that now he can see?"

²⁰"We know he is our son," the parents answered, "and we know he was born blind. ²¹But how he can see now, or who opened his eyes, we don't know. Ask him. He is of age; he will speak for himself." ²²His parents said this because they were afraid of the Jews, for already the Jews had decided that anyone who acknowledged that Jesus was the Christ ᵃ would be ʳput out of the synagogue. ²³That was why his parents said, "He is of age; ask him."

ᵖ(John 9:11) At this point the healed blind man has little apprehension of who Jesus is. As events unfold, however, his appreciation of him grows rapidly. In verse 17 (Sec. 100c) he calls him a prophet. In verses 27–28 (Sec. 100c) he has become his disciple. In verse 31 (Sec. 100c) he describes him as a godly man. In verse 33 (Sec. 100c) he acknowledges him to be from God. In verses 35 and 38 (Sec. 100d) he accepts him as the Son of Man.

ᵠ(John 9:16) The regress of the Pharisees during this encounter is pronounced. In verse 16 the dominant group says Jesus is not from God. In verse 18 they question his miracle. In verse 24 they call him a sinner. In verse 29 they acknowledge their ignorance about him. In verse 41 (Sec. 100e) they are pronounced to be blind sinners.

ʳ(John 9:22) A form of excommunication as a penalty for those who confessed Jesus to be the Messiah had by now been adopted by some Jewish leaders and perhaps by the Sanhedrin. Severe and final, the punishment resulted in severance from the religious and social life of Israel. This punishment was apparently not implemented with consistency; Christians in Acts moved in synagogue circles with a good bit of freedom.

John 9:13–34 (cont'd)

²⁴A second time they summoned the man who had been blind. "Give glory to God,ᵇ" they said. "We know this man is a sinner."

²⁵He replied, "Whether he is a sinner or not, I don't know. One thing I do know. I was blind but now I see!"

²⁶Then they asked him, "What did he do to you? How did he open your eyes?"

²⁷He answered, "I have told you already and you did not listen. Why do you want to hear it again? Do you want to become his disciples, too?"

²⁸Then they hurled insults at him and said, "You are this fellow's disciple! We are disciples of Moses! ²⁹We know that God spoke to Moses, but as for this fellow, we don't even know where he comes from."

³⁰The man answered, "Now that is remarkable! You don't know where he comes from, yet he opened my eyes. ³¹We know that God does not listen to sinners. He listens to the godly man who does his will. ³²Nobody has ever heard of opening the eyes of a man born blind. ³³If this man were not from God, he could do nothing."

³⁴To this they replied, "You were steeped in sin at birth; how dare you lecture us!" And they ˢthrew him out.

ᵃJn 9:22 Or Messiah   ᵇ24 A solemn charge to tell the truth (see Joshua 7:19)

Sec. 100d   Jesus' identification of himself to the blind man
—*Jerusalem*—

John 9:35–38

³⁵Jesus heard that they had thrown him out, and when he found him, he said, "Do you believe in the Son of Man?"

³⁶"Who is he, sir?" the man asked. "Tell me so that I may believe in him."

³⁷Jesus said, "You have now seen him; in fact, he is the one speaking with you."

³⁸Then the man said, "Lord, I believe," and he ᵗworshiped him.

Sec. 100e   Spiritual blindness of the Pharisees
—*Jerusalem*—

John 9:39–41

³⁹Jesus said, "For judgment I have come into this world, so that the blind will see and those who see will become blind."

⁴⁰Some Pharisees who were with him heard him say this and asked, "What? Are we blind too?"

⁴¹Jesus said, "ᵘIf you were blind, you would not be guilty of sin; but now that you claim you can see, your guilt remains.

ˢ(John 9:34) The excommunication so greatly feared by the parents (vv. 22–23) was here carried out against the son because of his tenacious defense of Jesus.

ᵗ(John 9:38) The man's devotion to Jesus here reaches its climax. In John's gospel the word for *worship* describes a reverence that is due God alone.

ᵘ(John 9:41) If the Pharisees had been willing to admit their spiritual blindness, they would have yearned for spiritual light and could have found forgiveness. Since they professed to see and consequently refused to acknowledge Jesus to be the Messiah, their case was hopeless. They were fully persuaded they were right and refused to learn the truth about him. Any prospect of being freed from sin was thereby removed (cf. Matt. 9:13; Mark 2:17; Luke 5:32, Sec. 47).

Sec. 101a   Allegory of the good shepherd and the thief
—*Jerusalem*—

John 10:1–18

[1]"I tell you the truth, the [v]man who does not enter the sheep pen by the gate, but climbs in by some other way, is a thief and a robber. [2]The man who enters by the gate is the shepherd of his sheep. [3]The watchman opens the gate for him, and the sheep listen to his voice. He calls his own sheep by name and leads them out. [4]When he has brought out all his own, he goes on ahead of them, and his sheep follow him because they know his voice. [5]But they will never follow a stranger; in fact, they will run away from him because they do not recognize a stranger's voice." [6]Jesus used this figure of speech, but they did not understand what he was telling them.

[7]Therefore Jesus said again, "I tell you the truth, I am the gate for the sheep. [8]All who ever came before me were thieves and robbers, but the sheep did not listen to them. [9]I am the gate; whoever enters through me will be saved.[a] He will come in and go out, and find pasture. [10]The thief comes only to steal and kill and destroy; I have come that they may have life, and have it to the full.

[11]"I am the good shepherd. The good shepherd lays down his life for the sheep. [12]The hired hand is not the shepherd who owns the sheep. So when he sees the wolf coming, he abandons the sheep and runs away. Then the wolf attacks the flock and scatters it. [13]The man runs away because he is a hired hand and cares nothing for the sheep.

[14]"I am the good shepherd; I know my sheep and my sheep know me— [15]just as the Father knows me and I know the Father—and I lay down my life for the sheep. [16]I have other sheep that are not of this sheep pen. I must bring them also. They too will listen to my voice, and there shall be one flock and one shepherd. [17]The reason my Father loves me is that I lay down my life—only to take it up again. [18]No one takes it from me, but I lay it down of my own accord. I have [w]authority to lay it down and authority to take it up again. This command I received from my Father."

[a]*Jn 10:9 Or kept safe*

Sec. 101b   Further division among the Jews
—*Jerusalem*—

John 10:19–21

[19]At these words the Jews were again [x]divided. [20]Many of them said, "He is demon-possessed and raving mad. Why listen to him?"

[21]But others said, "These are not the sayings of a man possessed by a demon. Can a demon open the eyes of the blind?"

---

[v](John 10:1) The occasion for this allegory was furnished by the excommunication of the blind man whom Jesus healed (John 9:34, Sec. 100c). The healed man was one of the sheep who are the godly remnant of Israel, and the Pharisees were identified with the thieves (10:1, 8), the stranger (10:5), and the hired hand (10:12–13). The "sheep pen" of which he spoke (10:1, 16) represented Judaism of Christ's day from which he led the remnant (10:3). The "other sheep" (10:16) were those of the Gentile world who were to believe in Christ. "One flock" (10:16) anticipated formation of the body of Christ composed of the godly remnant of Israel and Gentile believers. Jesus is both the door of access into the flock (10:7, 9) and the good shepherd who cares for the flock (10:11, 14).

[w](John 10:18) Only here and in John 2:19 (Sec. 31) does Jesus claim to raise himself or have authority to do so. Elsewhere the agent in raising the Son is always the Father.

[x](John 10:19) In John, earlier instances of such division include 6:52 (Sec. 76a), 7:43 (Sec. 96b), and 9:16 (Sec. 100c). Jesus' function as a divider of people had already become quite evident (Matt. 10:34–36, Sec. 70b; cf. Luke 12:51–53, Sec. 108d).

PRIVATE LESSONS ON LOVING SERVICE AND PRAYER

Sec. 102a   Commissioning of the seventy
(cf. Sec. 58—woes to the cities)
(cf. Secs. 70a, 70b—workers dispatched)
—*Probably in Judea*—

Luke 10:1–16

¹After this the Lord appointed ʸseventy-twoᵃ others and sent them two by two ahead of him to every town and place where he was about to go. ²He told them, "The harvest is plentiful, but the workers are few. Ask the Lord of the harvest, therefore, to send out workers into his harvest field. ³Go! I am sending you out like lambs among wolves. ⁴Do not take a purse or bag or sandals; and do not greet anyone on the road.

⁵"When you enter a house, first say, 'Peace to this house.' ⁶If a man of peace is there, your peace will rest on him; if not, it will return to you. ⁷Stay in that house, eating and drinking whatever they give you, for the worker deserves his wages. Do not move around from house to house.

⁸"When you enter a town and are welcomed, eat what is set before you. ⁹Heal the sick who are there and tell them, 'ᶻThe kingdom of God is near you.' ¹⁰But when you enter a town and are not welcomed, go into its streets and say, ¹¹'Even the dust of your town that sticks to our feet we wipe off against you. Yet be sure of this: The kingdom of God is near.' ¹²I tell you, it will be more bearable on that day for Sodom than for that town.

¹³"Woe to you, Korazin! Woe to you, Bethsaida! For if the miracles that were performed in you had been performed in Tyre and Sidon, they would have repented long ago, sitting in sackcloth and ashes. ¹⁴But it will be more bearable for Tyre and Sidon at the judgment than for you. ¹⁵And you, Capernaum, will you be lifted up to the skies? No, you will go down to the depths.ᵇ

¹⁶"He who listens to you listens to me; he who rejects you rejects me; but he who rejects me rejects him who sent me."

ᵃLk 10:1 Some manuscripts *seventy*; also in verse 17   ᵇ15 Greek *Hades*

Sec. 102b   Return of the seventy
—*Probably in Judea*—

Luke 10:17–24

¹⁷The seventy-two ᵃreturned with joy and said, "Lord, even the demons submit to us in your name."

¹⁸He replied, "I saw Satan fall like lightning from heaven. ¹⁹I have given you authority to trample on snakes and scorpions and to overcome all the power of the enemy; nothing will harm you. ²⁰However, do not rejoice that the spirits submit to you, but rejoice that your names are written in heaven."

²¹At that time Jesus, full of joy through the Holy Spirit, said, "I praise you, Father, Lord of heaven and earth, because you have hidden these things from the wise and

ʸ(Luke 10:1) Although the NIV follows those manuscripts that read "seventy-two," the revising editors prefer the reading "seventy." Just as Moses appointed seventy elders to help him, Jesus appointed a like number to expedite his mission in the brief time remaining before his arrest and crucifixion. Unlike the Twelve, whose ministry had been to Galilee, the seventy were to reach either Perea (Transjordan) or Judea. The Twelve had a more independent and permanent impact, but the seventy were commissioned to prepare the towns and villages for a coming visit by Christ.

ᶻ(Luke 10:9) The message is still about the nearness of the kingdom (cf. Matt. 10:7, Sec. 70b). The inhabitants of other areas had a right to this proclamation, just as did those in Galilee. This widespread ministry, particularly in Judea, served to prepare Israel for the official offer of its King in the triumphal entry, which was less than six months away (cf. Sec. 128b).

ᵃ(Luke 10:17) The seventy did not return all at once and probably did not return to the same place. They in all likelihood met him as he followed them into the places they had entered as his forerunners. After they were all back together, this dialogue took place.

Luke 10:17–24 (cont'd)

learned, and revealed them to little children. Yes, Father, for this was your good pleasure.

22"All things have been committed to me by my Father. No one knows who the Son is except the Father, and no one knows who the Father is except the Son and those to whom the Son chooses to reveal him."

23Then he turned to his disciples and said privately, "Blessed are the eyes that see what you see. 24For I tell you that many prophets and kings wanted to see what you see but did not see it, and to hear what you hear but did not hear it."

Sec. 103   Story of the good Samaritan
(cf. Sec. 135—greatest commandment in the Law)
—*Probably in Judea*—

Luke 10:25–37

25On one occasion an expert in the law stood up to test Jesus. "Teacher," he asked, "what must I do to inherit eternal life?"

26"What is written in the Law?" he replied. "How do you read it?"

27He answered: " 'Love the Lord your God with all your heart and with all your soul and with all your strength and with all your mind'ᵃ; and, 'Love your neighbor as yourself'ᵇ" [Lev. 19:18; Deut. 6:5].

28"You have answered correctly," Jesus replied. "Do this and you will live" [Lev. 18:5].

29But he wanted to justify himself, so he asked Jesus, "And who is my neighbor?"

30In reply Jesus said: "A ᵇman was going down from Jerusalem to Jericho, when he fell into the hands of robbers. They stripped him of his clothes, beat him and went away, leaving him half dead. 31A priest happened to be going down the same road, and when he saw the man, he passed by on the other side. 32So too, a Levite, when he came to the place and saw him, passed by on the other side. 33But a Samaritan, as he traveled, came where the man was; and when he saw him, he took pity on him. 34He went to him and bandaged his wounds, pouring on oil and wine. Then he put the man on his own donkey, took him to an inn and took care of him. 35The next day he took out two silver coinsᶜ and gave them to the innkeeper. 'Look after him,' he said, 'and when I return, I will reimburse you for any extra expense you may have.'

36"ᶜWhich of these three do you think was a neighbor to the man who fell into the hands of robbers?"

37The expert in the law replied, "The one who had mercy on him."

Jesus told him, "Go and do likewise."

ᵃLk 10:27 Deut. 6:5   ᵇ27 Lev. 19:18   ᶜ35 Greek *two denarii*

Sec. 104   Jesus' visit with Mary and Martha
—*Bethany, near Jerusalem*—

Luke 10:38–42

38As Jesus and his disciples were on their way, he came to a village where a woman named ᵈMartha opened her home to him. 39She had a sister called ᵈMary,

---

ᵇ(Luke 10:30) Though often referred to as a parable, the possibility of this being an actual occurrence is good. Jesus would have been unlikely to have attributed such unbecoming behavior to his enemies (i.e., a priest and a Levite) unless such a thing had actually happened. This is especially true because the expert in the law who asked was one of the scribes who was putting Jesus to the test (v. 25).

ᶜ(Luke 10:36) Jesus rephrased and corrected the expert's question from "Who is my neighbor?" (v. 29) to "To whom am I neighbor?" What the man should have asked himself was, "To whom do I prove myself to be a neighbor?" Jesus' answer in the story of the good Samaritan is, "Anyone in need, even if he is my avowed enemy." Love, not place, produces neighborhood.

ᵈ(Luke 10:38–39) The pictures of Mary and Martha in this episode agree perfectly with those in John 11:17–44 (Sec. 118b) when their brother Lazarus was raised. The former was characterized especially by

Luke 10:38–42 (cont'd)

who sat at the Lord's feet listening to what he said. [40]But Martha was distracted by all the preparations that had to be made. She came to him and asked, "Lord, don't you care that my sister has left me to do the work by myself? Tell her to help me!"

[41]"Martha, Martha," the Lord answered, "you are worried and upset about many things, [42]but only one thing is needed. [a] Mary has chosen what is better, and it will not be taken away from her."

[a]Lk 10:42 Some manuscripts *but few things are needed—or only one*

Sec. 105   Lesson on how to pray and parable of the °bold friend
        (cf. Sec. 54f—the disciple's prayer)
        (cf. Sec. 54h—ask, seek, knock)
        (cf. Sec. 121—persistent prayer)
        —Probably in Judea—

Luke 11:1–13

[1]One day Jesus was praying in a certain place. When he finished, one of his disciples said to him, "Lord, teach us to pray, just as John taught his disciples." [2]He said to them, "When you pray, say:

" 'Father, [a]
hallowed be your name,
your kingdom come. [b]
[3]Give us each day our daily bread.
[4]Forgive us our sins,
for we also forgive everyone who sins against us. [c]
And lead us not into temptation. [d] ' "

[5]Then he said to them, "Suppose one of you has a friend, and he goes to him at midnight and says, 'Friend, lend me three loaves of bread, [6]because a friend of mine on a journey has come to me, and I have nothing to set before him.'

[7]"Then the one inside answers, 'Don't bother me. The door is already locked, and my children are with me in bed. I can't get up and give you anything.' [8]I tell you, though he will not get up and give him the bread because he is his friend, yet because of the man's °boldness[e] he will get up and give him as much as he needs.

[9]"So I say to you: Ask and it will be given to you; seek and you will find; knock and the door will be opened to you. [10]For everyone who asks receives; he who seeks finds; and to him who knocks, the door will be opened.

[11]"Which of you fathers, if your son asks for[f] a fish, will give him a snake instead? [12]Or if he asks for an egg, will give him a scorpion? [13]If you then, though you are evil, know how to give good gifts to your children, how much more will your Father in heaven give the Holy Spirit to those who ask him!"

[a]Lk 11:2 Some manuscripts *Our Father in heaven*   [b]2 Some manuscripts *come. May your will be done on earth as it is in heaven.*   [c]4 Greek *everyone who is indebted to us*   [d]4 Some manuscripts *temptation but deliver us from the evil one*   [e]8 Or *persistence*   [f]11 Some manuscripts *for bread, will give him a stone; or if he asks for*

a life of worship and meditation, and the latter was given more to a life of activity and service. Both are legitimate. The error arose when Martha allowed anxiety to intervene and spoil what otherwise was a necessary service.

°Some uncertainty surrounds the meaning of the word translated *boldness* in Luke 11:8 (see NIV note on the text at that point). Perhaps this section should be entitled "Lesson on how to pray and parable of the *persistent* friend."

[f](Luke 11:8) The ideas of earnestness and urgency are found in the word. In the case of God, as in the case of the inconvenienced friend, the shamelessness of the asker who is thus motivated is what tips the balance in favor of granting the request.

SECOND DEBATE WITH THE TEACHERS OF THE LAW AND THE PHARISEES

Sec. 106   A third blasphemous accusation and a second debate
(cf. Secs. 54c, 64b—lighting a lamp)
(cf. Sec. 54g—lamp of the body)
(cf. Secs. 61, 91—being for and against)
(cf. Secs. 61, 68, 91—casting out demons, and blasphemous statements)
(cf. Secs. 62, 80—request for a sign)
(cf. Sec. 108a—blasphemous statements)
—*Probably in Judea*—

Luke 11:14–36

[14]Jesus was driving out a demon that was mute. When the demon left, the man who had been mute spoke, and the crowd was amazed. [15]But some of them said, "ᵍBy Beelzebub,[a] the prince of demons, he is driving out demons." [16]Others tested him by asking for a sign from heaven.

[17]Jesus knew their thoughts and said to them: "Any kingdom divided against itself will be ruined, and a house divided against itself will fall. [18]If Satan is divided against himself, how can his kingdom stand? I say this because you claim that I drive out demons by Beelzebub. [19]Now if I drive out demons by Beelzebub, by whom do your followers drive them out? So then, they will be your judges. [20]But if I drive out demons by the finger of God, then the kingdom of God has come to you.

[21]"When a strong man, fully armed, guards his own house, his possessions are safe. [22]But when someone stronger attacks and overpowers him, he takes away the armor in which the man trusted and divides up the spoils.

[23]"He who is not with me is against me, and he who does not gather with me, scatters.

[24]"When an evil[b] spirit comes out of a man, it goes through arid places seeking rest and does not find it. Then it says, 'I will return to the house I left.' [25]When it arrives, it finds the house swept clean and put in order. [26]Then it goes and takes seven other spirits more wicked than itself, and they go in and live there. And the final condition of that man is worse than the first."

[27]As Jesus was saying these things, a woman in the crowd called out, "Blessed is the mother who gave you birth and nursed you."

[28]He replied, "Blessed rather are those who hear the word of God and obey it."

[29]As the crowds increased, Jesus said, "This is a wicked generation. It asks for a miraculous sign, but none will be given it except the sign of Jonah. [30]For as Jonah was a sign to the Ninevites, so also will the Son of Man be to this generation. [31]The Queen of the South will rise at the judgment with the men of this generation and condemn them; for she came from the ends of the earth to listen to Solomon's wisdom, and now one[c] greater than Solomon is here. [32]The men of Nineveh will stand up at the judgment with this generation and condemn it; for they repented at the preaching of Jonah, and now one greater than Jonah is here.

[33]"No one lights a lamp and puts it in a place where it will be hidden, or under a bowl. Instead he puts it on its stand, so that those who come in may see the light. [34]Your eye is the lamp of your body. When your eyes are good, your whole body

---

ᵍ(Luke 11:15) The same accusation had been made about a year before, and a similar debate had ensued (Sec. 61). Jesus used the same three arguments he had used on the earlier occasion. That the two encounters were distinct from each other is seen by three factors:
1. Luke appears to place this debate in Judea, and the earlier one was in Galilee.
2. In Luke's account the man healed is dumb, but in Matthew's he is dumb and blind. Luke, in line with his medical orientation, would hardly have failed to mention the blindness if this were the man's condition.
3. Events that follow the two episodes are quite different, namely, the initiation of parabolic teaching in the earlier case and breakfast with a Pharisee in the later.

Luke 11:14–36. (cont'd)

also is full of light. But when they are bad, your body also is full of darkness. [35]See to it, then, that the light within you is not darkness. [36]Therefore, if your whole body is full of light, and no part of it dark, it will be completely lighted, as when the light of a lamp shines on you."

[a]Lk 11:15 Greek *Beezeboul* or *Beelzeboul*; also in verses 18 and 19   [b]24 Greek *unclean*   [c]31 Or *something*; also in verse 32

Sec. 107   Woes against the Pharisees and the teachers of the law while eating with a Pharisee
(cf. Sec. 137a—woes against teachers of the law and Pharisees)
—Probably in Judea—

Luke 11:37–54

[37]When Jesus had finished speaking, a Pharisee invited him to eat with him; so he went in and reclined at the table. [38]But the [h]Pharisee, noticing that Jesus did not first wash before the meal, was surprised.

[39]Then the Lord said to him, "Now then, you Pharisees clean the outside of the cup and dish, but inside you are full of greed and wickedness. [40]You foolish people! Did not the one who made the outside make the inside also? [41]But give what is inside ⌊the dish⌋[a] to the poor, and everything will be clean for you.

[42]"Woe to you Pharisees, because you give God a tenth of your mint, rue and all other kinds of garden herbs, but you neglect justice and the love of God. You should have practiced the latter without leaving the former undone.

[43]"Woe to you Pharisees, because you love the most important seats in the synagogues and greetings in the marketplaces.

[44]"Woe to you, because you are like unmarked graves, which men walk over without knowing it."

[45]One of the experts in the law answered him, "Teacher, when you say these things, you insult us also."

[46]Jesus replied, "And you experts in the law, woe to you, because you load people down with burdens they can hardly carry, and you yourselves will not lift one finger to help them.

[47]"Woe to you, because you build tombs for the prophets, and it was your forefathers who killed them. [48]So you testify that you approve of what your forefathers did; they killed the prophets, and you build their tombs. [49]Because of this, God in his wisdom said, 'I will send them prophets and apostles, some of whom they will kill and others they will persecute.' [50]Therefore this generation will be held responsible for the blood of all the prophets that has been shed since the beginning of the world, [51]from the blood of Abel to the blood of Zechariah, who was killed between the altar and the sanctuary. Yes, I tell you, this generation will be held responsible for it all.

[52]"Woe to you experts in the law, because you have [i]taken away the key to knowledge. You yourselves have not entered, and you have hindered those who were entering."

---

[h](Luke 11:38) The contrary inner disposition of Jesus' host is clear. Though the formal decision to destroy Jesus had not yet been reached (John 11:53, Sec. 119), the intentions of the Sanhedrin were obvious to its members (Sec. 96b, 99b). Thus the scribes and Pharisees had one of their number invite him to a meal so they could watch him more closely to find basis for a formal complaint. As a result of this encounter their hostility was intensified even more (vv. 53–54). At an earlier meal with a Pharisee in Galilee the host had not been so antagonistic (Sec. 59).

[i](Luke 11:52) Jesus' denunciation of the Pharisees (vv. 39–44) and the experts in the law (or scribes, vv. 45–51) was brought to a climax when he charged the experts with taking away the key of knowledge. The key to a knowledge of God was the Old Testament, the true meaning of which they had hidden by their erroneous interpretations and manmade traditions. These experts in the law refused to enter into an accurate appreciation of God and, in addition, kept those whom they taught from doing so by imposing their own ideas on the Scriptures.

Luke 11:37–54 (cont'd)

[53]When Jesus left there, the Pharisees and the teachers of the law began to oppose him fiercely and to besiege him with questions, [54]waiting to catch him in something he might say.

[a]Lk 11:41 Or *what you have*

Sec. 108a   Warning the disciples about hypocrisy
(cf. Secs. 54g, 70b—value of birds)
(cf. Secs. 54g, 61, 106—blasphemous statements)
(cf. Sec. 70b—confession before others)
(cf. Sec. 81a—the leaven of hypocrisy)
(cf. Sec. 139b—trials before courts and rulers)
—*Probably in Judea*—

Luke 12:1–12

[1]Meanwhile, when a crowd of many thousands had gathered, so that they were trampling on one another, Jesus began to speak first to his [j]disciples, saying: "Be on your guard against the yeast of the Pharisees, which is [k]hypocrisy. [2]There is nothing concealed that will not be disclosed, or hidden that will not be made known. [3]What you have said in the dark will be heard in the daylight, and what you have whispered in the ear in the inner rooms will be proclaimed from the roofs.

[4]"I tell you, my friends, do not be afraid of those who kill the body and after that can do no more. [5]But I will show you whom you should fear: Fear him who, after the killing of the body, has power to throw you into hell. Yes, I tell you, fear him. [6]Are not five sparrows sold for two pennies[a]? Yet not one of them is forgotten by God. [7]Indeed, the very hairs of your head are all numbered. Don't be afraid; you are worth more than many sparrows.

[8]"I tell you, whoever acknowledges me before men, the Son of Man will also acknowledge him before the angels of God. [9]But he who disowns me before men will be disowned before the angels of God. [10]And everyone who speaks a word against the Son of Man will be forgiven, but anyone who blasphemes against the Holy Spirit will not be forgiven.

[11]"When you are brought before synagogues, rulers and authorities, do not worry about how you will defend yourselves or what you will say, [12]for the Holy Spirit will teach you at that time what you should say."

[a]Lk 12:6 Greek *two assaria*

Sec. 108b   Warning about greed and trust in wealth
(cf. Sec. 54g—danger of riches, anxieties of life)
—*Probably in Judea*—

Luke 12:13–34

[13]Someone in the crowd said to him, "[j]Teacher, tell my brother to divide the inheritance with me."

[14]Jesus replied, "Man, who appointed me a judge or an arbiter between you?" [15]Then he said to them, "Watch out! Be on your guard against all kinds of greed; a man's life does not consist in the abundance of his possessions."

---

[j](Luke 12:1) Luke 12:1–59 (Secs. 108a–108e) is a continuous oration against the backdrop of strong opposition. A very large crowd, most of which was probably hostile, was present. What Jesus said, however, was largely addressed to his disciples (vv. 1–12, 22–53), though in the hearing of the crowd.

[k](Luke 12:1) Pharisaic pretense in general prompted by the fear of human beings (vv. 1–7) and pretense in particular in denying Jesus in word or work (vv. 8–12) are the two parts to this warning.

[l](Luke 12:13) This request reflected the pronounced tendency of the Pharisees toward avarice (Luke 16:14, Sec. 117b), with which Jesus had already dealt (Matt. 6:19–24, Sec. 54g).

Luke 12:13–34 (cont'd)

¹⁶And he told them this parable: "The ground of a certain rich man produced a good crop. ¹⁷He thought to himself, 'What shall I do? I have no place to store my crops.'

¹⁸"Then he said, 'This is what I'll do. I will tear down my barns and build bigger ones, and there I will store all my grain and my goods. ¹⁹And I'll say to myself, "You have plenty of good things laid up for many years. Take life easy; eat, drink and be merry."'

²⁰"But God said to him, 'You fool! This very night your life will be demanded from you. Then who will get what you have prepared for yourself?'

²¹"This is how it will be with anyone who stores up things for himself but is not rich toward God."

²²Then Jesus said to his disciples: "Therefore I tell you, do not worry about your life, what you will eat; or about your body, what you will wear. ²³Life is more than food, and the body more than clothes. ²⁴Consider the ravens: They do not sow or reap, they have no storeroom or barn; yet God feeds them. And how much more valuable are you than birds! ²⁵Who of you by worrying can add a single hour to his life*ᵃ*? ²⁶Since you cannot do this very little thing, why do you worry about the rest?

²⁷"Consider how the lilies grow. They do not labor or spin. Yet I tell you, not even Solomon in all his splendor was dressed like one of these. ²⁸If that is how God clothes the grass of the field, which is here today, and tomorrow is thrown into the fire, how much more will he clothe you, O you of little faith! ²⁹And do not set your heart on what you will eat or drink; do not worry about it. ³⁰For the pagan world runs after all such things, and your Father knows that you need them. ³¹But seek his kingdom, and these things will be given to you as well.

³²"Do not be afraid, little flock, for your Father has been pleased to give you the kingdom. ³³Sell your possessions and give to the poor. Provide purses for yourselves that will not wear out, a treasure in heaven that will not be exhausted, where no thief comes near and no moth destroys. ³⁴For where your treasure is, there your heart will be also.

ᵃLk 12:25 Or single cubit to his height

Sec. 108c **Warning against being unprepared for the Son of Man's coming (cf. Sec. 139f—readiness for Christ's return)**
—*Probably in Judea*—

Luke 12:35–48

³⁵"Be dressed ᵐready for service and keep your lamps burning, ³⁶like men waiting for their master to return from a wedding banquet, so that when he comes and knocks they can immediately open the door for him. ³⁷It will be good for those servants whose master finds them watching when he comes. I tell you the truth, he will dress himself to serve, will have them recline at the table and will come and wait on them. ³⁸It will be good for those servants whose master finds them ready, even if he comes in the second or third watch of the night. ³⁹But understand this: If the owner of the house had known at what hour the thief was coming, he would not have let his house be broken into. ⁴⁰You also must be ready, because the Son of Man will come at an hour when you do not expect him."

⁴¹Peter asked, "Lord, are you telling this parable to us, or to everyone?"

⁴²The Lord answered, "Who then is the faithful and wise manager, whom the master puts in charge of his servants to give them their food allowance at the proper time? ⁴³It will be good for that servant whom the master finds doing so when he returns. ⁴⁴I tell you the truth, he will put him in charge of all his possessions. ⁴⁵But

ᵐ(Luke 12:35) A state of constant readiness for the kingdom that is promised the "little flock" (Luke 12:31–32, Sec. 108b) and that will be ushered in by the coming of the Son of Man (Luke 12:40) is the only way to avoid future punishment (Luke 12:47–48)

Luke 12:35–48 (cont'd)

suppose the servant says to himself, 'My master is taking a long time in coming,' and he then begins to beat the menservants and maidservants and to eat and drink and get drunk. [46]The master of that servant will come on a day when he does not expect him and at an hour he is not aware of. He will cut him to pieces and assign him a place with the unbelievers.

[47]"That servant who knows his master's will and does not get ready or does not do what his master wants will be beaten with many blows. [48]But the one who does not know and does things deserving punishment will be beaten with few blows. From everyone who has been given much, much will be demanded; and from the one who has been entrusted with much, much more will be asked.

Sec. 108d   Warning about the coming division
(cf. Sec. 70b—divided households)
—Probably in Judea—

Luke 12:49–53

[49]"I have come to bring fire on the earth, and how I wish it were already kindled! [50]But I have a baptism to undergo, and how distressed I am until it is completed! [51]Do you think I came to bring peace on earth? No, I tell you, but [n]division. [52]From now on there will be five in one family divided against each other, three against two and two against three. [53]They will be divided, father against son and son against father, mother against daughter and daughter against mother, mother-in-law against daughter-in-law and daughter-in-law against mother-in-law."

Sec. 108e   Warning against failing to discern the present time
(cf. Sec. 54e—reconciliation)
—Probably in Judea—

Luke 12:54–59

[54]He said to the crowd: "When you see a cloud rising in the west, immediately you say, 'It's going to rain,' and it does. [55]And when the south wind blows, you say, 'It's going to be hot,' and it is. [56]Hypocrites! You know how to interpret the appearance of the earth and the sky. How is it that you don't know how to interpret this [o]present time?

[57]"Why don't you judge for yourselves what is right? [58]As you are going with your adversary to the magistrate, try hard to be reconciled to him on the way, or he may drag you off to the judge, and the judge turn you over to the officer, and the officer throw you into prison. [59]I tell you, you will not get out until you have paid the last penny.[a]"

[a]Lk 12:59 Greek *lepton*

---

[n](Luke 12:51) The division of which Jesus spoke was none other than the one represented in the crowd before him. Where there was adamant refusal to meet his terms of inner purity (refusal pictured by the self-indulgence of the wicked slave of the foregoing illustration [Luke 12:45, Sec. 108c]), nothing but division could result.

[o](Luke 12:56) "This present time" was a period characterized mainly by the nearness of the kingdom (cf. Sec. 108c). To the unfriendly members of the crowd, the signs of the times should have been just as obvious as the weather signs. Yet they pretended not to notice them, just as they purposely ignored the unambiguous evidence that Jesus was the Messiah.

Sec. 109   Two alternatives: repent or perish
—Probably in Judea—

Luke 13:1–9

[1]Now there were some present at that time who told Jesus about the Galileans whose blood Pilate had mixed with their sacrifices. [2]Jesus answered, "Do you think that these Galileans were worse sinners than all the other Galileans because they suffered this way? [3]I tell you, ᵖno! But unless you repent, you too will all perish. [4]Or those eighteen who died when the tower in Siloam fell on them—do you think they were more guilty than all the others living in Jerusalem? [5]I tell you, ᵖno! But unless you repent, you too will all perish."

[6]Then he told this parable: "A man had a ᑫfig tree, planted in his vineyard, and he went to look for fruit on it, but did not find any. [7]So he said to the man who took care of the vineyard, 'For three years now I've been coming to look for fruit on this fig tree and haven't found any. Cut it down! Why should it use up the soil?' [8]"'Sir,' the man replied, 'leave it alone for one more year, and I'll dig around it and fertilize it. [9]If it bears fruit next year, fine! If not, then cut it down.'"

Sec. 110   Opposition from a synagogue ruler for healing a woman on the Sabbath
(cf. Secs. 49a–51, 100c, 114—Sabbath controversies)
(cf. Sec. 64e—mustard tree)
(cf. Sec. 64f—leaven)
—Probably in Judea—

Luke 13:10–21

[10]On a Sabbath Jesus was teaching in one of the synagogues, [11]and a woman was there who had been crippled by a spirit for eighteen years. She was bent over and could not straighten up at all. [12]When Jesus saw her, he called her forward and said to her, "Woman, you are set free from your infirmity." [13]Then he put his hands on her, and immediately she straightened up and praised God.

[14]Indignant because Jesus had healed on the Sabbath, the synagogue ruler said to the people, "There are six days for work. So come and be healed on those days, not on the Sabbath."

[15]The Lord answered him, "You hypocrites! Doesn't each of you on the Sabbath untie his ox or donkey from the stall and lead it out to give it water? [16]Then should not this woman, a daughter of Abraham, whom Satan has kept bound for eighteen long years, be set free on the Sabbath day from what bound her?"

[17]When he said this, all his opponents were humiliated, but the people were delighted with all the wonderful things he was doing.

[18]ʳThen Jesus asked, "What is the kingdom of God like? What shall I compare it to? [19]It is like a mustard seed, which a man took and planted in his garden. It grew and became a tree, and the birds of the air perched in its branches"[Psalm 104:12; Ezek. 17:23; 31:6; Dan. 4:12].

ᵖ(Luke 13:3, 5) The false notion, prevailing from the time of Job, that a person's extreme sinfulness was always to blame for great calamity was flatly rejected by Jesus. Yet it was true that the suffering of a whole nation might be produced by that nation's sin. Christ foresaw the approaching judgment of Israel and therefore warned of the consequences of failure to repent.

ᑫ(Luke 13:6) In conjunction with the narrative of 13:1–5, the fig tree must symbolize this generation of Jewish people (cf. Hos. 9:10; Joel 1:7; Matt. 21:19 and Mark 11:13, Sec. 129a). Just as a fig tree has three years to reach maturity, so Israel had been exposed to three years of Christ's ministry. The additional year covered the remainder of Christ's ministry, his postresurrection ministry, and some of the post-Pentecostal ministry of the early church. If the symbolism is carried further, the owner of the vineyard is the Father, the vineyard-keeper is Christ, and the "using up" of the soil (v. 7) depicts Israel's standing in the way of God's merciful purpose to others (cf. Rom. 9:19).

ʳ(Luke 13:18) "Then" connects the two following parables with verses 11–17. With what it connects in those verses is not so easy to decide. Yet this determines the meaning of the parables. The two principal possibilities are the enthusiasm of the multitude for his miracles and the presence of opposition within the kingdom at this early stage.

Luke 13:10–21 (cont'd)

[20]Again he asked, "What shall I compare the kingdom of God to? [21]It is like yeast that a woman took and mixed into a large amount[a] of flour until it worked all through the dough."

> [a]Lk 13:21 Greek *three satas* (probably about 1/2 bushel or 22 liters)

[Healing of a man born blind

'John 9:1–41]

[Reaction of the blind man's neighbors

'John 9:8–12]

[Examination and excommunication of the blind man by the Pharisees

'John 9:13–34]

[Jesus' identification of himself to the blind man

'John 9:35–38]

[Spiritual blindness of the Pharisees

'John 9:39–41]

[Allegory of the good shepherd and the thief

'John 10:1–18]

[Further division among the Jews

'John 10:19–21]

Sec. 111   Another attempt to stone or arrest Jesus for blasphemy at the Feast of Dedication
—Jerusalem—

John 10:22–39

[22]Then came the Feast of Dedication[a] at Jerusalem. It was winter, [23]and Jesus was in the temple area walking in Solomon's Colonnade. [24]The Jews gathered around him, saying, "How long will you keep us in suspense? If you are the 'Christ,[b] tell us plainly."

[25]Jesus answered, "I did tell you, but you do not believe. The miracles I do in my Father's name speak for me, [26]but you do not believe because you are not my sheep. [27]My sheep listen to my voice; I know them, and they follow me. [28]I give them eternal life, and they shall never perish; no one can snatch them out of my hand.

___

> [s](John 9:1–10:21) See note o, Section 100a.
> [t](John 10:24) The heart of the whole dispute was whether Jesus was Israel's promised Messiah. As proofs that he was, Jesus offered his works (v. 25), his impartation of eternal life to his sheep (v. 28) and, as a climax, his unity with the Father (v. 30). This claim was more than his enemies could bear so they sought both to stone him again (v. 31) and to arrest him (v. 39).

John 10:22–39 (cont'd)

[29]My Father, who has given them to me, is greater than all[c]; no one can snatch them out of my Father's hand. [30]I and the Father are one."

[31]Again the Jews picked up stones to stone him, [32]but Jesus said to them, "I have shown you many great miracles from the Father. For which of these do you stone me?"

[33]"We are not stoning you for any of these," replied the Jews, "but for blasphemy, because you, a mere man, claim to be God."

[34]Jesus answered them, "Is it not written in your Law, 'I have said you are gods'[d] [Psalm 82:6]? [35]If he called them 'gods,' to whom the word of God came—and the Scripture cannot be broken— [36]what about the one whom the Father set apart as his very own and sent into the world? Why then do you accuse me of blasphemy because I said, '[u]I am God's Son'? [37]Do not believe me unless I do what my Father does. [38]But if I do it, even though you do not believe me, believe the miracles, that you may know and understand that the Father is in me, and I in the Father." [39]Again they tried to seize him, but he escaped their grasp.

[a]Jn 10:22 That is, Hanukkah   [b]24 Or *Messiah*   [c]29 Many early manuscripts *What my Father has given me is greater than all*   [d]34 Psalm 82:6

---

[u](John 10:36) It is wrong to conclude that Jesus was claiming to be no more than a man among men. His words mean that if the Psalm quoted in 10:35 applies the term *gods* to men, it may with even greater propriety be applied to him who is one in essence with the Father (cf. 10:30).

PART NINE
THE MINISTRY OF CHRIST IN AND AROUND PEREA
PRINCIPLES OF DISCIPLESHIP

Sec. 112   From Jerusalem to Perea
—*Perea*—

John 10:40–42

[40]Then Jesus [v]went back across the Jordan to the place where John had been baptizing in the early days. Here he stayed [41]and many people came to him. They said, "Though John never performed a miraculous sign, all that John said about this man was true." [42]And in that place many believed in Jesus.

Sec. 113a   Question about salvation and entering the kingdom
(cf. Sec. 54h—narrow entrance)
(cf. Secs. 124a, 124b—last first and first last)
—*Itineration toward Jerusalem while in Perea*—

Luke 13:22–30

[22]Then Jesus went through the towns and villages, teaching as he made his way to Jerusalem. [23]Someone asked him, "[w]Lord, are only a few people going to be saved?"
He said to them, [24]"Make every effort to enter through the narrow door, because many, I tell you, will try to enter and will not be able to. [25]Once the owner of the house gets up and closes the door, you will stand outside knocking and pleading, 'Sir, open the door for us.'
"But he will answer, 'I don't know you or where you come from.'
[26]"Then you will say, 'We ate and drank with you, and you taught in our streets.'
[27]"But he will reply, 'I don't know you or where you come from. Away from me, all you evildoers!' [Psalm 6:8].
[28]"There will be weeping there, and gnashing of teeth, when you see Abraham, Isaac and Jacob and all the prophets in the kingdom of God, but you yourselves thrown out. [29]People will come from east and west and north and south, and will take their places at the feast in the kingdom of God. [30]Indeed there are those who are last who will be first, and first who will be last."

Sec. 113b   Anticipation of Jesus' coming death and his sorrow over Jerusalem
(cf. Sec. 137b—sorrow over Jerusalem)
—*Itineration toward Jerusalem while in Perea*—

Luke 13:31–35

[31]At that time some Pharisees came to Jesus and said to him, "Leave this place and go somewhere else. [x]Herod wants to kill you."
[32]He replied, "Go tell that fox, 'I will drive out demons and heal people today and

---

[v](John 10:40) The period begun by this departure lasted about three and one-half months, from the Feast of Dedication until the week before Passover. Response to Jesus' ministry in Perea (v. 42) was in sharp contrast to the recent response in Jerusalem (John 10:37–39, Sec. 111).
[w](Luke 13:23) The question, provoked by the surprisingly small number who were following Messiah faithfully, related to being saved so as to enter Messiah's kingdom. Although Jesus only implied a positive answer here, he earlier had explicitly stated, "Only a few find it" (Matt. 7:14, Sec. 54h). Those who thought they could claim admission solely through their relation to Abraham will be excluded (Luke 13:28–29).
[x](Luke 13:31) Perea belonged to Herod Antipas' jurisdiction, as did Galilee. These Pharisees sought to capitalize on Jesus' past encounters with Antipas (Section 72b, note a) so as to force him back into Judea,

Luke 13:31–35 (cont'd)

tomorrow, and on the third day I will reach my goal.' [33]In any case, I ʸmust keep going today and tomorrow and the next day—for surely no prophet can die outside Jerusalem!
[34]"O Jerusalem, Jerusalem, you who kill the prophets and stone those sent to you, how often I have longed to gather your children together, as a hen gathers her chicks under her wings, but you were not willing! [35]Look, your house is left to you desolate. I tell you, you will not see me again until you say, 'Blessed is he who comes in the name of the Lord'[a]".

[a]Lk 13:35 Psalm 118:26

Sec. 114   Healing of a man with dropsy while eating with a prominent Pharisee on the Sabbath, and three parables suggested by the occasion (cf. Secs. 49a–51, 100c, 110—Sabbath controversies)
—Probably in Perea—

Luke 14:1–24

[1]One Sabbath, when Jesus went to eat in the house of a ᶻprominent Pharisee, he was being carefully watched. [2]There in front of him was a man suffering from dropsy. [3]Jesus asked the Pharisees and experts in the law, "Is it lawful to heal on the Sabbath or not?" [4]But they remained silent. So taking hold of the man, he healed him and sent him away.
[5]Then he asked them, "If one of you has a son[a] or an ox that falls into a well on the Sabbath day, will you not immediately pull him out?" [6]And they had nothing to say.
[7]When he noticed ᵃhow the guests picked the places of honor at the table, he told them this parable: [8]"When someone invites you to a wedding feast, do not take the place of honor, for a person more distinguished than you may have been invited. [9]If so, the host who invited both of you will come and say to you, 'Give this man your seat.' Then, humiliated, you will have to take the least important place. [10]But when you are invited, take the lowest place, so that when your host comes, he will say to you, 'Friend, move up to a better place.' Then you will be honored in the presence of all your fellow guests. [11]For everyone who exalts himself will be humbled, and he who humbles himself will be exalted."
[12]Then Jesus said to his host, "When you give a luncheon or dinner, do not invite your friends, your brothers or relatives, or your rich neighbors; if you do, they may invite you back and so you will be repaid. [13]But when you give a banquet, invite the poor, the crippled, the lame, the blind, [14]and you will be blessed. Although they cannot repay you, you will be repaid at the resurrection of the righteous."

---

where the Sanhedrin had more direct control. On the other hand, their story about Herod was not fabricated, because the Lord in his reply (vv. 32–35) refrained from denouncing them for deceit in the matter.
ʸ(Luke 13:33) Divine decree determined that Messiah's mission would not be cut short by Herod and that his death take place in Jerusalem, not Perea. In the process of carrying out this mission, therefore, he would not immediately flee because of Herod's animosity but would remain a few days longer in Perea before resuming that journey that would eventually carry him to his crucifixion in Jerusalem.
ᶻ(Luke 14:1) It is surprising to find Jesus eating at the home of a Pharisaic leader, in view of his recent denunciation of them (Luke 11:37–54, Sec. 107). Clearly the occasion was staged to furnish them an opportunity to watch him (v. 1) and thereby gain evidence against him. They wanted to catch him in the act of breaking the Sabbath when he healed the sick man.
ᵃ(Luke 14:7) Jesus used the occasion of this meal to teach three important lessons needed by those present:
1. the importance of humility instead of maneuvering to secure the places of honor (vv. 7–11);
2. the importance of impartiality in choosing whom to invite to such an occasion, (vv. 12–14); and
3. the importance of making the kingdom of God, viewed here as a "great banquet," one's highest priority and not forfeiting the right to enter the same (vv. 15–24).

Luke 14:1–24 (cont'd)

[15]When one of those at the table with him heard this, he said to Jesus, "Blessed is the man who will eat at the feast in the kingdom of God."

[16]Jesus replied: "A certain man was preparing a great banquet and invited many guests. [17]At the time of the banquet he sent his servant to tell those who had been invited, 'Come, for everything is now ready.'

[18]"But they all alike began to make excuses. The first said, 'I have just bought a field, and I must go and see it. Please excuse me.'

[19]"Another said, 'I have just bought five yoke of oxen, and I'm on my way to try them out. Please excuse me.'

[20]"Still another said, 'I just got married, so I can't come.'

[21]"The servant came back and reported this to his master. Then the owner of the house became angry and ordered his servant, 'Go out quickly into the streets and alleys of the town and bring in the poor, the crippled, the blind and the lame.'

[22]" 'Sir,' the servant said, 'what you ordered has been done, but there is still room.'

[23]"Then the master told his servant, 'Go out to the roads and country lanes and make them come in, so that my house will be full. [24]I tell you, not one of those men who were invited will get a taste of my banquet.' "

[a]Lk 14:5 Some manuscripts *donkey*

Sec. 115   Cost of discipleship
(cf. Secs. 54c, 91—salt of the earth)
(cf. Secs. 70b, 83—cost of discipleship)
—*Probably in Perea*—

Luke 14:25–35

[25b]Large crowds were traveling with Jesus, and turning to them he said: [26]"If anyone comes to me and does not hate his father and mother, his wife and children, his brothers and sisters—yes, even his own life—he cannot be my disciple. [27]And anyone who does not carry his cross and follow me cannot be my disciple.

[28]"Suppose one of you wants to build a tower. Will he not first sit down and estimate the cost to see if he has enough money to complete it? [29]For if he lays the foundation and is not able to finish it, everyone who sees it will ridicule him, [30]saying, 'This fellow began to build and was not able to finish.'

[31]"Or suppose a king is about to go to war against another king. Will he not first sit down and consider whether he is able with ten thousand men to oppose the one coming against him with twenty thousand? [32]If he is not able, he will send a delegation while the other is still a long way off and will ask for terms of peace. [33]In the same way, any of you who does not give up everything he has cannot be my disciple.

[34]"Salt is good, but if it loses its saltiness, how can it be made salty again? [35]It is fit neither for the soil nor for the manure pile; it is thrown out.

"He who has ears to hear, let him hear."

Jesus' host and fellow guests were in need of all three lessons.

[b](Luke 14:25) Jesus' ministry in Perea had attracted very wide attention. The people's persuasion that Jesus was Messiah dictated that they remain near him, especially in light of the nearing national crisis in relation to the kingdom of God. As he approached Jerusalem, they did not want to miss any blessings of the occasion. Jesus took this opportunity to discourage any who may have joined the throng for superficial reasons. His disciples had to be prepared to face adversity of the severest sort.

Sec. 116   Parables in defense of association with sinners
(cf. Sec. 91—the one lost sheep)
—*Probably in Perea*—

Luke 15:1–32

[1]Now the tax collectors and "sinners" were all gathering around to hear him. [2]But the Pharisees and the teachers of the law muttered, "ᶜThis man welcomes sinners and eats with them."

[3]Then Jesus told them this parable: [4]"Suppose one of you has a hundred sheep and loses one of them. Does he not leave the ninety-nine in the open country and go after the lost sheep until he finds it? [5]And when he finds it, he joyfully puts it on his shoulders [6]and goes home. Then he calls his friends and neighbors together and says, 'Rejoice with me; I have found my lost sheep.' [7]I tell you that in the same way there will be more rejoicing in heaven over one sinner who repents than over ninety-nine righteous persons who do not need to repent.

[8]"Or suppose a woman has ten silver coinsᵃ and loses one. Does she not light a lamp, sweep the house and search carefully until she finds it? [9]And when she finds it, she calls her friends and neighbors together and says, 'Rejoice with me; I have found my lost coin.' [10]In the same way, I tell you, there is rejoicing in the presence of the angels of God over one sinner who repents."

[11]Jesus continued: "There was a man who had two sons. [12]The younger one said to his father, 'Father, give me my share of the estate.' So he divided his property between them.

[13]"Not long after that, the younger son got together all he had, set off for a distant country and there squandered his wealth in wild living. [14]After he had spent everything, there was a severe famine in that whole country, and he began to be in need. [15]So he went and hired himself out to a citizen of that country, who sent him to his fields to feed pigs. [16]He longed to fill his stomach with the pods that the pigs were eating, but no one gave him anything.

[17]"When he came to his senses, he said, 'How many of my father's hired men have food to spare, and here I am starving to death! [18]I will set out and go back to my father and say to him: Father, I have sinned against heaven and against you. [19]I am no longer worthy to be called your son; make me like one of your hired men.' [20]So he got up and went to his father.

"But while he was still a long way off, his father saw him and was filled with compassion for him; he ran to his son, threw his arms around him and kissed him. [21]The son said to him, 'Father, I have sinned against heaven and against you. I am no longer worthy to be called your son.ᵇ'

[22]"But the father said to his servants, 'Quick! Bring the best robe and put it on him. Put a ring on his finger and sandals on his feet. [23]Bring the fattened calf and kill it. Let's have a feast and celebrate. [24]For this son of mine was dead and is alive again; he was lost and is found.' So they began to celebrate.

[25]"Meanwhile, the older son was in the field. When he came near the house, he heard music and dancing. [26]So he called one of the servants and asked him what was going on. [27]'Your brother has come,' he replied, 'and your father has killed the fattened calf because he has him back safe and sound.'

[28]"The older brother became angry and refused to go in. So his father went out and pleaded with him. [29]But he answered his father, 'Look! All these years I've been slaving for you and never disobeyed your orders. Yet you never gave me even a young goat so I could celebrate with my friends. [30]But when this son of yours who has squandered your property with prostitutes comes home, you kill the fattened calf for him!'

[31]"'My son,' the father said, 'you are always with me, and everything I have is

---

ᶜ(Luke 15:2) At least two significant features prompted the giving of three parables:
1. The enemies of Jesus were still scrutinizing his every move with evil intent.
2. They totally lacked the loving concern of Jesus that the tax collectors and sinners found so appealing. They lacked the loving heart of the Father and a readiness to receive one who repents (vv. 7, 10, 20–25).

Luke 14:25–35 (cont'd)

yours. [32]But we had to celebrate and be glad, because this brother of yours was dead and is alive again; he was lost and is found.' "

[a]Lk 15:8 Greek *ten drachmas*, each worth about a day's wages   [b]21 Some early manuscripts *son. Make me like one of your hired men.*

Sec. 117a   Parable to teach the proper use of money
(cf. Sec. 54g—impossibility of being a slave to two masters)
—*Probably in Perea*—

Luke 16:1–13

[1]Jesus told his disciples: "There was a rich man whose manager was accused of wasting his possessions. [2]So he called him in and asked him, 'What is this I hear about you? Give an account of your management, because you cannot be manager any longer.'

[3]"The manager said to himself, 'What shall I do now? My master is taking away my job. I'm not strong enough to dig, and I'm ashamed to beg— [4]I know what I'll do so that, when I lose my job here, people will welcome me into their houses.'

[5]"So he called in each one of his master's debtors. He asked the first, 'How much do you owe my master?'

[6]" 'Eight hundred gallons[a] of olive oil,' he replied.

"The manager told him, 'Take your bill, sit down quickly, and make it four hundred.'

[7]"Then he asked the second, 'And how much do you owe?'

" 'A thousand bushels[b] of wheat,' he replied.

"He told him, 'Take your bill and make it eight hundred.'

[8]"The master commended the dishonest manager because he had acted shrewdly. For the people of this world are more shrewd in dealing with their own kind than are the people of the light. [9]I tell you, use worldly wealth to [d]gain friends for yourselves, so that when it is gone, you will be welcomed into eternal dwellings.

[10]"Whoever can be trusted with very little can also be trusted with much, and whoever is dishonest with very little will also be dishonest with much. [11]So if you have not been trustworthy in handling worldly wealth, who will trust you with true riches? [12]And if you have not been trustworthy with someone else's property, who will give you property of your own?

[13]"No servant can serve two masters. Either he will hate the one and love the other, or he will be devoted to the one and despise the other. You cannot serve both God and Money.' "

[a]Lk 16:6 Greek *one hundred batous* (probably about 3 kiloliters)   [b]7 Greek *one hundred korous* (probably about 35 kiloliters)

---

[d](Luke 16:9) The wisdom of using material possessions to provide for the future is commended but not the dishonesty by which the steward procured the possessions. Money in itself is not sinful. Money can be used to bring blessing to others and thereby make provision for a warm welcome by others in an eternal home. Thereby perishable riches can be transformed into imperishable heavenly treasures.

Sec. 117b   Story to teach the danger of wealth
(cf. Sec. 54d—permanence of the Law)
(cf. Secs. 54e, 122—divorce and remarriage)
—*Probably in Perea*—

Luke 16:14–31

¹⁴ᵉThe Pharisees, who loved money, heard all this and were sneering at Jesus. ¹⁵He said to them, "You are the ones who justify yourselves in the eyes of men, but God knows your hearts. What is highly valued among men is detestable in God's sight.

¹⁶"The Law and the Prophets were proclaimed until John. Since that time, the good news of the kingdom of God is being preached, and everyone is forcing his way into it. ¹⁷It is easier for heaven and earth to disappear than for the least stroke of a pen to drop out of the Law.

¹⁸"Anyone who divorces his wife and marries another woman commits adultery, and the man who marries a divorced woman commits adultery.

¹⁹"There was a rich man who was dressed in purple and fine linen and lived in luxury every day. ²⁰At his gate was laid a beggar named ᶠLazarus, covered with sores ²¹and longing to eat what fell from the rich man's table. Even the dogs came and licked his sores.

²²"The time came when the beggar died and the angels carried him to Abraham's side. The rich man also died and was buried. ²³In ᵍhell,ᵃ where he was in torment, he looked up and saw Abraham far away, with Lazarus by his side. ²⁴So he called to him, 'Father Abraham, have pity on me and send Lazarus to dip the tip of his finger in water and cool my tongue, because I am in agony in this fire.'

²⁵"But Abraham replied, 'Son, remember that in your lifetime you received your good things, while Lazarus received bad things, but now he is comforted here and you are in agony. ²⁶And besides all this, between us and you a great chasm has been fixed, so that those who want to go from here to you cannot, nor can anyone cross over from there to us.'

²⁷"He answered, 'Then I beg you, father, send Lazarus to my father's house, ²⁸for I have five brothers. Let him warn them, so that they will not also come to this place of torment.'

²⁹"Abraham replied, 'They have Moses and the Prophets; let them listen to them.'

³⁰" 'No, father Abraham,' he said, 'but if someone from the dead goes to them, they will repent.'

³¹"He said to him, 'If they do not listen to Moses and the Prophets, they will not be convinced even if someone rises from the dead.' "

ᵃ23 Greek *Hades*

ᵉ(Luke 16:14) This highly condensed paragraph (vv. 14–18) introduces the story of the rich man and Lazarus. The avaricious Pharisees were addressed because of their reaction to his words to the disciples about money (Luke 16:13, Sec. 117a). He therefore spoke to the Pharisees in light of their persuasion that God had given them their wealth because they carefully kept the law. Their system of external observances did not satisfy God (v. 15) but amounted to an attempt to force their way into the kingdom of God (v. 16). By breaking the law, through such traditions as those that permitted divorce, they endeavored to change statutes that cannot be changed (vv. 17–18). Riches therefore were not a sign of God's favor, as the following story goes on to show (vv. 19–31).

ᶠ(Luke 16:20) Nowhere else does Jesus use a person's name in a parable. This story is often referred to as a parable, but is nowhere in the biblical text called one. It is therefore impossible to be sure that it was a parable and not a real happening.

ᵍ(Luke 16:23) "Hell" (literally, "Hades") in the New Testament is the abode of souls loosed from their bodies at death. For the ungodly it is a place of temporary retribution until their bodies are raised for judgment at the great white throne (Rev. 20:11–15). In this incident representing conditions before the resurrection of Christ, the godly are not specifically connected with Hades, but they are pictured in a state of rest in the underworld where Hades is located (Luke 16:26). Jesus was in Hades between his death and resurrection (Acts 2:27, 31). Since his resurrection, the godly are always found in his immediate presence (Phil. 1:23).

Sec. 117c Four lessons on discipleship
(cf. Sec. 91—warning against causing to sin)
—Probably in Perea—

Luke 17:1–10

[1]Jesus said to his disciples: "Things that cause people to sin are bound to come, but [h]woe to that person through whom they come. [2]It would be better for him to be thrown into the sea with a millstone tied around his neck than for him to cause one of these little ones to sin. [3]So watch yourselves.

"If your brother sins, rebuke him, and if he repents, forgive him. [4]If he sins against you seven times in a day, and seven times comes back to you and says, 'I repent,' forgive him."

[5]The apostles said to the Lord, "Increase our faith!"

[6]He replied, "If you have faith as small as a mustard seed, you can say to this mulberry tree, 'Be uprooted and planted in the sea,' and it will obey you.

[7]"Suppose one of you had a servant plowing or looking after the sheep. Would he say to the servant when he comes in from the field, 'Come along now and sit down to eat'? [8]Would he not rather say, 'Prepare my supper, get yourself ready and wait on me while I eat and drink; after that you may eat and drink'? [9]Would he thank the servant because he did what he was told to do? [10]So you also, when you have done everything you were told to do, should say, 'We are unworthy servants; we have only done our duty.' "

Sec. 118a Sickness and death of Lazarus
—From Perea to Bethany, near Jerusalem—

John 11:1–16

[1]Now a man named Lazarus was sick. He was from Bethany, the village of Mary and her sister Martha. [2]This Mary, whose brother Lazarus now lay sick, was the same one who poured perfume on the Lord and wiped his feet with her hair. [3]So the sisters sent word to Jesus, "Lord, the one you love is sick."

[4]When he heard this, Jesus said, "This sickness will not end in death. No, it is for God's glory so that God's Son may be glorified through it." [5]Jesus loved Martha and her sister and Lazarus. [6][i]Yet when he heard that Lazarus was sick, he stayed where he was two more days.

[7]Then he said to his disciples, "Let us go back to Judea."

[8]"But Rabbi," they said, "a short while ago [j]the Jews tried to stone you, and yet you are going back there?"

[9]Jesus answered, "Are there not twelve hours of daylight? A man who walks by day will not stumble, for he sees by this world's light. [10]It is when he walks by night that he stumbles, for he has no light."

[11]After he had said this, he went on to tell them, "Our friend Lazarus has fallen asleep; but I am going there to wake him up."

[12]His disciples replied, "Lord, if he sleeps, he will get better." [13]Jesus had been speaking of his death, but his disciples thought he meant natural sleep.

---

[h](Luke 17:1) The first of the four lessons is a warning against causing others to sin (vv. 1–2). The other three deal with the duty of forgiving a repentant brother (vv. 3–4), the power of faith (vv. 5–6), and the insufficiency of works to gain special honor (vv. 7–10).

[i](John 11:6) Although the NIV leaves it untranslated in three of the four occurrences, four unusual uses of the Greek particle *oun* mark the incident involving Lazarus. They apparently indicate four steps by which Jesus followed a sequence predetermined by the Father in carrying out this miracle:
1. Translated as *yet* in verse 6, it shows how he purposely delayed going to the scene.
2. In verse 17 (Sec. 118b) *oun* indicates the plan was for him to arrive four days after the death.
3. In verse 33 (Sec. 118b) *oun* points out his appointed response to the bereaved.
4. In verse 38 (Sec. 118b) *oun* shows the final step of going to the tomb to accomplish the miracle.
This procedure was clearly designed to bring glory to God and his son (v. 4).

[j](John 11:8) Bethany was only about two miles from Jerusalem, and the disciples remembered the recent attempted stoning in Jerusalem (John 10:31, Sec. 111). Jesus' response was that he, like everyone else, had to use his opportunities while present or else lose them. Danger could not be a deterrent.

John 11:1–16 (cont'd)

[14]So then he told them plainly, "Lazarus is dead, [15]and for your sake I am glad I was not there, so that you may believe. But let us go to him."

[16]Then Thomas (called Didymus) said to the rest of the disciples, "Let us also go, that we may die with him."

Sec. 118b   Lazarus raised from the dead
—Bethany, near Jerusalem—

John 11:17–44

[17]On his arrival, Jesus found that Lazarus had already been in the tomb for four days. [18]Bethany was less than two miles[a] from Jerusalem, [19]and many Jews had come to Martha and Mary to comfort them in the loss of their brother. [20]When Martha heard that Jesus was coming, she went out to meet him, but Mary stayed at home.

[21]"Lord," Martha said to Jesus, "if you had been here, my brother would not have died. [22]But I know that even now God will give you whatever you ask."

[23]Jesus said to her, "Your brother will rise again."

[24]Martha answered, "I know he will rise again in the resurrection at the last day."

[25]Jesus said to her, "I am the resurrection and the life. He who believes in me will live, even though he dies; [26]and whoever lives and believes in me will never die. Do you believe this?"

[27]"Yes, Lord," she told him, "[k]I believe that you are the Christ,[b] the Son of God, who was to come into the world."

[28]And after she had said this, she went back and called her sister Mary aside. "The Teacher is here," she said, "and is asking for you." [29]When Mary heard this, she got up quickly and went to him. [30]Now Jesus had not yet entered the village, but was still at the place where Martha had met him. [31]When the Jews who had been with Mary in the house, comforting her, noticed how quickly she got up and went out, they followed her, supposing she was going to the tomb to mourn there.

[32]When Mary reached the place where Jesus was and saw him, she fell at his feet and said, "Lord, if you had been here, my brother would not have died."

[33]When Jesus saw her weeping, and the Jews who had come along with her also weeping, he was deeply moved in spirit and troubled. [34]"Where have you laid him?" he asked.

"Come and see, Lord," they replied.

[35][l]Jesus wept.

[36]Then the Jews said, "See how he loved him!"

[37]But some of them said, "Could not he who opened the eyes of the blind man have kept this man from dying?"

[38]Jesus, once more deeply moved, came to the tomb. It was a cave with a stone laid across the entrance. [39]"Take away the stone," he said.

"But, Lord," said Martha, the sister of the dead man, "by this time there is a bad odor, for he has been there four days."

[40]Then Jesus said, "Did I not tell you that if you believed, you would see the glory of God?"

---

[k](John 11:27) Whatever fault she may have had (cf. Luke 10:41, Sec. 104), Martha was a woman of faith in and conviction about the person of Christ. Her threefold confession here represents the highest view of him one can hold.

[l](John 11:35) This verse has been subjected to a wide variety of interpretations. Certainly he did not weep because of the loss of Lazarus whom he was about to raise. His intense emotion (cf. v. 33) probably related somehow to the dominance of sin in these surroundings. Through sin, death had gained its power. Through it the mourners were misguided in their concept of death. Because of it he was about to call Lazarus from a far better existence back to mortality. Because of it Jesus himself became a criminal in the eyes of the authorities (Sec. 119). It is no wonder that John used a word usually reserved for anger when describing his response to the situation ("was deeply moved," v. 33).

John 11:17–44 (cont'd)

[41]So they took away the stone. Then Jesus looked up and said, "Father, I thank you that you have heard me. [42]I knew that you always hear me, but I said this for the benefit of the people standing here, that they may believe that you sent me." [43m]When he had said this, Jesus called in a loud voice, "Lazarus, come out!" [44m]The dead man came out, his hands and feet wrapped with strips of linen, and a cloth around his face.

Jesus said to them, "Take off the grave clothes and let him go."

   [a]Jn 11:18 Greek *fifteen stadia* (about 3 kilometers)   [b]27 Or *Messiah*

Sec. 119   Decision of the Sanhedrin to put Jesus to death
—*Jerusalem and [n]Ephraim, near the desert*—

John 11:45–54

[45]Therefore many of the Jews who had come to visit Mary, and had seen what Jesus did, put their faith in him. [46]But some of them went to the Pharisees and told them what Jesus had done. [47]Then the [o]chief priests and the Pharisees called a meeting of the Sanhedrin.

"What are we accomplishing?" they asked. "Here is this man performing many miraculous signs. [48]If we let him go on like this, everyone will believe in him, and then the Romans will come and take away both our place[a] and our nation."

[49]Then one of them, named Caiaphas, who was high priest that year, spoke up, "You know nothing at all! [50]You do not realize that [p]it is better for you that one man die for the people than that the whole nation perish."

[51]He did not say this on his own, but as high priest that year he prophesied that Jesus would die for the Jewish nation, [52]and not only for that nation but also for the scattered children of God, to bring them together and make them one. [53]So from that day on [q]they plotted to take his life.

[54]Therefore Jesus no longer moved about publicly among the Jews. Instead he withdrew to a region near the desert, to a village called Ephraim, where he stayed with his disciples.

   [a]Jn 11:48 Or *temple*

[m](John 11:44) It has been of great concern to many that the synoptic gospels say nothing of this highly significant miracle. For some reason the synoptic writers pass over other significant Jerusalem miracles (Secs. 49a, 100a) too. They are likewise noticeably silent about other happenings that came one to two months before Passion Week. Apparently they felt that the two resurrections already recorded (Secs. 56, 67) were sufficient to show Jesus' power over death.

   [n]Ephraim was probably in northern Judea and near the rough terrain that leads down to the Jordan Valley.

   [o](John 11:47) The chief priests belonged to the Sadducean hierarchy, which took the lead in opposing Jesus from this point until the end. (The Pharisees had now become secondary opponents.) Now that the resurrection of a dead person had become the center of attention in Jerusalem, the Sadducees could do no other because of their teaching that denied resurrection.

   [p](John 11:50) As Caiaphas intended them, these words meant that Jesus must be put to death for the privileged class of Jews to maintain its authority under Roman occupation. But John observes that God, because of Caiaphas' high priestly office, was using the high priest's cynicism to voice something altogether different. Unwittingly the high priest predicted the substitutionary death of Christ for Israel and for all Gentiles who were destined to believe in him (vv. 51–52; cf. John 10:16, Sec. 101a).

   [q](John 11:53) This occasion marked the official agreement of the Sanhedrin (cf. v. 47) to have Jesus executed, even though this may well not have been a formal meeting of the council. On the basis of Caiaphas' advice, these leaders came to a settled decision as to what must be done to rid themselves of this rival authority figure.

TEACHING WHILE ON FINAL JOURNEY
TO JERUSALEM

Sec. 120a Healing of ten lepers while passing through Samaria and Galilee
—Samaria and Galilee—

Luke 17:11–21

[11]Now on his way to Jerusalem, Jesus traveled [r]along the border between Samaria and Galilee. [12]As he was going into a village, ten men who had leprosy[a] met him. They stood at a distance [13]and called out in a loud voice, "Jesus, Master, have pity on us!"

[14]When he saw them, he said, "Go, show yourselves to the priests." And as they went, they were cleansed.

[15]One of them, when he saw he was healed, came back, praising God in a loud voice. [16]He threw himself at Jesus' feet and thanked him—and he was a Samaritan.

[17]Jesus asked, "Were not all ten cleansed? Where are the other nine? [18]Was no one found to return and give praise to God except this foreigner?" [19]Then he said to him, "Rise and go; your faith has made you well."

[20]Once, having been asked by the Pharisees when the kingdom of God would come, Jesus replied, "The kingdom of God does not come with your careful observation, [21]nor will people say, 'Here it is,' or 'There it is,' because the kingdom of God is [s]within[b] you."

[a]Lk 17:12 The Greek word was used for various diseases affecting the skin—not necessarily leprosy.   [b]21 Or *among*

Sec. 120b Instructions regarding the Son of Man's coming
(cf. Secs. 139c–139e—signs of Christ's return)
—Samaria or Galilee—

Luke 17:22–37

[22]Then he said to his disciples, "The time is coming when you will long to see one of the days of the Son of Man, but you will not see it. [23]Men will tell you, 'There he is!' or 'Here he is!' Do not go running off after them. [24]For the Son of Man in his day[a] will be like the lightning, which flashes and lights up the sky from one end to the other. [25]But first he must suffer many things and be rejected by this generation.

[26]"Just as it was in the days of Noah, so also will it be in the days of the Son of Man. [27]People were eating, drinking, marrying and being given in marriage up to the day Noah entered the ark. Then the flood came and destroyed them all.

[28]"It was the same in the days of Lot. People were eating and drinking, buying and selling, planting and building. [29]But the day Lot left Sodom, fire and sulfur rained down from heaven and destroyed them all.

---

[r](Luke 17:11) This verse may be translated so as to indicate either that Jesus passed between Samaria and Galilee, or that he passed through Samaria and Galilee. It is difficult to know what the former might mean, except perhaps that it might describe a journey through a stretch of disputed territory between Samaria and Galilee. The editors prefer the translation *through*. It fits best the probable sequence, so far as it can be reconstructed. Jesus had gone to Ephraim, a city in a remote northern district of Judea and near Samaria (Sec. 119). From there he went through Samaria and Galilee, probably to join the pilgrims traveling from Galilee, through Perea, to Jerusalem for the Passover. This explains why he would go north (through Samaria and Galilee) to go south (to Jerusalem).

[s](Luke 17:21) The kingdom of God was certainly not "within" the Pharisees, who were the ones addressed, though usage of the expression permits this meaning. Nor is it "with [their] careful observation," as the NIV proposes. The historical situation requires a reference to the kingdom as present "among you," i.e., the Pharisees. This is the kingdom whose arrival Jesus had already announced (Matt. 12:28, Sec. 61; Luke 11:20, Sec. 106), but that for the present was found in a form not predicted in the Old Testament (Matt. 13:1–52, Sec. 64a–64k) because of his rejection by Israel. In subsequent verses Jesus proceeds to speak of the coming of the kingdom as the disciples knew it from the Old Testament (Sec. 120b). This would come only after the Son of Man's rejection by that generation, however (Luke 17:24–25, Sec. 120b).

Luke 17:22–37 (cont'd)

[30]"It will be just like this on the day the Son of Man is revealed. [31]On that day no one who is on the roof of his house, with his goods inside, should go down to get them. Likewise, no one in the field should go back for anything. [32]Remember Lot's wife! [33]Whoever tries to keep his life will lose it, and whoever loses his life will preserve it. [34]I tell you, on that night two people will be in one bed; 'one will be taken and the other left. [35]Two women will be grinding grain together; 'one will be taken and the other left.[b]"

[37]"Where, Lord?" they asked.

He replied, "Where there is a dead body, there the vultures will gather."

[a]*Lk 17:24* Some manuscripts do not have *in his day.*   [b]35 Some manuscripts *left.* [36]*Two men will be in the field; 'one will be taken and the other left.*

Sec. 121 Two parables on prayer: the persistent widow, and the Pharisee and the tax collector
(cf. Sec. 54f—unhypocritical prayer)
(cf. Sec. 105—persistent prayer)
—*Itineration toward Jerusalem*—

Luke 18:1–14

[1]Then Jesus told his disciples a parable to show them that they should always pray and not give up. [2]He said: "In a certain town there was a judge who neither feared God nor cared about men. [3]And there was a widow in that town who kept coming to him with the plea, 'Grant me justice against my adversary.'

[4]"For some time he refused. But finally he said to himself, 'Even though I don't fear God or care about men, [5]yet because this widow keeps bothering me, I will see that she gets justice, so that she won't eventually wear me out with her coming!' "

[6]And the Lord said, "Listen to what the unjust judge says. [7]And will not God bring about justice for his chosen ones, who cry out to him day and night? Will he keep putting them off? [8]I tell you, [u]he will see that they get justice, and quickly. However, when the Son of Man comes, will he find faith on the earth?"

[9]To [v]some who were confident of their own righteousness and looked down on everybody else, Jesus told this parable: [10]"Two men went up to the temple to pray, one a Pharisee and the other a tax collector. [11]The Pharisee stood up and prayed about[a] himself: 'God, I thank you that I am not like other men—robbers, evildoers, adulterers—or even like this tax collector. [12]I fast twice a week and give a tenth of all I get.'

[13]"But the tax collector stood at a distance. He would not even look up to heaven, but beat his breast and said, 'God, have mercy on me, a sinner.'

[14]"I tell you that this man, rather than the other, went home justified before God. For everyone who exalts himself will be humbled, and he who humbles himself will be exalted."

[a]*Lk 18:11* Or *to*

[t](Luke 17:34–35) A final separation will come when the Son of Man is revealed. The unprepared, who are dominated by worldly pursuits, will be overtaken by judgment as in the illustrations above (vv. 26–29, 32), but the faithful will enter the joys of the kingdom.

[u](Luke 18:8) Continuing the theme of the previous section (Sec. 120b), the Lord went on to prepare his disciples for a delay in his return. The parable taught them not to be discouraged by the delay but to persist in faith and prayer, knowing that he will certainly return to institute justice speedily.

[v](Luke 18:9) The parable was probably addressed to Pharisees, perhaps the ones who had asked a little while earlier when the kingdom of God was coming (Luke 17:20, Sec. 120a). Their proud attitude prevented their prayers from being heard. Such as the tax collector, on the other hand, were heard because of their humility.

Sec. 122   Confict with Pharisaic teaching on divorce
(cf. Secs. 54e, 117b—divorce and remarriage)
—Perea—

Matthew 19:1–12

[1]When Jesus had finished saying these things, he left Galilee and went into the region of Judea to the other side of the Jordan. [2]Large crowds followed him, and he healed them there.

[3]Some Pharisees came to him to test him. They asked, "Is it lawful for a man to divorce his wife for any and every reason?"

[4]"Haven't you read," he replied, "that at the beginning the Creator 'made them male and female'[a] [Gen. 1:27; 5:2], [5]and said, 'For this reason a man will leave his father and mother and be united to his wife, and the two will become one flesh'[b]? [Gen. 2:24], [6]So they are no longer two, but one. Therefore what God has joined together, let man not separate."

[7]"[w]Why then," they asked, "did Moses command that a man give his wife a certificate of divorce and send her away?" [Deut. 24:1–4].

[8]Jesus replied, "Moses permitted you to divorce your wives because your hearts were hard. But it was not this way from the beginning. [9]I tell you that anyone who divorces his wife, except for marital unfaithfulness, and marries another woman commits adultery."

[10]The disciples said to him, "If this is the situation between a husband and wife, it is better not to marry."

[11]Jesus replied, "Not everyone can accept this word, but only those to whom it has been given. [12]For some are eunuchs because they were born that way; others were made that way by men; and others have renounced marriage[c] because of the kingdom of heaven. The

Mark 10:1–12

[1]Jesus then left that place and went into the region of Judea and across the Jordan. Again crowds of people came to him, and as was his custom, he taught them.

[2]Some Pharisees came and tested him by asking, "Is it lawful for a man to divorce his wife?"

[3]"What did Moses command you?" he replied.

[4]They said, "Moses permitted a man to write a certificate of divorce and send her away" [Deut. 24:1–4].

[5]"It was because your hearts were hard that Moses wrote you this law," Jesus replied. [6]"But at the beginning of creation God 'made them male and female'[d] [Gen. 1:27; 5:2]. [7]For this reason a man will leave his father and mother and be united to his wife,[e] [8]and the two will become one flesh'[f] [Gen. 2:24]. So they are no longer two, but one. [9]Therefore what God has joined together, let man not separate."

[10]When they were in the house again, the disciples asked Jesus about this.

[11]He answered, "Anyone who divorces his wife and marries another woman commits adultery against her. [12]And if she divorces her husband and marries another man, she commits adultery."

---

[w](Matt. 19:7) In light of Jesus' view of the indissolubility of the marriage union, his enemies thought they had finally caught him teaching contrary to Moses. Jesus easily relieved the contradiction, however, by showing that Moses only permitted divorce because of the moral insensitivity that prevailed following the slavery in Egypt. The Pharisees gave more attention to the *concession* of Deuteronomy 24:1–4 than they did to the *institution* of marriage of Genesis 2:24. Moses commanded the latter (Mark 10:3), but he only permitted the former (Matt. 19:8).

Matthew 19:1–12 (cont'd)

one who can accept this should accept
it."

^aMt 19:4 Gen. 1:27   ^b5 Gen. 2:24   ^c12 Or *have made themselves eunuchs*   ^dMk 10:6 Gen. 1:27
^e7 Some early manuscripts do not have *and be united to his wife.*   ^f8 Gen. 2:24

Sec. 123   Example of little children in relation to the kingdom
(cf. Sec. 90—example of little children)
—Perea—

Matthew 19:13–15	Mark 10:13–16	Luke 18:15–17
¹³Then little children were brought to Jesus for him to place his hands on them and pray for them. But the disciples rebuked those who brought them. ¹⁴Jesus said, "Let the little children come to me, and do not hinder them, for the kingdom of heaven belongs to such as these."	¹³People were bringing little children to Jesus to have him touch them, but the disciples rebuked them. ¹⁴When Jesus saw this, he was indignant. He said to them, "Let the little children come to me, and do not hinder them, for the kingdom of God belongs to such as these. ¹⁵I tell you the truth, anyone who will not receive the kingdom of God like a little child will never enter it." ¹⁶And he took the children in his arms, put his hands on them and blessed them.	¹⁵People were also bringing babies to Jesus to have him touch them. When the disciples saw this, they rebuked them. ¹⁶But Jesus called the children to him and said, "Let the little children come to me, and do not hinder them, for the kingdom of God belongs to such as these. ¹⁷I tell you the truth, anyone who will not receive the kingdom of God like a little child will never enter it."
¹⁵When he had placed his hands on them, he went on from there.		

Sec. 124a   Riches and the kingdom
(cf. Secs. 113a, 124b—last first and first last)
—Perea—

Matthew 19:16–30	Mark 10:17–31	Luke 18:18–30
¹⁶Now a man came up to Jesus and asked, "Teacher, what good thing must I do to get eternal life?" ¹⁷"Why do you ask me about what is good?" Jesus replied. "There is only One who is good. If you want to enter life, obey the commandments." ¹⁸"Which ones?" the man inquired. Jesus replied, " 'Do not murder, do not commit adultery, do not steal, do	¹⁷As Jesus started on his way, a man ran up to him and fell on his knees before him. "Good teacher," he asked, "what must I do to inherit eternal life?" ¹⁸"Why do you call me good?" Jesus answered. "No one is good—except God alone. ¹⁹You know the commandments: 'Do not murder, do not commit adultery, do not steal, do not give false testimony, do not defraud, honor your father and moth-	¹⁸A certain ruler asked him, "Good teacher, what must I do to inherit eternal life?" ¹⁹"Why do you call me good?" Jesus answered. "No one is good—except God alone. ²⁰You know the commandments: 'Do not commit adultery, do not murder, do not steal, do not give false testimony, honor your father and mother'^f" [Exod. 20:12–16; Deut. 5:16–20].

Matthew 19:16–30(cont'd)

Mark 10:17–31(cont'd)

Luke 18:18–30 (cont'd)

not give false testimony, [19]honor your father and mother'[a] [Exod. 20:12–16; Deut. 5:16–20], and 'love your neighbor as yourself'[b]" [Lev. 19:18].

er'[d]" [Exod. 20:12–16; Deut. 5:16–20].

[20]"All these I have kept," the young man said. "What do I still lack?"
[21]Jesus answered, "If you want to be perfect, go, sell your possessions and give to the poor, and you will have treasure in heaven. Then come, follow me."
[22]When the young man heard this, he went away sad, because he had great wealth.
[23]Then Jesus said to his disciples, "I tell you the truth, it is hard for a rich man to enter the kingdom of heaven.

[20]"Teacher," he declared, "all these I have kept since I was a boy."
[21]Jesus looked at him and loved him. "One thing you lack," he said. "Go, sell everything you have and give to the poor, and you will have treasure in heaven. Then come, follow me."
[22]At this the man's face fell. He went away sad, because he had great wealth.
[23]Jesus looked around and said to his disciples, "How hard it is for the rich to enter the kingdom of God!"
[24]The disciples were amazed at his words. But Jesus said again, "Children, how hard it is[e] to enter the kingdom of God!

[21]"All these I have kept since I was a boy," he said.
[22]When Jesus heard this, he said to him, "You still lack one thing. Sell everything you have and give to the poor, and you will have treasure in heaven. Then come, follow me."
[23]When he heard this, he became very sad, because he was a man of great wealth. [24]Jesus looked at him and said, "How hard it is for the rich to enter the kingdom of God!

[24]Again I tell you, it is easier for a camel to go through the eye of a needle than for a rich man to enter the kingdom of God."
[25]When the disciples heard this, they were [x]greatly astonished and asked, "Who then can be saved?"
[26]Jesus looked at them and said, "With man this is impossible, but with God all things are possible."
[27]Peter answered him, "We have left everything to follow you! What then will there be for us?"

[25]It is easier for a camel to go through the eye of a needle than for a rich man to enter the kingdom of God."
[26]The disciples were [x]even more amazed, and said to each other, "Who then can be saved?"
[27]Jesus looked at them and said, "With man this is impossible, but not with God; all things are possible with God."
[28]Peter said to him, "We have left everything to follow you!"

[25]Indeed, it is easier for a camel to go through the eye of a needle than for a rich man to enter the kingdom of God."
[26]Those who heard this asked, "Who then can be saved?"
[27]Jesus replied, "What is impossible with men is possible with God."
[28]Peter said to him, "We have left all we had to follow you!"

---

[x](Matt. 19:25; Mark 10:26) It was inconceivable in contemporary Judaism that wealth should be a hindrance to entering the kingdom of God, because this was considered to be a sign of God's favor. When properly used to help the needy (Deut. 15:7–8, 11), wealth did give opportunity for demonstrating personal piety and could be construed as a work of God's blessing (Job 1:10; 42:10), but too many of Jesus' day, including this ruler, had succumbed to the temptation to place a higher premium on material things than on God.

Matthew 19:16–30(cont'd)	Mark 10:17–31 (cont'd)	Luke 18:18–30 (cont'd)
[28]Jesus said to them, "I tell you the truth, at the ʸrenewal of all things, when the Son of Man sits on his glorious throne, you who have followed me will also sit on twelve thrones, judging the twelve tribes of Israel. [29]And everyone who has left houses or brothers or sisters or father or mother[c] or children or fields for my sake will receive a hundred times as much and	[29]"I tell you the truth," Jesus replied, "no one who has left home or brothers or sisters or mother or father or children or fields for me and the gospel [30]will fail to receive a hundred times as much in this present age (homes, brothers, sisters, mothers, children and fields—and with them, persecutions) and in the age to come, eternal life. [31]But many who are first will be last, and the last first."	[29]"I tell you the truth," Jesus said to them, "no one who has left home or wife or brothers or parents or children for the sake of the kingdom of God [30]will fail to receive many times as much in this age and, in the age to come, eternal life."
will inherit eternal life. [30]But many who are first will be last, and many who are last will be first.		

[a]Mt 19:19 Exodus 20:12-16; Deut. 5:16-20   [b]19 Lev. 19:18   [c]29 Some manuscripts *mother or wife*
[d]Mk 10:19 Exodus 20:12-16 Deut. 5:16-20   [e]24 Some manuscripts *is for those who trust in riches*
[f]Lk 18:20 Exodus 20:12-16; Deut. 5:16-20

Sec. 124b Parable of the landowner's sovereignty
   (cf. Secs. 113a, 124a—last first and first last)
   —Perea—

Matthew 20:1–16

[1]"For the kingdom of heaven is like a landowner who went out early in the morning to hire men to work in his vineyard. [2]He agreed to pay them a denarius for the day and sent them into his vineyard.

[3]"About the third hour he went out and saw others standing in the marketplace doing nothing. [4]He told them, 'You also go and work in my vineyard, and I will pay you whatever is right.' [5]So they went.

"He went out again about the sixth hour and the ninth hour and did the same thing. [6]About the eleventh hour he went out and found still others standing around. He asked them, 'Why have you been standing here all day long doing nothing?'

[7]" 'Because no one has hired us,' they answered.

"He said to them, 'You also go and work in my vineyard.'

[8]"When evening came, the owner of the vineyard said to his foreman, 'Call the workers and pay them their wages, beginning with the last ones hired and going on to the first.'

[9]"The workers who were hired about the eleventh hour came and each received a denarius. [10]So when those came who were hired first, they expected to receive more. But each one of them also received a denarius. [11]When they received it, they

ʸ(Matt. 19:28) "Renewal of all things" (literally, *regeneration*) describes the world's restored condition when Messiah returns to fulfill the long-anticipated Old Testament promises of the kingdom. The people of Israel will once again be central objects in God's dealings with the world, and these twelve (excluding Judas, of course) will occupy places of authority over them. This teaching, following Jesus' shocking statement about how hard it is to enter the kingdom of God (Mark 10:24), must have been quite a relief to them.

Matthew 20:1–16 (cont'd)

began to grumble against the landowner. [12]'These men who were hired last worked only one hour,' they said, 'and you have made them equal to us who have borne the burden of the work and the heat of the day.'

[13]"But he answered one of them, 'Friend, I am not being unfair to you. Didn't you agree to work for a denarius? [14]Take your pay and go. I want to give the man who was hired last the same as I gave you. [15z]Don't I have the right to do what I want with my own money? Or are you envious because I am generous?'

[16]"So the last will be first, and the first will be last."

Sec. 125a   Third prediction of Jesus' death and resurrection
(cf. Secs. 83, 85, 86, 88—prophecies of death and resurrection)
—On the road up to Jerusalem—

Matthew 20:17–19	Mark 10:32–34	Luke 18:31–34
[17]Now as Jesus was going up to Jerusalem,	[32]They were on their way up to Jerusalem, with Jesus leading the way, and the disciples were astonished, while those who followed were [a]afraid. Again he took the	[31]Jesus took the Twelve aside and told them, "We are going up to Jerusalem, and everything that is written by the prophets about the Son of Man will be fulfilled. [32]He will be handed over to the Gentiles. They will mock him, insult him, spit on him, flog him and kill him.
he took the twelve disciples aside and said to them, [18]"We are going up to Jerusalem, and the Son of Man will be betrayed to the chief priests and the teachers of the law. They will condemn him to death [19]and will turn him over to the Gentiles to be mocked and flogged and crucified. On the third day he will be raised to life!"	Twelve aside and told them what was going to happen to him. [33]"We are going up to Jerusalem," he said, "and the Son of Man will be betrayed to the chief priests and teachers of the law. They will condemn him to death and will hand him over to the Gentiles, [34]who will mock him and spit on him, flog him and kill him. Three days later he will rise."	[33]On the third day he will rise again." [34]The disciples did not understand any of this. Its meaning was hidden from them, and they did not know what he was talking about.

z(Matt. 20:15) In further response to Peter's question of Matt. 19:27 (Sec. 124a), Jesus warned against the Twelve's assuming that their favored position in the kingdom would be the result of longer service or more work performed. Ultimately all rewards will issue from the sovereign grace of God, who may, on the basis of his judgment of motives, grant richer rewards to those who have labored less.

a(Mark 10:32) This was probably a fear of what Jesus' enemies would do to him once he arrived in Jerusalem (cf. John 11:8, Sec. 118a). In spite of his reiterated prophecy of suffering and resurrection, the Twelve did not comprehend yet (Luke 18:34) because they still anticipated a mighty Messianic conqueror who would establish his kingdom on earth. In three years of instruction Jesus had not denied them this hope, but taught them that this hope must wait a little longer before realization (cf. Sec. 127b).

Sec. 125b   Warning against ambitious pride
(cf. Sec. 144—rivalry over greatness)
—On the road up to Jerusalem—

Matthew 20:20–28	Mark 10:35–45
[20]Then the mother of Zebedee's sons came to Jesus with her sons and, kneeling down, [b]asked a favor of him. [21]"What is it you want?" he asked. She said, "Grant that one of these two sons of mine may sit at your right and the other at your left in your kingdom."	[35]Then James and John, the sons of Zebedee, came to him. "Teacher," they [b]said, "we want you to do for us whatever we ask." [36]"What do you want me to do for you?" he asked. [37]They replied, "Let one of us sit at your right and the other at your left in your glory."
[22]"You don't know what you are asking," Jesus said to them. "Can you drink the cup I am going to drink?" "We can," they answered. [23]Jesus said to them, "You will indeed drink from my cup,	[38]"You don't know what you are asking," Jesus said. "Can you drink the cup I drink or be baptized with the baptism I am baptized with?" [39]"We can," they answered. Jesus said to them, "You will drink the cup I drink and be baptized with the baptism I am baptized with, [40]but to sit at my right or left is not for me to grant. These places belong to those for whom they have been prepared."
but to sit at my right or left is not for me to grant. These places belong to those for whom they have been prepared by my Father." [24]When the ten heard about this, they were indignant with the two brothers. [25]Jesus called them together and said, "You know that the rulers of the Gentiles lord it over them, and their high officials exercise authority over them. [26]Not so with you. Instead, whoever wants to become great among you must be your servant, [27]and whoever wants to be first must be your slave— [28]just as the Son of Man did not come to be served, but to serve, and to give his life as a ransom for many."	[41]When the ten heard about this, they became indignant with James and John. [42]Jesus called them together and said, "You know that those who are regarded as rulers of the Gentiles lord it over them, and their high officials exercise authority over them. [43]Not so with you. Instead, whoever wants to become great among you must be your servant, [44]and whoever wants to be first must be slave of all. [45]For even the Son of Man did not come to be served, but to serve, and to give his life as a ransom for many."

Sec. 126   Healing of blind Bartimaeus and his companion
(cf. Sec. 68—healing the blind)
—Jericho—

Matthew 20:29–34	Mark 10:46–52	Luke 18:35–43
[29]As Jesus and his disciples were leaving Jericho, a large crowd followed him.	[46]Then they came to Jericho. As Jesus and his disciples, together with a large crowd, were leaving the city, [c]a blind man, Bar-	[35]As Jesus approached Jericho,

---

[b](Matt. 20:20; Mark 10:35) This request for places of honor showed a continuing feeling among the disciples that Jesus was going to Jerusalem to restore the glory of the fallen throne and kingdom of David. This was a normal, though selfish, reaction to Jesus' recent words about the Twelve's occupancy of twelve thrones in that kingdom (Matt. 19:28, Sec. 124a). Not only had James and John missed the point in regard to humility, they had also failed to grasp the necessity of delay because of Messiah's coming passion.

[c](Matt. 20:30; Mark 10:46; Luke 18:35) As in an earlier case, Matthew describes two victims and Mark and Luke write about only one (Sec. 66). The second and third gospels single out the more vocal of the pair. The miracle was apparently performed as Jesus left the city (Matt. 20:29; Mark 10:46), though he first encountered the men when he approached the city (Luke 18:35).

Matthew 20:29–34 (cont'd)	Mark 10:46–52 (cont'd)	Luke 18:35–43 (cont'd)
	timaeus (that is, the Son of Timaeus), was sitting by the roadside begging.	ᶜa blind man was sitting by the roadside begging. ³⁶When he heard the crowd going by, he asked what was happening. ³⁷They told him,
³⁰ᶜTwo blind men were sitting by the roadside, and when they heard that Jesus was going by, they shouted, "Lord, Son of David, have mercy on us!"	⁴⁷When he heard that it was Jesus of Nazareth, he began to shout, "Jesus, Son of David, have mercy on me!"	"Jesus of Nazareth is passing by." ³⁸He called out, "Jesus, Son of David, have mercy on me!"
³¹The crowd rebuked them and told them to be quiet, but they shouted all the louder, "Lord, ᵈSon of David, have mercy on us!"	⁴⁸Many rebuked him and told him to be quiet, but he shouted all the more, "ᵈSon of David, have mercy on me!"	³⁹Those who led the way rebuked him and told him to be quiet, but he shouted all the more, "ᵈSon of David, have mercy on me!"
³²Jesus stopped and called them.	⁴⁹Jesus stopped and said, "Call him." So they called to the blind man, "Cheer up! On your feet! He's calling you." ⁵⁰Throwing his cloak aside, he jumped to his feet and came to Jesus.	⁴⁰Jesus stopped and ordered the man to be brought to him. When he came near, Jesus asked him, ⁴¹"What do you want me to do for you?"
"What do you want me to do for you?" he asked.	⁵¹"What do you want me to do for you?" Jesus asked him. The blind man said, "Rabbi, I want to see."	"Lord, I want to see," he replied. ⁴²Jesus said to him, "Receive your sight; your faith has healed you."
³³"Lord," they answered, "we want our sight." ³⁴Jesus had compassion on them and touched their eyes. Immediately they received their sight and followed him.	⁵²"Go," said Jesus, "your faith has healed you." Immediately he received his sight and followed Jesus along the road.	⁴³Immediately he received his sight and followed Jesus, praising God. When all the people saw it, they also praised God.

Sec. 127a   Salvation of Zaccheus
—Jericho—

Luke 19:1–10

¹Jesus entered Jericho and was passing through. ²A man was there by the name of Zacchaeus; he was a chief tax collector and was wealthy. ³He wanted to see who Jesus was, but being a short man he could not, because of the crowd. ⁴So he ran ahead and climbed a sycamore-fig tree to see him, since Jesus was coming that way.

⁵When Jesus reached the spot, he looked up and said to him, "Zacchaeus, come down immediately. I must stay at your house today." ⁶So he came down at once and welcomed him gladly.

⁷All the people saw this and began to mutter, "He has gone to be the guest of a 'sinner.' "

ᵈ(Matt. 20:31; Mark 10:48; Luke 18:38) The title *Son of David* is a Messianic title. Like the Twelve, these blind men looked upon Jesus not only as one who could restore their sight (Isa. 35:5) but also as one who would fulfill the promises made to David (2 Sam. 7:12–16; Psalm 89; Isa. 11:1–9; Jer. 23:5–6; Ezek. 34:23–24).

Luke 19:1–10 (cont'd)

⁸But Zacchaeus stood up and said to the Lord, "Look, Lord! Here and now I give half of my possessions to the poor, and if I have cheated anybody out of anything, I will pay back four times the amount."

⁹Jesus said to him, "Today salvation has come to this house, because this man, too, is a ᵉson of Abraham. ¹⁰For the Son of Man came to seek and to save what was lost."

Sec. 127b Parable to teach responsibility while the kingdom is delayed (cf. Sec. 139f—faithful handling of the Lord's possessions)
—Jericho and the final trip up to Jerusalem—

Luke 19:11–28

¹¹While they were listening to this, he went on to tell them a parable, because he was near Jerusalem and the people thought that the kingdom of God was going to appear ᶠat once. ¹²He said: "ᵍA man of noble birth went to a distant country to have himself appointed king and then to return. ¹³So he called ten of his servants and gave them ten minas.ᵃ 'Put this money to work,' he said, 'until I come back.'

¹⁴"But his subjects hated him and sent a delegation after him to say, 'We don't want this man to be our king.'

¹⁵"He was made king, however, and returned home. Then he sent for the servants to whom he had given the money, in order to find out what they had gained with it.

¹⁶"The first one came and said, 'Sir, your mina has earned ten more.'

¹⁷" 'Well done, my good servant!' his master replied. 'Because you have been trustworthy in a very small matter, take charge of ten cities.'

¹⁸"The second came and said, 'Sir, your mina has earned five more.'

¹⁹"His master answered, 'You take charge of five cities.'

²⁰"Then another servant came and said, 'Sir, here is your mina; I have kept it laid away in a piece of cloth. ²¹I was afraid of you, because you are a hard man. You take out what you did not put in and reap what you did not sow.'

²²"His master replied, 'I will judge you by your own words, you wicked servant! You knew, did you, that I am a hard man, taking out what I did not put in, and reaping what I did not sow? ²³Why then didn't you put my money on deposit, so that when I came back, I could have collected it with interest?'

²⁴"Then he said to those standing by, 'Take his mina away from him and give it to the one who has ten minas.'

²⁵" 'Sir,' they said, 'he already has ten!'

²⁶"He replied, 'I tell you that ʰto everyone who has, more will be given, but as for the one who has nothing, even what he has will be taken away. ²⁷But those enemies of mine who did not want me to be king over them—bring them here and kill them in front of me.' "

²⁸After Jesus had said this, he went on ahead, going up to Jerusalem.

ᵃLk 19:13 A mina was about three months' wages.

ᵉ(Luke 19:9) The despised calling of tax collector could not nullify the birthright of Zaccheus. It was a matter of divine compulsion (cf. "must," v. 5) that he be offered an opportunity to repent. Jesus' insistence on reaching out to the tax collectors, (Luke 15:1–2, Sec. 116) had visible fruit in this instance.

ᶠ(Luke 19:11) Spoken when the party was in Jericho, only fifteen miles from Jerusalem, these words were designed to prepare the listeners for what might be an extended delay before institution of the kingdom on earth. By this time Jesus' followers expected him to ascend the throne of David upon his arrival in Jerusalem.

ᵍ(Luke 19:12) Archelaus, son of Herod the Great, who had built a palace at Jericho, had made a similar visit to Rome to receive for himself a vassal kingdom from the Roman government (cf. Matt. 2:22, Sec. 16). That historical incident may have suggested the structuring of this parable.

ʰ(Luke 19:26) The lesson of the parable is twofold:
1. While awaiting the kingdom to be ushered in by the King's return, the disciples were to apply themselves diligently to the King's business.
2. The Jews who refused to acknowledge him as King were given a stern warning regarding the heavy retribution brought on by their rejection (v. 27).

PART TEN
THE FORMAL PRESENTATION OF CHRIST TO ISRAEL AND THE RESULTING CONFLICT

TRIUMPHAL ENTRY AND THE FIG TREE

Sec. 128a   Arrival at Bethany
—Bethany, near Jerusalem—

John 11:55–12:1, 9–11

[55]When it was almost time for the Jewish Passover, many went up from the country to Jerusalem for their ceremonial cleansing [i]before the Passover. [56]They kept looking for Jesus, and as they stood in the temple area they asked one another, "What do you think? [j]Isn't he coming to the Feast at all?" [57]But the chief priests and Pharisees had given orders that if anyone found out where Jesus was, he should report it so that they might arrest him.

[1k]Six days before the Passover, Jesus arrived at Bethany, where Lazarus lived, whom Jesus had raised from the dead.

[9]Meanwhile a large crowd of Jews found out that Jesus was there and came, not only because of him [l]but also to see Lazarus, whom he had raised from the dead. [10]So the chief priests made plans to kill Lazarus as well, [11]for on account of him many of the Jews were going over to Jesus and putting their faith in him.

[Mary's anointing of Jesus for burial
—Bethany, in the home of Simon the Leper—]

[m]Matthew 26:6–13   [m]Mark 14:3–9   [m]John 12:2–8

---

[i](John 11:55) Because of the large number making this pilgrimage, ceremonial purification for the feast required more time than otherwise. Hence many came early, as much as a full week in some cases.

[i](John 11:56) General opinion appears to have been that Jesus would not come to this feast. The command of the authorities (John 11:57) served to incriminate anyone who withheld information as to his whereabouts. Under such conditions Jesus' presence in Jerusalem was difficult for all who knew him.

[k](John 12:1) Jesus probably arrived on the Saturday before Passover, if we assume that the Passover fell on Friday that year. He must have already been in the vicinity. Otherwise, he would have exceeded the limit set for a Sabbath day's journey.

[l](John 12:9) The raising of Lazarus played a large part in attracting the throngs that witnessed the triumphal entry of Christ (cf. John 12:17–18, Sec. 128b). The notoriety of Lazarus' resurrection resulted in an official decision to have him executed (John 12:10), a decision like the earlier one against Jesus (John 11:53, Sec. 119).

[m](Matt. 26:6–13; Mark 14:3–9; John 12:2–8) See Section 141 for the text of these passages. A. T. Robertson's *Harmony* accepts the possibility that this episode may have occurred later, two days before Passover, as Matthew and Mark may imply (cf. Matt. 26:2; Mark 14:1, Sec. 140), instead of six days before, as John places it. Hence the text of these three passages is printed as Section 141 in this revision of Robertson's *Harmony*. This placement sees John as anticipating an event that actually came six days later, perhaps because of Jesus' presence in Bethany six days before the Passover (cf. John 12:1, Sec. 128a). The revisers of Robertson's *Harmony*, however, prefer another option: They understand the placement of John to give the chronological sequence, because it is easier to construe the synoptic accounts as flashbacks than to interpret John's account as an anticipation. Matthew and Mark, on the other hand, introduce the material out of sequence, either to contrast the worship of Mary with the animosity of the high priest, chief priests, and teachers of the law (Matt. 26:3–4; Mark 14:1; Luke 22:2, Sec. 140) or to show why Judas was so interested in obtaining additional funds (cf. Matt. 26:9; Mark 14:5; John 12:5–6 with Matt. 26:15; Mark 14:11; Luke 22:5, Sec. 142). If the sequence preferred by the revisers is correct, John 12:9–11 should be relocated to follow John 12:2–8 instead of being put at the end of Section 128a, as it is currently.

Sec. 128b   Triumphal entry into Jerusalem
—From Bethany to Jerusalem to Bethany—

Matthew 21:1–3, 6–7, 4–5, 8–11, 14–17	Mark 11:1–11	Luke 19:29–44	John 12:12–19
[1]As they approached Jerusalem and came to Bethphage on the Mount of Olives, Jesus sent two disciples, [2]saying to them, "[n]Go to the village ahead of you, and at once you will find a [o]donkey tied there, with her colt by her. Untie them and bring them to me.	[1]As they approached Jerusalem and came to Bethphage and Bethany at the Mount of Olives, Jesus sent two of his disciples, [2]saying to them, "[n]Go to the village ahead of you, and just as you enter it, you will find a [o]colt tied there, which no one has ever ridden. Untie it and bring it here.	[29]As he approached Bethphage and Bethany at the hill called the Mount of Olives, he sent two of his disciples, saying to them, [30]"[n]Go to the village ahead of you, and as you enter it, you will find a [o]colt tied there, which no one has ever ridden. Untie it and bring it here.	[12]The next day the great crowd that had come for the Feast heard that Jesus was on his way to Jerusalem.
[3]If anyone says anything to you, tell him that the Lord needs them, and he will send them right away."	[3]If anyone asks you, 'Why are you doing this?' tell him, 'The Lord needs it and will send it back here shortly.' "	[31]If anyone asks you, 'Why are you untying it?' tell him, 'The Lord needs it.' "	
[6]The disciples went and did as Jesus had instructed them.	[4]They went and found a colt outside in the street, tied at a doorway. As they untied it, [5]some people standing there asked, "What are you doing, untying that colt?" [6]They answered as Jesus had told them to, and the people let them go. [7]When	[32]Those who were sent ahead went and found it just as he had told them. [33]As they were untying the colt, its owners asked them, "Why are you untying the colt?" [34]They replied, "The Lord needs it." [35]They brought it	[13]They took palm branches and went out to meet him, shouting,
[7]They brought the don-			

[n](Matt. 21:2; Mark 11:2; Luke 19:30) Jesus took great pains to demonstrate his office as King of Israel in fulfillment of Zechariah 9:9, a point that was not missed by the crowds (Matt. 21:9; Mark 11:9–10; Luke 19:38; John 12:13). According to John, the crowds who assembled came from three sources. In 12:12 a pilgrim throng approached Jerusalem from more distant areas. Probably most of them came from Galilee, where they had witnessed a large part of Jesus' ministry. In 12:17 the crowd that had been in Bethany when Lazarus was raised bore witness (cf. John 11:42, Sec. 118b). In 12:18 a large Jerusalem crowd flocked out of the city to see the one who had raised Lazarus.

The people's understanding of his mission was only partial, however. They grasped its political significance, namely, deliverance from foreign oppression, but failed to catch the spiritual requirements of his kingdom. Therefore the national aspirations of their generation were doomed to disappointment. This failure brought grief to Jesus, even in his hour of great public acclamation (Luke 19:41).

[o](Matt. 21:2; Mark 11:2; Luke 19:30; John 12:14) Matthew tells about two animals, a donkey and a colt, but the other writers mention only the colt. Here is another instance where Matthew recalls a second participant whereas the other accounts are more general and speak of one only (cf. note k, Sec. 66, and note c, Sec. 126). Matthew adds this detail to tie the event more closely with Zechariah 9:9 (Matt. 21:4–5), which mentions two animals. Jesus apparently rode on the colt only, as the other three gospels stipulate. The second occurrence of "on them" in verse 7 means that he sat on the garments, not on both donkey and colt. The mother of the colt was probably led in front to make the colt more at ease in carrying its first rider.

Matthew 21:1–3, 6–7, 4–5, 8–11, 14–17 (cont'd)	Mark 11:1–11 (cont'd)	Luke 19:29–44 (cont'd)	John 12:12–19 (cont'd)
key and the colt, placed their cloaks on them, and Jesus sat on them.	they brought the colt to Jesus and threw their cloaks over it, he sat on it.	to Jesus, threw their cloaks on the colt and put Jesus on it.	"Hosanna![h]"

Matthew (cont'd):

[4]This took place to fulfill what was spoken through the prophet:

[5]"Say to the
Daughter of
Zion,
'See, your king
comes to
you,
gentle and riding
on a donkey,
on a colt, the
foal of a
donkey' "[a]
[Isa. 62:11;
Zech. 9:9].

John (cont'd):

"Blessed is he
who comes
in the name
of the
Lord!"[i]
[Psalm
118:25,26].

"Blessed is the
King of
Israel!"

[14]Jesus found a young donkey and sat upon it, as it is written,

[15]"Do not be
afraid, O
Daughter of
Zion;
see, your king
is coming,
seated on a
donkey's
colt"[j]
[Zech. 9:9].

[16]At first his disciples did not understand all this. Only after Jesus was glorified did they realize that these things had been written about him and that they had done these things to him. [17]Now the crowd that was with him when he called Lazarus from the tomb and raised him from the dead continued to spread the word. [18]Many people, because they had heard that he had given this miraculous sign, went out to meet him. [19]So the Pharisees said to one another, "See, this is getting us nowhere. Look

Matthew 21:1–3, 6–7, 4–5, 8–11, 14–17 (cont'd)	Mark 11:1–11 (cont'd)	Luke 19:29–44 (cont'd)	John 12:12–19 (cont'd)
			how the whole world has gone after him!"
⁸A very large crowd spread their cloaks on the road, while others cut branches from the trees and spread them on the road. ⁹The crowds that went ahead of him and those that followed shouted, "Hosanna *b* to the Son of David!" "Blessed is he who comes in the name of the Lord!" *c* [Psalm 118:26]. "Hosanna *b* in the highest!"	⁸Many people spread their cloaks on the road, while others spread branches they had cut in the fields. ⁹Those who went ahead and those who followed shouted, "Hosanna! *e*" "Blessed is he who comes in the name of the Lord!" *f* [Psalm 118:26]. ¹⁰"Blessed is the coming kingdom of our father David!" "Hosanna in the highest!"	³⁶As he went along, people spread their cloaks on the road. ³⁷When he came near the place where the road goes down the Mount of Olives, the whole crowd of disciples began joyfully to praise God in loud voices for all the miracles they had seen: ³⁸"Blessed is the king who comes in the name of the Lord!" *g* [Psalm 118:26]. "Peace in heaven and glory in the highest!" ³⁹Some of the Pharisees in the crowd said to Jesus, "Teacher, rebuke your disciples!" ⁴⁰"I tell you," he replied, "if they keep quiet, the stones will cry out." ⁴¹As he approached Jerusalem and saw the city, he wept over it ⁴²and said, "If you, even you, had only known on this day what would bring you peace— but now it is hidden from your eyes. ⁴³The days will come upon you when your enemies will build	

Matthew 21:1–3, 6–7, 4–5, 8–11, 14–17 (cont'd)	Mark 11:1–11 (cont'd)	Luke 19:29–44 (cont'd)
		an embankment against you and encircle you and hem you in on every side. ⁴⁴They will dash you to the ground, you and the children within your walls. They will not leave one stone on another, because you did not recognize the time of God's coming to you."
against you and encircle you and hem		
¹⁰When Jesus entered Jerusalem, the whole city was stirred and asked, "Who is this?" ¹¹The crowds answered, "This is Jesus, the prophet from Nazareth in Galilee." ¹⁴The blind and the lame came to him at the temple, and he healed them. ¹⁵But when the chief priests and the teachers of the law saw the wonderful things he did and the children shouting in the temple area, "Hosanna to the Son of David," they were indignant. ¹⁶"Do you hear what these children are saying?" they asked him. "Yes," replied Jesus, "have you never read,	¹¹Jesus entered Jerusalem	
	and went to the temple.	

" 'From the lips
   of children
   and infants
you have
   ordained
   praise'ᵈ?"
[Psalm 8:2].

¹⁷And he left   He looked around

Matthew 21:1–3, 6–7, 4–5, 8–11, 14–17 (cont'd)	Mark 11:1–11 (cont'd)
them and went out of the city to Bethany, where he spent the night.	at everything, but since it was already late, he went out to Bethany with the Twelve.

[a]*Mt 21:5* Zech. 9:9 [b]9 A Hebrew expression meaning "Save!" which became an exclamation of praise; also in verse 15 [c]9 Psalm 118:26 [d]16 Psalm 8:2 [e]*Mk 11:9* A Hebrew expression meaning "Save!" which became an exclamation of praise; also in verse 10 [f]9 Psalm 118:25,26 [g]*Lk 19:38* Psalm 118:26 [h]*Jn 12:13* A Hebrew expression meaning "Save!" which became an exclamation of praise [i]13 Psalm 118:25, 26 [j]15 Zech. 9:9

Sec. 129a Cursing of the fig tree having leaves but no figs

—From Bethany to Jerusalem—

Matthew 21:18–19a	Mark 11:12–14
[18]Early in the morning, as he was on his way back to the city, he was hungry. [19]Seeing a fig tree by the road, he went up to it but found nothing on it except leaves.	[12]The next day as they were leaving Bethany, Jesus was hungry. [13]Seeing in the distance a fig tree in leaf, he went to find out if it had any fruit. When he reached it, he found nothing but leaves, because it was [p]not the season for figs.
Then he said to it, "May you never bear fruit again!"	[14]Then he said to the tree, "May no one ever eat fruit from you again." And his disciples heard him say it.

Sec. 129b Second cleansing of the temple (cf. Sec. 31—cleansing the temple)

—Jerusalem, in the temple—

Matthew 21:12–13	Mark 11:15–18	Luke 19:45–48
[12]Jesus entered the [q]temple area and drove out all who were buying and selling there. He overturned the tables of the money changers and the benches of those selling doves.	[15]On reaching Jerusalem, Jesus entered the [q]temple area and began driving out those who were buying and selling there. He overturned the tables of the money changers and the benches of those selling doves, [16]and would not allow anyone to carry merchandise through the temple courts. [17]And as he taught them, he said, "Is it not written:	[45]Then he entered the [q]temple area and began driving out those who were selling.
[13]"It is written," he	" 'My house will be	[46]"It is written," he said to them, " 'My house will be a

[p](Mark 11:13) Jesus knew that Passover time was not the season for figs, but he used his own hunger and this leafy fig tree as an object lesson for the disciples. In the Old Testament the fig tree is often a symbol for Israel (Jer. 8:13; 29:17; Hos. 9:10, 16; Joel 1:7; Mic. 7:1–6). Such is the case here. The ritualism of national worship was hiding the absence of genuine piety among the people (cf. Sec. 129b). Hence Jesus' curse of this fig tree (Matt. 21:19; Mark 11:14) was emblematic of God's judgment that was going to fall on Jerusalem (cf. Sec. 131).

[q](Matt. 21:12; Mark 11:15; Luke 19:45) The Court of the Gentiles was the scene of the cleansing. After his dramatic entrance into the city (Sec. 128b), the King went right to the heart of the nation's problem: corruption in worship. This lack of true devotion to God was what kept his triumphal entry from being triumphal in a permanent sense.

Matthew 21:12–13 (cont'd)	Mark 11:15–18 (cont'd)	Luke 19:45–48 (cont'd)
said to them, " 'My house will be called a house of prayer,'ᵃ but you are making it a 'den of robbers'ᵇ" [Isa. 56:7; Jer. 7:11].	called a house of prayer for all nations'ᶜ? But you have made it 'a den of robbers'ᵈ" [Isa. 56:7; Jer. 7:11]. ¹⁸The chief priests and the teachers of the law heard this and began looking for a way to kill him, for they feared him, because the whole crowd was amazed at his teaching.	house of prayer'ᶜ; but you have made it 'a den of robbers'ᵈ" [Isa. 56:7; Jer. 7:11]. ⁴⁷Every day he was teaching at the temple. But the chief priests, the teachers of the law and the leaders among the people were trying to kill him. ⁴⁸Yet they could not find any way to do it, because all the people hung on his words.

ᵃMt 21:13; Mk 11:17; Lk 19:46 Isaiah 56:7   ᵇMt 21:13; Mk 11:17; Lk 19:46 Jer. 7:11
ᶜMk 11:17; Lk 19:46 Isaiah 56:7   ᵈMk 11:17; Lk 19:46 Jer. 7:11

Sec. 130a   Request of some Greeks to see Jesus and necessity of the Son of Man's being lifted up
(cf. Sec. 83—loving and hating life)
—*Jerusalem*—

John 12:20–36a

²⁰Now there were some Greeks among those who went up to worship at the Feast. ²¹They came to Philip, who was from Bethsaida in Galilee, with a request. "Sir," they said, "we would like to see Jesus." ²²Philip went to tell Andrew; Andrew and Philip in turn told Jesus.

²³Jesus replied, "ʳThe hour has come for the Son of Man to be glorified. ²⁴I tell you the truth, unless a kernel of wheat falls to the ground and dies, it remains only a single seed. But if it dies, it produces many seeds. ²⁵The man who loves his life will lose it, while the man who hates his life in this world will keep it for eternal life. ²⁶Whoever serves me must follow me; and where I am, my servant also will be. My Father will honor the one who serves me.

²⁷"Now my heart is troubled, and what shall I say? 'Father, save me from this hour'? No, it was for this very reason I came to this hour. ²⁸Father, glorify your name!"

Then a voice came from heaven, "I have glorified it, and will glorify it again." ²⁹The crowd that was there and heard it said it had thundered; others said an angel had spoken to him.

³⁰Jesus said, "This voice was for your benefit, not mine. ³¹Now is the time for judgment on this world; now the prince of this world will be driven out. ³²But I, when I am lifted up from the earth, will draw all men to myself." ³³He said this to show the kind of death he was going to die.

³⁴The crowd spoke up, "We have heard from the Law that the Christᵃ will remain forever, so how can you say, 'The Son of Man must be lifted up'? Who is this 'Son of Man'?"

³⁵Then Jesus told them, "You are going to have the light just a little while longer. Walk while you have the light, before darkness overtakes you. The man who walks in the dark does not know where he is going. ³⁶Put your trust in the light while you have it, so that you may become sons of light."

ᵃJn 12:34 Or Messiah

ʳ(John 12:23) Jesus' answer totally ignored the Greeks and their request. John's inclusion of the incident, however, clearly indicates their importance. Indirectly, their coming to seek Jesus indicated to him that the climax of his ministry had come. The time had now come for him to conclude his ministry limited to the Jews and move out to include others such as these Greeks. This, however, could happen only after his crucifixion (cf. John 12:24, 32).

Sec. 130b   Different responses to Jesus and Jesus' response to the crowds
(cf. Sec. 64b—deadened hearts and blinded eyes)
—Jerusalem—

John 12:36b–50

When he had finished speaking, Jesus left and hid himself from them.

[37]Even after Jesus had done all these miraculous signs in their presence, they still would not believe in him. [38]This was to fulfill the word of Isaiah the prophet:

"Lord, who has believed our message
and to whom has the arm of the Lord been revealed?"[a] [Isa. 53:1].

[39]For this reason they could not believe, because, as Isaiah says elsewhere:

[40]"He has blinded their eyes
and deadened their hearts,
so they can neither see with their eyes,
nor understand with their hearts,
nor turn—and I would heal them"[b] [Isa. 6:10].

[41]Isaiah said this because he saw Jesus' glory and spoke about him.

[42]Yet at the same time [s]many even among the leaders believed in him. But because of the Pharisees they would not confess their faith for fear they would be put out of the synagogue; [43]for they loved praise from men more than praise from God.

[44]Then Jesus cried out, "When a man [t]believes in me, he does not believe in me only, but in the one who sent me. [45]When he looks at me, he sees the one who sent me. [46]I have come into the world as a light, so that no one who believes in me should stay in darkness.

[47]"As for the person who hears my words but does not keep them, I do not judge him. For I did not come to judge the world, but to save it. [48]There is a judge for the one who rejects me and does not accept my words; that very word which I spoke will condemn him at the last day. [49]For I did not speak of my own accord, but the Father who sent me commanded me what to say and how to say it. [50]I know that his command leads to eternal life. So whatever I say is just what the Father has told me to say."

[a]Jn 12:38 Isaiah 53:1   [b]40 Isaiah 6:10

Sec. 131   Withered fig tree and the lesson on faith
(cf. Sec. 54f—forgiveness of others and forgiveness by God)
—Back to Bethany and return to Jerusalem—

Matthew 21:19b–22	Mark 11:19–25	[u]Luke 21:37–38
	[19]When evening came, they[a] went out of the city. [20]In the morning, as they went along, they saw	
Immediately the tree withered.	the fig tree withered from the roots. [21]Peter remem-	

---

[s](John 12:42) Nicodemus and Joseph of Arimathea must have been only two of a much larger number of leaders who had trusted Christ. What a pity that misplaced values (cf. John 12:43) may have kept them from speaking up in his defense.

[t](John 12:44) Fittingly, John closes his description of Jesus' public ministry with a final plea to believe. This along with other emphases of the earlier chapters are picked up in this summary paragraph (e.g., his being sent by the Father [vv. 44–45, 49], light and darkness [v. 46], present and future judgment [vv. 47–48], salvation for the world [v. 47], eternal life [v. 50]).

[u](Luke 21:37–38) Following A. T. Robertson's Harmony, this revision includes the text of these verses at this point. In the opinion of the revisers, however, the order of Luke's gospel is chronological at this point and the two verses should immediately precede Luke 22:1–2 at the beginning of Section 140. They fit into the sequence of Christ's life well at that point.

Matthew 21:19b–22 (cont'd)	Mark 11:19–25 (cont'd)	Luke 21:37–38 (cont'd)
[20]When the disciples saw this, they were amazed. "How did the fig tree wither so quickly?" they asked. [21]Jesus replied, "I tell you the truth, if you have faith and do not doubt, not only can you do what was done to the fig tree, but also you can say to this [v]mountain, 'Go, throw yourself into the sea,' and it will be done. [22]If you believe, you will receive whatever you ask for in prayer."	bered and said to Jesus, "Rabbi, look! The fig tree you cursed has withered!" [22]"Have[b] faith in God," Jesus answered. [23]"I tell you the truth, if anyone says to this [v]mountain, 'Go, throw yourself into the sea,' and does not doubt in his heart but believes that what he says will happen, it will be done for him. [24]Therefore I tell you, whatever you ask for in prayer, believe that you have received it, and it will be yours. [25]And when you stand praying, if you hold anything against anyone, forgive him, so that your Father in heaven may forgive you your sins.[c]"	[37]Each day Jesus was teaching at the temple, and each evening he went out to spend the night on the hill called the Mount of Olives, [38]and all the people came early in the morning to hear him at the temple.

[a]Mk 11:19 Some early manuscripts *he*   [b]22 Some early manuscripts *If you have*   [c]25 Some manuscripts *sins.* [26]*But if you do not forgive, neither will your Father who is in heaven forgive your sins.*

OFFICIAL CHALLENGE TO CHRIST'S AUTHORITY

Sec. 132a   Questioning of Jesus' authority by the chief priests, teachers of the law, and elders
   —Jerusalem, in the temple—

Matthew 21:23–27	Mark 11:27–33	Luke 20:1–8
[23]Jesus entered the temple courts, and, while he was teaching, the chief priests and the elders of	[27]They arrived again in Jerusalem, and while Jesus was walking in the temple courts, the chief	[1]One day as he was teaching the people in the temple courts and preaching the [w]gospel, the chief

[v](Matt. 21:21; Mark 11:23) The mountain referred to was the Mount of Olives, from which one could see the Dead Sea. For this mountain to have been cast into the sea would have meant a fall of about four thousand feet. Whether Jesus intended a physical miracle or used the mountain only in a symbolic way is uncertain. The important lesson in either case was for the disciples to believe God.
[w](Luke 20:1) It was probably the gospel of the kingdom (Matt. 9:35; 24:14) to which these representatives of the Sanhedrin objected, but the cleansing of the temple the day before was probably included also in "these things" (Matt. 21:23; Mark 11:28; Luke 20:2) about which they asked. This is the first in a series of verbal encounters with various groups of Jewish leaders. All of these came on Tuesday of Passion Week.

Matthew 21:23–27 (cont'd)	Mark 11:27–33 (cont'd)	Luke 20:1–8 (cont'd)
the people came to him. "By what authority are you doing these things?" they asked. "And who gave you this authority?" 24Jesus replied, "I will also ask you one question. If you answer me, I will tell you by what authority I am doing these things. 25John's baptism—where did it come from? Was it from heaven, or from men?" They discussed it among themselves and said, "If we say, 'From heaven,' he will ask, 'Then why didn't you believe him?' 26But if we say, 'From men'—we are afraid of the people, for they all hold that John was a prophet." 27So they answered Jesus, "We don't know." Then he said, "Neither will I tell you by what authority I am doing these things.	priests, the teachers of the law and the elders came to him. 28"By what authority are you doing these things?" they asked. "And who gave you authority to do this?" 29Jesus replied, "I will ask you one question. Answer me, and I will tell you by what authority I am doing these things. 30John's baptism—was it from heaven, or from men? Tell me!" 31They discussed it among themselves and said, "If we say, 'From heaven,' he will ask, 'Then why didn't you believe him?' 32But if we say, 'From men'. . . ." (They feared the people, for everyone held that John really was a prophet.) 33So they answered Jesus, "We don't know." Jesus said, "Neither will I tell you by what authority I am doing these things."	priests and the teachers of the law, together with the elders, came up to him. 2"Tell us by what authority you are doing these things," they said. "Who gave you this authority?" 3He replied, "I will also ask you a question. Tell me, 4John's baptism—was it from heaven, or from men?" 5They discussed it among themselves and said, "If we say, 'From heaven,' he will ask, 'Why didn't you believe him?' 6But if we say, 'From men,' all the people will stone us, because they are persuaded that John was a prophet." 7So they answered, "We don't know where it was from." 8Jesus said, "Neither will I tell you by what authority I am doing these things."

Sec. 132b   Jesus' response with his own question and three parables
—Jerusalem, in the temple—

Matthew 21:28–22:14	Mark 12:1–12	Luke 20:9–19
28"What do you think? There was a man who had two sons. He went to the first and said, 'Son, go and work today in the vineyard.' 29" 'I will not,' he answered, but later he changed his mind and went. 30"Then the father went to the other son and said the same thing. He answered, 'I will, sir,' but he did not go. 31"Which of the two did what his father wanted?" "The first," they answered.		

Matthew 21:28–22:14 (cont'd)	Mark 12:1–12 (cont'd)	Luke 20:9–19 (cont'd)

Jesus said to them, "I tell you the truth, the tax collectors and the prostitutes are entering the kingdom of God ahead of you. 32For John came to you to show you the way of righteousness, and you did not believe him, but the tax collectors and the prostitutes did. And even after you saw this, you did not repent and believe him.

33"Listen to another ˣparable: There was a landowner who planted a vineyard. He put a wall around it, dug a winepress in it and built a watchtower [Isa. 5:2]. Then he rented the vineyard to some farmers and went away on a journey. 34When the harvest time approached, he sent his servants to the tenants to collect his fruit.

35"The tenants seized his servants; they beat one, killed another, and stoned a third. 36Then he sent other servants to them, more than the first time, and the tenants treated them the same way.

37Last of all, he sent his son to them. 'They will respect my son,' he said.

38"But when the tenants saw the son, they said to each other, 'This is the heir. Come, let's kill him and take his inheritance.' 39So they took him and threw him out of the vineyard and killed him.

40"Therefore, when the

1He then began to speak to them in ˣparables: "A man planted a vineyard. He put a wall around it, dug a pit for the winepress and built a watchtower [Isa. 5:2]. Then he rented the vineyard to some farmers and went away on a journey. 2At harvest time he sent a servant to the tenants to collect from them some of the fruit of the vineyard. 3But they seized him, beat him and sent him away empty-handed. 4Then he sent another servant to them; they struck this man on the head and treated him shamefully. 5He sent still another, and that one they killed. He sent many others; some of them they beat, others they killed.

6"He had one left to send, a son, whom he loved. He sent him last of all, saying, 'They will respect my son.'

7"But the tenants said to one another, 'This is the heir. Come, let's kill him, and the inheritance will be ours.' 8So they took him and killed him, and threw him out of the vineyard.

9He went on to tell the people this ˣparable: "A man planted a vineyard, rented it to some farmers and went away for a long time. 10At harvest time he sent a servant to the tenants so they would give him some of the fruit of the vineyard. But the tenants beat him and sent him away empty-handed. 11He sent another servant, but that one also they beat and treated shamefully and sent away empty-handed. 12He sent still a third, and they wounded him and threw him out.

13"Then the owner of the vineyard said, 'What shall I do? I will send my son, whom I love; perhaps they will respect him.'

14"But when the tenants saw him, they talked the matter over. 'This is the heir,' they said. 'Let's kill him, and the inheritance will be ours.' 15So they threw him out of the vineyard and killed him.

ˣ(Matt. 21:33; Mark 12:1; Luke 20:9) This parable pictures the rejection of God's 'beloved son' (Luke 20:13), and that of the two sons (Matt. 21:28–32) charges the listeners with the rejection of John the Baptist.

Matthew 21:28–22:14 (cont'd)	Mark 12:1–12 (cont'd)	Luke 20:9–19 (cont'd)

owner of the vineyard comes, what will he do to those tenants?"

⁴¹"He will bring those wretches to a wretched end," they replied, "and he will rent the vineyard to other tenants, who will give him his share of the crop at harvest time."

⁴²Jesus said to them, "Have you never read in the Scriptures:

" 'The stone the
builders rejected
has become the
capstone ᵃ;
the Lord has done this,
and it is marvelous in
our eyes' ᵇ? [Psalm
118:22–23].

⁴³"Therefore I tell you that the kingdom of God will be ʸtaken away from you and given to a people who will produce its fruit. ⁴⁴He who falls on this stone will be broken to pieces, but he on whom it falls will be crushed." ᶜ

⁴⁵When the chief priests and the Pharisees heard Jesus' parables, they knew he was talking about them. ⁴⁶They looked for a way to arrest him, but they were afraid of the crowd because the people held that he was a prophet.

⁹"What then will the owner of the vineyard do? He will come and kill those tenants and give the vineyard to others.

¹⁰Haven't you read this scripture:

" 'The stone the
builders rejected
has become the
capstone ᵈ;
¹¹the Lord has done this,
and it is marvelous in
our eyes' ᵉ?"
[Psalm 118:22–23].

¹²Then they looked for a way to arrest him because they knew he had spoken the parable against them. But they were afraid of the crowd; so they left him and went away.

"What then will the owner of the vineyard do to them? ¹⁶He will come and kill those tenants and give the vineyard to others."

When the people heard this, they said, "May this never be!"

¹⁷Jesus looked directly at them and asked, "Then what is the meaning of that which is written:

" 'The stone the
builders rejected
has become the
capstone ᵈ ʼ ᶠ?
[Psalm 118:22].

¹⁸Everyone who falls on that stone will be broken to pieces, but he on whom it falls will be crushed."

¹⁹The teachers of the law and the chief priests looked for a way to arrest him immediately, because they knew he had spoken this parable against them. But they were afraid of the people.

¹Jesus spoke to them again in parables, saying: ²"The kingdom of heaven is like a king who prepared a wedding banquet for his son. ³He sent his servants to those who had been invited to the banquet to tell them to come, but they refused to come.

⁴"Then he sent some more servants and said, 'Tell those who have been invited that I have prepared my dinner: My oxen and fattened cattle have been butchered, and everything is ready. Come to the wedding banquet.'

⁵"But they paid no attention and went off—one to his field, another to his business. ⁶The rest seized his servants, mistreated them and killed them. ⁷The king

---

ʸ(Matt. 21:43) God's rejection of this generation of Israelites because of their rejection of Jesus and his spiritual standards has received attention already (cf. Luke 19:41–44, Sec. 128b; Matt. 21:19; Mark 11:14, Sec. 129a). The new "people" to whom the kingdom will be given is either those who respond to the gospel during the present, whether they be Jews or Gentiles (cf. Matt. 22:8–10), or that future generation of Israel that will respond to his call to repentance (Matt. 23:39, Sec. 137b). The Greek word translated *people* (literally, *nation*) (v. 43) is without a definite article and hence stresses the quality of people to whom the kingdom will be given, rather than the identity of the nation.

ᶻ(Matt. 22:7) This parabolic reference to the destruction of Jerusalem, which came in A.D. 70, is one

Matthew 21:28–22:14 (cont'd)

was enraged. He sent his army and destroyed those murderers and ᶻburned their city.

⁸"Then he said to his servants, 'The wedding banquet is ready, but those I invited did not deserve to come. ⁹Go to the street corners and invite to the banquet anyone you find.' ¹⁰So the servants went out into the streets and gathered all the people they could find, both good and bad, and the wedding hall was filled with guests.

¹¹"But when the king came in to see the guests, he noticed a man there who was not wearing wedding clothes. ¹²'Friend,' he asked, 'how did you get in here without wedding clothes?' The man was speechless.

¹³"Then the king told the attendants, 'Tie him hand and foot, and throw him outside, into the darkness, where there will be weeping and gnashing of teeth.'

¹⁴"For many are invited, but few are chosen."

ᵃMt 21:42 Or cornerstone   ᵇ42 Psalm 118:22,23   ᶜ44 Some manuscripts do not have verse 44.
ᵈMk 12:10; Lk 20:17 Or cornerstone   ᵉMk 12:11 Psalm 118:22,23   ᶠLk 20:17 Psalm 118:22

Sec. 133   Attempts by Pharisees and Herodians to trap Jesus with a question about paying taxes to Caesar
—*Jerusalem, probably in the temple*—

Matthew 22:15–22	Mark 12:13–17	Luke 20:20–26
¹⁵Then the Pharisees went out and laid plans to trap him in his words. ¹⁶They sent their disciples to him along with the ᵃHerodians. "Teacher," they said, "we know you are a man of integrity and that you teach the way of God in accordance with the truth. You aren't swayed by men, because you pay no attention to who they are. ¹⁷Tell us then, what is your opinion? Is it right to pay taxes to Caesar or not?" ¹⁸But Jesus, knowing their evil intent, said, "You hypocrites, why are you trying to trap me? ¹⁹Show me the coin used for paying the tax." They brought him a denarius, ²⁰and he asked them, "Whose portrait is this? And whose inscription?" ²¹"Caesar's," they replied.	¹³Later they sent some of the ᵃPharisees and Herodians to Jesus to catch him in his words. ¹⁴They came to him and said, "Teacher, we know you are a man of integrity. You aren't swayed by men, because you pay no attention to who they are; but you teach the way of God in accordance with truth. Is it right to pay taxes to Caesar or not? ¹⁵Should we pay or shouldn't we?" But Jesus knew their hypocrisy. "Why are you trying to trap me?" he asked. "Bring me a denarius and let me look at it." ¹⁶They brought the coin, and he asked them, "Whose portrait is this? And whose inscription?" "Caesar's," they replied.	²⁰Keeping a close watch on him, they sent spies, who pretended to be honest. They hoped to catch Jesus in something he said so that they might hand him over to the power and authority of the governor. ²¹So the spies questioned him: "Teacher, we know that you speak and teach what is right, and that you do not show partiality but teach the way of God in accordance with the truth. ²²Is it right for us to pay taxes to Caesar or not?" ²³He saw through their duplicity and said to them, ²⁴"Show me a denarius. Whose portrait and inscription are on it?" ²⁵"Caesar's," they replied. He said to them, "Then give to Caesar what is Caesar's, and to God what is God's."

of several predictions about that event. Jesus had already referred to it (Luke 19:43–44, Sec. 128b) and was to do so again (Matt. 23:37–38, Sec. 137b; Matt. 24:1–2; Mark 13:1–2; Luke 21:5–6, Sec. 139a).

ᵃ(Matt. 22:16; Mark 12:13) For the Pharisees and Herodians to unite in a common cause was quite unusual. The Pharisees were strongly resentful of the Roman occupation of Palestine—particularly of Judea, where the poll tax was required (cf. Matt. 22:17; Mark 12:14). In contrast, the Herodians strongly supported the Roman presence in the land, because this was the source of power by which the Herod family ruled. In whatever way Jesus answered their question (Matt. 22:17; Mark 12:15; Luke 20:22), they assumed he must violate the tenets of one of the two groups. He would be proven guilty in the eyes of either the people (Luke 20:26) if he disagreed with the Pharisees or the governor (Luke 20:20) if he disagreed with the Herodians. But Jesus avoided both pitfalls with his perceptive answer.

| Matthew 22:15–22 | Mark 12:13–17 | Luke 20:20–26 |
| (cont'd) | (cont'd) | (cont'd) |

Then he said to them, "Give to Caesar what is Caesar's, and to God what is God's." [22]When they heard this, they were amazed. So they left him and went away.

[17]Then Jesus said to them, "Give to Caesar what is Caesar's and to God what is God's." And they were amazed at him.

[26]They were unable to trap him in what he had said there in public. And astonished by his answer, they became silent.

Sec. 134   Sadducees' puzzling question about the resurrection
—Jerusalem, probably in the temple—

| Matthew 22:23–33 | Mark 12:18–27 | Luke 20:27–40 |

[23]That same day the Sadducees, [b]who say there is no resurrection, came to him with a question. [24]"Teacher," they said, "Moses told us that if a man dies without having children, his brother must marry the widow and have children for him [Deut. 25:5]. [25]Now there were seven brothers among us. The first one married and died, and since he had no children, he left his wife to his brother. [26]The same thing happened to the second and third brother, right on down to the seventh. [27]Finally, the woman died. [28]Now then, at the resurrection, whose wife will she be of the seven, since all of them were married to her?"

[29]Jesus replied, "You are in error because you do not know the Scriptures or the power of God.

[18]Then the Sadducees, [b]who say there is no resurrection, came to him with a question. [19]"Teacher," they said, "Moses wrote for us that if a man's brother dies and leaves a wife but no children, the man must marry the widow and have children for his brother [Deut. 25:5]. [20]Now there were seven brothers. The first one married and died without leaving any children. [21]The second one married the widow, but he also died, leaving no child. It was the same with the third. [22]In fact, none of the seven left any children. Last of all, the woman died too. [23]At the resurrection[b] whose wife will she be, since the seven were married to her?"

[24]Jesus replied, "Are you not in error because you do not know the Scriptures or the power of God?

[27]Some of the Sadducees, [b]who say there is no resurrection, came to Jesus with a question. [28]"Teacher," they said, "Moses wrote for us that if a man's brother dies and leaves a wife but no children, the man must marry the widow and have children for his brother [Deut. 25:5]. [29]Now there were seven brothers. The first one married a woman and died childless. [30]The second [31]and then the third married her, and in the same way the seven died, leaving no children. [32]Finally, the woman died too. [33]Now then, at the resurrection whose wife will she be, since the seven were married to her?"

[34]Jesus replied,

"The people of this age marry and are given in marriage. [35]But those who are considered worthy of taking part in that age and in the

---

[b](Matt. 22:23; Mark 12:18; Luke 20:27) On a Tuesday filled with conflicts, the Sadducees thought they had a theological question that could not be answered by anyone who believed in resurrection, as did Jesus (cf. John 11:23–26, Sec. 118b). The law of levirate marriage (Deut. 25:7–10), they held, ruled out the possibility of resurrection. In response Jesus authoritatively expounded Exodus 3:6 (Matt. 22:32; Mark 12:26) and Exodus 3:15–16 (Luke 20:37) to show that Moses' words would have been entirely inappropriate if the Sadducean doctrine of extinction without hope of resurrection held true for Abraham, Isaac, and Jacob after their deaths.

Matthew 22:23–33 (cont'd)	Mark 12:18–27 (cont'd)	Luke 20:27–40 (cont'd)
30At the resurrection people will neither marry nor be given in marriage; they will be like the angels in heaven.	25When the dead rise, they will neither marry nor be given in marriage; they will be like the angels in heaven.	resurrection from the dead will neither marry nor be given in marriage, 36and they can no longer die; for they are like the angels. They are God's children, since they are children of the resurrec-
31But about the resurrection of the dead —have you not read what God said to you, 32'I am the God of Abraham, the God of Isaac, and the God of Jacob'a? [Exod. 3:6]. He is not the God of the dead but of the living." 33When the crowds heard this, they were astonished at his teaching.	26Now about the dead rising—have you not read in the book of Moses, in the account of the bush, how God said to him, 'I am the God of Abraham, the God of Isaac, and the God of Jacob'c? [Exod. 3:6]. 27He is not the God of the dead, but of the living. You are badly mistaken!"	tion. 37But in the account of the bush, even Moses showed that the dead rise, for he calls the Lord 'the God of Abraham, and the God of Isaac, and the God of Jacob'c [Exod. 3:6]. 38He is not the God of the dead, but of the living, for to him all are alive." 39Some of the teachers of the law responded, "Well said, teacher!" 40And no one dared to ask him any more questions.

aMt 22:32; Mk 12:26; Lk 20:37 Exodus 3:6   bMk 12:23 Some manuscripts *resurrection, when men rise from the dead,*

Sec. 135   A Pharisee's legal question
(cf. Sec. 103—greatest commandment in the law)
—Jerusalem, probably in the temple—

Matthew 22:34–40	Mark 12:28–34
34Hearing that Jesus had silenced the Sadducees, the Pharisees got together. 35One of them, an expert in the law, tested him with this question: 36"Teacher, which is the greatest commandment in the Law?" 37Jesus replied: " 'Love the Lord your God with all your heart and with all your soul and with all your mind'a [Deut. 6:5]. 38This is the first and greatest commandment. 39And the second is like it: 'Love your neighbor as yourself'b [Lev. 19:18]. 40All the Law and the Prophets hang on these two commandments."	28One of the teachers of the law came and heard them debating. Noticing that Jesus had given them a good answer, he asked him, "Of all the commandments, which is the most important?" 29"The most important one," answered Jesus, "is this: 'Hear, O Israel, the Lord our God, the Lord is one.c 30Love the Lord your God with all your heart and with all your soul and with all your mind and with all your strength'd [Deut. 6:4–5]. 31The second is this: 'Love your neighbor as yourself'b [Lev. 19:18]. There is no commandment greater than these." 32"Well said, teacher," the man replied. "You are right in saying that God is one and there is no other but him. 33To love him with all your heart, with all your understanding and with all your strength, and to love your neighbor as yourself [Lev. 19:18; Deut. 4:35; 6:5] is more important than all burnt offerings and sacrifices."

Mark 12:28–34
(cont'd)

[34]When Jesus saw that [c]he had answered wisely, he said to him, "You are not far from the kingdom of God." And from then on no one dared ask him any more questions.

[a]Mt 22:37 Deut. 6:5   [b]39,31 Lev. 19:18   [c]Mk 12:29 Or the Lord our God is one Lord   [d]30 Deut. 6:4,5

CHRIST'S RESPONSE TO HIS ENEMIES' CHALLENGES

Sec. 136   Christ's relationship to David as son and Lord
—*Jerusalem, in the temple*—

Matthew 22:41–46	Mark 12:35–37	Luke 20:41–44
[41]While the Pharisees were gathered together, [d]Jesus asked them, [42]"What do you think about the Christ[a]? Whose son is he?" "The son of David," they replied. [43]He said to them, "How is it then that David, speaking by the Spirit, calls him 'Lord'? For he says,	[35]While Jesus was teaching in the temple courts, he asked, "How is it that the teachers of the law say that the Christ[c] is the son of David? [36]David himself, speaking by the Holy Spirit, declared:	[41]Then Jesus said to them, "How is it that they say the Christ[a] is the Son of David? [42]David himself declares in the Book of Psalms:
[44]" 'The Lord said to my Lord: "Sit at my right hand until I put your enemies under your feet" '[b] [Psalm 110:1].	" 'The Lord said to my Lord: "Sit at my right hand until I put your enemies under your feet" '[d] [Psalm 110:1].	" 'The Lord said to my Lord: "Sit at my right hand [43]until I make your enemies a footstool for your feet" '[b] [Psalm 110:1].
[45]If then David calls him 'Lord,' how can he be his son?" [46]No one could say a word in reply, and from that day on no one dared to ask him any more questions.	[37]David himself calls him 'Lord.' How then can he be his son?" The large crowd listened to him with delight.	[44]David calls him 'Lord.' How then can he be his son?"

[a]Mt 22:42; Mk 12:35; Lk 20:41 Or Messiah   [b]Mt 22:44; Mk 12:36; Lk 20:43 Psalm 110:1

[c](Mark 12:34) The favorable response of this expert in the law to Jesus' answer must have caused alarm among his fellow Pharisees. It is a sign of Jesus' remarkable perception that he was able to recognize among such vicious opponents one whose heart was still open to the gospel, and who might still qualify for entrance into the kingdom of God.

[d](Matt. 22:41) Having repulsed his opponents, Jesus now took the initiative. To the dismay of his enemies (Matt. 22:46) and the enjoyment of the crowd (Mark 12:37), by a single rhetorical question he proved from Old Testament Scripture that the Messiah must be both God and man ("Lord" and "son," Matt. 22:45; Mark 12:37; Luke 20:44).

Sec. 137a   Seven woes against the teachers of the law and Pharisees
(cf. Sec. 54e—taking an oath)
(cf. Sec. 107—woes against teachers of the law and Pharisees)
—Jerusalem, in the temple—

Matthew 23:1–36	Mark 12:38–40	Luke 20:45–47
[1]Then Jesus said to the crowds and to his disciples: [2]"The teachers of the law and the Pharisees sit in Moses' seat. [3]So you must obey them and do eeverything they tell you. But do not do what they do, for they do not practice what they preach. [4]They tie up heavy loads and put them on men's shoulders, but they themselves are not willing to lift a finger to move them.	[38]As he taught, Jesus said, "Watch out for the teachers of the law.	[45]While all the people were listening, Jesus said to his disciples, [46]"Beware of the teachers of the law.
[5]"Everything they do is done for men to see: They make their phylacteriesᵃ wide and the tassels on their garments long; [6]they love the place of honor at banquets and the most important seats in the synagogues; [7]they love to be greeted in the marketplaces and to have men call them 'Rabbi.'	They like to walk around in flowing robes and be greeted in the marketplaces, [39]and have the most important seats in the synagogues and the places of honor at banquets. [40]They devour widows' houses and for a show make lengthy prayers. Such men will be punished most severely."	They like to walk around in flowing robes and love to be greeted in the marketplaces and have the most important seats in the synagogues and the places of honor at banquets. [47]They devour widows' houses and for a show make lengthy prayers. Such men will be punished most severely."

[8]"But you are not to be called 'Rabbi,' for you have only one Master and you are all brothers. [9]And do not call anyone on earth 'father,' for you have one Father, and he is in heaven. [10]Nor are you to be called 'teacher,' for you have one Teacher, the Christ.ᵇ [11]The greatest among you will be your servant. [12]For whoever exalts himself will be humbled, and whoever humbles himself will be exalted.

[13]"Woe to ᶠyou, teachers of the law and Pharisees, you hypocrites! You shut the kingdom of heaven in men's faces. You yourselves do not enter, nor will you let those enter who are trying to.ᶜ

[15]"Woe to you, teachers of the law and Pharisees, you hypocrites! You travel over land and sea to win a single convert, and when he becomes one, you make him twice as much a son of hell as you are.

[16]"Woe to you, blind guides! You say, 'If anyone swears by the temple, it means nothing; but if anyone swears by the gold of the temple, he is bound by his oath.'

ᵉ(Matt. 23:3) Even though he was about to denounce the teachers of the law and Pharisees as hypocrites (Matt. 23:13, 15, 23, 25, 27, 29) and "blind guides" (Matt. 23:16), Jesus still recognized their official capacity as propagators of the law of Moses. To the extent that they taught the law faithfully, they were to be obeyed, but wherever their traditions missed the point of the law (Matt. 5:21–48, Sec. 54e) or nullified the teaching of the law (Matt. 15:1–20; Mark 7:1–23, Sec. 77), they were not to be obeyed.

ᶠ(Matt. 23:13) Whether the teachers of the law and Pharisees were still present to hear these words has been debated. The natural impression is that they must have been, because the "woes" are addressed to the second person ("you"). Because Jesus was still in the temple, it would be surprising if they had not been at least within earshot of his words. Aside from his two cleansings of the temple (Secs. 31, 129b), the wrath of Jesus shows itself more clearly here than at any other time. The failure of these religious leaders to qualify for entering the kingdom of God was clearly delineated on this occasion.

Matthew 23:1–36 (cont'd)

[17]You blind fools! Which is greater: the gold, or the temple that makes the gold sacred? [18]You also say, 'If anyone swears by the altar, it means nothing; but if anyone swears by the gift on it, he is bound by his oath.' [19]You blind men! Which is greater: the gift, or the altar that makes the gift sacred? [20]Therefore, he who swears by the altar swears by it and by everything on it. [21]And he who swears by the temple swears by it and by the one who dwells in it. [22]And he who swears by heaven swears by God's throne and by the one who sits on it.

[23]"Woe to you, teachers of the law and Pharisees, you hypocrites! You give a tenth of your spices—mint, dill and cummin. But you have neglected the more important matters of the law—justice, mercy and faithfulness. You should have practiced the latter, without neglecting the former. [24]You blind guides! You strain out a gnat but swallow a camel.

[25]"Woe to you, teachers of the law and Pharisees, you hypocrites! You clean the outside of the cup and dish, but inside they are full of greed and self-indulgence. [26]Blind Pharisee! First clean the inside of the cup and dish, and then the outside also will be clean.

[27]"Woe to you, teachers of the law and Pharisees, you hypocrites! You are like whitewashed tombs, which look beautiful on the outside but on the inside are full of dead men's bones and everything unclean. [28]In the same way, on the outside you appear to people as righteous but on the inside you are full of hypocrisy and wickedness.

[29]"Woe to you, teachers of the law and Pharisees, you hypocrites! You build tombs for the prophets and decorate the graves of the righteous. [30]And you say, 'If we had lived in the days of our forefathers, we would not have taken part with them in shedding the blood of the prophets.' [31]So you testify against yourselves that you are the descendants of those who murdered the prophets. [32]Fill up, then, the measure of the sin of your forefathers!

[33]"You snakes! You brood of vipers! How will you escape being condemned to hell? [34]Therefore I am sending you prophets and wise men and teachers. Some of them you will kill and crucify; others you will flog in your synagogues and pursue from town to town. [35]And so upon you will come all the righteous blood that has been shed on earth, from the blood of righteous Abel to the blood of Zechariah son of Berekiah, whom you murdered between the temple and the altar. [36]I tell you the truth, all this will come upon this generation.

[a]Mt 23:5 That is, boxes containing Scripture verses, worn on forehead and arm   [b]10 Or *Messiah*
[c]13 Some manuscripts *to.* [14]*Woe to you, teachers of the law and Pharisees, you hypocrites! You devour widows' houses and for a show make lengthy prayers. Therefore you will be punished more severely.*

Sec. 137b   Jesus' sorrow over Jerusalem
(cf. Sec. 113b—sorrow over Jerusalem)
—Jerusalem, in the temple—

Matthew 23:37–39

[37]"[g]O Jerusalem, Jerusalem, you who kill the prophets and stone those sent to you, how often I have longed to gather your children together, as a hen gathers her chicks under her wings, but you were not willing. [38]Look, your house is left to you desolate. [39]For I tell you, you will not see me again until [h]you say, 'Blessed is he who comes in the name of the Lord'[a]" [Psalm 118:26].

[a]Mt 23:39 Psalm 118:26

[g](Matt. 23:37) Jesus' deep concern for Jerusalem was voiced in similar language about three months earlier (Luke 13:34–35, Sec. 113b) and also two days before in somewhat different language (Luke 19:41–44, Sec. 128b). This city represented the whole nation of Israel, for whom Jesus was deeply burdened, especially in light of its coming judgment.

[h](Matt. 23:39) At his second coming a far greater proportion of Israel will joyfully recognize Jesus as Messiah than did so at his first coming. This lament over Jerusalem was preparatory to what Jesus wanted to tell his disciples about his future coming and its relation to Jerusalem (cf. Sec. 139a).

Sec. 138   A poor widow's gift of all she had
—Jerusalem, in the temple—

Mark 12:41–44

[41]Jesus sat down opposite the place where the offerings were put and watched the crowd putting their money into the temple treasury. Many rich people threw in large amounts. [42]But a poor widow came and put in two very small copper coins,[a] worth only a fraction of a penny.[b]

[43]Calling his disciples to him, Jesus said, "I tell you the truth, this poor widow has put more into the treasury than all the others. [44]They all gave out of their wealth; but [i]she, out of her poverty, put in everything—all she had to live on."

Luke 21:1–4

[1]As he looked up, Jesus saw the rich putting their gifts into the temple treasury. [2]He also saw a poor widow put in two very small copper coins.[c]

[3]"I tell you the truth," he said, "this poor widow has put in more than all the others. [4]All these people gave their gifts out of their wealth; but [i]she out of her poverty put in all she had to live on."

[a]Mk 12:42; Lk 21:2 Greek *two lepta*   [b]Mk 12:42 Greek *kodrantes*

---

[i](Mark 12:44; Luke 21:4) Here was an example of true piety. In contrast to the corrupt leadership (cf. Matt. 23:23–24, Sec. 137a), this woman gave from her heart, as evidenced by her self-sacrifice.

THE OLIVET DISCOURSE: JESUS SPEAKS PROPHETICALLY ABOUT THE TEMPLE AND HIS OWN SECOND COMING

Sec. 139a Setting of the discourse
—From the temple to the Mount of Olives—

Matthew 24:1–3	Mark 13:1–4	Luke 21:5–7
¹Jesus left the temple and was walking away when his disciples came up to him to call his attention to its buildings.	¹As he was leaving the temple, one of his disciples said to him, "Look, Teacher! What massive stones! What magnificent buildings!"	⁵Some of his disciples were remarking about how the temple was adorned with beautiful stones and with gifts dedicated to God. But Jesus
²"Do you see all these things?" he asked. "I tell you the truth, not one stone here will be left on another; every one will be thrown down."	²"Do you see all these great buildings?" replied Jesus. "Not one stone here will be left on another; every one will be thrown down."	said, ⁶"As for what you see here, the time will come when not one stone will be left on another; every one of them will be thrown down."
³As Jesus was sitting on the Mount of Olives, the disciples came to him privately.	³As Jesus was sitting on the Mount of Olives opposite the temple, Peter, James, John and Andrew asked him privately,	
"Tell us," they said, "ⁱwhen will this happen, and what will be the sign of your coming and of the end of the age?"	⁴"Tell us, ⁱwhen will these things happen? And what will be the sign that they are all about to be fulfilled?"	⁷"Teacher," they asked, "ⁱwhen will these things happen? And what will be the sign that they are about to take place?"

Sec. 139b Beginning of birth pains
(cf. Sec. 70b—divided households)
(cf. Sec. 108a—trials before courts and rulers)
—Mount of Olives—

Matthew 24:4–14	Mark 13:5–13	Luke 21:8–19
⁴Jesus answered: "Watch out that no one deceives you. ⁵For many will come in my name,	⁵Jesus said to them: "Watch out that no one deceives you. ⁶Many will come in my name, claim-	⁸He replied: "Watch out that you are not deceived. For many will come in my name, claiming, 'I am he,'

ⁱ(Matt. 24:3; Mark 13:4; Luke 21:7) The disciples apparently asked three questions. The first pertained to the destruction of the temple (cf. Matt. 24:1–2; Mark 13:1–2; Luke 21:5–6), which subsequently happened in A.D. 70 at the hands of the Roman army. Another pertained to Jesus' future personal return and the consummation of the age associated with it. Though separated by many years, the two events are closely related in that both are part of God's ongoing program for the people of Israel. The other question related to the sign when "these things," probably the destruction of the temple, were about to happen. The disciples assumed that the destruction of the temple would be the prelude to Messiah's return to consummate that age and initiate his kingdom on earth. Jesus did not deny a relationship between the two events, nor did he in the subsequent discourse reveal the long interval that would separate the two. Some predictions were fulfilled a few years after he spoke the words (e.g., Luke 21:20, Sec. 139c), but others have as yet to be fulfilled (e.g., Matt. 24:30, Sec. 139d).

Matthew 24:4–14 (cont'd)

Mark 13:5–13 (cont'd)

Luke 21:8–19 (cont'd)

claiming, 'I am the Christ,ᵃ' and will deceive many. ⁶You will hear of wars and rumors of wars, but see to it that you are not alarmed. Such things must happen, but the end is still to come. ⁷Nation will rise against nation, and kingdom against kingdom. There will be famines and earthquakes in various places. ⁸All these are the beginning of ᵏbirth pains.

⁹"Then you will be handed over to be persecuted and put to death, and you will be hated by all nations because of me. ¹⁰At that time many will turn away from the faith and will betray and hate each other,

ing, 'I am he,' and will deceive many. ⁷When you hear of wars and rumors of wars, do not be alarmed. Such things must happen, but the end is still to come. ⁸Nation will rise against nation, and kingdom against kingdom. There will be earthquakes in various places, and famines. These are the beginning of ᵏbirth pains.

⁹"You must be on your guard. You will be handed over to the local councils and flogged in the synagogues. On account of me you will stand before governors and kings as witnesses to them.

¹⁰And the gospel must first be preached to all nations. ¹¹Whenever you are arrested and brought to trial, do not worry beforehand about what to say. Just say whatever is given you at the time, for it is not you speaking, but the Holy Spirit. ¹²"Brother will betray brother to death, and a father his child. Children will rebel against their parents and have them put to death. ¹³All men will hate you because of me,

and, 'The time is near.' Do not follow them. ⁹When you hear of wars and revolutions, do not be frightened. These things must happen first, but the end will not come right away."

¹⁰Then he said to them: "Nation will rise against nation, and kingdom against kingdom. ¹¹There will be great earthquakes, famines and pestilences in various places, and fearful events and great signs from heaven.

¹²"But before all this, they will lay hands on you and persecute you. They will deliver you to synagogues and prisons, and you will be brought before kings and governors, and all on account of my name. ¹³This will result in your being witnesses to them.

¹⁴But make up your mind not to worry beforehand how you will defend yourselves. ¹⁵For I will give you words and wisdom that none of your adversaries will be able to resist or contradict. ¹⁶You will be betrayed even by parents, brothers, relatives and friends, and they will put some of you to death. ¹⁷All men will hate you because of me. ¹⁸But not a hair of your head will perish. ¹⁹By standing firm you will gain life.

¹¹and many false prophets will appear and deceive many people. ¹²Because of the increase

---

ᵏ(Matt. 24:8; Mark 13:8) "Birth pains" is a frequent figure of speech to depict the time of Israel's tribulation, which is the initial phase of "the day of the Lord" in Scripture (Isa. 13:8; 26:17–19; 66:7–9; Jer. 30:7–8; Mic. 4:9–10; 1 Thess. 5:3). This period of growing human agony will be climaxed by Messiah's second coming to earth.

Matthew 24:4–14 (cont'd)   Mark 13:5–13 (cont'd)

of wickedness, the love of most will grow cold, ¹³but he who stands firm to the end will be saved. ¹⁴And this gospel of the kingdom will be preached in the whole world as a testimony to all nations, and then the end will come.

but he who stands firm to the end will be saved.

ᵃMt 24:5 or *Messiah;* also in verse 23

Sec. 139c   Abomination of desolation and subsequent distress (cf. Sec. 120b—signs of Christ's return)
—*Mount of Olives*—

Matthew 24:15–28   Mark 13:14–23   Luke 21:20–24

¹⁵"So when you see standing in the holy place 'the ¹abomination that causes desolation'ᵃ [Dan. 9:27; 11:31; 12:11], spoken of through the prophet Daniel—let the reader understand—

¹⁴"When you see 'the ¹abomination that causes desolation'ᵇ [Dan. 9:27; 11:31; 12:11] standing where itᶜ does not belong—let the reader understand

²⁰"When you see Jerusalem being surrounded by armies, you will know that its desolation is near. ²¹Then let those who are in Judea flee to the mountains, let those in the city get out, and let those in the country not enter the city. ²²For this is the time of punishment in fulfillment of all that has been written. ²³How dreadful it will be in those days for pregnant women and nursing mothers!

¹⁶then let those who are in Judea flee to the mountains. ¹⁷Let no one on the roof of his house go down to take anything out of the house. ¹⁸Let no one in the field go back to get his cloak.

—then let those who are in Judea flee to the mountains. ¹⁵Let no one on the roof of his house go down or enter the house to take anything out. ¹⁶Let no one in the field go back to get his cloak.

¹⁹How dreadful it will be in those days for pregnant women and nursing mothers! ²⁰Pray that your flight will not take place in winter or on the Sabbath. ²¹For then there will be great distress, unequaled from the beginning of the world until now—and never to be equaled again. ²²If those days had not been cut short, no one would sur-

¹⁷How dreadful it will be in those days for pregnant women and nursing mothers! ¹⁸Pray that this will not take place in winter, ¹⁹because those will be days of distress unequaled from the beginning, when God created the world, until now—and never to be equaled again. ²⁰If the Lord had not cut short those days, no one would

---

¹(Matt. 24:15; Mark 13:14) This feature of Daniel's seventy-week prophecy (Dan. 9:27) had not been fulfilled by this time. Neither has it been fulfilled since Jesus' time. As the midpoint of the future seventieth week of the prophecy, the "abomination that causes desolation" furnishes one of the most conspicuous signs of Jesus' coming (cf. Matt. 24:3, Sec. 139a).

Matthew 24:15–28
(cont'd)

vive, but for the sake of
the elect those days will
be shortened.

Mark 13:14–23
(cont'd)

survive. But for the sake
of the elect, whom he has
chosen, he has shortened
them.

Luke 21:20–24
(cont'd)

There
will be great distress in
the land and wrath
against this people.
24They will fall by the
sword and will be taken
as prisoners to all the nations. Jerusalem will be
trampled on by the Gen-
tiles until the times of the
Gentiles are fulfilled.

23At that
time if anyone says to
you, 'Look, here is the
Christ!' or, 'There he is!'
do not believe it. 24For
false Christs and false
prophets will appear and
perform great signs and
miracles to deceive even
the elect—if that were
possible. 25See, I have told
you ahead of time.
26"So if anyone tells
you, 'There he is, out in
the desert,' do not go out;
or, 'Here he is, in the inner
rooms,' do not believe it.
27For as lightning that
comes from the east is visible even in the west, so
will be the coming of the
Son of Man. 28Wherever
there is a carcass, there
the vultures will gather.

21At that time if
anyone says to you, 'Look,
here is the Christ d!' or,
'Look, there he is!' do not
believe it. 22For false
Christs and false prophets
will appear and perform
signs and miracles to de-
ceive the elect—if that
were possible. 23So be on
your guard; I have told
you everything ahead of
time.

aMt 24:15; Mk 13:14 Daniel 9:27; 11:31; 12:11   bMk 13:14 Or he; also in verse 29   c21 Or Messiah

Sec. 139d   Coming of the Son of Man
(cf. Sec. 120b—signs of Christ's return)
—Mount of Olives—

Matthew 24:29–31

29"Immediately after
the distress of those days

" 'the sun will be
    darkened,
and the moon will not
    give its light;
the stars will fall [Isa.
    13:10; 34:4; Ezek.
    32:7; Joel 2:10, 31;

Mark 13:24–27

24"But in those days,
following that distress,

" 'the sun will be
    darkened,
and the moon will not
    give its light;
25the stars will fall [Isa.
    13:10; 34:4; Ezek.
    32:7; Joel 2:10, 31;

Luke 21:25–27

25"There will be signs
in the sun, moon and
stars. On the earth, na-
tions will be in anguish
and perplexity at the roar-
ing and tossing of the sea.
26Men will faint from ter-
ror, apprehensive of what
is coming on the world,

Matthew 24:29–31 (cont'd)	Mark 13:24–27 (cont'd)	Luke 21:25–27 (cont'd)
3:15] from the sky, and the heavenly bodies will be shaken.'[a]	3:15] from the sky, and the heavenly bodies will be shaken.'[b]	for the heavenly bodies will be shaken.
[30]"At that time the sign of the [m]Son of Man will appear in the sky, and all the nations of the earth will mourn. They will see the [m]Son of Man coming on the clouds of the sky [Dan. 7:13], with power and great glory. [31]And he will send his angels with a loud trumpet call, and they will gather [Isa. 27:13] his elect from the four winds, from one end of the heavens to the other.	[26]"At that time men will see the [m]Son of Man coming in clouds [Dan. 7:13] with great power and glory. [27]And he will send his angels and gather his elect from the four winds, from the ends of the earth to the ends of the heavens.	[27]At that time they will see the [m]Son of Man coming in a cloud [Dan. 7:13] with power and great glory.

[a]Mt 24:29; Mk 13:25 Isaiah 13:10; 34:4

Sec. 139e   Signs of nearness but unknown time (cf. Sec. 120b—signs of Christ's return)
—*Mount of Olives*—

Matthew 24:32–41	Mark 13:28–32	Luke 21:28–33
		[28]When these things begin to take place, stand up and lift up your heads, because your redemption is drawing near."
[32]"Now learn this lesson from the fig tree: As soon as its twigs get tender and its leaves come out, you know that summer is near. [33]Even so, when you see all [n]these things, you know that it[a] is near, right at the door. [34]I tell you the truth, this generation[b] will certainly not pass away until all these things have hap-	[28]"Now learn this lesson from the fig tree: As soon as its twigs get tender and its leaves come out, you know that summer is near. [29]Even so, when you see [n]these things happening, you know that it is near, right at the door. [30]I tell you the truth, this generation[d] will certainly not pass away until all these things	[29]He told them this parable: "Look at the fig tree and all the trees. [30]When they sprout leaves, you can see for yourselves and know that summer is near. [31]Even so, when you see [n]these things happening, you know that the kingdom of God is near. [32]"I tell you the truth, this generation[d] will certainly not pass away until

---

[m](Matt. 23:40; Mark 13:26; Luke 21:27) The return of "the Son of Man" to earth will climax all the hopes and aspirations of Israel. Coming, as it does, immediately after her time of tribulation (Matt. 24:29), the return will be the occasion for regathering the dispersed of Israel (Matt. 24:31; Mark 13:27). Throughout the Old Testament this national deliverance is a recurring theme of Jewish eschatological hope (Deut. 30:3–4; Isa. 11:12; 27:13; 56:8; Jer. 23:3; 31:8; Ezek. 11:17; 20:34, 41; 28:25; 34:13; cf. Rom. 11:26).

[n](Matt. 24:33; Mark 13:29; Luke 21:31) "These things" are events the Lord has described in earlier verses of this discourse, such as the "birth pains" (Matt. 24:8; Mark 13:9, Sec. 139b), and "the abomination that causes desolation" (Matt. 24:15; Mark 13:14, Sec. 139c). When Israel sees these things beginning to happen, it can recognize that its "redemption is drawing near" (Luke 21:28) and that "the kingdom of God is near" (Luke 21:31). It will experience this national deliverance through the coming of the Son of Man (cf. Sec. 139d).

Matthew 24:32–41 (cont'd)	Mark 13:28–32 (cont'd)	Luke 21:28–33 (cont'd)
pened. [35]Heaven and earth will pass away, but my words will never pass away. [36]"No one knows about that day or hour, not even the angels in heaven, nor the Son,[c] but only the Father. [37]As it was in the days of Noah, so it will be at the coming of the Son of Man. [38]For in the days before the flood, people were eating and drinking, marrying and giving in marriage, up to the day Noah entered the ark [Gen. 7:7]; [39]and they knew nothing about what would happen until the flood came and took them all away. That is how it will be at the coming of the Son of Man. [40]Two men will be in the field; one will be taken and the other left. [41]Two women will be grinding with a hand mill; one will be taken and the other left.	have happened. [31]Heaven and earth will pass away, but my words will never pass away. [32]"No one knows about that day or hour, not even the angels in heaven, nor the Son, but only the Father.	all these things have happened. [33]Heaven and earth will pass away, but my words will never pass away.

[a]Mt 24:33 Or he   [b]Mt 24:34; Mk 13:30; Lk 21:32 Or race   [c]Mt 24:36 Some manuscripts do not have nor the Son.

Sec. 139f [o]**Five parables to teach watchfulness and faithfulness**
(cf. Sec. 108c—readiness for Christ's return)
(cf. Sec. 127b—faithful handling of the Lord's possessions)
—Mount of Olives—

Matthew 24:42–25:30	Mark 13:33–37	Luke 21:34–36
	[33]Be on guard! Be alert[b]! You do not know when that time will come. [34]It's like a man going away: He leaves his house and puts his servants in charge, each with his assigned task, and tells the one at the door to keep watch.	[34]"Be careful, or your hearts will be weighed down with dissipation, drunkenness and the anxieties of life, and that day will close on you unexpectedly like a trap. [35]For it will come upon all those who live on the face of the whole earth. [36]Be always on the watch, and pray that you may be able to escape all that is about
[42]"Therefore keep watch, because you do	[35]"Therefore keep watch because you do not	

[o]Of the five parables, one is in Mark alone (13:34–36) and four are in Matthew only (24:43, 45–51; 25:1–12, 14–30). In the first, second, and fourth parables the dominant lesson is watchfulness. The lesson of the third and fifth parables is that faithfulness in service must accompany alertness for the Lord's return.

Matthew 24:42–25:30	Mark 13:33–37	Luke 21:34–36
(cont'd)	(cont'd)	(cont'd)

not know on what day your Lord will come.	know when the owner of the house will come back —whether in the evening, or at midnight, or when the rooster crows, or at dawn. [36]If he comes suddenly, do not let him find you sleeping. [37]What I say to you, I say to everyone: 'Watch!' "	to happen, and that you may be able to stand before the Son of Man.''

[43]But understand this: If the owner of the house had known at what time of night the thief was coming, he would have kept watch and would not have let his house be broken into. [44]So you also must be ready, because the Son of Man will come at an hour when you do not expect him.

[45]"Who then is the faithful and wise servant, whom the master has put in charge of the servants in his household to give them their food at the proper time? [46]It will be good for that servant whose master finds him doing so when he returns. [47]I tell you the truth, he will put him in charge of all his possessions. [48]But suppose that servant is wicked and says to himself, 'My master is staying away a long time,' [49]and he then begins to beat his fellow servants and to eat and drink with drunkards. [50]The master of that servant will come on a day when he does not expect him and at an hour he is not aware of. [51]He will cut him to pieces and assign him a place with the hypocrites, where there will be weeping and gnashing of teeth.

[1]"At that time the kingdom of heaven will be like ten virgins who took their lamps and went out to meet the bridegroom. [2]Five of them were foolish and five were wise. [3]The foolish ones took their lamps but did not take any oil with them. [4]The wise, however, took oil in jars along with their lamps. [5]The bridegroom was a long time in coming, and they all became drowsy and fell asleep.

[6]"At midnight the cry rang out: 'Here's the bridegroom! Come out to meet him!'

[7]"Then all the virgins woke up and trimmed their lamps. [8]The foolish ones said to the wise, 'Give us some of your oil; our lamps are going out.'

[9]" 'No,' they replied, 'there may not be enough for both us and you. Instead, go to those who sell oil and buy some for yourselves.'

[10]"But while they were on their way to buy the oil, the bridegroom arrived. The virgins who were ready went in with him to the wedding banquet. And the door was shut.

[11]"Later the others also came. 'Sir! Sir!' they said. 'Open the door for us!'

[12]"But he replied, 'I tell you the truth, I don't know you.'

[13]"Therefore keep watch, because you do not know the day or the hour.

[14]"Again, it will be like a man going on a journey, who called his servants and entrusted his property to them. [15]To one he gave five talents[a] of money, to another two talents, and to another one talent, each according to his ability. Then he went on his journey. [16]The man who had received the five talents went at once and put his money to work and gained five more. [17]So also, the one with the two talents gained two more. [18]But the man who had received the one talent went off, dug a hole in the ground and hid his master's money.

[19]"After a long time the master of those servants returned and settled accounts with them. [20]The man who had received the five talents brought the other five. 'Master,' he said, 'you entrusted me with five talents. See, I have gained five more.'

Matthew 24:42–25:30 (cont'd)

[21]"His master replied, 'Well done, good and faithful servant! You have been faithful with a few things; I will put you in charge of many things. Come and share your master's happiness!'

[22]"The man with the two talents also came. 'Master,' he said, 'you entrusted me with two talents; see, I have gained two more.'

[23]"His master replied, 'Well done, good and faithful servant! You have been faithful with a few things; I will put you in charge of many things. Come and share your master's happiness!'

[24]"Then the man who had received the one talent came. 'Master,' he said, 'I knew that you are a hard man, harvesting where you have not sown and gathering where you have not scattered seed. [25]So I was afraid and went out and hid your talent in the ground. See, here is what belongs to you.'

[26]"His master replied, 'You wicked, lazy servant! So you knew that I harvest where I have not sown and gather where I have not scattered seed? [27]Well then, you should have put my money on deposit with the bankers, so that when I returned I would have received it back with interest.

[28]" 'Take the talent from him and give it to the one who has the ten talents. [29]For everyone who has will be given more, and he will have an abundance. Whoever does not have, even what he has will be taken from him. [30]And throw that worthless servant outside, into the darkness, where there will be weeping and gnashing of teeth.'

[a]Mt 24:15 A talent was worth more than a thousand dollars.   [b]Mk 13:33 Some manuscripts *alert and pray*

Sec. 139g   Judgment at the Son of Man's coming
—*Mount of Olives*—

Matthew 25:31–46

[31]"When the Son of Man comes in his glory, and all the angels with him, he will sit on his [p]throne in heavenly glory. [32]All the nations will be gathered before him, and he will separate the people one from another as a shepherd separates the sheep from the goats. [33]He will put the sheep on his right and the goats on his left.

[34]"Then the King will say to those on his right, 'Come, you who are blessed by my Father; take your inheritance, the kingdom prepared for you since the creation of the world. [35]For I was hungry and you gave me something to eat, I was thirsty and you gave me something to drink, I was a stranger and you invited me in, [36]I needed clothes and you clothed me, I was sick and you looked after me, I was in prison and you came to visit me.'

[37]"Then the righteous will answer him, 'Lord, when did we see you hungry and feed you, or thirsty and give you something to drink? [38]When did we see you a stranger and invite you in, or needing clothes and clothe you? [39]When did we see you sick or in prison and go to visit you?'

[40]"The King will reply, 'I tell you the truth, whatever you did for one of the least of these brothers of mine, you did for me.'

[41]"Then he will say to those on his left, 'Depart from me, you who are cursed, into the eternal fire prepared for the devil and his angels. [42]For I was hungry and you gave me nothing to eat, I was thirsty and you gave me nothing to drink, [43]I was a stranger and you did not invite me in, I needed clothes and you did not clothe me, I was sick and in prison and you did not look after me.'

[44]"They also will answer, 'Lord, when did we see you hungry or thirsty or a stranger or needing clothes or sick or in prison, and did not help you?'

[p](Matt. 25:31) The throne on which the Son of Man will sit when he comes (cf. Matt. 24:30; Mark 13:26; Luke 21:27, Sec. 139d) will be located at his destination, that is, on earth ("heavenly" in v. 31 is not supported by the Greek text). It is the throne of his father David, to which he is heir (Luke 1:32–33, Sec. 5). From here he will judge the survivors of the period of the Great Tribulation ("great distress," Matt. 24:21–22; Mark 13:19–20, Sec. 139c; Matt. 24:29; Mark 13:24, Sec. 139d).

Matthew 25:31–46 (cont'd)

⁴⁵"He will reply, 'I tell you the truth, whatever you did not do for one of the least of these, you did not do for me.'

⁴⁶"Then they will go away to eternal punishment, but the righteous to eternal life."

ARRANGEMENTS FOR BETRAYAL

Sec. 140 Plot by the Sanhedrin to arrest and kill Jesus
—*Mount of Olives and the palace of the high priest*—

Matthew 26:1–5	Mark 14:1–2	Luke q[21:37–38]; 22:1–2
¹When Jesus had finished saying all these things, he said to his disciples, ²"As you know, the Passover is two days away—and the Son of Man will be handed over to be crucified." ³Then ʳthe chief priests and the elders of the people assembled in the palace of the high priest, whose name was Caiaphas, ⁴and they plotted to arrest Jesus in some sly way and kill him. ⁵"But not during the Feast," they said, "or there may be a riot among the people."	¹Now the Passover and the Feast of Unleavened Bread were only two days away, and the chief priests and the teachers of the law were looking for some sly way to arrest Jesus and kill him. ²"But not during the Feast," they said, "or the people may riot."	¹Now the Feast of Unleavened Bread, called the Passover, was approaching, ²and the chief priests and the teachers of the law were looking for some way to get rid of Jesus, for they were afraid of the people.

Sec. 141 Mary's anointing of Jesus for burial
(cf. Sec. 59—anointing with perfume)
—*Bethany, in the home of Simon the leper*—

ˢMatthew 26:6–13	ˢMark 14:3–9	ˢJohn 12:2–8
⁶While Jesus was in Bethany in the home of a man known as Simon the Leper, ⁷a woman came to him with an alabaster jar	³While he was in Bethany, reclining at the table in the home of a man known as Simon the Leper, a woman came with an	²Here a dinner was given in Jesus' honor. Martha served, while Lazarus was among those reclining at the table with him. ³Then

q(Luke 21:37–38) For the text of these two verses, see Section 131 and note u associated with that section.

r(Matt. 26:3) The Sanhedrin, represented by two of its three groups and presided over by Caiaphas, met to lay plans as to how it could impl ment the decision already reached (cf. John 11:53, Sec. 119). Because of Jesus' great popularity (Luke 21:38; 22:2), particularly among the visitors from Galilee and Perea, they decided to wait until after the feast (Matt. 26:5; Mark 14:2), when these pilgrims would have gone home. Their schedule of action was accelerated, however, when they received an unexpected offer of cooperation from one of the Twelve (Sec. 142). This enabled them to arrest Jesus privately (Luke 22:6, Sec. 142; Sec. 153). In this way God's predetermined schedule for the Lamb of God to be slain on the Passover, and not after, (Matt. 26:2) was kept.

s(Matt. 26:6–13; Mark 14:3–9; John 12:2–8) See note m just after Section 128a.

Matthew 26:6–13 (cont'd)	*Mark 14:3–9 (cont'd)	*John 12:2–8 (cont'd)

of very expensive perfume, which she poured on his head as he was reclining at the table.

⁸When the disciples saw this, they were indignant. "Why this waste?" they asked. ⁹"This perfume could have been sold at a high price and the money given to the poor."

¹⁰Aware of this, Jesus said to them, "Why are you bothering this woman? She has done a beautiful thing to me. ¹¹The poor you will always have with you, but you will not always have me. ¹²When she poured this perfume on my body, she did it to prepare me for burial. ¹³I tell you the truth, wherever this gospel is preached throughout the world, what she has done will also be told, in memory of her."

alabaster jar of very expensive perfume, made of pure nard. She broke the jar and poured the perfume on his head.

⁴Some of those present were saying indignantly to one another, "Why this waste of perfume? ⁵It could have been sold for more than a year's wages ͣ and the money given to the poor." And they rebuked her harshly.

⁶"Leave her alone," said Jesus. "Why are you bothering her? She has done a beautiful thing to me. ⁷The poor you will always have with you, and you can help them any time you want. But you will not always have me. ⁸She did what she could. She poured perfume on my body beforehand to prepare for my burial. ⁹I tell you the truth, wherever the gospel is preached throughout the world, what she has done will also be told, in memory of her."

Mary took about a pint ᵇ of pure nard, an expensive perfume; she poured it on Jesus' feet and wiped his feet with her hair. And the house was filled with the fragrance of the perfume.

⁴But one of his disciples, Judas Iscariot, who was later to betray him, objected, ⁵"Why wasn't this perfume sold and the money given to the poor? It was worth a year's wages. ͨ" ⁶He did not say this because he cared about the poor but because he was a thief; as keeper of the money bag, he used to help himself to what was put into it.

⁷"Leave her alone," Jesus replied. "It was intended that she should save this perfume for the day of my burial. ⁸You will always have the poor among you, but you will not always have me."

ͣMk 14:5 Greek *than three hundred denarii*   ᵇJn 12:3 Greek *a litra* (probably about 0.5 liter)
ͨ5 Greek *three hundred denarii*

Sec. 142   Judas' agreement to betray Jesus
—*Jerusalem*—

Matthew 26:14–16	Mark 14:10–11	Luke 22:3–6

¹⁴Then one of the Twelve—the one called Judas Iscariot—went to the chief priests ¹⁵and asked, "What are you

¹⁰Then Judas Iscariot, one of the Twelve, went to the chief priests to betray Jesus to them.

³Then ᵗSatan entered Judas, called Iscariot, one of the Twelve. ⁴And Judas went to the chief priests and the officers of the

ᵗ(Luke 22:3) The Scripture does not tell what form of deception Satan used to persuade Judas to follow this calamitous course. Judas could have been moved by any one of a number of motives or a combination of several. Covetousness seems to have played some part (John 12:6, Sec. 141). He may have wanted to make it appear to the rest of the Twelve that he, like them, was concerned for the poor (Matt. 26:8–9; Mark 14:4–5, Sec. 141). He possibly felt his obligation as a citizen to obey the recent ruling about reporting Jesus' whereabouts to the authorities (John 11:57, Sec. 128a). He may have been more disappointed than the rest of the Twelve over the outcome of the triumphal entry: that Jesus and the Jewish leaders did not enter into an agreement to make him King (Matt. 21:15–17; Luke 19:39–40, Sec. 128b). Perhaps he thought by this action he could force Jesus to assume the throne. After what he had witnessed over the past three years, in all likelihood he never dreamed that his action would result in Jesus' crucifixion (Sec. 158). Whatever the case, his motives must have been selfish. Otherwise, Satan could not have gained control over him.

Matthew 26:14–16 (cont'd)	Mark 14:10–11 (cont'd)	Luke 22:3–6 (cont'd)
willing to give me if I hand him over to you?" So they counted out for him thirty silver coins. [16]From then on Judas watched for an opportunity to hand him over.	[11]They were delighted to hear this and promised to give him money. So he watched for an opportunity to hand him over.	temple guard and discussed with them how he might betray Jesus. [5]They were delighted and agreed to give him money. [6]He consented, and watched for an opportunity to hand Jesus over to them when no crowd was present.

THE LAST SUPPER

Sec. 143   Preparation for the Passover meal
—*Jerusalem*—

Matthew 26:17–19	Mark 14:12–16	Luke 22:7–13
[17]On the first day of the Feast of Unleavened Bread, the disciples came to Jesus and asked, "Where do you want us to ᵘmake preparations for you to eat the Passover?" [18]He replied,	[12]On the first day of the Feast of Unleavened Bread, when it was customary to sacrifice the Passover lamb, Jesus' disciples asked him, "Where do you want us to go and ᵘmake preparations for you to eat the Passover?" [13]So he sent two of his disciples, telling them,	[7]Then came the day of Unleavened Bread on which the Passover lamb had to be sacrificed. [8]Jesus sent Peter and John, saying, "Go and ᵘmake preparations for us to eat the Passover." [9]"Where do you want us to prepare for it?" they asked. [10]He replied, "As you enter the city, a man carrying a jar of water will meet you. Follow him to the house that he enters, [11]and say to the owner of the house, 'The Teacher asks: Where is the guest room, where I may eat the Passover with my disciples?' [12]He will show you a large upper room, all furnished. Make preparations there." [13]They left and found things just as Jesus had told them. So they prepared the Passover.
"Go into the city to a certain man and tell him, 'The Teacher says: My appointed time is near. I am going to celebrate the Passover with my disciples at your house.'" [19]So the disciples did as Jesus had directed them and prepared the Passover.	"Go into the city, and a man carrying a jar of water will meet you. Follow him. [14]Say to the owner of the house he enters, 'The Teacher asks: Where is my guest room, where I may eat the Passover with my disciples?' [15]He will show you a large upper room, furnished and ready. Make preparations for us there." [16]The disciples left, went into the city and found things just as Jesus had told them. So they prepared the Passover.	

ᵘ(Matt. 26:17; Mark 14:12; Luke 22:8) These preparations came during the daylight hours on Thursday, the fourteenth of Nisan. Lambs were customarily sacrificed in the afternoon in preparation for the Passover supper, which was eaten in the evening.

Sec. 144   Beginning of the Passover meal and dissension among the disciples over greatness
(cf. Sec. 125b—rivalry over greatness)
—*Jerusalem, in the upper room*—

Matthew 26:20	Mark 14:17	Luke 22:14–16, ᵛ24–30
²⁰When evening came, Jesus was reclining at the table with the Twelve.	¹⁷When evening came, Jesus arrived with the Twelve.	¹⁴When the hour came, Jesus and his apostles reclined at the table. ¹⁵And he said to them, "I have eagerly desired to eat this ʷPassover with you before I suffer. ¹⁶For I tell you, I will not eat it again until it finds fulfillment in the kingdom of God." ²⁴Also a dispute arose among them as to which of them was considered to be greatest. ²⁵Jesus said to them, "The kings of the Gentiles lord it over them; and those who exercise authority over them call themselves Benefactors. ²⁶But you are not to be like that. Instead, the greatest among you should be like the youngest, and the one who rules like the one who serves. ²⁷For who is greater, the one who is at the table or the one who serves? Is it not the one who is at the table? But I am among you as one who serves. ²⁸You are those who have stood by me in my trials. ²⁹And I confer on you a kingdom, just as my Father conferred one on me, ³⁰so that you may eat and drink at my table in my kingdom and sit on thrones, judging the twelve tribes of Israel.

ᵛ(Luke 22:24–30) The text of these verses is printed here in agreement with A. T. Robertson's placement. The dispute among the disciples described therein may have immediately preceded and have been the occasion for the example of foot washing (Sec. 145). Yet, in the opinion of the revisers of Robertson's *Harmony*, there is not ample reason for departing from Luke's placement of the argument after the identification of the betrayer (Sec. 146). At this later time Jesus' words about the destruction of Jerusalem and his second coming (Secs. 139a–g) again provoked the disciples to ambition in relation to their roles of leadership when the promised kingdom on earth would become a reality (Sec. 125b). On the night before his crucifixion, Jesus' patience must have been taxed, because they still had not learned his oft repeated lesson on humility. Jesus, nevertheless, corrected them in regard to this important character trait once again (Luke 22:26–27) but did not correct their anticipations about the kingdom. He rather confirmed them (Luke 22:28–30).

ʷ(Luke 22:15) Matthew, Mark, and Luke leave no doubt that this Last Supper was the Passover meal. This means that it took place on the fifteenth of Nisan (Lev. 23:5), that is, Thursday evening after sundown, which was the evening that closed the fourteenth and began the fifteenth.

Sec. 145   Washing the disciples' feet
(cf. Secs. 54g, 70b, 150b—followers not above the leader)
(cf. Sec. 90—to receive the Son is to receive the Father)
—Jerusalem, in the upper room—

John 13:1–20

[1]It was just [x]before the Passover Feast. Jesus knew that the time had come for him to leave this world and go to the Father. Having loved his own who were in the world, he now showed them the full extent of his love.[a]

[2]The evening meal was being served, and the devil had already prompted Judas Iscariot, son of Simon, to betray Jesus. [3]Jesus knew that the Father had put all things under his power, and that he had come from God and was returning to God; [4]so he got up from the meal, took off his outer clothing, and wrapped a towel around his waist. [5]After that, he poured water into a basin and began to wash his disciples' feet, drying them with the towel that was wrapped around him.

[6]He came to Simon Peter, who said to him, "Lord, are you going to wash my feet?"

[7]Jesus replied, "You do not realize now what I am doing, but later you will understand."

[8]"No," said Peter, "you shall never wash my feet."

Jesus answered, "Unless I wash you, you have no part with me."

[9]"Then, Lord," Simon Peter replied, "not just my feet but my hands and my head as well!"

[10]Jesus answered, "A person who has had a bath needs only to wash his feet; his whole body is clean. And you are clean, though not every one of you." [11]For he knew who was going to betray him, and that was why he said not every one was clean.

[12]When he had finished washing their feet, he put on his clothes and returned to his place. "Do you understand what I have done for you?" he asked them. [13]"You call me 'Teacher' and 'Lord,' and rightly so, for that is what I am. [14]Now that I, your Lord and Teacher, have washed your feet, you also should wash one another's feet. [15]I have set you an [y]example that you should do as I have done for you. [16]I tell you the truth, no servant is greater than his master, nor is a messenger greater than the one who sent him. [17]Now that you know these things, you will be blessed if you do them.

[18]"I am not referring to all of you; I know those I have chosen. But this is to fulfill the scripture: 'He who shares my bread has lifted up his heel against me'[b] [Psalm 41:9].

[19]"I am telling you now before it happens, so that when it does happen you will believe that I am He. [20]I tell you the truth, whoever accepts anyone I send accepts me; and whoever accepts me accepts the one who sent me."

[a]Jn 13:1 Or *he loved them to the last*   [b]18 Psalm 41:9

Sec. 146   Identification of the betrayer
—Jerusalem, in the upper room—

Matthew 26:21–25	Mark 14:18–21	Luke 22:21–23	John 13:21–30
	[18]While they were reclining at the table eating, he said,		[21]After he had said this, Jesus was troubled in spirit

[x](John 13:1) Apparently John intends this as a chronological note to locate the supper (John 13:2) described in the rest of the chapter. It is also apparent that this is the same supper described as the Passover in the synoptic gospels (cf. Secs. 143–144). Therefore John seems to have in mind a different scheme for reckoning when the Passover began. For further discussion, see essay 10, "The Day and Year of Christ's Crucifixion" (pp. 311–14).

[y](John 13:15) What Jesus did while the supper was in progress was intended to be an example of self-sacrificing humility. The disciples would do well to imitate their Teacher in possessing this quality (John 13:14, 16–17; cf. Secs. 125b, 144).

Matthew 26:21–25 (cont'd)	Mark 14:18–21 (cont'd)	Luke 22:21–23 (cont'd)	John 13:21–30 (cont'd)

Matthew 26:21–25 (cont'd)

21And while they were eating, he said, "I tell you the truth, one of you will betray me."

22They were very sad and began to say to him one after the other, "Surely not I, Lord?"
23Jesus replied, "ᶻThe one who has dipped his hand into the bowl with me will betray me. 24The Son of Man will go just as it is written about him. But woe to that man who betrays the Son of Man! It would be better for him if he had not been born."

Mark 14:18–21 (cont'd)

"I tell you the truth, one of you will betray me—one who is eating with me."

19They were saddened, and one by one they said to him, "Surely not I?"
20"ᶻIt is one of the Twelve," he replied, "one who dips bread into the bowl with me. 21The Son of Man will go just as it is written about him. But woe to that man who betrays the Son of Man! It would be better for him if he had not been born."

Luke 22:21–23 (cont'd)

21But ᶻthe hand of him who is going to betray me is with mine on the table. 22The Son of Man will go as it has been decreed, but woe to that man who betrays him." 23They began to question among themselves which of them it might be who would do this.

John 13:21–30 (cont'd)

and testified, "I tell you the truth, one of you is going to betray me."

22His disciples stared at one another, at a loss to know which of them he meant.

23One of them, the disciple whom Jesus loved, was reclining next to him. 24Simon Peter motioned to this disciple and said, "Ask him which one he means."
25Leaning back against Jesus, he asked him, "Lord, who is it?"
26Jesus answered, "ᶻIt is the one to whom I will give this piece of bread when I have dipped it in the dish." Then, dipping the piece of

---

ᶻ(Matt. 26:23, 25; Mark 14:20; Luke 22:21; John 13:26) Mark and Luke do not identify the traitor by name, but Matthew and John do. The rest present apparently did not grasp that Judas was the betrayer (John 13:28). Judas was an honored member of the Twelve. He was their treasurer (John 13:29; cf. John 12:6, Sec. 141), and normally was the one to administer benevolences to the poor on their behalf (John 13:29; cf. John. 12:4–5, Sec. 141). In fact, he seemingly was seated in the place of honor at this supper, that is, at Jesus' left hand, and John the apostle was on his right (John 13:23, 26). Surely, the rest of the disciples must have reasoned, one so respected as Judas could not be the betrayer.

Matthew 26:21–25
(cont'd)

John 13:21–30
(cont'd)

bread, he gave it to Judas Iscariot, son of   Simon.

[25]Then Judas, the one who would betray   him,   said, "Surely not I, Rabbi?"

Jesus   answered, "Yes, it is you."[a]

[27]As soon as Judas took the   bread,   Satan entered into him.

"What   you   are about   to   do,   do quickly,"   Jesus told him, [28]but no one at the meal understood   why Jesus said this to him. [29]Since Judas had charge of the money,   some thought Jesus was telling him to buy what   was   needed for the Feast, or to give something to the poor. [30]As soon as Judas had taken the bread, he went out.   And   it   was night.

[a]Mt 26:25 Or *"You yourself have said it"*

[Dissension among the disciples over greatness
—*Jerusalem, in the upper room*—

[a]Luke 22:24–30]

Sec. 147   Prediction of Peter's denial
(cf. Sec. 156—Peter's denials)
—*Jerusalem, in the upper room*—

John 13:31–36

[31]When he was gone, Jesus said, "Now is the Son of Man glorified and God is glorified in him. [32]If God is glorified in him,[a] God will glorify the Son in himself, and will glorify him at once.

[a](Luke 22:24–30) For the text of these verses, see Section 144 and note v associated with that section.

John 13:31–36 (cont.)

[33]"My children, I will be with you only a little longer. You will look for me, and just as I told the Jews, so I tell you now: Where I am going, you cannot come. [34]"A new command I give you: Love one another. As I have loved you, so you must love one another. [35]By this all men will know that you are my disciples, if you love one another."

[36]Simon Peter asked him, "Lord, where are you going?"

Jesus replied, "Where I am going, you cannot follow now, but you will follow later."

[b]Matthew 26:31–35	[b]Mark 14:27–31	Luke 22:31–38	John 13:37–38

[31]Then Jesus told them, "This very night you will all fall away on account of me, for it is written:

" 'I will strike the shepherd, and the sheep of the flock will be scattered'[b] [Zech. 13:7].

[32]But after I have risen, I will go ahead of you into Galilee."

[33]Peter replied, "Even if all fall away on account of you, I never will."

[34]"I tell you the truth," Jesus answered, "this very night, before the [c]rooster crows, you will disown me three times."

[35]But Peter declared, "Even if I have to die with you, I will never disown you." And

[27]"You will all fall away," Jesus told them, "for it is written:

" 'I will strike the shepherd, and the sheep will be scattered'[b] [Zech. 13:7].

[28]But after I have risen, I will go ahead of you into Galilee."

[29]Peter declared, "Even if all fall away, I will not."

[30]"I tell you the truth," Jesus answered, "today— yes, tonight—before the [c]rooster crows twice[c] you yourself will disown me three times."

[31]But Peter insisted emphatically, "Even if I have to die with you, I will never disown

[31]"Simon, Simon, Satan has asked to sift you[d] as wheat. [32]But I have prayed for you, Simon, that your faith may not fail. And when you have turned back, strengthen your brothers."

[33]But he replied, "Lord, I am ready to go with you to prison and to death."

[34]Jesus answered, "I tell you, Peter, before the [c]rooster crows today, you will deny three times that you know me."

[37]Peter asked, "Lord, why can't I follow you now? I will lay down my life for you."

[38]Then Jesus answered, "Will you really lay down your life for me? I tell you the truth, before the [c]rooster crows, you will disown me three times!

---

[b](Matt. 26:31–35; Mark 14:27–31) In compliance with A. T. Robertson's *Harmony*, these two passages are printed as part of Section 147. This places Matthew's and Mark's predictions of Peter's denial in parallel with the similar predictions found in Luke and John. In the opinion of the revisers of this *Harmony*, however, Jesus made at least two predictions of Peter's denials, the earlier one coming in Luke and John (Luke 22:34; John 13:38) and the later one described in Matthew and Mark (Matthew 26:34; Mark 14:30). The reason two distinct predictions are seen relates to their placement by the writers. Luke and John make Jesus' prediction of Peter's denial an integral part of the events in the upper room (cf. Luke 22:39; John 18:1, Sec. 152), and Matthew and Mark locate a comparable prediction at the Mount of Olives (cf. Matt. 26:30; Mark 14:26, Sec. 152). In connection with this second prediction, Peter and the other disciples claimed they would never deny Jesus (Matt. 26:35; Mark 14:31, Sec. 147). If this conclusion is valid, the Matthean and Marcan accounts of the prediction relate more closely to Section 152 than they do to the current section.

Matt. 26:31–35 (cont'd)	Mark 14:27–31 (cont'd)	Luke 22:31–38 (cont'd)
all the other disciples said the same.	you." And all the others said the same.	

[Luke 22:31-38 continued:]

35Then Jesus asked them, "When I sent you without purse, bag or sandals, did you lack anything?"

"Nothing," they answered.

36He said to them, "But now if you have a purse, take it, and also a bag; and if you don't have a sword, sell your cloak and buy one. 37It is written: 'And he was numbered with the transgressors'e; [Isa. 53:12]; and I tell you that this must be fulfilled in me. Yes, what is written about me is reaching its fulfillment."

38The disciples said, "See, Lord, here are two swords."

"That is enough," he replied.

---

aJn 13:32 Many early manuscripts do not have *If God is glorified in him.* bMt 26:31; Mk 14:27 Zech. 13:7 cMk 14:30 Some early manuscripts do not have *twice.* dMk 14:31 The Greek is plural. eLk 22:37 Isaiah 53:12

---

c(Matt. 26:34; Mark 14:30; Luke 22:34; John 13:38) The third of the four "watches" of the night (12:00 A.M. to 3:00 A.M.) was called "rooster crowing" (cf. Mark 13:35, Sec. 139f). The rooster would crow early in this period and again toward the period's end. In Mark's account Jesus referred to the second crowing so as to be quite specific. Matthew, Luke, and John record a reiteration of his prediction in more general terms, that is, they refer to only one crowing, the second, which was the more commonly known of the two. Before dawn the next morning Peter was to deny his Lord three times.

Sec. 148   Conclusion of the meal and the Lord's Supper instituted
—Jerusalem, in the upper room—

Matthew 26:26–29	Mark 14:22–25	Luke 22:17–20	1 Corinthians 11:23–26
		[17]After taking the cup, he gave thanks and said, "Take this and divide it among you. [18]For I tell you I will not drink again of the fruit of the vine until the kingdom of God comes."	[23]For I received from the Lord what I also passed on to you: The Lord Jesus, on the night
[26]While they were eating, Jesus took bread, gave thanks and broke it, and gave it to his disciples, saying, "Take and eat; this is my body." [27]Then he took the [d]cup, gave thanks and offered it to them, saying, "Drink from it, all of you. [28]This is my blood of the[a] covenant, which is poured out for many for the forgiveness of sins. [29]I tell you, I will not drink of this fruit of the vine from now on until that day when I drink it anew with you in my Father's kingdom."	[22]While they were eating, Jesus took bread, gave thanks and broke it, and gave it to his disciples, saying, "Take it; this is my body." [23]Then he took the [d]cup, gave thanks and offered it to them, and they all drank from it. [24]"This is my blood of the[b] covenant, which is poured out for many," he said to them. [25]"I tell you the truth, I will not drink again of the fruit of the vine until that day when I drink it anew in the kingdom of God."	[19]And he took bread, gave thanks and broke it, and gave it to them, saying, "This is my body given for you; do this in remembrance of me." [20]In the same way, after the supper he took the [d]cup, saying, "This cup is the new covenant in my blood, which is poured out for you.	he was betrayed, took bread, [24]and when he had given thanks, he broke it and said, "This is my body, which is for you; do this in remembrance of me." [25]In the same way, after supper he took the [d]cup, saying, "This cup is the new covenant in my blood; do this, whenever you drink it, in remembrance of me." [26]For whenever you eat this bread and drink this cup, you proclaim the Lord's death until he comes.

[a]Mt 26:28; Mk 14:24 Some manuscripts *the new*

[d](Matt. 26:27; Mark 14:23; Luke 22:20; 1 Cor. 11:25) Like the bread (Matt. 26:26; Mark 14:22; Luke 22:19; 1 Cor. 11:23), this cup was part of the traditional Passover meal among the Jews. It was the third of four times that participants took the cup during the meal. Traditionally the third cup related to the third of four promises of God to Israel in Exodus 6:6–7: "I will free you from being slaves to them, and I will redeem you with an outstretched arm and with mighty acts of judgment." It becomes symbolic of the shedding of Jesus' blood for redemption (Matt. 26:28; Mark 14:24; Luke 22:20; 1 Cor. 11:25). The final cup, relating to the fourth promise, that of the restoration of Israel, will not be taken by Jesus until the establishing of the kingdom of God (Matt. 26:29; Mark 14:25).

DISCOURSE AND PRAYERS FROM THE UPPER ROOM
TO GETHSEMANE

Sec. 149   Questions about his destination, the Father, and the Holy Spirit answered

—Jerusalem, in the upper room—

John 14:1–31

[1]"*Do not let your hearts be troubled. Trust in God[a]; trust also in me. [2]In my Father's house are many rooms; if it were not so, I would have told you. I am going there to prepare a place for you. [3]And if I go and prepare a place for you, I will come back and take you to be with me that you also may be where I am. [4]You know the way to the place where I am going."

[5]Thomas said to him, "Lord, we don't know where you are going, so how can we know the way?"

[6]Jesus answered, "I am the way and the truth and the life. No one comes to the Father except through me. [7]If you really knew me, you would know[b] my Father as well. From now on, you do know him and have seen him."

[8]Philip said, "Lord, show us the Father and that will be enough for us."

[9]Jesus answered: "Don't you know me, Philip, even after I have been among you such a long time? Anyone who has seen me has seen the Father. How can you say, 'Show us the Father'? [10]Don't you believe that I am in the Father, and that the Father is in me? The words I say to you are not just my own. Rather, it is the Father, living in me, who is doing his work. [11]Believe me when I say that I am in the Father and the Father is in me; or at least believe on the evidence of the miracles themselves. [12]I tell you the truth, anyone who has faith in me will do what I have been doing. He will do even greater things than these, because I am going to the Father. [13]And I will do whatever you ask in my name, so that the Son may bring glory to the Father. [14]You may ask me for anything in my name, and I will do it.

[15]"If you love me, you will obey what I command. [16]And I will ask the Father, and he will give you another Counselor to be with you forever— [17]the Spirit of truth. The world cannot accept him, because it neither sees him nor knows him. But you know him, for he lives with you and will be[c] in you. [18]I will not leave you as orphans; I will come to you. [19]Before long, the world will not see me anymore, but you will see me. Because I live, you also will live. [20]On that day you will realize that I am in my Father, and you are in me, and I am in you. [21]Whoever has my commands and obeys them, he is the one who loves me. He who loves me will be loved by my Father, and I too will love him and show myself to him."

[22]Then Judas (not Judas Iscariot) said, "But, Lord, why do you intend to show yourself to us and not to the world?"

[23]Jesus replied, "If anyone loves me, he will obey my teaching. My Father will love him, and we will come to him and make our home with him. [24]He who does not love me will not obey my teaching. These words you hear are not my own; they belong to the Father who sent me.

[25]"All this I have spoken while still with you. [26]But the Counselor, the Holy Spirit, whom the Father will send in my name, will teach you all things and will remind you of everything I have said to you. [27]Peace I leave with you; my peace I give you. I do not give to you as the world gives. Do not let your hearts be troubled and do not be afraid.

[28]"You heard me say, 'I am going away and I am coming back to you.' If you loved

---

e(John 14:1) This discourse (Secs. 149–151), given on Thursday evening of Passion Week, was delivered to the same group as the Olivet discourse given on Tuesday (Secs. 139a–139g). Yet the two differ radically from one another. A good reason for this difference lies in the dual capacity in which they were addressed. On Tuesday the focus of interest was the future of the nation of Israel, of which those in the group were members (cf. Sec. 139a). On Thursday the issue was the state of the disciples and other believers during the period of Jesus' absence (John 13:33, 36, Sec. 147; John 16:5–7, Sec. 150c). Anticipations of the latter group, many of whom are not Israelites, differ markedly from those concerned with the national expectations of Israel.

John 14:1–31 (cont'd)

me, you would be glad that I am going to the Father, for the Father is greater than I. [29]I have told you now before it happens, so that when it does happen you will believe. [30]I will not speak with you much longer, for the prince of this world is — coming. He has no hold on me, [31]but the world must learn that I love the Father and that I do exactly what my Father has commanded me.

"[f]Come now; let us leave."

[a]Jn 14:1 Or *You trust in God*   [b]7 Some early manuscripts *If you really have known me, you will know*   [c]17 Some early manuscripts *and is*

Sec. 150a   The vine and the branches
—Jerusalem, in the upper room—

John 15:1–17

[1]"I am the [g]true vine, and my Father is the gardener. [2]He cuts off every branch in me that bears no fruit, while every branch that does bear fruit he prunes[a] so that it will be even more fruitful. [3]You are already clean because of the word I have spoken to you. [4]Remain in me, and I will remain in you. No branch can bear fruit by itself; it must remain in the vine. Neither can you bear fruit unless you remain in me.

[5]"I am the vine; you are the branches. If a man remains in me and I in him, he will bear much fruit; apart from me you can do nothing. [6]If anyone does not remain in me, he is like a branch that is thrown away and withers; such branches are picked up, thrown into the fire and burned. [7]If you remain in me and my words remain in you, ask whatever you wish, and it will be given you. [8]This is to my Father's glory, that you bear much fruit, showing yourselves to be my disciples.

[9]"As the Father has loved me, so have I loved you. Now remain in my love. [10]If you obey my commands, you will remain in my love, just as I have obeyed my Father's commands and remain in his love. [11]I have told you this so that my joy may be in you and that your joy may be complete. [12]My command is this: Love each other as I have loved you. [13]Greater love has no one than this, that he lay down his life for his friends. [14]You are my friends if you do what I command. [15]I no longer call you servants, because a servant does not know his master's business. Instead, I have called you friends, for everything that I learned from my Father I have made known to you. [16]You did not choose me, but I chose you and appointed you to go and bear fruit—fruit that will last. Then the Father will give you whatever you ask in my name. [17]This is my command: Love each other.

[a]Jn 15:2 The Greek for *prunes* also means *cleans.*

---

[f](John 14:31) Apparently Jesus' words, "Come now; let us leave," expressed the intent to leave the upper room shortly, not the actual departure. Thus the discourse and prayer of John 15–17 was given while they were still in the upper room, and their actual departure was recorded in Matthew 26:30, Mark 14:26, Luke 22:39, and John 18:1 (Sec. 152). However, it is also possible to argue that their departure from the upper room is indicated by John 14:31, with Matthew 26:30, Mark 14:26, and Luke 22:39 as parallels. John 18:1 would then refer to departure from the city. This, of course, would mean that the discourse and prayer of John 15–17 were given as they walked in the city on the way to Gethsemane. Although such a reconstruction of events is possible, it has certain problems. It introduces an unnatural change of subject (a possible second prediction of Peter's denial, Matt. 26:30–35; Mark 14:26–31; cf. note b, Sec. 147) between John 14 and 15. Also, is it likely that such a long discourse and prayer (John 15–17) would be delivered while walking through the streets?

[g](John 15:1) The vine as a symbol for Israel was well known from the Old Testament (Psalm 80:8; Isa. 5:1–7; Jer. 2:21; Ezek. 15:1–8; 19:10; Hos. 10:1), but the generation of the nation at Jesus' first coming turned its back on him. Hence they were not a part of the "true" vine. Only by abiding in him who is the true vine does one belong to it (John 15:4). Through such a spiritual relationship, the disciples were enabled to bear fruit after his departure (John 15:16).

Sec. 150b   Opposition from the world
(cf. Secs. 54g, 70b, 145—followers not above the leader)
—Jerusalem, in the upper room—

John 15:18–16:4

[18]"If [h]the world hates you, keep in mind that it hated me first. [19]If you belonged to the world, it would love you as its own. As it is, you do not belong to the world, but I have chosen you out of the world. That is why the world hates you. [20]Remember the words I spoke to you: 'No servant is greater than his master.'[a] If they persecuted me, they will persecute you also. If they obeyed my teaching, they will obey yours also. [21]They will treat you this way because of my name, for they do not know the One who sent me. [22]If I had not come and spoken to them, they would not be guilty of sin. Now, however, they have no excuse for their sin. [23]He who hates me hates my Father as well. [24]If I had not done among them what no one else did, they would not be guilty of sin. But now they have seen these miracles, and yet they have hated both me and my Father. [25]But this is to fulfill what is written in their Law: 'They hated me without reason'[b] [Psalm 35:19; 69:4].

[26]"When the Counselor comes, whom I will send to you from the Father, the Spirit of truth who goes out from the Father, he will testify about me. [27]And you also must testify, for you have been with me from the beginning.

[1]"All this I have told you so that you will not go astray. [2]They will put you out of the synagogue; in fact, a time is coming when anyone who kills you will think he is offering a service to God. [3]They will do such things because they have not known the Father or me. [4]I have told you this, so that when the time comes you will remember that I warned you. I did not tell you this at first because I was with you.

[a]Jn 15:20 John 13:16   [b]25 Psalms 35:19; 69:4

Sec. 150c   Coming and ministry of the Spirit
—Jerusalem, in the upper room—

John 16:5–15

[5]"Now I am going to him who sent me, yet [i]none of you asks me, 'Where are you going?' [6]Because I have said these things, you are filled with grief. [7]But I tell you the truth: It is for your good that I am going away. Unless I go away, the Counselor will not come to you; but if I go, [j]I will send him to you. [8]When he comes, he will convict the world of guilt[a] in regard to sin and righteousness and judgment: [9]in regard to sin, because men do not believe in me; [10]in regard to righteousness, because I am going to the Father, where you can see me no longer; [11]and in regard to judgment, because the prince of this world now stands condemned.

[12]"I have much more to say to you, more than you can now bear. [13]But when he, the Spirit of truth, comes, he will guide you into all truth. He will not speak on his own; he will speak only what he hears, and he will tell you what is yet to come. [14]He will bring glory to me by taking from what is mine and making it known to you. [15]All that belongs to the Father is mine. That is why I said the Spirit will take from what is mine and make it known to you.

[a]Jn 16:8 Or *will expose the guilt of the world*

[h](John 15:18) Because of his departure Jesus had to add this word about opposition. As long as he was present there was no need (John 16:4b), for the persecution fell on him, not them. After his departure they would have to rely on the Holy Spirit to help them (John 15:26–27).

[i](John 16:5) This statement at first appears to ignore the questions already asked by Peter (John 13:36, Sec. 147) and Thomas (John 14:5, Sec. 149). What Jesus meant by this statement was that the earlier questions were prompted by their concern over being separated from him, not by a genuine interest in where he was going. Now that he had explained about his return to the Father, they should have asked more intelligently about the meaning of such a destination.

[j](John 16:7) The coming of the Holy Spirit (i.e., the "Counselor") to inaugurate the new age beginning at Pentecost would mark a new phase of his ministry. His new activity was to be a leading characteristic of that age. The ministry of the Spirit is described here in a twofold manner: his ministry to the world (John 16:7–11) and his ministry to the disciples and others who would become believers through their testimony (John 16:12–15; cf. John 17:20, Sec. 151).

Sec. 150d   Prediction of joy over his resurrection
—Jerusalem, in the upper room—

John 16:16–22

[16]"In a little while you will see me no more, and then after a little while [k]you will see me."

[17]Some of his disciples said to one another, "What does he mean by saying, 'In a little while you will see me no more, and then after a little while you will see me,' and 'Because I am going to the Father'?" [18]They kept asking, "What does he mean by 'a little while'? We don't understand what he is saying."

[19]Jesus saw that they wanted to ask him about this, so he said to them, "Are you asking one another what I meant when I said, 'In a little while you will see me no more, and then after a little while you will see me'? [20]I tell you the truth, you will weep and mourn while the world rejoices. You will grieve, but your grief will turn to joy. [21]A woman giving birth to a child has pain because her time has come; but when her baby is born she forgets the anguish because of her joy that a child is born into the world. [22]So with you: Now is your time of grief, but I will see you again and you will rejoice, and no one will take away your joy.

Sec. 150e   Promise of answered prayer and peace
—Jerusalem, in the upper room—

John 16:23–33

[23]In that day you will no longer ask me anything. I tell you the truth, my Father will give you whatever you ask in my name. [24]Until now you have not asked for anything in my name. Ask and you will receive, and your joy will be complete.

[25]"Though I have been speaking figuratively, a time is coming when I will no longer use this kind of language but will tell you plainly about my Father. [26]In that day you will ask in my name. I am not saying that I will ask the Father on your behalf. [27]No, the Father himself loves you because you have loved me and have believed that I came from God. [28]I came from the Father and entered the world; now I am leaving the world and going back to the Father."

[29]Then Jesus' disciples said, "Now you are speaking clearly and without figures of speech. [30]Now we can see that you know all things and that you do not even need to have anyone ask you questions. This makes us believe that you came from God."

[31]"You believe at last!"[a] Jesus answered. [32]"But a time is coming, and has come, when you will be scattered, each to his own home. You will leave me all alone. Yet I am not alone, for my Father is with me.

[33]"I have told you these things, so that in me you may have peace. In this world you will have trouble. But take heart! I have overcome the world."

[a]Jn 16:31 Or *"Do you now believe?"*

---

[k](John 16:16) It is difficult to be sure what Jesus meant by these words. Though elsewhere in the discourse he seemed to refer to the coming of the Spirit as his own coming (John 14:17–18, Sec. 149), the promise "you will see me" is an unlikely way of referring to the Spirit's coming at Pentecost. He also referred to his second advent earlier in the address (John 14:3, Sec. 149), but "a little while" (John 16:17) seems inadequate to refer to the entire present age that separates his two comings. The impending sorrow over his death followed quickly by an impartation of joy (John 16:20–21) favors a reference to the historical experience of the disciples when they viewed the resurrected Christ (John 16:22).

Sec. 151   Jesus' prayer for his disciples and all who believe
—Jerusalem, in the upper room—

John 17:1–26

[1]After Jesus said this, he looked toward heaven and prayed:

"[1]Father, the time has come. Glorify your Son, that your Son may glorify you. [2]For you granted him authority over all people that he might give eternal life to all those you have given him. [3]Now this is eternal life: that they may know you, the only true God, and Jesus Christ, whom you have sent. [4]I have brought you glory on earth by completing the work you gave me to do. [5]And now, Father, glorify me in your presence with the glory I had with you before the world began.

[6]"I have revealed you[a] to those whom you gave me out of the world. They were yours; you gave them to me and they have obeyed your word. [7]Now they know that everything you have given me comes from you. [8]For I gave them the words you gave me and they accepted them. They knew with certainty that I came from you, and they believed that you sent me. [9]I pray for them. I am not praying for the world, but for those you have given me, for they are yours. [10]All I have is yours, and all you have is mine. And glory has come to me through them. [11]I will remain in the world no longer, but they are still in the world, and I am coming to you. Holy Father, protect them by the power of your name—the name you gave me—so that they may be one as we are one. [12]While I was with them, I protected them and kept them safe by that name you gave me. None has been lost except the one doomed to destruction so that Scripture would be fulfilled.

[13]"I am coming to you now, but I say these things while I am still in the world, so that they may have the full measure of my joy within them. [14]I have given them your word and the world has hated them, for they are not of the world any more than I am of the world. [15]My prayer is not that you take them out of the world but that you protect them from the evil one. [16]They are not of the world, even as I am not of it. [17]Sanctify[b] them by the truth; your word is truth. [18]As you sent me into the world, I have sent them into the world. [19]For them I sanctify myself, that they too may be truly sanctified.

[20]"My prayer is not for them alone. I pray also for those who will believe in me through their message, [21]that all of them may be one, Father, just as you are in me and I am in you. May they also be in us so that the world may believe that you have sent me. [22]I have given them the glory that you gave me, that they may be one as we are one: [23]I in them and you in me. May they be brought to complete unity to let the world know that you sent me and have loved them even as you have loved me.

[24]"Father, I want those you have given me to be with me where I am, and to see my glory, the glory you have given me because you loved me before the creation of the world.

[25]"Righteous Father, though the world does not know you, I know you, and they know that you have sent me. [26]I have made you known to them, and will continue to make you known in order that the love you have for me may be in them and that I myself may be in them."

---

[a]Jn 17:6 Greek *your name;* also in verse 26   [b]17 Greek *hagiazo (set apart for sacred use or make holy);* also in verse 19

---

[1](John 17:1) The prayer of this chapter is high priestly in the sense of Romans 8:34 and Hebrews 7:25. In his own thoughts Jesus was at this point thrust forward beyond the time of being offered as a sacrifice for sin to the time when in heaven he would engage in a continuing ministry of intercession. In other words, we have here a preview of his work as our advocate (1 John 2:1). The three parts of the prayer are: his prayer for his own glorification (17:1–5), his prayer for the disciples (17:6–19), and his prayer for future believers (17:20–26).

Sec. 152   Jesus' three agonizing prayers in Gethsemane
—Garden of Gethsemane on the Mount of Olives—

Matthew 26:30, m[31–35], 36–46	Mark 14:26, m[27–31], 32–42	Luke 22:39–46	John 18:1

[30]When they had sung a hymn, they went out to the Mount of Olives.

[26]When they had sung a hymn, they went out to the Mount of Olives.

[39]Jesus went out as usual to the Mount of Olives, and his disciples followed him. [40]On reaching the place, he said to them,

[1]When he had finished praying, Jesus left with his disciples and crossed the Kidron Valley. On the other side there was an olive grove, and he and his disciples went into it.

[36]Then Jesus went with his disciples to a place called Gethsemane, and he said to them, "Sit here while I go over there and pray." [37]He took Peter and the two sons of Zebedee along with him, and he began to be [n]sorrowful and troubled. [38]Then he said to them, "My soul is overwhelmed with sorrow to the point of death. Stay here and keep watch with me." [39]Going a little farther, he fell with his face to the ground and prayed, "My Father, if it is possible, may this cup be taken from me. Yet not as I will, but as you will."

[32]They went to a place called Gethsemane, and Jesus said to his disciples, "Sit here while I pray." [33]He took Peter, James and John along with him, and he began to be deeply [n]distressed and troubled. [34]"My soul is overwhelmed with sorrow to the point of death," he said to them. "Stay here and keep watch." [35]Going a little farther, he fell to the ground and prayed that if possible the hour might pass from him. [36]"*Abba*,[a] Father," he said, "everything is possible for you. Take this cup from me. Yet not what I will, but what you will."

"Pray that you will not fall into temptation." [41]He withdrew about a stone's throw beyond them, knelt down and prayed, [42]"Father, if you are willing, take this cup from me; yet not my will, but yours be done." [43]An angel from heaven appeared to him and strengthened him. [44]And being [n]in anguish, he prayed more earnestly, and his sweat was like drops of blood falling to the ground.[b]

---

m(Matt. 26:31–35; Mark 14:27–31) For the text of these two passages, see Section 147 and note b associated with that section.

n(Matt. 26:37; Mark 14:33; Luke 22:44) Jesus' agony is not attributable primarily to his dread of physical pain or to the prospect of being deserted by his friends and associates. The "cup" from which he prayed three times to be delivered (Matt. 26:39, 42, 44; Mark 14:36, 39; Luke 22:42) was the ultimate horror of separation from the Father (Matt. 27:46; Mark 15:34, Sec. 165). He was willing to undergo even this, however, if it were the Father's will, and it was (cf. Acts. 2:22–23).

Matthew 26:30, [31–35], 36–46 (cont'd)	Mark 14:26, [27–31], 32–42 (cont'd)	Luke 22:39–46 (cont'd)
40Then he returned to his disciples and found them sleeping. "Could you men not keep watch with me for one hour?" he asked Peter. 41"Watch and pray so that you will not fall into temptation. The spirit is willing, but the body is weak."	37Then he returned to his disciples and found them sleeping. "Simon," he said to Peter, "are you asleep? Could you not keep watch for one hour? 38Watch and pray so that you will not fall into temptation. The spirit is willing, but the body is weak."	45When he rose from prayer and went back to the disciples, he found them asleep, exhausted from sorrow. 46"Why are you sleeping?" he asked them. "Get up and pray so that you will not fall into temptation."
42He went away a second time and prayed, "My Father, if it is not possible for this cup to be taken away unless I drink it, may your will be done."	39Once more he went away and prayed the same thing.	
43When he came back, he again found them sleeping, because their eyes were heavy. 44So he left them and went away once more and prayed the third time, saying the same thing.	40When he came back, he again found them sleeping, because their eyes were heavy. They did not know what to say to him.	
45Then he returned to the disciples and said to them, "Are you still sleeping and resting? Look, the hour is near, and the Son of Man is betrayed into the hands of sinners. 46Rise, let us go! Here comes my betrayer!"	41Returning the third time, he said to them, "Are you still sleeping and resting? Enough! The hour has come. Look, the Son of Man is betrayed into the hands of sinners. 42Rise! Let us go! Here comes my betrayer!"	

aMk 26:36 Aramaic for *Father*   bLk 22:44 Some early manuscripts do not have verses 43 and 44.

PART TWELVE
THE DEATH OF CHRIST
BETRAYAL AND ARREST

Sec. 153 Jesus betrayed, arrested, and forsaken
—Gethsemane—

Matthew 26:47–56   Mark 14:43–52   Luke 22:47–53   John 18:2–12

			[2]Now Judas, who betrayed him, knew the place, because Jesus had often met there with
[47]While he was still speaking, Judas, one of the Twelve, arrived. With him was a large crowd armed with swords and clubs, sent from the chief priests and the elders of the people.	[43]Just as he was speaking, Judas, one of the Twelve, appeared. With him was a crowd armed with swords and clubs, sent from the chief priests, the teachers of the law, and the elders.	[47]While he was still speaking a crowd came up, and the man who was called Judas, one of the Twelve, was leading them.	his disciples. [3]So Judas came to the grove, guiding a [o]detachment of soldiers and some officials from the chief priests and Pharisees. They were carrying torches, lanterns and weapons.

[4]Jesus, knowing all that was going to happen to him, went out and asked them, "Who is it you want?"

[5]"Jesus of Nazareth," they replied.

"I am he," Jesus said. (And Judas the traitor was standing there with them.) [6]When Jesus said, "I am he," they drew back and fell to the ground.

[7]Again he asked them, "Who is it you want?"

And they said, "Jesus of Nazareth."

[8]"I told you that I am he," Jesus answered. "If you are looking for me,

---

[o](John 18:3) In connection with their intention of putting Jesus to death, the Sanhedrin, represented by the chief priests and Pharisees, had called upon the Romans to help in the arrest. A Roman cohort (NIV, "detachment of soldiers") was normally made up of six hundred soldiers. Although the Romans were known to use large numbers to handle one prisoner (cf. Acts 23:23), it is doubtful that the whole cohort was involved in this arrest. In light of Matthew's "large crowd" (Matt. 26:47) and the "crowd" of Mark and Luke (Mark 14:43; Luke 22:47), the number of soldiers probably was still quite substantial.

212

Matthew 26:47–56 (cont'd)	Mark 14:43–52 (cont'd)	Luke 22:47–53 (cont'd)	John 8:2–12 (cont'd)
			then let these men go." [9]This happened so that the words he had spoken would be fulfilled: "I have not lost one of those you gave me."[b]
[48]Now the betrayer had arranged a signal with them: "The one I kiss is the man; arrest him." [49]Going at once to Jesus, Judas said, "Greetings, Rabbi!" and kissed him.	[44]Now the betrayer had arranged a signal with them: "The one I kiss is the man; arrest him and lead him away under guard." [45]Going at once to Jesus, Judas said, "Rabbi!" and kissed him.	He approached Jesus to kiss him, [48]but Jesus asked him, "Judas, are you betraying the Son of Man with a kiss?" [49]When Jesus' followers saw what was going to happen, they said, "Lord, should we strike with our swords?"	
[50]Jesus replied, "Friend, do what you came for."[a] Then the men stepped forward, seized Jesus and arrested him. [51]With that, one of Jesus' companions reached for his sword, drew it out and struck the servant of the high priest, cutting off his ear. [52]"Put your sword back in its place," Jesus said to him, "for all who draw the sword will die by the sword. [53]Do you think I cannot call on my Father, and he will at once put at my disposal more than twelve legions of angels? [54]But how then would the Scrip-	[46]The men seized Jesus and arrested him. [47]Then one of those standing near drew his sword and struck the servant of the high priest, cutting off his ear.	[50]And one of them struck the servant of the high priest, cutting off his right ear. [51]But Jesus answered, "No more of this!" And he touched the man's ear and healed him.	[10]Then Simon Peter, who had a sword, drew it and struck the high priest's servant, cutting off his right ear. (The servant's name was Malchus.) [11]Jesus commanded Peter, "Put your sword away! Shall I not drink the cup the Father has given me?" [12]Then the detachment of soldiers with its commander and the Jewish officials arrested Jesus. They bound him

Matthew 26:47–56
(cont'd)

tures be fulfilled
that say it must
happen in this
way?"
55At that time
Jesus said to the
crowd, "Am I lead-
ing a rebellion, that
you have come out
with swords and
clubs to capture
me? Every day I sat
in the temple
courts teaching,
and you did not ar-
rest me. 56But this
has all taken place
that the writings of
the prophets might
be fulfilled." Then
all the disciples
deserted him and
fled.

Mark 14:43–52
(cont'd)

48"Am I leading
a rebellion," said
Jesus, "that you
have come out
with swords and
clubs to capture
me? 49Every day I
was with you,
teaching in the
temple courts, and
you did not arrest
me. But the Scrip-
tures must be ful-
filled." 50Then ev-
eryone deserted
him and fled.
51A young man,
wearing nothing
but a linen gar-
ment, was follow-
ing Jesus. When
they seized him,
52he fled naked,
leaving his gar-
ment behind.

Luke 22:47–53
(cont'd)

52Then Jesus said
to the chief priests,
the officers of the
temple guard, and
the elders, who
had come for him,
"Am I leading a re-
bellion, that you
have come with
swords and clubs?
53Every day I was
with you in the
temple courts, and
you did not lay a
hand on me. But
this is your hour
—when darkness
reigns."

[a]*Mt 26:50* Or *"Friend, why have you come?"* [b]*Jn 8:9* John 6:39

TRIAL

Sec. 154 First Jewish phase, before Annas
—Jerusalem, courtyard of Annas—

[p]John 18:13–14, [q][15–18], 19–23

13and brought him first to Annas, who was the father-in-law of Caiaphas, the high
priest that year. 14Caiaphas was the one who had advised the Jews that it would be
good if one man died for the people.
19Meanwhile, the high priest questioned Jesus about his disciples and his teaching.
20"I have spoken openly to the world," Jesus replied. "I always taught in syna-

[p](John 18:13–14) Robertson's *Harmony* repeats John 18:12 from Section 153 so that this section will begin with a complete sentence, but the revisers of this *Harmony* have chosen to avoid confusion by not repeating the text of that verse here.

[q](John 18:15–18) The text of these verses is printed as part of Section 156. A. T. Robertson's *Harmony* placed them there so as to incorporate all of Peter's denials into one section. The current revisers of Robertson's *Harmony*, however, prefer to locate them in Section 154, thereby maintaining the sequence and circumstances of the first denial that are indicated in John's gospel. Each writer, including John, records three denials to show the fulfillment of Jesus' predictions, but John records only two denials at the house of Caiaphas as compared with three described by the others (cf. John 18:25–27, Sec. 156). John places the first of his three denials in the court of Annas (cf. John 18:13). If this understanding of the writers is correct, Peter apparently denied Jesus at least four times. Yet this does not create great difficulty, because Jesus' prediction of at least three denials need not exclude a fourth.

John 18:13–14, [15–18], 19–23 (cont'd)

gogues or at the temple, where all the Jews come together. I said nothing in secret. [21]Why question me? Ask those who heard me. Surely they know what I said."

[22]When Jesus said this, one of the officials nearby struck him in the face. "Is this the way you answer the high priest?" he demanded.

[23]"If I said something wrong," Jesus replied, "testify as to what is wrong. But if I spoke the truth, why did you strike me?"

Sec. 155 Second Jewish phase, before Caiaphas and the Sanhedrin
—*Jerusalem, house of Caiaphas*—

Matthew 26:57, 59–68	Mark 14:53, 55–65	Luke 22:54a, 63–65	John 18:24
[57]Those who had arrested Jesus took him to Caiaphas, the high priest, where the teachers of the law and the elders had assembled. [59]The chief priests and the whole Sanhedrin were looking for false evidence against Jesus so that they could put him to death. [60]But they did not find any, though many false witnesses came forward. Finally two came forward [61]and declared, "This fellow said, 'I am able to destroy the temple of God and rebuild it in three days.'"	[53]They took Jesus to the high priest, and all the [r]chief priests, elders and teachers of the law came together. [55]The chief priests and the whole Sanhedrin were looking for evidence against Jesus so that they could put him to death, but they did not find any. [56]Many testified falsely against him, but their statements did not agree. [57]Then some stood up and gave this false testimony against him: [58]"We heard him say, 'I will destroy this man-made temple and in three days will build another, not made by man.'" [59]Yet even then their testimony did not agree.	[54]Then seizing him, they led him away and took him into the house of the high priest.	[24]Then Annas sent him, still bound, to Caiaphas the high priest. [c]

---

[r](Mark 14:53) Mark lists the three groups who composed the Sanhedrin of Jerusalem, the supreme Jewish court of law:

  1. "chief priests," comprising those who were former high priests (including Annas probably), the commander of the temple guard, the steward of the temple, and the three temple treasurers;
  2. "elders," some of the wealthy and influential lay persons of Jerusalem;
  3. "teachers of the law," who were primarily drawn from the middle class.

The first two groups were predominantly Sadducean and the last Pharisaic. In meeting at the house of Caiaphas rather than in its usual meeting place, the Sanhedrin evidenced its haste to carry out its predetermined plan to convict Jesus (Mark 14:55; cf. Matt. 26:4; Mark 14:1, Sec. 140). For further discussion of Jesus' arrest and trial, see essay 12 (pp. 320–28).

Matthew 26:57, 59–68 (cont'd)	Mark 14:53, 55–65 (cont'd)	Luke 22:54a, 63–65 (cont'd)
[62]Then the high priest stood up and said to Jesus, "Are you not going to answer? What is this testimony that these men are bringing against you?" [63]But Jesus remained silent.	[60]Then the high priest stood up before them and asked Jesus, "Are you not going to answer? What is this testimony that these men are bringing against you?" [61]But Jesus remained silent and gave no answer.	
The high priest said to him, "I charge you under oath by the living God: Tell us if you are the Christ,[a] the Son of God."	Again the high priest asked him, "Are you the Christ,[b] the Son of the Blessed One?"	
[64]"Yes, it is as you say," Jesus replied. "But I say to all of you: In the future you will see the Son of Man sitting at the right hand of the Mighty One and coming on the clouds of heaven" [Psalm 110:1; Dan. 7:13].	[62]"I am," said Jesus. "And you will see the Son of Man sitting at the right hand of the Mighty One and coming on the clouds of heaven" [Psalm 110:1; Dan. 7:13].	
[65]Then the high priest tore his clothes and said, "He has spoken blasphemy! Why do we need any more witnesses? Look, now you have heard the blasphemy. [66]What do you think?"	[63]The high priest tore his clothes. "Why do we need any more witnesses?" he asked. [64]"You have heard the blasphemy. What do you think?"	
"He is worthy of death," they answered.	They all condemned him as worthy of death. [65]Then some began to spit at him; they blindfolded him, struck him with their fists, and said, "Prophesy!" And the guards took him and beat him.	[63]The men who were guarding Jesus began mocking and beating him. [64]They blindfolded him and demanded, "Prophesy! Who hit you?" [65]And they said many other insulting things to him.
[67]Then they spit in his face and struck him with their fists. Others slapped him [68]and said, "Prophesy to us, Christ. Who hit you?"		

[a]Mt 26:63 Or Messiah; also in verse 68   [b]Mk 14:61 Or Messiah   [c]Jn 18:24 Or (Now Annas had sent him, still bound, to Caiaphas the high priest.)

Sec. 156   Peter's denials
(cf. Sec. 147—Peter's denials)
—Jerusalem, courtyard of Caiaphas—

Matthew 26:58, 69–75	Mark 14:54, 66–72	Luke 22:54b–62	John 18:[s]15–18, 25–27
[58]But Peter followed him at a distance, right	[54]Peter followed him at a distance, right into the	Peter followed at a distance.	[15]Simon Peter and another disciple were following Jesus. Because this disciple was known to the [t]high priest, he went with Jesus into the
up to the courtyard of the high priest. He entered	courtyard of the high priest.		high priest's courtyard, [16]but Peter had to wait outside at the door. The other disciple, who was known to the high priest, came back, spoke to the girl on duty there and brought Peter in.
			[17]"You are not one of his disciples, are you?" the girl at the door asked Peter.
			He replied, "I am not."
and sat down with the guards to see the outcome.	There he sat with the guards and warmed himself at the fire.	[55]But when they had kindled a fire in the middle of the courtyard and had sat down together, Peter sat down with them.	[18]It was cold, and the servants and officials stood around a fire they had made to keep warm. Peter also was standing with them, warming himself.
[69]Now Peter was sitting out in the courtyard, and a servant girl came to him.	[66]While Peter was below in the courtyard, one of the servant girls of the high priest came by. [67]When she saw Peter warming himself, she looked closely at him.	[56]A servant girl saw him seated there in the firelight. She looked closely at him and said, "This man was with him."	
"You also were with Jesus of Galilee," she said.	"You also were with that Nazarene, Jesus," she said.		[25]As Simon Peter stood warming himself, he was asked, "You are not one of his disciples, are you?"

---

[s](John 18:15–18) Though the text of these verses is printed as part of this section, the revisers prefer to think of this first denial as happening earlier, at the house of Annas. For further discussion of this issue, see note q, Section 154.

[t](John 18:15) Here and in verses 16, 19, and 22 John calls Annas "the high priest," but he says in 18:13 (Sec. 154) that Caiaphas was high priest. Caiaphas was the official high priest, having taken the office in A.D. 18, three years after his father-in-law, Annas, had been deposed. Though no longer in office, Annas still wielded great influence and bore the title of courtesy granted to former high priests.

Matthew 26:58, 69–75 (cont'd)	Mark 14:54, 66–72 (cont'd)	Luke 22:54b–62 (cont'd)	John 18: 15–18, 25–27 (cont'd)
[70]But he denied it before them all. "I don't know what you're talking about," he said.	[68]But he denied it. "I don't know or understand what you're talking about," he said, and went out into the entryway.[a]	[57]But he denied it. "Woman, I don't know him," he said.	He denied it, saying, "I am not."
[71]Then he went out to the gateway, where another girl saw him and said to the people there, "This fellow was with Jesus of Nazareth." [72]He denied it again, with an oath: "I don't know the man!"	[69]When the servant girl saw him there, she said again to those standing around, "This fellow is one of them." [70]Again he denied it.	[58]A little later someone else saw him and said, "You also are one of them." "Man, I am not!" Peter replied.	
[73]After a little while, those standing there went up to Peter and said, "Surely you are one of them, for your accent gives you away." [74]Then he began to call down curses on himself and he swore to them, "I don't know the man!" Immediately a rooster crowed. [75]Then Peter remembered the word Jesus had spoken: "Before the rooster crows, you will disown me [u]three times." And he went outside and wept bitterly.	After a little while, those standing near said to Peter, "Surely you are one of them, for you are a Galilean." [71]He began to call down curses on himself, and he swore to them, "I don't know this man you're talking about." [72]Immediately the rooster crowed the second time.[b] Then Peter remembered the word Jesus had spoken to him: "Before the rooster crows twice[c] you will disown me [u]three times." And he broke down and wept.	[59]About an hour later another asserted, "Certainly this fellow was with him, for he is a Galilean." [60]Peter replied, "Man, I don't know what you're talking about!" Just as he was speaking, the rooster crowed. [61]The Lord turned and looked straight at Peter. Then Peter remembered the word the Lord had spoken to him: "Before the rooster crows today, you will disown me [u]three times." [62]And he went outside and wept bitterly.	[26]One of the high priest's servants, a relative of the man whose ear Peter had cut off, challenged him, "Didn't I see you with him in the olive grove?" [27]Again Peter denied it, and at that moment a rooster began to crow.

[a]Mk 14:68 Some early manuscripts *entryway and the rooster crowed*   [b]72 Some early manuscripts do not have *the second time.*   [c]72 Some early manuscripts do not have *twice.*

[u](Matt. 26:75; Mark 14:72; Luke 22:61) Jesus' prediction of a threefold denial by Peter need not exclude a fourth denial. See Note q, Section 154.

Sec. 157 Third Jewish phase, before the Sanhedrin
—Jerusalem, meeting place of the Sanhedrin—

Matthew 27:1	Mark 15:1a	Luke 22:66–71

¹Early in the morning, all the chief priests and the elders of the people came to the decision to put Jesus to death.

¹Very early in the morning, the chief priests, with the elders, the teachers of the law and the whole Sanhedrin, reached a decision.

⁶⁶At ᵛdaybreak the council of the elders of the people, both the chief priests and teachers of the law, met together, and Jesus was led before them. ⁶⁷"If you are the Christ,ᵃ" they said, "tell us."

Jesus answered, "If I tell you, you will not believe me, ⁶⁸and if I asked you, you would not answer. ⁶⁹But from now on, the Son of Man will be seated at the right hand [Psalm 110:1] of the mighty God." mighty God."

⁷⁰They all asked, "Are you then the Son of God?"

He replied, "You are right in saying I am."

⁷¹Then they said, "Why do we need any more testimony? We have heard it from his own lips."

ᵃ67 Or Messiah

Sec. 158 Remorse and suicide of Judas Iscariot
—In the temple and the potter's field—

Matthew 27:3–10	Acts 1:18–19

³When Judas, who had betrayed him, saw that Jesus was condemned, he was seized with remorse and returned the thirty silver coins to the chief priests and the elders. ⁴"I have sinned," he said, "for I have betrayed innocent blood."

"What is that to us?" they replied. "That's your responsibility."

⁵So Judas threw the money into the temple and left. Then he went away and ʷhanged himself.

⁶The chief priests picked up the coins

ᵛ(Luke 22:66) The traditional Christian explanation has been that no trial of the Jewish Sanhedrin was legal if held during the hours of darkness. Hence the council had to get together again and formalize the illegal verdict it had already settled upon a few hours earlier (Matt. 26:66; Mark 14:64, Sec. 155). The question of legality, however, is a moot point, and is discussed in essay 12 (pp. 320–28).

ʷ(Matt. 27:5; Acts 1:18) There is no reason to question the usual harmonization of these two accounts of Judas' death, that is, that he hanged himself from a tree on a cliff overlooking a valley, and that the tree limb or rope broke, causing him to plunge to the valley below.

Matthew 27:3–10 (cont'd)

and said, "It is against the law to put this into the treasury, since it is blood money." [7]So they decided to use the money to buy the potter's field as a burial place for foreigners. [8]That is why it has been called the Field of Blood to this day. [9]Then what was spoken by Jeremiah the prophet was fulfilled: "They took the thirty silver coins, the price set on him by the people of Israel, [10]and they used them to buy the potter's field, as the Lord commanded me"[a] [Zech. 11:12–13; cf. Jer. 18:2, 11; 32:6–9].

[a]Mt 27:10 See Zech. 11:12,13; Jer. 19:1-13; 32:6-9.

Acts 1:18–19 (cont'd)

[18](With the reward he got for his wickedness, Judas bought a field; there he fell headlong, his body burst open and all his intestines spilled out. [19]Everyone in Jerusalem heard about this, so they called that field in their language Akeldama, that is, Field of Blood.)

Sec. 159   First Roman phase, before Pilate
—Jerusalem, at the Praetorium (the palace of the Roman governor)—

Matthew 27:2, 11–14	Mark 15:1b–5	Luke 23:1–5	John 18:28–38
[2]They bound him, led him away and handed him over to Pilate, the governor.	They bound Jesus, led him away and handed him over to Pilate.	[1]Then the whole assembly rose and led him off to Pilate.	[28]Then the Jews led Jesus from Caiaphas to the palace of the Roman governor. By now it was early morning, and to avoid ceremonial uncleanness the Jews did not enter the palace; they wanted to be able to eat the Passover. [29]So Pilate came out to them and asked, "What charges are you bringing against this man?"
		[2]And they began to accuse him, saying, "We have found this man subverting our nation. He opposes payment of taxes to Caesar and claims to be Christ,[a] a king."	[30]"If he were not a criminal," they replied, "we would not have handed him over to you." [31]Pilate said, "Take him yourselves and judge him by your own law." "But we have no right to execute anyone," the Jews objected. [32]This happened so that the words Jesus

Matthew 27:2, 11–14(cont'd)	Mark 15:1b–5 (cont'd)	Luke 23:1–5 (cont'd)	John 18:28–38 (cont'd)
			had spoken indicating the kind of death he was going to die would be fulfilled.
			[33]Pilate then went back inside the palace, summoned Jesus and
[11]Meanwhile Jesus stood before the governor, and the governor asked him, "Are you the king of the Jews?"	[2]"Are you the king of the Jews?" asked Pilate.	[3]So Pilate asked Jesus, "Are you the king of the Jews?"	
"Yes, it is as you say," Jesus replied.	"Yes, it is as you say," Jesus replied.	"Yes, it is as you say," Jesus replied.	asked him, "Are you the king of the Jews?"
			[34]"Is that your own idea," Jesus asked, "or did others talk to you about me?"
			[35]"Am I a Jew?" Pilate replied. "It was your people and your chief priests who handed you over to me. What is it you have done?"
			[36]Jesus said, "My kingdom is not [x]of this world. If it were, my servants would fight to prevent my arrest by the Jews. But now my kingdom is from another place."
			[37]"You are a king, then!" said Pilate.
			Jesus answered, "You are right in saying I am a king. In fact, for this reason I was born, and for this I came into the world, to testify to the truth. Ev-

---

[x](John 18:36) Jesus denied that his kingdom had an earthly origin. If it had, he would have proceeded to round up and equip a conventional army to set it into operation. He did not deny, however, that the kingdom will consist of an earthly realm such as the scripturally oriented Jew expected Messiah to establish (Dan. 7:13–14, 22–23, 27). Because this kingdom on earth did not represent a rebellion against his Roman authority, Pilate was willing to release Jesus (Luke 23:4; John 18:38).

Matthew 27:2, 11–14 (cont'd)	Mark 15:1b–5 (cont'd)	Luke 23:1–5 (cont'd)	John 18:28–38 (cont'd)
			eryone on the side of truth listens to me."
		⁴Then Pilate announced to the chief priests and the crowd, "I find no basis for a charge against this man."	³⁸"What is truth?" Pilate asked. With this he went out again to the Jews and said, "I find no basis for a charge against him.
¹²When he was accused by the chief priests and the elders, he gave no answer. ¹³Then Pilate asked him, "Don't you hear the testimony they are bringing against you?" ¹⁴But Jesus made no reply, not even to a single charge—to the great amazement of the governor.	³The chief priests accused him of many things. ⁴So again Pilate asked him, "Aren't you going to answer? See how many things they are accusing you of." ⁵But Jesus still made no reply, and Pilate was amazed.	⁵But they insisted, "He stirs up the people all over Judea*b* by his teaching. He started in Galilee and has come all the way here."	

ᵃLk 23:2 Or *Messiah*; also in verses 35 and 39   ᵇ5 Or *over the land of the Jews*

Sec. 160   Second Roman phase, before Herod Antipas
—Jerusalem, before Herod Antipas—

Luke 23:6–12

⁶On hearing this, Pilate asked if the man was a Galilean. ⁷When he learned that Jesus was under ʸHerod's jurisdiction, he sent him to Herod, who was also in Jerusalem at that time.

⁸When Herod saw Jesus, he was greatly pleased, because for a long time he had been wanting to see him. From what he had heard about him, he hoped to see him perform some miracle. ⁹He plied him with many questions, but Jesus gave him no answer. ¹⁰The chief priests and the teachers of the law were standing there, vehemently accusing him. ¹¹Then Herod and his soldiers ridiculed and mocked him. Dressing him in an elegant robe, they sent him back to Pilate. ¹²That day Herod and Pilate became friends—before this they had been enemies.

ʸ(Luke 23:7) This is Herod Antipas, tetrarch of Galilee and Perea, who rather than repenting because of the preaching of John, had the Baptist beheaded (cf. Sec. 71b). Because much of Jesus' public ministry had been in Galilee, Pilate thought he had found a way to avoid condemning an innocent person, but Herod did not pronounce Jesus guilty or innocent. Luke had contacts within Herod's household (cf. Luke 8:3, Sec. 60) that enabled him to describe a phase of the trial not found in the other gospels, just as John had access to information about what happened at Annas' house (cf. Sec. 154).

Sec. 161 Third Roman phase, before Pilate
—*Jerusalem, at the Praetorium*—

Matthew 27:15–26	Mark 15:6–15	Luke 23:13–25	John 18:39–19:16a
[15]Now it was the governor's custom at the Feast to release a prisoner chosen by the crowd. [16]At that time they had a notorious prisoner, called [z]Barabbas.	[6]Now it was the custom at the Feast to release a prisoner whom the people requested. [7]A man called [z]Barabbas was in prison with the insurrectionists who had committed murder in the uprising. [8]The crowd came up and asked Pilate to do for them what he usually did.		
		[13]Pilate called together the chief priests, the rulers and the people, [14]and said to them, "You brought me this man as one who was inciting the people to rebellion. I have examined him in your presence and have found no basis for your charges against him. [15]Neither has Herod, for he sent him back to us; as you can see, he has done nothing to deserve death. [16]Therefore, I will punish him and then release him.[a]"	
[17]So when the crowd had gathered, Pilate asked them, "Which one do you want me to release to you: Barabbas, or Jesus who is called Christ?" [18]For he knew it was out of envy that they had handed Jesus over to him. [19]While Pilate	[9]"Do you want me to release to you the king of the Jews?" asked Pilate, [10]knowing it was out of envy that the chief priests had handed Jesus over to him.		[39]But it is your custom for me to release to you one prisoner at the time of the Passover. Do you want me to release 'the king of the Jews'?"

---

[z](Matt. 27:16; Mark 15:7; Luke 23:19; John 18:40) Barabbas was a well-known member of a local resistance movement dedicated to overthrowing Roman rule in Judea. Even though he was a thief and a murderer, he was a hero to many Jews who disliked Roman control. Hence the chief priests and elders had little difficulty persuading the crowd to prefer the release of Barabbas (Matt. 27:20; Mark 15:11). It is ironic that these leaders sought the release of one who was clearly guilty of the crime they had accused Jesus of committing (cf. Luke 23:2, Sec. 159; John 19:12).

Matthew 27:15–26 (cont'd)	Mark 15:6–15 (cont'd)	Luke 23:13–25 (cont'd)	John 18:39–19:16a (cont'd)
was sitting on the judge's seat, his wife sent him this message: "Don't have anything to do with that innocent man, for I have suffered a great deal today in a dream because of him." ²⁰But the chief priests and the elders persuaded the crowd to ask for Barabbas and to have Jesus executed. ²¹"Which of the two do you want me to release to you?" asked the governor. "Barabbas," they answered.	¹¹But the chief priests stirred up the crowd to have Pilate release Barabbas instead.	¹⁸With one voice they cried out, "Away with this man! Release Barabbas to us!" ¹⁹(ᶻBarabbas had been thrown into prison for an insurrection in the city, and for murder.)	⁴⁰They shouted back, "No, not him! Give us Barabbas!" Now ᶻBarabbas had taken part in a rebellion. ¹Then Pilate took Jesus and had him flogged. ²The soldiers twisted together a crown of thorns and put it on his head. They clothed him in a purple robe ³and went up to him again and again, saying, "Hail, king of the Jews!" And they struck him in the face. ⁴Once more Pilate came out and said to the Jews, "Look, I am bringing him out to you to let you know that I find no basis for a charge against him." ⁵When Jesus came out wearing the crown of thorns and the purple robe, Pilate said to them, "Here is the man!"

Matthew 27:15–26 (cont'd)	Mark 15:6–15 (cont'd)	Luke 23:13–25 (cont'd)	John 18:39– 19:16a (cont'd)
[22]"What shall I do, then, with Jesus who is called Christ?" Pilate asked. They all answered, "Crucify him!" [23]"Why? What crime has he committed?" asked Pilate. But they shouted all the louder, "Crucify him!"	[12]"What shall I do, then, with the one you call the king of the Jews?" Pilate asked them. [13]"Crucify him!" they shouted. [14]"Why? What crime has he committed?" asked Pilate. But they shouted all the louder, "Crucify him!"	[20]Wanting to release Jesus, Pilate appealed to them again. [21]But they kept shouting, "Crucify him! Crucify him!" [22]For the third time he spoke to them: "Why? What crime has this man committed? I have found in him no grounds for the death penalty. Therefore I will have him punished and then release him."	 [6]As soon as the chief priests and their officials saw him, they shouted, "Crucify! Crucify!" But Pilate answered, "You take him and crucify him. As for me, I find no basis for a charge against him." [7]The Jews insisted, "We have a law, and according to that law he must die, because he claimed to be the Son of God." [8]When Pilate heard this, he was even more afraid, [9]and he went back inside the palace. "Where do you come from?" he asked Jesus, but Jesus gave him no answer. [10]"Do you refuse to speak to me?" Pilate said. "Don't you realize I have power either to free you or to crucify you?" [11]Jesus answered, "You would have no power over me if it were not given to you from above. Therefore the one who handed me over to you is guilty of a greater sin."

Matthew 27:15–26 (cont'd)	Mark 15:6–15 (cont'd)	Luke 23:13–25 (cont'd)	John 18:39– 19:16a (cont'd)
			[12]From then on, Pilate tried to set Jesus free, but the Jews kept shouting, "If you let this man go, you are no friend of Caesar. Anyone who claims to be a king opposes Caesar." [13]When Pilate heard this, he brought Jesus out and sat down on the judge's seat at a place known as the Stone Pavement (which in Aramaic is Gabbatha). [14]It was the day of Preparation of Passover Week, about the sixth hour. "Here is your king," Pilate said to the Jews.
[24]When Pilate saw that he was getting nowhere, but that instead an uproar was starting, he took water and washed his hands in front of the crowd. "I am innocent of this man's blood," he said. "It is your responsibility!" [25]All the people answered, "Let his blood be on us and on our children!" [26]Then he released Barabbas to them. But he had Jesus flogged, and handed him over to be crucified.	[15]Wanting to satisfy the crowd, Pilate released Barabbas to them. He had Jesus flogged, and handed him over to be crucified.	[23]But with loud shouts they insistently demanded that he be crucified, and their shouts prevailed. [24]So Pilate decided to grant their demand. [25]He released the man who had been thrown into prison for insurrection and murder, the one they asked for, and surrendered Jesus to [a]their will.	[15]But they shouted, "Take him away! Take him away! Crucify him!" "Shall I crucify your king?" Pilate asked. "We have no king but Caesar," the chief priests answered. [16]Finally Pilate handed him over to [a]them to be crucified.

[a]*Lk 23:16* Some manuscripts *him." [17]Now he was obliged to release one man to them at the Feast.*

[a](Luke 23:25; John 19:16) "Their" and "them" naturally refer to the chief priests, the rulers, and the people mentioned in Luke 23:13 and John 19:15. Yet the Jews had no authority to carry out capital punishment (John 18:31, Sec. 159). Even if they had had such authority, their method of execution was by stoning (cf. Acts 7:58–60). Luke and John obviously mean that Pilate acceded to the wishes of the Jews in delivering Jesus to the Roman soldiers, who would execute him by crucifixion (Luke 23:36; John 19:23, Sec. 164).

CRUCIFIXION

Sec. 162   Mockery by the Roman soldiers
—Jerusalem, in the Praetorium—

Matthew 27:27–30

[27]Then the governor's soldiers took Jesus into the Praetorium and gathered the whole company of soldiers around him. [28]They stripped him and put a scarlet robe on him, [29]and then twisted together a crown of thorns and set it on his head. They put a staff in his right hand and knelt in front of him and mocked him. "[b]Hail, king of the Jews!" they said. [30]They spit on him, and took the staff and struck him on the head again and again.

Mark 15:16–19

[16]The soldiers led Jesus away into the palace (that is, the Praetorium) and called together the whole company of soldiers. [17]They put a purple robe on him, then twisted together a crown of thorns and set it on him. [18]And they began to call out to him, "[b]Hail, king of the Jews!" [19]Again and again they struck him on the head with a staff and spit on him. Falling on their knees, they paid homage to him.

Sec. 163   Journey to Golgotha
—From the Praetorium to Golgotha—

Matthew 27:31–34

[31]After they had mocked him, they took off the robe and put his own clothes on him. Then they led him away to crucify him.

[32]As they were going out, they met a man from Cyrene, named Simon, and they [c]forced him to carry the cross.

Mark 15:20–23

[20]And when they had mocked him, they took off the purple robe and put his own clothes on him. Then they led him out to crucify him.

[21]A certain man from Cyrene, Simon, the father of Alexander and Rufus, was passing by on his way in from the country, and they [c]forced him to carry the cross.

Luke 23:26–33a

[26]As they led him away, they seized Simon from Cyrene, who was on his way in from the country, and [c]put the cross on him and made him carry it behind esus. [27]A large number of people followed him, including women who mourned and wailed for him.

John 19:16b–17

So the soldiers took charge of Jesus. [17c]Carrying his own cross,

---

[b](Matt. 27:29; Mark 15:18) The mockery and crude treatment of Jesus came in two stages, of which this is the second. Before his condemnation, Pilate seems to have allowed ill treatment in hopes of provoking the crowd's sympathy toward Jesus and thereby persuading them to ask for his release (John 19:1–5, Sec. 161). In this section, however, following his condemnation the soldiers took the initiative and carried the brutal mockery to a much greater extreme.

[c](Matt. 27:32; Mark 15:21; Luke 23:26; John 19:17) At the outset of the journey to Golgotha, Jesus appears to have carried the cross (or the transverse beam of the cross) himself, in accordance with John's description. Being so weakened from lack of sleep and the cruel scourging, however, he was unable to complete the journey. The soldiers therefore forced Simon of Cyrene to carry it for him. It is possible that Simon's son Rufus, who appears to have been known to Mark's Roman readers (Mark 15:21), is the person whom Paul greets in Roman 16:13.

Matthew 27:31–34 (cont'd)	Mark 15:20–23 (cont'd)	Luke 23:26–33a (cont'd)	John 19:16b–17 (cont'd)
		[28]Jesus turned and said to them, "Daughters of Jerusalem, do not weep for me; weep for yourselves and for your children. [29]For the time will come when you will say, 'Blessed are the barren women, the wombs that never bore and the breasts that never nursed!' [30]Then	
		" 'they will say to the mountains, "Fall on us!" and to the hills, "Cover us!" '[a] [Hos. 10:8].	
		[31]For if men do these things when the tree is green, what will happen when it is dry?" [32]Two other men, both criminals, were also led	
[33]They came to a place called Golgotha (which means The Place of the Skull). [34]There they offered Jesus wine to drink, mixed with gall; but after tasting it, he refused to drink it.	[22]They brought Jesus to the place called Golgotha (which means The Place of the Skull). [23]Then they offered him wine mixed with myrrh, but he did not take it.	out with him to be executed. [33]When they came to the place called the Skull,	he went out to the place of the Skull (which in Aramaic is called Golgotha).

[a]Lk 23:30 Hosea 10:8

Sec. 164   First three hours of crucifixion
—*Golgotha*—

Matthew 27:35–44	Mark 15:24–32	Luke 23:33b–43	John 19:18, 23–24, 19–22, 25–27
35When they had crucified him, they divided up his clothes by casting lots.ᵃ 36And sitting down, they kept watch over him there.	24And they crucified him. Dividing up his clothes, they cast lots to see what each would get.	there they crucified him, along with the criminals —one on his right, the other on his left. 34Jesus said, "ᵈFather, forgive them, for they do not know what they are doing."ᵈ And they divided up his clothes by casting lots.	18Here they crucified him, and with him two others— one on each side and Jesus in the middle. 23When the soldiers crucified Jesus, they took his clothes, dividing them into four shares, one for each of them, with the undergarment remaining. This garment was seamless, woven in one piece from top to bottom. 24"Let's not tear it," they said to one another. "Let's decide by lot who will get it." This happened that the scripture might be fulfilled which said, "They divided my garments among them and cast lots for my clothing"ᶠ [Psalm 22:18]. So this is what the soldiers did.
37Above his head they placed the written charge against him: ᶠTHIS IS JESUS, THE KING OF THE JEWS. 38Two robbers	25It was the ᵉthird hour when they crucified him. 26The written notice of the charge against him read: ᶠTHE KING OF THE JEWS.	38There was a written notice above him, which read: ᶠTHIS IS THE KING OF THE JEWS.	19Pilate had a notice prepared and fastened to the cross. It read: ᶠJESUS OF NAZARETH, THE KING

ᵈ(Luke 23:34) This prayer for forgiveness is the first of Jesus' sayings from the cross. The others are the promise to the repentant criminal (Luke 23:43), the provision for his mother (John 19:26–27), the cry of separation from the Father (Matt. 27:46; Mark 15:34, Sec. 165), the acknowledgement of thirst (John 19:28, Sec. 165), the cry of accomplishment (John 19:30, Sec. 165), and the cry of resignation (Luke 23:46, Sec. 165).

ᵉ(Mark 15:25) Jesus' hours on the cross extended from 9:00 A.M. to 3:00 P.M. The last three hours were distinct because of a darkness into which the area was plunged beginning at noon (Matt. 27:45; Mark 15:33; Luke 23:44–45a, Sec. 165).

ᶠ(Matt. 27:37; Mark 15:26; Luke 23:38; John 19:19) Each writer records only a portion of the inscription. The full inscription is reconstructed by combining the four accounts: "This is Jesus of Nazareth, the King of the Jews."

Matthew 27:35–44 (cont'd)	Mark 15:24–32 (cont'd)	Luke 23:33b–43 (cont'd)	John 19:18, 23–24, 19–22, 25–27 (cont'd)
were crucified with him, one on his right and one on his left.	²⁷They crucified two robbers with him, one on his right and one on his left.ᵇ		OF THE JEWS. ²⁰Many of the Jews read this sign, for the place where Jesus was crucified was near the city, and the sign was written in Aramaic, Latin and Greek. ²¹The chief priests of the Jews protested to Pilate, "Do not write 'The King of the Jews,' but that this man claimed to be king of the Jews." ²²Pilate answered, "What I have written, I have written."
³⁹Those who passed by hurled insults at him, shaking their heads ⁴⁰and saying, "You who are going to destroy the temple and build it in three days, save yourself! Come down from the cross, if you are the Son of God!" ⁴¹In the same way the chief priests, the teachers of the law and the elders mocked him. ⁴²"He saved others," they said, "but he can't save himself! He's the King of Israel! Let him come down now from the cross, and we will believe in him. ⁴³He trusts in God. Let God rescue him now if he wants him, for he said, 'I am the Son of God'" [Psalm 22:8]. ⁴⁴In the same way the robbers	²⁹Those who passed by hurled insults at him, shaking their heads and saying, "So! You who are going to destroy the temple and build it in three days, ³⁰come down from the cross and save yourself!" ³¹In the same way the chief priests and the teachers of the law mocked him among themselves. "He saved others," they said, "but he can't save himself! ³²Let this Christ,ᶜ this King of Israel, come down now from the cross, that we may see and believe."	³⁵The people stood watching, and the rulers even sneered at him. They said, "He saved others; let him save himself if he is the Christ of God, the Chosen One." ³⁶The soldiers also came up and mocked him. They offered him wine vinegar ³⁷and said, "If you are the king of the Jews, save yourself."	

Matthew 27:35–44 (cont'd)	Mark 15:24–32 (cont'd)	Luke 23:33b–43 (cont'd)	John 19:18, 23–24, 19–22, 25–27 (cont'd)
who were crucified with him also heaped insults on him.	Those crucified with him also heaped insults on him.		

Luke (cont'd):

[39]One of the criminals who hung there hurled insults at him: "Aren't you the Christ? Save yourself and us!"

[40]But the other criminal rebuked him. "Don't you fear God," he said, "since you are under the same sentence? [41]We are punished justly, for we are getting what our deeds deserve. But this man has done nothing wrong."

[42]Then he said, "Jesus, remember me when you come into your kingdom.[e]"

[43]Jesus answered him, "I tell you the truth, today you will be with me in paradise."

John (cont'd):

[25]Near the cross of Jesus stood his mother, his mother's sister, Mary the wife of Clopas, and Mary Magdalene. [26]When Jesus saw his mother there, and the disciple whom he loved standing nearby, he said to his mother, "Dear woman, here is your son," [27]and to the disciple, "Here is your mother." From that time on, this disciple took her into his home.

---

[a]Mt 27:35 A few late manuscripts *lots that the word spoken by the prophet might be fulfilled: "They divided my garments among themselves and cast lots for my clothing"* (Psalm 22:18)
[b]Mk 15:27 Some manuscripts *left,* [28]*and the scripture was fulfilled which says, "He was counted with the lawless ones"* (Isaiah 53:12)   [c]32 Or *Messiah*   [d]Lk 23:34 Some early manuscripts do not have this sentence.   [e]42 Some manuscripts *come with your kingly power*   [f]Jn 19:24 Psalm 22:18

Sec. 165   Last three hours of crucifixion
—*Golgotha*—

Matthew 27:45–50	Mark 15:33–37	Luke 23:44–45a, 46	John 19:28–30
[45]From the sixth hour until the ninth hour darkness came over all the land. [46]About the ninth hour Jesus cried out in a loud voice, "[g]*Eloi, Eloi,*[a] *lama sabachthani?*"— which means, "My God, my God, why have you forsaken me?"[b] [Psalm 22:1].	[33]At the sixth hour darkness came over the whole land until the ninth hour. [34]And at the ninth hour Jesus cried out in a loud voice, "[g]*Eloi, Eloi, lama sabachthani?*"— which means, "My God, my God, why have you forsaken me?"[c] [Psalm 22:1].	[44]It was now about the sixth hour, and darkness came over the whole land until the ninth hour, [45]for the sun stopped shining.	
[47]When some of those standing there heard this, they said, "He's calling Elijah." [48]Immediately one of them ran and got a sponge. He filled it with wine vinegar, put it on a stick, and offered it to Jesus to drink. [49]The rest said, "Now leave him alone. Let's see if Elijah comes to save him." [50]And when Jesus had cried out again in a loud voice, he gave up his spirit.	[35]When some of those standing near heard this, they said, "Listen, he's calling Elijah." [36]One man ran, filled a sponge with wine vinegar, put it on a stick, and offered it to Jesus to drink. "Now leave him alone. Let's see if Elijah comes to take him down," he said. [37]With a loud cry, Jesus breathed his last.		[28]Later, knowing that all was now completed, and so that the Scripture would be fulfilled, Jesus said, "I am thirsty." [29]A jar of wine vinegar was there, so they soaked a sponge in it, put the sponge on a stalk of the hyssop plant, and lifted it to Jesus' lips. [30]When he had received the drink, Jesus said, "[h]It is finished." With that, he bowed his head and gave up his spirit.
		[46]Jesus called out with a loud voice, "Father, into your hands I commit my spirit" [Psalm 31:5]. When he had said this, he breathed his last.	

[a]Mt 27:46 Some manuscripts *Eli, Eli*   [b]Mt 27:46; Mk 15:34 Psalm 22:1

---

[g](Matt. 27:46; Mark 15:34) This cry of dereliction reflects the heart of Jesus' purpose in his first advent and death: to bear the penalty for human sin (Heb. 9:28). Because sin separates from a holy God, he had to endure that separation in the moment of his death. Otherwise, the penalty could not have been paid.
   [h](John 19:30) These words look back to the words "all was now completed" in John 19:28. They refer to all things that the Father had given Jesus to do (John 17:4, Sec. 151; cf. John 3:35, Sec. 33; John 13:3, Sec. 145). Included in his commission was the complete fulfillment of Scripture (John 19:28), which the words *it is finished* also reflect.

Sec. 166   Witnesses of Jesus' death
—Temple and Golgotha—

Matthew 27:51–56	Mark 15:38–41	Luke 23:45b, 47–49
[51]At that moment the curtain of the temple was torn in two from top to bottom. The earth shook and the rocks split. [52]The tombs broke open and the bodies of many holy people who had died were raised to life. [53]They came out of the tombs, and after Jesus' resurrection they went into the holy city and appeared to many people.	[38]The curtain of the temple was torn in two from top to bottom.	And the curtain of the temple was torn in two.
[54]When the centurion and those with him who were guarding Jesus saw the earthquake and all that had happened, they were terrified, and exclaimed, "Surely he was the Son[a] of God!"	[39]And when the centurion, who stood there in front of Jesus, heard his cry and[b] saw [i]how he died, he said, "Surely this man was the Son[c] of God!"	[47]The centurion, seeing what had happened, praised God and said, "Surely this was a righteous man." [48]When all the
[55]Many women were there, watching from a distance. They had followed Jesus from Galilee to care for his needs. [56]Among them were [j]Mary Magdalene, Mary the mother of James and Joses, and the mother of Zebedee's sons.	[40]Some women were watching from a distance. Among them were [j]Mary Magdalene, Mary the mother of James the younger and of Joses, and Salome. [41]In Galilee these women had followed him and cared for his needs. Many other women who had come up with him to Jerusalem were also there.	people who had gathered to witness this sight saw what took place, they beat their breasts and went away. [49]But all those who knew him, including the [j]women who had followed him from Galilee, stood at a distance, watching these things.

[a]Mt 27:54; Mk 15:39 Or *a son*   [b]Mk 15:39 Some manuscripts do not have *heard his cry and*.

[i](Mark 15:39) The centurion was impressed not only by the earthquake and other signs (Matt. 27:54), but also by the manner of Jesus' death. That Jesus possessed enough strength to cry loudly at the moment of death (Matt. 27:50; Mark 15:37; Luke 23:46, Sec. 165) was remarkable to one who was accustomed to seeing crucified criminals die from sheer exhaustion.

[j](Matt. 27:56; Mark 15:40; Luke 23:49) These women were eyewitnesses to the events that compose the heart of the gospel message: Jesus' death (in this section), his burial (Matt. 27:61; Mark 15:47; Luke 23:55, Sec. 168), and his resurrection (Matt. 28:1; Mark 16:1, Sec. 169). Compare 1 Corinthians 15:3–4.

BURIAL

Sec. 167a   Certification of Jesus' death and procurement of his body
—Golgotha and the Praetorium—

Matthew 27:57–58   Mark 15:42–45   Luke 23:50–52   John 19:31–38

[31]Now it was the day of Preparation, and the next day was to be a special Sabbath. Because the Jews did not want the bodies left on the crosses during the Sabbath, they asked Pilate to have the legs broken and the bodies taken down. [32]The soldiers therefore came and broke the legs of the first man who had been crucified with Jesus, and then those of the other. [33]But when they came to Jesus and found that he was already dead, they did not break his legs. [34]Instead, one of the soldiers pierced Jesus' side with a spear, bringing a sudden flow of [k]blood and water. [35]The man who saw it has given testimony, and his testimony is true. He knows that he tells the truth, and he testifies so that you also may believe. [36]These things happened so that the scripture would be fulfilled: "Not one of his bones will be broken"[a] [Psalm

[k](John 19:34) The flow of blood and water from Jesus' side, though difficult to explain medically, actually happened as John describes it (John 19:35). This signified that Jesus was already dead and was the basis for a report to this effect brought back to Pilate (Mark 15:44–45). In the midst of uncertainty regarding the cause of this phenomenon, the possibility that Jesus died of a ruptured heart must remain one of the possible explanations (cf. Psalm 69:20).

Matthew 27:57–58 (cont'd)	Mark 15:42–45 (cont'd)	Luke 23:50–52 (cont'd)	John 19:31–38 (cont'd)
			34:20], [37]and, as another scripture says, "They will look on the one they have pierced"[b] [Zech. 12:10].
[57]As evening approached,	[42]It was Preparation Day (that is, the day before the Sabbath). So as evening approached, [43]Joseph of Arimathea, a prominent member of the Council,		
there came a rich man from Arimathea, named Joseph,		[50]Now there was a man named Joseph, a member of the Council, a good and upright man, [51]who had not consented to their decision and action. He came from the Judean town of Arimathea and he was waiting for the kingdom of God. [52]Going to Pilate, he asked for Jesus' body.	[38]Later, Joseph of Arimathea
who had himself become a disciple of Jesus. [58]Going to Pilate, he asked for Jesus' body,	who was himself waiting for the kingdom of God, went boldly to Pilate and asked for Jesus' body. [44]Pilate was surprised to hear that he was already dead. Summoning the centurion, he asked him if Jesus had already died. [45]When he learned from the centurion that it was so, he		asked Pilate for the body of Jesus. Now Joseph was a disciple of Jesus, but secretly because he feared the Jews.
and Pilate ordered that it be given to him.	gave the body to Joseph.		With Pilate's permission, he came and took the body away.

[a]Jn 19:36 Exodus 12:46; Num. 9:12; Psalm 34:20   [b]37 Zech. 12:10

Sec. 167b   Jesus' body placed in a tomb
—The garden tomb at Golgotha—

Matthew 27:59–60	Mark 15:46	Luke 23:53–54	John 19:39–42
			[39]He was accompanied by [l]Nicodemus, the man who earlier had visited Jesus at night. Nicodemus

[l](Matt. 27:59; John 19:39) The disciples who had openly followed Jesus during his lifetime ran away at the end, but Joseph and Nicodemus, who had kept their faith secret while he was alive (cf. John 19:38, Sec. 167a), came forward publicly to give him an appropriate burial.

Matthew 27:59–60 (cont'd)	Mark 15:46 (cont'd)	Luke 23:53–54 (cont'd)	John 19:39–42 (cont'd)
⁵⁹Joseph took the body, wrapped it in a clean linen cloth,	⁴⁶So Joseph bought some linen cloth, took down the body, wrapped it in the linen,	⁵³Then he took it down, wrapped it in linen cloth	brought a mixture of myrrh and aloes, about seventy-five pounds.ᵃ ⁴⁰Taking Jesus' body, the two of them wrapped it, with the spices, in strips of linen. This was in accordance with Jewish burial cus-
⁶⁰and placed it in his own new tomb that he had cut out of the rock. He rolled a big stone in front of the entrance to the tomb and went away.	and placed it in a tomb cut out of rock. Then he rolled a stone against the entrance of the tomb.	and placed it in a tomb cut in the rock, one in which no one had yet been laid. ⁵⁴It was Preparation Day, and the	toms. ⁴¹At the place where Jesus was crucified, there was a garden, and in the garden a new tomb, in which no one had ever been laid. ⁴²Because it was the Jewish day of Preparation and since the tomb was nearby, they laid Jesus there.

ᵃJn 19:39 Greek *a hundred litrai* (about 34 kilograms)

Sec. 168   The tomb watched by the women and guarded by the soldiers
—Bethany, Golgotha, and the Praetorium—

Matthew 27:61–66	Mark 15:47	Luke 23:55–56
⁶¹Mary Magdalene and the other Mary were sitting there opposite the tomb.	⁴⁷Mary Magdalene and Mary the mother of Joses saw where he was laid.	⁵⁵The women who had come with Jesus from Galilee followed Joseph and saw the tomb and how his body was laid in it. ⁵⁶Then they went home and prepared spices and perfumes. But they rested on the Sabbath in obedience to the commandment.

⁶²The next day, the one after Preparation Day, the chief priests and the Pharisees went to Pilate. ⁶³"Sir," they said, "ᵐwe remember that while he was still alive that deceiver said, 'After three days I will rise again.' ⁶⁴So give the order for the tomb to be made secure until the third day. Otherwise, his disciples may come and steal the body and tell the people that he has been raised from the dead. This last deception will be worse than the first."

⁶⁵"Take a guard," Pilate answered. "Go, make the tomb as secure as you know how." ⁶⁶So they went and made the tomb secure by putting a seal on the stone and posting the guard.

ᵐ(Matt. 27:63) How strange it is that Jesus' disciples failed to grasp his plainly spoken prophecies to them about his resurrection (cf. Secs. 83, 88, 125a), whereas these Sadducees and Pharisees understood and remembered the ones he had spoken to them in figurative language (Matt. 12:40, Sec. 62; Matt. 16:4, Sec. 80; John 2:19–20, Sec. 31).

PART THIRTEEN
THE RESURRECTION AND ASCENSION OF CHRIST
THE EMPTY TOMB

Sec. 169 The tomb visited by the women
—Bethany and Golgotha—

Matthew 28:1

¹After the Sabbath, at dawn on the first day of the week, ⁿMary Magdalene and the other Mary went to look at the tomb.

Mark 16:1

¹When the Sabbath was over, ⁿMary Magdalene, Mary the mother of James, and Salome bought spices so that they might go to anoint Jesus' body.

Sec. 170 The stone rolled away
—Golgotha—

Matthew 28:2–4

²There was a ᵒviolent earthquake, for an angel of the Lord came down from heaven and, going to the tomb, rolled back the stone and sat on it. ³His appearance was like lightning, and his clothes were white as snow. ⁴The guards were so afraid of him that they shook and became like dead men.

Sec. 171 The tomb found to be empty by the women
—Golgotha—

Matthew 28:5–8	Mark 16:2–8	Luke 24:1–8	John 20:1
	²Very early on the first day of the week, ᵖjust after sunrise, they were on their way to the tomb ³and they asked each other, "Who will roll the stone away from the entrance of the tomb?" ⁴But when they	¹On the first day of the week, very early in the morning, the women took the spices they had prepared and went to the tomb. ²They found the stone rolled away from the tomb, ³but when they entered, they did not find the	¹Early on the first day of the week, ᵖwhile it was still dark, Mary Magdalene went to the tomb and saw that the stone had been removed from the entrance.

ⁿ(Matt. 28:1; Mark 16:1) The number of women involved in various visits to the tomb is indefinite. The following are named: Mary Magdalene (Matt. 28:1; Mark 16:1; Luke 24:10, Sec. 172; John 20:1, Sec. 171), Mary the mother of James or "the other Mary" (Matt. 28:1; Mark 16:1; Luke 24:10, Sec. 172), Salome (Mark 16:1), and Joanna (Luke 24:10, Sec. 172). How many "others" (Luke 24:10, Sec. 172) were with them we are not told.

ᵒ(Matt. 28:2) Perhaps the moment of Christ's resurrection coincided with this "violent earthquake," because so often in Scripture the earthquake signifies a divine visitation (cf. Matt. 27:51, 54, Sec. 166). Yet the exact time cannot be fixed with certainty, because no one saw Jesus rise. The early witnesses of his resurrection (cf. Acts 1:22) were those who saw him after he rose (cf. Secs. 173–174, 176, 178–184), not when he rose. The angel's coming to roll away the stone was not designed to allow the risen Jesus to leave. He did not need this (cf. John 20:19, Sec. 178). Removal of the stone was designed to let witnesses see the empty tomb (cf. Mark 16:5; Luke 24:3, Sec. 171; John 20:5–8, Sec. 172).

ᵖ(Mark 16:2; John 20:1) "Just after sunrise" in Mark 16:2 does not contradict "while it was still dark" in John 20:1. Quite possibly Mary Magdalene ran ahead of the other women and arrived before the sun rose, as John describes it, whereas the rest reached the tomb after sunrise, as Mark records it. Another possible explanation is that it was dark when the party of women departed, and after sunrise when they arrived at the tomb.

237

Matthew 28:5–8 (cont'd)	Mark 16:2–8 (cont'd)	Luke 24:1–8 (cont'd)	John 20:1 (cont'd)
	looked up, they saw that the stone, which was very large, had been rolled away. ⁵As they entered the tomb, they saw a young man dressed in a white	body of the Lord Jesus. ⁴While they were wondering about this, sudden- ly two men in clothes that gleamed like light- ning stood beside	
⁵The angel said to the women, "Do not be afraid, for I know that you are looking for Jesus, who was crucified. ⁶He is not here; he has risen, just as he said. Come and see the place where he lay. ⁷Then go quickly and tell his disciples: 'He has risen from the dead and is going ahead of you into Galilee. There you will see him.' Now I have told you." ⁸So the women hurried away from the tomb, afraid yet filled with joy, and ran to tell his disci- ples.	robe sitting on the right side, and they were alarmed. ⁶"Don't be alarmed," he said. "You are looking for Jesus the Naza- rene, who was cru- cified. He has ris- en! He is not here. See the place where they laid him. ⁷But go, tell his disciples and Peter, 'He is going ahead of you into Galilee. There you will see him, just as he told you.'" ⁸Trembling and bewildered, the women went out and fled from the tomb. They said nothing to anyone, because they were afraid.	them. ⁵In their fright the women bowed down with their faces to the ground, but the men said to them, "Why do you look for the living among the dead? ⁶He is not here; he has risen! Remem- ber how he told you, while he was still with you in Galilee: ⁷'The Son of Man must be de- livered into the hands of sinful men, be crucified and on the third day be raised again.'" ⁸Then they remembered his words.	

Sec. 172   The tomb found to be empty by Peter and John
—Golgotha—

Luke 24:9–11, ⁹12

⁹When they came back from the tomb, they told all these things to the Eleven and to all the others. ¹⁰It was Mary Mag- dalene, Joanna, Mary the mother of James, and the others with them who told this to the apostles. ¹¹But they did not believe the women, because their words seemed to them like nonsense. ¹²Peter, however, got up and ran to the tomb. Bending over, he saw the strips of linen lying by themselves, and he went

John 20:2–10

²So she came running to Simon Peter and the other disciple, the one Jesus loved, and said, "They have taken the Lord out of the tomb, and we don't know where they have put him!"

³So Peter and the other disciple start- ed for the tomb. ⁴Both were running, but the other disciple outran Peter and reached the tomb first. ⁵He bent over and looked in at the strips of linen lying

ᵠ(Luke 24:12) An impressive group of ancient sources omits this verse from the text of Luke 24, though witnesses for its inclusion are also strong.

Luke 24:9–11, 12 (cont'd)

John 20:2–10 (cont'd)

away, wondering to himself what had happened.

there but did not go in. [6]Then Simon Peter, who was behind him, arrived and went into the tomb. He saw the strips of [r]linen lying there, [7]as well as the burial cloth that had been around Jesus' head. The cloth was folded up by itself, separate from the linen. [8]Finally the other disciple, who had reached the tomb first, also went inside. He saw and believed. [9](They still did not understand from Scripture that Jesus had to rise from the dead.)

[10]Then the disciples went back to their homes,

THE POSTRESURRECTION APPEARANCES

Sec. 173   Appearance to Mary Magdalene
—Golgotha and Jerusalem—

[s][Mark 16:9–11]

John 20:11–18

[11]but Mary stood outside the tomb crying. As she wept, she bent over to look into the tomb [12]and saw two angels in white, seated where Jesus' body had been, one at the head and the other at the foot.

[13]They asked her, "Woman, why are you crying?"

[9When Jesus rose early on the first day of the week, he appeared first to Mary Magdalene, out of whom he had driven seven demons.

"They have taken my Lord away," she said, "and I don't know where they have put him." [14]At this, she turned around and saw Jesus standing there, but she did not realize that it was Jesus.

[15]"Woman," he said, "why are you crying? Who is it you are looking for?"

Thinking he was the gardener, she said, "Sir, if you have carried him away, tell me where you have put him, and I will get him."

[16]Jesus said to her, "Mary."

She turned toward him and cried out in Aramaic, "Rabboni!" (which means Teacher).

[17]Jesus said, "[t]Do not hold on to me,

---

[r](John 20:6) John's description of the linen wrappings and face cloth (John 20:7) does not necessarily mean that Jesus rose from the dead without disturbing the grave clothes in which he was wrapped. The record rather presents a picture of the orderly arrangement of these grave clothes, such as would not have been the case if grave robbers, the disciples, or anyone else had taken the body away. This neatness was sufficient to convince John that Jesus had risen (John 20:8).

[s](Mark 16:9–20) The two most reliable early manuscripts and other ancient witnesses do not have Mark 16:9–20.

[t](John 20:17) The force of Jesus' words apparently was to inform Mary that he was not returning to the old life as Lazarus had (cf. John 12:2, Sec. 141; John 12:9, Sec. 128a). By holding on to him, Mary responded to his presence as though he were. His postresurrection appearances were to occupy only a brief time because he must soon return to the Father's house (cf. Sec. 184; John 14:2, Sec. 149). He therefore instructed Mary to go and tell the disciples this.

[Mark 16:9–11] (cont'd)

John 20:11–18 (cont'd)

for I have not yet returned to the Father. Go instead to my brothers and tell them, 'I am returning to my Father and your Father, to my God and your God.' "

¹⁰She went and told those who had been with him and who were mourning and weeping. ¹¹When they heard that Jesus was alive and that she had seen him, they did not believe it.]

¹⁸Mary Magdalene went to the disciples with the news: "I have seen the Lord!" And she told them that he had said these things to her.

Sec. 174   Appearance to the other women
—*Jerusalem*—

Matthew 28:9–10

⁹Suddenly Jesus met ^uthem. "Greetings," he said. They came to him, clasped his feet and worshiped him. ¹⁰Then Jesus said to them, "Do not be afraid. Go and tell my brothers to go to Galilee; there they will see me."

Sec. 175   Report of the soldiers to the Jewish authorities
—*Jerusalem*—

Matthew 28:11–15

¹¹While the women were on their way, some of the guards went into the city and reported to the chief priests everything that had happened. ¹²When the chief priests had met with the elders and devised a plan, they gave the soldiers a large sum of money, ¹³telling them, "You are to say, ^v'His disciples came during the night and stole him away while we were asleep.' ¹⁴If this report gets to the governor, we will satisfy him and keep you out of trouble." ¹⁵So the soldiers took the money and did as they were instructed. And this story has been widely circulated among the Jews to this very day.

Sec. 176   Appearance to the two disciples traveling to Emmaus
—*On the road to Emmaus*—

[Mark 16:12–13]

[¹²Afterward Jesus appeared in a different form to two of them while they were walking in the country. ¹³These returned and reported it to the rest; but they did not believe them either.]

Luke 24:13–32

¹³Now that same day two of them were going to a village called Emmaus, about seven miles^a from Jerusalem. ¹⁴They were talking with each other about everything that had happened.

---

^u(Matt. 28:9) Mary Magdalene had returned to the tomb after contacting Peter and John (John 20:11, Sec. 173) and was therefore no longer with this company of women when they left the tomb (Matt. 28:8; Mark 16:8, Sec. 171). This group now could report to the disciples not only the empty tomb and the words of the angelic messenger (Matt. 28:7–8; Mark 16:7, Sec. 171), but also that they themselves had seen their risen Lord (Matt. 28:10).

^v(Matt. 28:13) The absurdity of this story invented by the Sanhedrin in official session (Matt. 28:11–12) reveals the desperation to which they had been driven by recent developments. Surely the disciples in removing the heavy stone from the tomb would have made enough noise to have awakened at least one of the soldiers. Furthermore, if the soldiers were asleep, how could they have known the grave robbers to be the disciples? Yet for twenty centuries attempts to explain the empty tomb have continued and have proven just as futile as this original one. The only plausible explanation is that God raised Jesus from the dead, thus allowing him to leave the tomb under his own power.

Luke 24:13–32 (cont'd)

[15]As they talked and discussed these things with each other, Jesus himself came up and walked along with them; [16]but they were kept from recognizing him.

[17]He asked them, "What are you discussing together as you walk along?"

They stood still, their faces ʷdowncast. [18]One of them, named Cleopas, asked him, "Are you only a visitor to Jerusalem and do not know the things that have happened there in these days?"

[19]"What things?" he asked.

"About Jesus of Nazareth," they replied. "He was a prophet, powerful in word and deed before God and all the people. [20]The chief priests and our rulers handed him over to be sentenced to death, and they crucified him; [21]but we had hoped that he was the one who was going to redeem Israel. And what is more, it is the third day since all this took place. [22]In addition, some of our women amazed us. They went to the tomb early this morning [23]but didn't find his body. They came and told us that they had seen a vision of angels, who said he was alive. [24]Then some of our companions went to the tomb and found it just as the women had said, but him they did not see."

[25]He said to them, "How foolish you are, and how slow of heart to believe all that the prophets have spoken! [26]Did not the Christ[b] have to suffer these things and then enter his glory?" [27]And beginning with Moses and all the Prophets, he explained to them what was said in all the Scriptures concerning himself.

[28]As they approached the village to which they were going, Jesus acted as if he were going farther. [29]But they urged him strongly, "Stay with us, for it is nearly evening; the day is almost over." So he went in to stay with them.

[30]When he was at the table with them, he took bread, gave thanks, broke it and began to give it to them. [31]Then their eyes were opened and they recognized him, and he disappeared from their sight. [32]They asked each other, "Were not our hearts burning within us while he talked with us on the road and opened the Scriptures to us?"

[a]Lk 24:13 Greek *sixty stadia* (about 11 kilometers)   [b]26 Or *Messiah*; also in verse 46

Sec. 177   Report of the two disciples to the rest
—*Jerusalem*—

Luke 24:33–35	1 Corinthians 15:5a
[33]They got up and returned at once to Jerusalem. There they found the Eleven and those with them, assembled together [34]and saying, "It is true! The Lord has risen ₌and has appeared to ˣSimon." [35]Then the two told what had happened on the way, and how Jesus was recognized by them when he broke the bread.	[5]and that he appeared to ˣPeter,[a]

[a]5 Greek *Cephas*

ʷ(Luke 24:17) The sorrow and despondency of Jesus' followers, even after they had received word about the empty tomb, show how ridiculous is the explanation that they invented the story of Jesus' resurrection. Their state of mind was completely opposed to the possibility of doing such a thing.

ˣ(Luke 24:34; 1 Cor. 15:5a) This private appearance to Peter is not described in the four gospels, though Paul alludes to it in his first Corinthian epistle. It apparently happened after the two disciples started for Emmaus (Luke 24:13, Sec. 176), but before the eleven disciples assembled in Jerusalem (Luke 24:33).

Sec. 178   Appearance to the ten assembled disciples
(cf. Secs. 181, 183—postresurrection appearances to the disciples)
—*Jerusalem*—

[Mark 16:14]	Luke 24:36–43	John 20:19–25
[[14]Later Jesus appeared to the Eleven as they were eating; he rebuked them for their lack of faith and their stubborn refusal to believe those who had seen him after he had risen.]	[36]While they were still talking about this, Jesus himself stood among them and said to them, "Peace be with you." [37]They were startled and frightened, thinking they saw a ghost. [38]He said to them, "Why are you troubled, and why do doubts rise in your minds? [39]Look at my hands and my feet. It is I myself! Touch me and see; a ghost does not have flesh and bones, as you see I have." [40]When he had said this, he showed them his hands and feet. [41]And while they still did not believe it because of joy and amazement, he asked them, "Do you have anything here to eat?" [42]They gave him a piece of broiled fish, [43]and he took it and ate it in their presence.	[19]On the evening of that first day of the week, when the disciples were together, with the doors locked for fear of the Jews, Jesus came and [y]stood among them and said, "Peace be with you!" [20]After he said this, he showed them his hands and side. The disciples were overjoyed when they saw the Lord. [21]Again Jesus said, "Peace be with you! As the Father has sent me, I am sending you." [22]And with that he breathed on them and said, "Receive the Holy Spirit. [23]If you forgive anyone his sins, they are forgiven; if you do not forgive them, they are not forgiven." [24]Now Thomas (called Didymus), one of the Twelve, was not with the disciples when Jesus came. [25]So the other disci-

[y](John 20:19) This section reveals several things about Jesus' resurrection body. In this verse he was able to pass through a locked door. The wounds of his crucifixion were still visible (Luke 24:39; John 20:20). The body was composed of material substance that could be felt (Luke 24:39; John 20:25, 27, Secs. 178–179). It consisted of flesh and bone as contrasted with flesh and blood (Luke 24:39). It was capable of consuming food as a mortal body does (Luke 24:43).

John 20:19–25 (cont'd)

ples told him, "We have seen the Lord!"

But he said to them, "Unless I see the nail marks in his hands and put my finger where the nails were, and put my hand into his side, I will not believe it."

Sec. 179   Appearance to the eleven assembled disciples
—Jerusalem—

John 20:26–31

²⁶A week later his disciples were in the house again, and Thomas was with them. Though the doors were locked, Jesus came and stood among them and said, "Peace be with you!"

1 Corinthians 15:5b

and then to the Twelve.

²⁷Then he said to Thomas, "Put your finger here; see my hands. Reach out your hand and put it into my side. Stop doubting and believe."

²⁸Thomas said to him, "My Lord and ᶻmy God!"

²⁹Then Jesus told him, "Because you have seen me, you have believed; blessed are those who have not seen and yet have believed."

³⁰Jesus did many other miraculous signs in the presence of his disciples, which are not recorded in this book. ³¹But these are written that you may[a] believe that Jesus is the Christ, the Son of God, and that by believing you may have life in his name.

a Jn 20:31 Some manuscripts may continue to

Sec. 180   Appearance to the seven disciples while fishing
—Sea of Galilee—

John 21:1–25

¹ᵃAfterward Jesus appeared again to his disciples, by the Sea of Tiberias.[a] It happened this way: ²Simon Peter, Thomas (called Didymus), Nathanael from Cana in Galilee, the sons of Zebedee, and two other disciples were together. ³"I'm going out to fish," Simon Peter told them, and they said, "We'll go with you." So they went out and got into the boat, but that night they caught nothing.

⁴Early in the morning, Jesus stood on the shore, but the disciples did not realize that it was Jesus.

⁵He called out to them, "Friends, haven't you any fish?"

"No," they answered.

⁶He said, "Throw your net on the right side of the boat and you will find some." When they did, they were unable to haul the net in because of the large number of fish.

ᶻ(John 20:28) Once he overcame his skepticism, Thomas made the strongest confession of all. Prior to this no one had addressed Jesus in this way. To call Jesus God put him on an equal plane with the Father (cf. John 5:23, Sec. 49c).

ᵃ(John 21:1) The viewpoint that makes John 21 a later addition to the fourth gospel cannot be substantiated. The absence of manuscript support for this theory and the fact that the writing style used in chapters 1–20 continues in chapter 21 strongly support the traditional position that this chapter was an integral part of the gospel from the time John the apostle penned it.

John 21:1–25 (cont'd)

[7]Then the disciple whom Jesus loved said to Peter, "It is the Lord!" As soon as Simon Peter heard him say, "It is the Lord," he wrapped his outer garment around him (for he had taken it off) and jumped into the water. [8]The other disciples followed in the boat, towing the net full of fish, for they were not far from shore, about a hundred yards.[b] [9]When they landed, they saw a fire of burning coals there with fish on it, and some bread.

[10]Jesus said to them, "Bring some of the fish you have just caught."

[11]Simon Peter climbed aboard and dragged the net ashore. It was full of large fish, 153, but even with so many the net was not torn. [12]Jesus said to them, "Come and have breakfast." None of the disciples dared ask him, "Who are you?" They knew it was the Lord. [13]Jesus came, took the bread and gave it to them, and did the same with the fish. [14]This was now the third time Jesus appeared to his disciples after he was raised from the dead.

[15]When they had finished eating, Jesus said to Simon Peter, "Simon son of John, do you truly love me more than these?"

"Yes, Lord," he said, "you know that I love you."

Jesus said, "Feed my lambs."

[16]Again Jesus said, "Simon son of John, do you truly love me?"

He answered, "Yes, Lord, you know that I love you."

Jesus said, "Take care of my sheep."

[17]The third time he said to him, "Simon son of John, do you love me?"

Peter was hurt because Jesus asked him the third time, "Do you love me?" He said, "Lord, you know all things; you know that I love you."

Jesus said, "Feed my sheep. [18]I tell you the truth, when you were younger you dressed yourself and went where you wanted; but when you are old you will stretch out your hands, and someone else will dress you and lead you where you do not want to go." [19]Jesus said this to indicate the kind of death by which Peter would glorify God. Then he said to him, "Follow me!"

[20]Peter turned and saw that the disciple whom Jesus loved was following them. (This was the one who had leaned back against Jesus at the supper and had said, "Lord, who is going to betray you?") [21]When Peter saw him, he asked, "Lord, what about him?"

[22]Jesus answered, "If I want him to remain alive until I return, what is that to you? You must follow me." [23]Because of this, the rumor spread among the brothers that this disciple would not die. But Jesus did not say that he would not die; he only said, "If I want him to remain alive until I return, what is that to you?"

[24]This is the disciple who testifies to these things and who wrote them down. We know that his testimony is true.

[25]Jesus did many other things as well. If every one of them were written down, I suppose that even the whole world would not have room for the books that would be written.

[a]Jn 21:1 That is, Sea of Galilee   [b]8 Greek *about two hundred cubits* (about 90 meters)

Sec. 181   Appearance to the eleven in Galilee
(cf. Secs. 178, 183—postresurrection appearances to the disciples)
—*A mountain in Galilee*—

Matthew 28:16–20	[Mark 16:15–18]	1 Corinthians 15:6
[16]Then the eleven disci-ples went to [b]Galilee, to		

[b](Matt. 28:16) For some reason great prominence is given to this rendezvous in Galilee (Matt. 26:32; Mark 14:38, Sec. 147; Matt. 28:7; Mark 16:7, Sec. 171; Matt. 28:10, Sec. 174; cf. John 21:1, Sec. 180). Perhaps this site was chosen because it was convenient to many of Jesus' loyal followers who lived in Galilee. In addition, the mountain probably furnished a location that would be free from distractions and outside disturbances.

Matthew 28:16–20 (cont'd)	[Mark 16:15–18] (cont'd)	1 Corinthians 15:6 (cont'd)
the mountain where Jesus had told them to go. ¹⁷When they saw him, they worshiped him; but some doubted. ¹⁸Then Jesus came to them and said, "All authority in heaven and on earth has been given to me. ¹⁹Therefore go and make disciples of all nations, baptizing them in^a the name of the Father and of the Son and of the Holy Spirit, ²⁰and teaching them to obey everything I have commanded you. And surely I am with you always, to the very end of the age."	[¹⁵He said to them, "Go into all the world and preach the good news to all creation. ¹⁶Whoever believes and is baptized will be saved, but whoever does not believe will be condemned. ¹⁷And these signs will accompany those who believe: In my name they will drive out demons; they will speak in new tongues; ¹⁸they will pick up snakes with their hands; and when they drink deadly poison, it will not hurt them at all; they will place their hands on sick people, and they will get well."]	⁶After that, he appeared to more than five hundred of the brothers at the same time, most of whom are still living, though some have fallen asleep.

^aMt 28:19 Or *into*; see Acts 8:16; 19:5; Romans 6:3; 1 Cor. 1:13; 10:2 and Gal. 3:27.

Sec. 182   Appearance to James, Jesus' brother

1 Corinthians 15:7

⁷Then he appeared to ^cJames, then to all the apostles,

^c(1 Cor. 15:7) This is probably James, the half-brother of Jesus. The time of this appearance is not given, but that it happened was well known. James, an unbeliever before Jesus' crucifixion, became a believer and leader of the Jerusalem church after this experience. Seeing the risen Jesus not only resulted in his conversion but was also a basis for his appointment to the apostolic office (cf. Gal. 1:19).

Sec. 183   Appearance to the disciples in Jerusalem
(cf. Secs. 178, 181—postresurrection appearances to the disciples)
—Jerusalem—

Luke 24:44–49

⁴⁴ᵈHe said to them, "This is what I told you while I was still with you: Everything must be fulfilled that is written about me in the Law of Moses, the Prophets and the Psalms." ⁴⁵Then he opened their minds so they could understand the Scriptures. ⁴⁶He told them, "This is what is written: The Christ will suffer and rise from the dead on the third day, ⁴⁷and repentance and forgiveness of sins will be preached in his name to all nations, beginning at Jerusalem.

⁴⁸You are witnesses of these things. ⁴⁹I am going to send you what my Father has promised; but stay in the city until you have been clothed with power from on high."

Acts 1:3–8

³After his suffering, he showed himself to these men and gave many convincing proofs that he was alive. He appeared to them over a period of forty days and spoke about the kingdom of God. ⁴On one occasion, while he was eating with them, he gave them this command: "Do not leave Jerusalem, but wait for the gift my Father promised, which you have heard me speak about. ⁵For John baptized with ᵃ water, but in a few days you will be baptized with the Holy Spirit."
⁶So when they met together, they asked him, "Lord, are you at this time going to restore the kingdom to Israel?"
⁷He said to them: "It is not for you to know the times or dates the Father has set by his own authority. ⁸But you will receive power when the Holy Spirit comes on you; and you will be my witnesses in Jerusalem, and in all Judea and Samaria, and to the ends of the earth."

ᵃActs 1:5 Or in

THE ASCENSION

Sec. 184   Christ's parting blessing and departure
—From Jerusalem to the Mount of Olives (the vicinity of Bethany)—

[Mark 16:19–20]

[¹⁹After the Lord Jesus had spoken to them, he was taken up into heaven and he sat at the right hand of God.

Luke 24:50–53

⁵⁰When he had led them out to the vicinity of Bethany, he lifted up his hands and blessed them. ⁵¹While he was blessing them, he left them and was taken up into heaven.

Acts 1:9–12

⁹After he said this, he was taken up before their very eyes, and a cloud hid him from their sight. ¹⁰They were looking intently up into the sky as he was going, when suddenly two men dressed in white stood beside them.

ᵈ(Luke 24:44) It must not be surmised that this meeting was the same as that in Section 178 and therefore took place on the same day as the resurrection. Luke clarifies this point in his second book when he points out that forty days had transpired since the resurrection (Acts 1:3). Hence there was ample time for a journey to Galilee (Secs. 180–181) and back.

[Mark 16:19–20] (cont'd)   Luke 24:50–53 (cont'd)   Acts 1:9–12 (cont'd)

[11]"Men of Galilee," they said, "why do you stand here looking into the sky? This same Jesus, who has been taken from you into heaven, will come back in the same way you have seen him go into heaven."

[52]Then they worshiped him and returned to Jerusalem with great joy. [53]And they stayed continually at the [e]temple, praising God.

[12]Then they returned to Jerusalem from the hill called the Mount of Olives, a Sabbath day's walk[a] from the city.

[20]Then the disciples went out and preached everywhere, and the Lord worked with them and confirmed his word by the signs that accompanied it.]

[a]*Acts 1:12* That is, about 3/4 mile (about 1,100 meters)

[e](Luke 24:53) Only gradually did the earliest Christians learn that they had been freed from the old forms of temple worship (cf. Heb. 8:13). Hence right after Jesus' ascension they went back to the only form of worship they knew. Over a period of years, however, their understanding grew to the point that the temple's destruction in A.D. 70 proved no hindrance to their worship.

ESSAYS RELATED TO HARMONISTIC STUDIES

ESSAY 1

Is a Harmony of the Gospels Legitimate?

Until the nineteenth or possibly the twentieth century, it was a foregone conclusion that constructing a harmony of the gospels was a legitimate undertaking. Since the rise of modern criticism, however, harmonization is no longer universally admitted to be a valid procedure. An increasing number of people are concerned about whether research into the life of Jesus—in other words, compiling a harmony of the biblical records of that life—can or should be undertaken.

Opposition to this type of project has followed various approaches:

1. One thrust has been to emphasize that the four gospels were not designed to be histories, but gospels. With such bias on the part of the writers admitted, it is held, one could hardly expect to derive much value in drawing up a biography of Jesus. This objection to harmonization is, however, logically weak. An evangelistic interest and purpose does not preclude historical accuracy. In fact, the wise evangelist will compose an accurate account so that the cause being promoted will not be undermined by being shown to be fallacious (Luke 1:3–4). Furthermore, a principal ethic of Christianity and the gospels is honesty. Because the evangelists intended to give accurate reports based on thorough investigation (Luke 1:3–4), it is unlikely that those who wrote about this ethic would have practiced distortions of historical truth in the very books where it is taught.

2. Another attempt to discredit the harmonizing approach to the gospels has come from some who doubt that the historical Jesus ever existed. To these extremists, who incidentally are few in number, Jesus is no more than a mythological figure such as those encountered in the nature myths and mystery religions of the Graeco-Roman world. That Jesus Christ was a historical person is subscribed to by an impressive collection of ancient documents, however, including those from Jewish and Roman writers as well as Christian. In addition, the existence of the Christian church is explicable only on the ground of his being a historical person.

3. Others attempt to demonstrate the fruitlessness of harmonies by placing strong emphasis on alleged loose handling of traditions by the earliest Christian churches. Supposedly the church took fragmentary

reports about the person Jesus and elaborated upon them so as to attribute to Jesus sayings and actions that would meet its own needs. The process held to be necessary in separating the facts from the elaborations is called Form Criticism (see essay 4, pp. 268–74). Several difficulties confront such criticism of the gospels' historical worth. Among them is the critics' assumption that those who had the strongest reason for being interested in the historical facts of Jesus' life had little or no interest in ascertaining and transmitting those facts. Form Criticism also maintains that eyewitnesses of Jesus' life stood by in silence while falsehood about Jesus was promoted as the truth. This is inconceivable.

4. A more recent theory, Redaction Criticism, has also proposed obstacles to accepting the gospels at face value (see essay 5, pp. 275–84). This discipline takes special note of the gospel writers and their distinctive theological purposes. The writers purportedly took the traditions handed down to them and molded them so as to reflect the church's and their own understanding of the kerygma ("proclamation; the preached Word; gospel"). In so doing, Redaction Criticism claims, they beclouded the historical Jesus and his teachings even more than the generation before them had done. It may be agreed that each gospel writer had a distinctive purpose in mind, but it is unwarranted to conclude that he altered the facts at hand in order to attain this purpose. Matthew, Mark, Luke, and John were truthful men writing about a system of truth built around him who is the Truth. To arbitrarily attribute to them an almost endless stream of lies, even "white lies," as does the redaction critic, is to impugn the truth itself. No tangible grounds have as yet been forthcoming to support this objection to harmonizing the gospels.

5. Closely akin to number 4 is the position of some evangelicals who advocate redaction critical methodology. They do not agree that the evangelists altered the facts at hand, but still maintain that the gospel narratives and other connective features are of questionable value in constructing a chronological sequence of the life of Christ. These scholars do not label the gospels as unhistorical, but they do assume an agnostic stance, expressing doubts about the possibility of harmonizing the gospel accounts. They find themselves occupying an in-between position regarding the historical accuracy of the gospels and continually struggle to reconcile their views with a high view of biblical authority (see the section entitled "Evangelical Use of Redaction Criticism" in essay 5, pp. 281–83). If the gospels are historical documents, this must include the connective portions and chronological indicators also, these objectors notwithstanding.

6. Another problem, insuperable to some, is the extreme difficulty encountered in attempting to harmonize parallel accounts (see essay

7, "Problems and Principles of Harmonization," pp. 293–99). So difficult are some areas that the only solution is the presumption that there is no solution. This viewpoint is often associated with a lower estimate of biblical inspiration than orthodox Christianity has traditionally held. It unfortunately reflects a willingness to concede a point here and there to those who actively support biblical errancy. Yet this is not necessary. For those who are willing to approach the Bible from the perspective of what it says about itself, namely, that it is free from error, satisfactory explanations for most problems of harmonization can be found. The remaining problems can be explained reasonably, although it is granted that completely satisfying solutions to them must await further discoveries.

7. Others, who represent a more conservative approach to the gospels, object to attempts to harmonize them on the basis of not wishing to "tamper" with the text of Scripture. If God had wanted us to have a harmony of the life of Christ, they say, he would have given us one gospel instead of four. In response, it should be noted that a harmony of the gospels, especially one such as this where the text of each gospel is retained in its entirety in a separate column, is not an attempt to destroy the distinctive contribution of each gospel. The grammatical and historical interpretation of each gospel as an entity must remain the basic element in understanding God's revelation of Jesus Christ. At the same time, however, much can be added to that grammatical-historical understanding through a systematic comparison of the light the gospels shed on each other. Harmonization is not contradictory, but supplementary, to exegesis of the individual books.

8. One last objection may be cited. Some contend that the gospel writers, principally Luke, disagree with secular sources on points of history, and that it is thus foolish to try to combine the four gospels as though they were historical documents. Although discrepancies of this type have been proposed, however, none has as yet been verified. In fact, the findings of archaeological and historical research have consistently certified the accuracy of the scriptural record. No convincing reason, therefore, has emerged for believing that the gospels err by violating nonbiblical evidence. In fact, it is possible that the evidence from nonbiblical sources, or our interpretation of it, may at times be in error.

On the other hand, good reasons exist for arranging the gospels so as to point out their parallels as well as their distinctive contributions.

1. In the first place, harmonization grants deserved recognition to these writings as historical documents. Places in the gospels have geographical significance. Dates and chronological notations are also

components worthy of historical note (see essay 10, "The Day and Year of Christ's Crucifixion," pp. 311–14, and essay 11, "Chronology of the Life of Christ," pp. 315–19). The people mentioned in the gospels were actual people. A harmony clarifies relationships among these places, times, and people, resulting in a better understanding of the separate writings.

2. Also, a harmony highlights the historical basis of Christianity. Without such a factual basis, Christianity becomes just another world religion, something that has been concocted by the human imagination. Unfortunately, a delusion widely propagated today reasons that it does not matter what Jesus said and did; the important thing is that Christianity meet human needs now. What Jesus said and did, however, does matter. It is essential that Christianity have the historical Jesus as he is described in the four gospels. It is essential that Christianity be built on the foundation of his Resurrection from the dead. Without historical foundation, Christianity would be just another sham. A harmony of the gospels helps demonstrate how very solid is the historical foundation of Christianity.

3. Further, a harmony of the gospels enhances our knowledge of the historical Jesus. Much additional insight is gained by allowing each gospel to fill in gaps in the others' accounts. The result is a fuller record of the Lord's life. Some instances of this type of mutual help are discussed in the explanatory footnotes of this work.

4. Finally, the twentieth-century church should note that the Body of Christ has found harmonies to be conducive to its growth since very early in its existence (see essay 2, "A History of Harmonies," pp. 254–259). Though the nature of these harmonies has varied, the principle of the need for them remains. The replacement of harmonies by synopses in more recent years is doubtless attributable to the rise of the aforementioned objections. But the church can hardly afford to deprive itself of this means of growth because some have unjustifiably doubted the validity of harmonization. Furthermore, the church can rejoice in this added opportunity to know Jesus Christ better, especially in a day when historical research is enhancing our knowledge of the times in which he lived.

In summary, let it be recalled that the objections to the practice of harmonizing the gospels are not formidable. Each argument seems to be based on ill-founded presuppositions about Jesus, the gospels, or the objectives of harmonization. On the other side, good reasons exist for study of the gospels in relation to one another. In fact, it may be affirmed that harmonies of the gospels are not only legitimate but necessary to the fullest comprehension of the person and work of Jesus Christ.

Selected Reading List

Guthrie, Donald. *A Shorter Life of Christ*. Grand Rapids: Zondervan, 1970.
Harrison, Everett F. *A Short Life of Christ*. Grand Rapids: Eerdmans, 1968.

ESSAY 2

A History of Harmonies

Harmonies of the gospels are by no means recent innovations. In spite of the difficulties and limitations involved in putting together the four accounts of the life, death, and resurrection of Jesus, obvious practical advantages were recognized early in the history of the church. The earliest known attempt at combination was Tatian's *Diatessaron*, compiled about A.D. 170. Present knowledge of the *Diatessaron* is sketchy and indirect. Nevertheless, Tatian appears to have woven the four gospel accounts into one continuous narrative of the life and words of Jesus Christ. He retained so far as possible the words of all the evangelists. On what principles or with what success he carried out his work is simply not known.

In the early third century, Ammonius of Alexandria devised a system that made it possible to compare passages in Mark, Luke, and John with parallel passages in Matthew. He gave the full text of Matthew and then copied alongside what he regarded as the parallel portions of the other gospels. Consequently, only those portions of Mark, Luke, and John that parallel Matthew were reproduced, and they were presented in the sequence of Matthew. In the next century, Eusebius of Caesarea developed a system of cross-references that preserved the sequential arrangement of each gospel and yet allowed the reader to find and study similar passages in the other gospels.

Although a few occasional attempts were made in subsequent centuries to establish sequence and parallels among the gospels, an outpouring of harmonies has appeared since the Protestant Reformation. In the sixteenth century itself, such works came from Andreas Osiander, R. Stephanus, John Calvin, Cornelis Jansen, Molinaeus, Codomanus, Paul Crell, and Martin Chemnitz. Between the time that Chemnitz's work appeared and the nineteenth century, the trickle of harmonies became a flood. Well-known scholars producing harmonies during this period were John Clericus, John Lightfoot, Jean LeClerc, J. A. Bengel, Joseph Priestly, and J. J. Griesbach. Griesbach's work is especially noteworthy; in 1776 he established a new format for published harmonies with his *Synopsis Evangeliorum Matthaei Marci et Lucae una cum iis Johannis pericopis*. He hit upon the device of printing the gospels in parallel columns when they recorded the same or similar material.

Since Griesbach's time, most harmonies have either been of the diatessaron type (one continuous narrative with the material from the four accounts interwoven and changed as little as possible) or of the parallel column type. The parallel column format has two variations. One type attempts no rearrangement of the text to achieve a probable chronological order. Instead, the text of each gospel is given in its original sequence. Most who have taken this approach, however, also print the same or similar material that occurs in a different sequence in the other gospels alongside the material with which it seems to be at least a secondary parallel. Usually some printer's device (brackets, or smaller or lighter type) is used to indicate that such material has been removed from its original context. Works taking this approach often have the word *synopsis* in their title. This saves the editor from the necessity of making difficult, and sometimes arbitrary, decisions of probable chronological sequence, and yet allows the reader to have on one page an overview of all primary and secondary parallels for comparative purposes. Sometimes, however, this approach also reflects the editor's skepticism that harmonization is possible or that basically accurate chronological sequence can be established.

New Testament scholars have a primary concern for the Greek text of the gospels, and there has been no lack of harmonies placing the Greek text in parallel columns. The better known of these were prepared by Robinson (1846), Tischendorf (1851), Anger (1852), Stroud (1853), Strong (1859), Gardiner (1876), Rushbrooke (1880–1882), Huck (1892), Wright (1896), Veit (1897), Campbell (1899), Burton and Goodspeed (1920), Huck, Lietzmann, and Cross (1935), Mgr. de Solages (edition with notes in English, 1959), and Aland (1963). Some of these would be more accurately described as synopses rather than harmonies, and some deal only with the text of the first three gospels. Several were issued in more than one edition. The work of Edward Robinson had an especially long and useful history. In the twentieth century, *A Harmony of the Synoptic Gospels in Greek* by Ernest De Witt Burton and Edgar Johnson Goodspeed long held the field, and Huck's *Synopsis of the First Three Gospels* has been periodically revised and is still widely used. The thirteenth edition of Huck, fundamentally revised by Heinrich Greeven, appeared in 1981. But Kurt Aland's *Synopsis Quattuor Evangeliorum* (1972) is presently unmatched in utility and completeness. It has also been published with the English Revised Standard Version text on facing pages. For the serious student who uses Greek, Aland's work is indispensable for a comparative study of the gospels.

A more recent addition to the reservoir of Greek harmonies is the one by John Bernard Orchard, *A Synopsis of the Four Gospels* (Macon, GA: Mercer University Press, 1983). Orchard's work is influenced both in its arrangement and in the selection of its Greek text by the Griesbach or "two-gospel" hypothesis regarding the origin of the synoptic gospels.

255

The average reader, though, must use a harmony of the English text. Since the mid-nineteenth century English harmonies have been even more numerous than Greek. Unfortunately, the care with which many of these have been executed leaves much to be desired, and results are mixed. This is especially true of the diatessaron type. Their primary purpose is to create a continuous narrative of the life, works, and words of Jesus Christ. If done carefully, this method can communicate a sense of the course of development of Christ's life and ministry. But the approach, even in its best forms, also has severe limitations. Passages are presented out of their original contexts. The distinctive purposes of each evangelist are almost hopelessly obscured. The method does not allow for comparative study of parallel passages. And when their wording differs, the texts of parallel passages are combined in an arbitrary manner. But apparently the desire to produce such "lives of Christ" has been compelling. The following is a partial listing of such works appearing since the mid-nineteenth century:

C. F. Holley and J. E. Holley, *Jesus the Christ: A Complete Gospel Harmony* (n.d.), KJV.

R. Mimpriss, *A Harmony of the Four Gospels, Arranged as a Continuous History* (1845), KJV.

J. Glentworth Butler, *Bible Reader's Commentary, New Testament*, vol. 1, The Fourfold Gospel (1878), KJV.

Arthur T. Pierson, *The One Gospel* (1889), KJV.

William Pittenger, *The Interwoven Gospels* (1890), ERV.

Fred'k L. Chapman, *The True Life of Christ* (1899), KJV.

Horace J. Cossar, *The Four Gospels Unified* (1911), KJV.

Eva Livingston, *His Life: The Story of Christ's Life* (1912), ASV.

Helen Barrett Montgomery, *The Story of Jesus As Told by His Four Friends* (1927), Centenary translation.

Robert Edgar Beall, *The Short Story Combined Gospels, and Reference Harmony Supplement* (1928), ASV.

Andrew J. Reynolds, *Jesus of Nazareth, "The Prince of Life"* (1933), KJV.

Loraine Boettner, *A Summary of the Gospels* (1933), ASV.

Vaughan Stock, *The Life of Christ* (1934), KJV.

J. W. Lea, *The Unified Gospels: The Complete Life of Christ in the Words of the Evangelist* (1935), KJV.

Russell Hubbard White, *The Combined Gospels of Matthew, Mark, Luke and John* (1947), KJV.

Fred Fisher, *A Composite Gospel* (1948), an original translation.

Freeman Wills Crofts, *The Four Gospels in One Story* (1949), an original paraphrase.

Edward F. Cary, *The Life of Jesus in the Words of the Four Gospels* (1951), an original translation.

Thomas U. Fann, *Behold the Son of Man! Or the Complete Gospel Interwoven from the Four Gospels* (1955), ASV.

William F. Beck, *The Christ of the Gospels* (1959), an original translation.

Who is This Man Jesus? The Complete Life of Jesus from the Living Bible (1967).

Johnston M. Cheney, *The Life of Christ in Stereo: The Four Gospels Combined as One*, ed. Stanley A. Ellison (1969). "We have sought to preserve the beauty of the 'King James' version, testing each rendering by the original."

Chester Wilkins, *The Four Gospels Arranged as a Single Narrative* (1976), KJV.

Baird W. Whitlock, *The Gospel of the Life of Jesus* (1984), KJV.

Harmonies using the parallel column format are obviously more useful for careful comparative study of the text of the gospels. When skillfully arranged and outlined, they can also portray the course of development in Christ's life and ministry. Although rearrangement of some of the materials is necessary if there is to be a chronological account of Christ's life in the text of the harmony, the wording of each evangelist is allowed to stand in its own integrity rather than being amalgamated with the others. Still, the individual success of a harmony primarily depends on the care the editor has taken. The following harmonies appearing since the mid-nineteenth century are of varying value:

Lent Carpenter, *A Harmony of the Gospels* (1831), KJV.

Benjamin Davies, *Harmony of the Four Gospels* (n.d.), KJV.

Adam Fahling, *A Harmony of the Gospels* (n.d.), KJV.

J. M. Fuller, *The Four Gospels Arranged in the Form of a Harmony* (n.d.), KJV.

Edward Robinson, *A Harmony of the Four Gospels in English* (1846), KJV.

Simon Greenleaf, *The Testimony of the Evangelists Examined by the Rules of Evidence Administered in Courts of Justice* (1874), KJV.

John A. Broadus, *A Harmony of the Gospels* (1893), ERV.

William Arnold Stevens and Ernest De Witt Burton, *A Harmony of the Gospels for Historical Study* (1893), ERV.

I. N. Johns and J. F. Kempfer, *The Parallel Gospels* (1896), KJV.

E. S. Young, *The Life of Christ: A Harmony of the Four Gospels* (1898), KJV.

John A. Broadus, *A Harmony of the Gospels* (1903) (a minor revision of Broadus's 1893 work by A. T. Robertson), ERV.

John H. Kerr, *A Harmony of the Gospels* (1903), ASV.

Ernest De Witt Burton and Edgar Johnson Goodspeed, *A Harmony of the Synoptic Gospels for Historical and Critical Study* (1917), ASV.

A. T. Robertson, *A Harmony of the Gospels for Students of the Life of Christ* (1922), ERV.

G. C. Savage, *Time and Place Harmony of the Gospels* (1927), original translation.

Walter E. Bundy, *A Syllabus and Synopsis of the First Three Gospels* (1932), ASV.

Ralph Daniel Heim, *A Harmony of the Gospels for Students* (1947), RSV.

Albert Cassel Wieand, *A New Harmony of the Gospels: The Gospel Records of the Message and Mission of Jesus Christ* (1947), RSV.

Henry J. Cadbury, Frederick C. Grant, and Clarence T. Craig, *Gospel Parallels: A Synopsis of the First Three Gospels* (1949), RSV.

Throckmorton, Burton H., Jr., *Gospel Parallels: A Synopsis of the First Three Gospels* (1949), RSV.

John Franklin Carter, *A Layman's Harmony of the Gospels* (1961), ASV.

H. F. D. Sparks, *A Synopsis of the Gospels* (1964), ERV.

Frederick R. Coulter, *A Harmony of the Gospels in Modern English* (1974), original translation.

Robert L. Thomas and Stanley N. Gundry, *A Harmony of the Gospels with Explanations and Essays* (1978), NASB.

J. Dwight Pentecost, *A Harmony of the Words and Works of Jesus Christ* (1981), NIV.

Edward Robinson's work went through many editions, and was eventually revised by M. B. Riddle; it also served as the basis for the work of other harmonists. The year 1893 marked the advent of two harmonies that were long to be standards, those by Broadus, and Stevens and Burton. Both used the English Revised Version of 1881, and both used divisions that showed the historical unfolding of Christ's life; previous practice had been to divide according to the feasts. Broadus's work of 1903 contained endnotes by his younger colleague, A. T. Robertson. Robertson's major revision (in 1922) of Broadus's work and the Burton and Goodspeed harmony of 1917 became the new standards in the field. Robertson's revision has had an especially long and useful life, even in the face of more recent entries into the field, such as Sparks's widely used *Synopsis*.

In 1975 Reuben J. Swanson presented to students of the gospels a completely new concept in *The Horizontal Line Synopsis of the Gospels* (Dillsboro, NC: Western North Carolina). He followed this up with Volume I, *The Gospel of Matthew*, of *The Horizontal Line Synopsis of the Gospels, Greek Edition* in 1982. Swanson's innovation grew out of the frustration students experience in identifying the details of similarity and differences among the gospel accounts. Even when put in parallel columns, one's eye must still jump from column to column to pick out the points of comparison and contrast. To eliminate this tedious work, Swanson hit upon the idea of placing the parallel material in parallel horizontal lines rather than in parallel vertical columns. Thus the similarities and differences would be immediately apparent. Using the text of the Revised Standard Version for the English edition and the third edition of the United Bible Societies' *The Greek New Testament* in the Greek edition, he gives the text of Matthew line by line. Parallel with each line he gives whatever corresponding material there may be from any of the other three gospels, again line by line. The same procedure is then followed in the English edition with the texts of Mark, Luke, and John, the Greek version of these three gospels being unpublished at the time of this writing. This method has obvious advantages for the kind of detailed comparison Swanson has in mind. Also, each gospel in its original sequence can be examined and compared with line-by-line parallels from the other gospels placed there for easy reference.

If such detailed comparison is not one's primary purpose, however, the horizontal line format has severe limitations. It is difficult to read with any feeling for continuity of thought even in the lead line of the lead gospel. Furthermore, because the method presents each gospel line by line with parallels to each line, it does not integrate all the materials and give an overall picture of the historical unfolding of Christ's life and ministry.

Thus although Swanson's innovation should receive appropriate recognition, its value is limited for the general reader. Unless one primarily wishes to discover possible literary interrelationships among the gospels, the parallel column format, in spite of its own limitations, is still superior for general study of the life of Christ, because the material from all four gospels is integrated.

In 1985 another variation in format appeared. It was *New Gospel Parallels, The Synoptic Gospels* in two volumes, designed and edited by Robert W. Funk (Philadelphia: Fortress). Using the Revised Standard Version, this work follows sequentially the text of each gospel in turn, placing a paragraph or two at the upper left corner of the page. In the center and right of the page tops are whatever may be parallel in Mark and Luke, with parallel expressions indicated in boldface type. The lower left corner is reserved for parallels from the gospel of John, with the lower center and right reserved for parallels from the gospel of Thomas and other noncanonical works. The goal of this format is to avoid neglecting the narrative setting in which each segment appears. It also seeks to avoid "the artificial chronology of the harmonies and the arbitrary sequences of the synopses" (vol. I, p. viii).

The advantages of Funk's format are obvious. Beginning with either gospel, one can move quickly to parallels in the other two. Every text is easy to locate, too. On the other side, however, it is more difficult to make detailed comparisons because of the distance on a page the eye must travel to find agreements in wording. Also, no help regarding chronological sequence of the Lord's life is derived from this type of work. And, of course, a work of this type is more bulky because of the necessity to cite some of the same portions two, three, or even four times.

Selected Reading List

Ebrard, J. H. A. *The Gospel History: A Compendium of Critical Investigations in Support of the Historical Character of the Four Gospels.* Edinburgh: T. and T. Clark, 1873. Pp. 47–55.

Fabricus, J. A. *Bibliotheca Graece.* Hamburg: 1790/1809. Pp. 4.882–4.889.

Youngblood, Ronald. "From Tatian to Swanson, from Calvin to Bendavid: The Harmonization of Biblical History," *Journal of the Evangelical Theological Society* 25 (1982): 415–23.

ESSAY 3

Source Criticism

Matthew, Mark, and Luke have in modern times been referred to as the synoptic gospels because the three take a more or less common view of the Lord Jesus' life. Supposing that extensive agreement among the three indicates some sort of direct literary collaboration, much New Testament scholarship of the past century or so has attempted to explain the nature of that literary relationship. A complicating factor in these studies, however, has been a substantial number of instances where one gospel describes matters differently from one or both of the others. The difficulty encountered in devising a scheme of literary dependence to account for the combinations of similarities and dissimilarities has been labeled the Synoptic Problem and the field of studies devoted to solving the problem as Source Criticism.

Ancient Christianity was not concerned about this difficulty. It was generally assumed that the gospel writers drew upon personal memory and firsthand reports rather than upon one another's writings or some common written source. The church historian Eusebius indicated that Matthew, one of the twelve apostles, was the first to write. About to leave the Palestinian area, he supplied a written substitute for his oral ministry, which apparently in turn was drawn largely from his apostolic experience. Luke, according to his own word (Luke 1:1–4), drew from a number of sources, both oral and written, none of which had the authority of Matthew or Mark. Mark is said by Clement of Alexandria to have based his gospel on the apostolic tradition through Peter. John alone, writing at a much later time a gospel quite different from the synoptics, was in possession of the other gospels before he wrote. He could have copied from them, yet he did not. Instead, he verified their truthfulness and supplemented their contents with material not found in the other three.

This near-unanimous consensus in the church that the synoptic gospel writers did not see each other's works before writing lasted until the mid-eighteenth century, when scholars began exploring various hypotheses as to how one writer may have depended on others or on a single source also available to the others. Theories of one source used by all three and of various orders of writing, with the second writer depending on the first and the third on the other two, were typical forerunners of the Two-Source Theory, an approach that eventually gained wide acceptance among New Testament scholars. This theory advocates that Mark was written first, and that Matthew and Luke were based on this and another source called Q, now nonextant.

B. H. Streeter's five considerations given in *The Four Gospels: A Study of Origins* are the most widely cited supports for the prior writing of Mark. These considerations, along with possible responses to each one, are:

1. Most of the material in Mark (93 percent, according to Westcott) is found in Matthew and Luke. Because it seemed inconceivable to Streeter that Mark would have abbreviated the other two, Streeter concluded that Matthew and Luke must have expanded Mark.

   In answer, it should be noted that Mark may have had a special reason for condensing one or both of the other gospels. In fact, literary practice in English writings indicates the tendency of a writer to shorten the work of another when editing it. If there was literary dependence, the likelihood of Mark's being last rather than first is just as strong, if not stronger.

   Another possible answer postulates no literary dependence. Material common to two or three gospels may conceivably be traced to a common oral tradition, in which case Mark may never have seen Matthew's and Luke's gospels before writing his own, and vice versa.

2. Though agreeing often with Mark in actual words used, Matthew and Luke do not agree with each other when they diverge from Mark. Allowing for exceptions to this generalization, Streeter explained these exceptions as either irrelevant, deceptive, agreements because of an overlap of Mark and Q (Matthew's and Luke's other major source), or agreements because of textual corruption. Matthean-Lucan diversity is taken to prove their dependence on Mark.

   Like Streeter's first proposition, this one too can be turned to prove the priority of Matthew or Luke, if literary dependence is assumed. Depending on the parallel passages chosen and on which two gospels are pitted against the other, one can prove the priority of either Matthew or Luke as well. Though not as numerous, agreements between Matthew and Luke where Mark says something different are substantial enough to indicate their independence of Mark in almost all sections where the Two-Source Theory says they were dependent. The absence of a convincing explanation of these "exceptions" forces this premise to fail.

   Furthermore, it need not be granted that copying among the three writers took place. Many accounts, both written and oral, of the events and discourses of Christ's life were in circulation for the writers to draw upon without borrowing from each other. This is the most plausible explanation of the randomness of their agreements and disagreements with each other, that is, Matthew and Mark against Luke, Matthew and Luke against Mark, and Mark and Luke against Matthew.

3. The order of events in Mark is original, for wherever Matthew departs from Mark, Luke supports Mark's order, and wherever Luke departs from Mark, Matthew agrees with Mark's order. This, it is said, demonstrates Marcan priority and that the other two gospels are secondary, because they never follow each other when departing from Mark's order.

Again, however, the conclusion does not necessarily follow. For example, if copying was involved, Mark may have worked from Matthew and Luke; he may have followed their order when they agreed and followed one or the other of them when they disagreed.

Other explanations are also plausible. One option is that all three were working from an order dictated by a tradition agreed upon by eyewitnesses and transmitted in varieties of ways among early Christians. All three writers, then, as the occasion arose, deviated from this traditional sequence in their gospels.

4. The primitive nature of Mark as compared with Matthew and Luke demonstrates Mark's priority. To illustrate, Matthew uses *kurie* ("lord") nineteen times and Luke sixteen times, compared with the word's appearing only once in Mark. This is taken to indicate a more developed reverential attitude and hence a later date for the two longer gospels.

This evidence is neutralized, however, when it is noted that *kurie* lacks the alleged reverential connotation, because Matthew uses such an address seven times when referring to mere man (Matt. 13:27; 21:29; 25:11, 20, 24; 27:63). Certainly this was not a form of address Matthew reserved for deity. Consequently, no chronological argument can be built on its use or nonuse in any of the gospels.

The same disposition may be made of other alleged signs of primitivity, such as Mark's Aramaisms. According to most standards of judgment, Matthew is much more Semitic than Mark. Couple with this indications of Mark's lateness (his Latinisms and his translation of Aramaic expressions for the sake of those who knew no Aramaic), and one has good reason for postulating the priority of Matthew.

5. The distribution of Marcan and non-Marcan material in Matthew and Luke shows their dependence on Mark. Matthew uses Mark as a framework and arranges his material into that structure, and Luke gives Marcan and non-Marcan material in alternate blocks.

If literary borrowing transpired, however, it is just as reasonable to suppose the opposite procedure. Rather than Matthew's picking words or phrases here and there and weaving them into a smooth, polished narrative, Mark, in coming up with his account, just as feasibly may have taken the book of Matthew and added details for vividness. If the assumption of Mark's priority is dropped, it can be shown how Luke could have extracted sections from Matthew and, in turn, Mark could have done the same from Luke.

Another possible explanation is that all three could have drawn from a common core of tradition among early Christians.

Thus Streeter's support of the Two-Source Theory, though enjoying wide acceptance for a long time, in some cases presupposes the point to be proven and in others rests on overgeneralizations that fail to account for substantial exceptions. His case has therefore met with increasing opposition. Realizing the demise of Streeter's supports, other proponents of Marcan priority have advanced arguments to try to sustain this century-old theory, but none of these attempts has had enough merit to earn significant attention.

Aside from the weakness of evidence supporting the Two-Source Theory, it also clashes directly with the unanimous testimony of more than eighteen hundred years of Christian history to the effect that Matthew was the first gospel written. That the apostle by this name composed an Aramaic work before his Greek gospel did not concern the early Fathers. They apparently took the Greek writing to be a natural sequel of the Aramaic, written after Matthew left Palestine to undertake a ministry among non-Aramaic-speaking people. Coupled with this, inherent weaknesses in support of Mark and Q as sources for Matthew and Luke have given rise to growing opposition that questions the Two-Source Theory's validity. Five of the theory's more prominent shortcomings may be mentioned:

1. The Two-Source Theory cannot account for what has been labeled "The Great Omission." If Luke used Mark as a source, no adequate explanation has as yet come as to why he omitted any reference to Mark 6:45–8:26. This important section includes Jesus' walking on the water, the healing at Gennesaret, a major conflict over the tradition of the elders, the Syrophoenician woman's faith, the healing of a deaf and dumb man, the feeding of the four thousand, the Pharisees' demand for a sign, the instruction regarding the leaven of the Pharisees and that of Herod, and the healing of a blind man at Bethsaida. Though Luke may have had reasons for omitting such a long, consecutive body of material, it is simpler to suppose he had no access to Mark's gospel when he wrote.
2. Recent archaeological findings and increased knowledge about first-century Palestinian conditions have made it increasingly difficult to sustain the argument for Q as a single written body of tradition. Ancient historical records indicate that in this locale traditions did not tend to unify, but they proliferated in a random manner. They

did not coalesce into a homogeneous body.

Furthermore, if Q is insisted upon as a single written source, the changes made by Matthew and Luke are anomalous. Attempts to analyze the alleged use of this source by these two writers are frustrated by the absence of any consistent rational procedure.

If the symbol Q must be retained, a doubtful necessity, it is more satisfying to explain it as gospel material belonging to many different strands of tradition, both written and oral. Far from being homogeneous, it has no definable limits. Because the Two-Source Theory rests on the foundation of a homogeneous Q, it is essentially disproved by such a redefinition of Q.

3. In sections of triple tradition (that is, those covered by Matthew, Mark, and Luke) a considerable number (about two hundred thirty) of agreements between Matthew and Luke are different from a parallel portion of Mark. ("Different from" does not mean that Mark contradicts the other two, but that his wording varies.) Such agreements are admittedly not as numerous as agreements of Matthew and Mark where Luke differs, and Mark and Luke where Matthew differs, but they are sufficient, and their arrangement is such as to prove a common source other than Mark for Matthew and Luke. For example, Matthew 9:1–8 and Luke 5:17–26 agree with one another verbatim in nine separate expressions, whereas Mark 2:1–12 records different wording in its parallels. In Matthew 8:1–4 and Luke 5:12–16, seven identical words or expressions are found, but Mark deviates from these. Perhaps these agreements could be explained individually as accidental or as a textual corruption, but when their proximity to one another is considered, the possibility of coincidence is rendered quite remote. The fact of the matter is that the Two-Source Theory cannot account for such agreements between Matthew and Luke when Mark reads differently.

These first three weaknesses should be apparent to people of any theological persuasion, including the extremely liberal. The last two that follow have special impact upon those who are evangelicals.

4. The priority of Mark poses a serious challenge to the heretofore unchallenged testimony of early Christianity that Matthew the apostle wrote the first gospel. It necessitates understanding that Matthew, an eyewitness of Jesus' ministry, depended on Mark, a noneyewitness, for his information. The dependence extends even to Matthew's reliance on Mark for a description of his own conversion! Even excluding this last, such dependence is improbable, even though Mark did have the highly respected Peter as his source.

It boils down to accepting what the early Fathers said about Matthean authorship or accepting the "findings" of nineteenth-century rationalism. The latter, unconcerned about retaining Matthean authorship of Matthew, placed the first gospel's composition much later than the traditional date of writing, even into the second century. In such a choice, probability of accuracy is on the side of the ancient church, because this generation of the church was much nearer and had access to better information about the authorship of the gospels. No good reason for doubting the accuracy of these ancient sources has been forthcoming, so the Two-Source Theory falls short in another respect.

5. The Two-Source Theory takes insufficient notice of personal contacts between the synoptic writers. Unless one rejects the traditional authorship of the three synoptics, he or she must be impressed by the opportunities available to the three writers to exchange information about the life of Christ orally, without having to resort to a form of documentary dependence. Matthew and Mark must have been close associates immediately following Pentecost, while Jerusalem Christians used Mark's home as a meeting place (cf. Acts 12:12). Mark and Luke were associated during Paul's Roman imprisonment (Col. 4:10, 14; Philem. 24). Possibly Luke encountered Matthew during his two-year stay with Paul in Palestine in the late A.D. 50s (cf. Acts 24:27). If not, in the process of his gospel research he must have talked to some people close to Matthew. Personal contacts such as these render unnecessary the literary dependence advocated by the Two-Source Theory.

These and other weaknesses reflect the inadequacy of the Two-Source Theory and have contributed to the recent decline in its popularity. No one theory has emerged to replace it, but an approach that treats the gospels as independent entities is growing in appeal. This approach is superior, not only because of evidence cited, but also because it is an endorsement of the tradition of ancient Christianity: each of the three synoptic gospels arose in relatively independent circumstances.

The writers probably exchanged information in personal contacts, but each had sources of information different from the other two. Matthew's contacts with the Lord were primarily personal. Mark's were predominantly through Peter. Luke utilized what he could derive through interviews and whatever accurate written records he could find. All three drew heavily on various oral traditions that accumulated rapidly around Jerusalem through the concentrated post-Pentecostal preaching of the first Christians. Constant repetition directed toward Spirit-quickened minds (John 14:26; 16:13) was more than adequate to account for the large number of agreements in the synoptic gospels. It was unnecessary for the writers to see each other's work, or for all three to draw upon one or two common sources. The times and places of composition were sufficiently scattered that these three can be called independent witnesses of Jesus' life.

Selected Reading List

Albright, C. F., and C. S. Mann. *Matthew*. Vol. 26 of The Anchor Bible. Garden City, NY: Doubleday, 1971. Pp. xix–cxcvii.

Bellinzoni, Arthur J. *The Two-Source Hypothesis*. Macon, GA: Mercer University Press, 1985.

Boismard, M.-E. "The Two-Source Theory at an Impasse," *New Testament Studies* 26 (1980): 1–17.

Cole, R. A. *The Gospel According to Mark*. The Tyndale New Testament Commentaries. Grand Rapids: Eerdmans, 1961. Pp. 23–48.

Dyer, Charles H. "Do the Synoptics Depend on Each Other?" *Bibliotheca Sacra* 138 (1981): 230–45.

Farmer, William R. *The Synoptic Problem*. New York: Macmillan, 1964. Pp. 1–198.

Farmer, William R., ed. *New Synoptic Studies*. Macon, GA: Mercer University Press, 1983.

Fuller, Reginald. "What Is Happening in New Testament Studies?" *St. Luke's Journal of Theology* 23 (1980): 90–100.

Hiebert, D. Edmond. *An Introduction to the New Testament: The Gospels and Acts*. Vol. 1. Chicago: Moody, 1975. Pp. 160–90.

Lowe, Malcolm. "The Demise of Arguments from Order for Markan Priority," *Novum Testamentum* 24 (1982): 27–36.

Maier, G. *The End of the Historical-Critical Method*. Translated by E. W. Leverenz and R. F. Norden. St. Louis: Concordia, 1977.

Pamphilus, Eusebius. *The Ecclesiastical History of Eusebius Pamphilus*. Translated by Christian Frederick Cruse. Grand Rapids: Baker, 1955. Pp. 12–478.

Rist, J. M. *On the Independence of Matthew and Mark*. Cambridge: Cambridge University Press, 1978.

Sanders, E. P. "New Testament Studies Today," *Colloquy on New Testament Studies*. Edited by Bruce C. Corley. Macon, GA: Mercer University Press, 1983. Pp. 11–28.

————. *The Tendencies of the Synoptic Tradition*. Cambridge: Cambridge University Press, 1969. Pp. 1–285.

Stein, Robert H. *The Synoptic Problem*. Grand Rapids: Baker, 1987.

Stoldt, Hans-Herbert. *History and Criticism of the Marcan Hypothesis*. Macon, GA: Mercer University Press, 1980.

Streeter, B. H. *The Four Gospels: A Study of Origins*. London: Macmillan, 1936. Pp. 150–360.

Styler, G. M. "The Priority of Mark," *The Birth of the New Testament*. Edited by C. F. D. Moule, 3rd ed. San Francisco: Harper & Row, 1982. Pp. 285–87, 288–90.

Thomas, Robert L. "An Investigation of the Agreements Between Matthew and Luke Against Mark," *Journal of the Evangelical Theological Society* 19 (1976): 103–12.

————. "The Rich Young Man in Matthew," *Grace Theological Journal* 3 (1982): 235–60.

Walker, William O., ed. *The Relationships Among the Gospels*. San Antonio: Trinity University Press, 1978.

Wenham, David. "The Synoptic Problem Revisited: Some Suggestions About the Composition of Mark 4:1–34," *Tyndale Bulletin* 23 (1972): 3–38.

Form Criticism

THE NATURE OF FORM CRITICISM

In the early twentieth century a new variety of gospel criticism came on the scene. In Germany, its place of origin, it is known as *Formges-chicte* ("form history"). Its English name is Form Criticism. Source Criticism attempted to solve the Synoptic Problem by analysis of the gospels in terms of positing source documents upon which the gospel writers were supposedly dependent. Thus Source Criticism generally held that Mark was the earliest gospel and that Matthew and Luke drew upon Mark and another conjectural written source known as Q, which mainly contained sayings. By this means the similarities and divergencies among the synoptics were explained. Form critics for the most part accept some form of Source Criticism theory, but they have not been content to let the matter rest there.

The reasons for this discontent are significant. In the effort to account for all the phenomena of the synoptics, source critics found it necessary to multiply the hypothetical written sources; this in itself tended to discredit the theory as an adequate solution. Furthermore, as a literary method Source Criticism could not push behind the written sources. Yet the written sources did not appear for at least twenty years following Jesus' death. What had been the status of the gospel tradition during this period? In addition, W. Wrede and others challenged the historicity of the Marcan account by arguing that the framework of Mark was the author's own creation. Thus Mark could not be considered reliable chronologically or geographically; Mark and those dependent upon him were not biographically accurate. With the elimination of the integrity of the chronological-geographical framework of the synoptics, the units of gospel material that had been tied together by that framework were left in isolation, subject to critical analysis in their own right.

The intent of Form Criticism has been to investigate these units of gospel tradition in the twenty-year oral period before they were edited into the first written sources proposed by source critics. Form critics attempt to classify this material into forms of oral tradition and to discover the historical situation (*Sitz im Leben*) within the early church that gave rise to each of these forms. In other words, Form Criticism generally accepts Source Criticism as far as it goes, but Form Criticism aims to push the inquiry of gospel origins behind the written sources into the oral period. New Testament scholars most readily identified as form critics have been Martin Dibelius, Rudolf Bultmann, Burton S. Easton, Frederick C. Grant, Edwin B. Redlick, R. H. Lightfoot, Vincent Taylor, and D. E. Nineham.

Even these leading advocates, however, represent widely different perspectives. For some form critics the study of the forms of gospel material is simply and only a matter of literary analysis. At the other extreme are those whose theories are highly speculative and who are skeptical in their evaluation of the historical worth of the material. To such scholars the units of tradition are products of the earliest Christian community. The units usually reflect more of the life and teaching of the early church than of the life and teaching of Jesus. The forms in which the units are cast are clues to their relative historical value. Among form critics there are also differences of judgment as to what forms the units of tradition are cast in, what they should be named, and what the significance of each form is. Dibelius spoke of paradigms, tales, legends, sayings, and myths. Bultmann divided the traditional material into three general categories: miracle stories, *apophthegmata* (utterances of Jesus resulting from controversies that followed Jesus' miracles), and sayings of Jesus.

Analysis and comparison of the form critical theories of classification and interpretation would require detailed discussion and are outside the scope of this essay. This type of discussion, however, is not necessary to an evaluation of Form Criticism. To get to the heart of the matter, one must evaluate the fundamental assumption of Form Criticism in its more thoroughgoing forms as typified by Dibelius and Bultmann. If the foundation of radical Form Criticism is without footing, there is little point in giving serious consideration to the details of its superstructure. And if Form Criticism is viewed only as a method of literary analysis devoid of value judgments, there is no cause for it to create much stir.

But what is the fundamental assumption of Form Criticism? It is that form tradition first existed as brief, rounded units, circulating orally in the Christian community, and that their contextual connections in the gospels are the creations of the evangelists. This assumption in itself could be innocuous. Indeed, when stated in this manner, it nearly corresponds to the oral tradition theory regarding the origin of the gospels. But by this assumption, the thoroughgoing form critic means something entirely different. He or she means that the primitive Christian church not only transmitted the accounts of the words and deeds of Jesus, but also molded and changed the tradition to fit its own changing perspectives and needs. It even created new words and deeds of Jesus if the occasion demanded. The evangelists, in turn, took over the units of this tradition with little change or discrimination. They arranged the material in an artificial context so as to serve the purposes of their compositions.

This assumption contains two key elements. First, it holds that the early Christian community was so lacking in genuine biographical interest or honesty that it thought nothing of creating and transforming the tradition that it passed on. Supposedly this was done in order to meet certain types of needs within the community. These needs allegedly are discernible now from the various forms that the units of the tradition assumed. Thus, the gospels become primary sources of knowledge concerning the life of the primitive church and only secondary sources concerning the words and deeds of Jesus. The second element of the basic assumption is that the evangelists were merely editors of these individual, isolated units of tradition (though not much attention was focused on their editorial changes until the advent of Redaction Criticism; see essay 5). Without regard for historical reality, they likewise arranged and rearranged material to suit their own purposes. Virtually all descriptions of place and time that connect the individual units are regarded as editorial creations and therefore historically unreliable. This view of the early church and of the gospel writers is open to serious challenge because of a number of weaknesses, which are outlined in the following discussion.

The Evidence of Eyewitnesses

The first and most obvious factor to be considered in an evaluation of Form Criticism is the evidence from eyewitnesses of the life of Jesus. The failure of this discipline to account adequately for the role of eyewitnesses in the early church is sufficient to discredit its basic assumption and implications. The presence of eyewitnesses means that there could have been no "creative" community that formed and transformed tradition to suit its own needs without attention to readily accessible facts.

In effect, form critics see Christianity as cut off from its founder and his disciples by either an inexplicable ignorance or an unexplainable silence on the part of eyewitnesses. The new sect had to invent situations for the words of Jesus and put into his mouth words that memory could not check and that he may not have spoken. But leaders and disciples who had heard and seen what they recounted (Acts 2:1–4) were still alive during the time of the early church. The form critic either forgets or ignores the fact that Jesus had a surviving mother and followers, who had many vivid memories of his life and ministry. There is no reason to suppose that the individuals mentioned in Mark 3:31–35; 4:10; 15:40; and 16:1–8 would not have remembered Jesus.

By their theory form critics call into question the integrity of the disciples, who had seen and heard Jesus and even been personally involved in his ministry. Yet, if form critics are correct, the disciples did not control the accuracy of the tradition. Such, however, could hardly have been the case. Is it conceivable that in its own discussions and disputes the early church would not have examined doubtful statements concerning Jesus' ministry? If the church, in fact, did not scrutinize such statements, why is there such close agreement as to the nature and details of that ministry? A community that was purely imaginative and lacking in discrimination would have found it impossible to form a consistent tradition. The tradition must have been under the control of eyewitnesses within the church.

Equally important is the fact that outside the church opponents of Christianity also had been eyewitnesses of Jesus' ministry. Again, is it possible that opponents would have allowed false statements to pass as facts concerning his life as they knew it? Christianity would have become hopelessly vulnerable if it had created stories in order to perpetuate itself. Peter not only said, "We are all witnesses" (Acts 2:32), but he also said to the men of Israel, "You yourselves know" (Acts 2:22).

THE BIOGRAPHICAL INTEREST OF THE COMMUNITY

The assumption of Form Criticism that the primitive Christian community was imaginative not only disregards the eyewitnesses, who could have checked the accuracy of the developing tradition, but also, as its second weakness, disregards the fact that the early church would surely have wanted to guard the accuracy of the tradition. In other words, the early church did have biographical interest in the life of Jesus. Form Criticism, asserting the opposite, claims that early Christians were so absorbed in the possibility of the Lord's return that they were not interested in the facts of the life of Jesus. It is inconceivable, however, that memories of Jesus would not have been carefully and accurately retained. No solid evidence proves that the early church was preoccupied with other interests. In fact, all indicators point to the opposite conclusion.

If no biographical interest in Jesus existed among them, why did Paul distinguish between his words and those of the Lord (1 Cor. 7:10, 12, 25)? Why had many taken pen in hand to draw up narratives of the events of Jesus' life, and why had they used the material of eyewitnesses (Luke 1:1–2)? Why did Luke, after careful research, add to this collection his own accurate account of the Lord's ministry (Luke 1:3–4)? Why did early Christians appeal constantly to the fact that they were eyewitnesses of the events about which they spoke (Acts 2:32; 3:15; 10:41)? The form critics must thoroughly discredit Luke's prologue and his Acts account if they are to eliminate a case for the early church's biographical interest.

Besides the evidence of eyewitnesses spoken of in Acts, the book also directly proves that the early church had a biographical interest extending beyond the bounds of the passion story. This is seen in the choice of Matthias to replace Judas (Acts 1:21–22), in Peter's sermon at Pentecost (Acts 2:12–24), in Peter's words to Cornelius's household (Acts 10:36–43), and in Paul's message in Antioch of Pisidia (Acts 13:23–31).

Contrary to what form critics say, it can be confidently asserted that early Christians had an intense desire to know about Jesus. The form critic forgets that the person of Jesus is central to the Christian faith. That faith would have no meaning if an accurate picture of him were not drawn. Faith in Christ is central, but this is impossible without a knowledge of who and what he was. Thus the historical Jesus, being identical with the Christ of Christianity (and not a mere shadow of him, as the form critic holds), was the heart of the Christian message, no matter who was preaching (cf. Acts 2:32; 3:12–26; 4:10–20; 5:30–32; 8:35).

THE IMPOSSIBILITY OF A CREATIVE COMMUNITY

A third weakness of the fundamental assumption of Form Criticism is that it involves the concept of an imaginative, creative community; that is, the primitive Christian church supposedly exercised the power of creating and changing tradition about Jesus to suit its own needs.

To the form critic, Jesus is a faint and remote figure. The community was supposedly alert and ready for every enterprise of creation or corruption. But could this have been the case? Sayings as striking and pointed as those preserved in the gospels are not created by communities but by individuals. In this case the individual could only have been Jesus. Nor would the sayings necessarily have been taken from Hellenistic or rabbinic sources and put into Jesus' mouth. The occasional similarities in Jesus' teachings to teachings from other sources is no proof of borrowing on the part of the early church. Even great teachers may say familiar things.

Nevertheless, for the sake of argument, let it be supposed that the community did have the inclination to create a tradition about Jesus, including sayings and stories about him. If such were the case, where did the community get the wisdom to select the best? That such a selection would have had to be made is evident from the consistency of synoptic tradition. No contradiction is found between Jesus' doctrine and actions. A logical and chronological sequence marks the gospel story from beginning to end. Accuracy in the descriptions of Palestine is acknowledged. But if the early church had been "creative," it would have had no standard by which to govern its selections and thus form such a harmonious tradition.

The impossibility of such a creative church is demonstrated by noting that gospel history created the community, not vice versa. To put it another way, if early Christian faith created the gospel record, what created Christian faith? The idea of a creative community responsible for originating synoptic tradition supposes the almost spontaneous appearance of an organized religious life built upon an intense faith in the deity of a crucified Jew—all without the dominant influence of Jesus or any other person. Such speculation contradicts the facts.

THE EVIDENCE FOR RELIABLE HISTORICAL CONTEXTS

A fourth weakness surfaces when it is noted that form critics question the reliability of historical contexts into which the units of tradition are woven. In fact, their first task is to free the units from alleged artificial contexts. But allegations of such artificiality are without proof. The character of the gospels themselves leads to the opposite conclusion.

To support the idea of artificial contexts, the form critics hold that most historical, geographical, chronological, and biographical references in the gospels are a fictional means by which the evangelists combined isolated units of tradition. An examination of the references to place, time, sequence, and persons, however, shows these to be so interwoven with the other material of the units, and to present such a natural ordered sequence when considered separately, that to view them as editorial creations of the evangelists is highly speculative. The contexts, as well as the sayings and events, are rooted in history.

The gospel of Mark is a good example. Close examination of its sequence and its chronological and geographical notations reveals an integration and development that is natural, not artificial, and that is confirmed by close parallels with the outlines, or partial outlines, of the gospel story in Acts. These accounts cover the period from the preaching of John the Baptist to the resurrection of Christ, and especially emphasize the passion story (cf. Acts 10:37–40; 13:23–31). Here is the heart of the message of the early church. This is also exactly the scope of the gospel of Mark.

THE REAL SIGNIFICANCE OF STEREOTYPED FORMS

It would be difficult to deny that some parts included in the gospels originally circulated in the early church as isolated units. Even form critics, however, recognize that the passion story existed as a long, continuous narrative. Why not also recognize other continuous sections, such as Mark 1:21–39 and 2:1–3:6? It is evident from synoptic material that probably some stereotyped forms existed, although the extent of these has been exaggerated by form critics. The real question is, Do the stereotyped forms indicate particular historical situations (*Sitz im Leben*) of the church in which each kind of form originated to fill certain needs of that primitive church? That is, do these forms sometimes indicate the nonhistoricity of what is recounted?

The answer to this question can only be an emphatic No, and herein lies a fifth weakness of Form Criticism. Forms do not give the material of the text a relative historical value. Form is in no way related to truth or falsity. Nothing can be inferred from stereotyped forms other than that the church customarily related episodes in a certain way or that Jesus taught in certain patterns.

Accounts of miracles would naturally be related in similar ways, for the general outline of conditions and events is likely to be the same. The same may be said of controversies with the scribes and the Pharisees. As for the poetic form of many of Jesus' sayings, what would have been more natural for him, speaking to Jews, than to cast his declarations in poetic form? Such, in fact, was normal Semitic style. This practice made it easier for his followers, whether Jews or not, to remember his words. It makes just as much sense, perhaps more, to say that the real originator of the forms of those sayings attributed to Jesus is Jesus himself.

In summary, it is noted that Form Criticism as a method for study of the synoptic gospels falls short in five respects: its failure to account for the evidence of eyewitnesses, its lack of acknowledgment of the biographical interest of the community, the impossibility of its theory of a creative community, its questioning of the evidence for the reliability of the gospels' historical contexts, and its conclusions about historical worth based on stereotyped forms.

Selected Reading List

Bultmann, Rudolf. *History of the Synoptic Tradition.* New York: Harper & Row, 1963.
Dibelius, Martin. *From Tradition to Gospel.* New York: Scribner's, 1935.
————. *Gospel Criticism and Christology.* London: Nicholson and Watson, 1935.
Easton, Burton Scott. *The Gospel Before the Gospels.* New York: Scribner's, 1928.
Gundry, Stanley N. "A Critique of the Fundamental Assumption of Form Criticism," *Bibliotheca Sacra* 123 (1966): 32–39, 140–49.
Guthrie, Donald. *New Testament Introduction.* Downers Grove, IL: InterVarsity, 1970. Pp. 188–219.

ESSAY 5

Redaction Criticism

Just as Form Criticism originated as a further refinement of Source Criticism, so Form Criticism has itself given birth to a further sub-discipline called Redaction Criticism (*Redaktionsgeschichte*). With the amount of attention being devoted to synoptic gospel forms and church theology (*Gemeindetheologie*), the question was not *whether* but *when* the scrutiny of New Testament scholarship would be redirected to the gospel writers who put together Matthew, Mark, and Luke. Though not recognized immediately as separate from Form Criticism, Redaction Criticism eventually earned the status of a separate discipline.

As compared with Form Criticism, the primary focus of Redaction Criticism is the theology of the evangelists as distinguished from that of the Christian community. A clear-cut line of demarcation between the two is not easily drawn. In fact, in some cases overlap must be acknowledged. Because the gospel writers were part of the community, inevitably they would reflect the community's theological outlook, at least in part. Otherwise these composers must be unnaturally separated from the people whom they served.

Redaction critics, for the most part, do not embrace traditional viewpoints of authorship. They look upon the originators of the synoptics as later theological editors to whose works the names of Matthew, Mark, and Luke were attached for the sake of prestige. These anonymous writers are, then, the ones whose theological views are in question in this type of research. Such views are assumed to be distinct from any specific, systematic teaching delivered by Jesus.

The emergence of Redaction Criticism as a separate discipline dates from the mid-twentieth century. Most prominent among its early advocates are Gunther Bornkamm, Hans Conzelmann, and Willi Marxsen. Each of these has concentrated his efforts on one gospel—Bornkamm on Matthew, Conzelmann on Luke, and Marxsen on Mark. In the discussion to follow, these three along with Werner Kummel and Norman Perrin will be representatives of Redaction Criticism.

THEOLOGY OF MARK

Because the Two-Source Theory and Form Criticism endorse the priority of Mark, so does Redaction Criticism. This gospel is then a suitable starting point for theological analysis. Redactional analysis of Mark is more difficult because of the unavailability of sources used by its writer.

According to Marxsen, Mark joins, edits, and expands isolated units of tradition in accordance with four guidelines:

1. The passion story is linked to the rest by his addition of predictions of its coming.
2. He invents the Messianic-secret theory to explain the late (post-Easter) emergence of Messianic teaching.
3. He introduces the new literary concept of a "gospel" (*euangelion*). It is the "proclamation of a message of salvation" and is derived from Paul.
4. He weaves into the narrative a geographical orientation toward Galilee. The resultant force of the gospel is, therefore, not a historical account of Jesus' life but a proclamation of the salvation to be expected by Christians subsequent to the Easter (that is, resurrection) "experience." The evangelist anticipates an imminent return of Christ and directs his readers to make their way to Galilee, where he expects the *parousia* ("coming") to happen.

THEOLOGY OF MATTHEW

For the redaction critic the theologies of Matthew and Luke are more easily discernible, because these gospels were based on a known source (Mark) and a reconstructed source (Q). Bornkamm contends that Matthew was written in the A.D. 80s or A.D. 90s, somewhere between Palestine and Syria. The book reflects a deep cleavage between Judaism and Christianity and, more specifically, a turmoil within the church between Jewish Christianity and Gentile Christianity. In siding with the Gentile position, this evangelist arranges his sources (Mark and Q plus some special Matthean material) and adds material so as to create a Teacher who has captured the true essence of the Law that had been missed by Pharisaic Judaism. Unlike his predecessors, this "rabbi" teaches with authority supported by miracles, and his disciples never cease to be pupils. Although having much in common with Judaism, this new system is distinct from it and earns its own title of "church" (*ekklesia*), a term put into the mouth of the earthly Jesus by the Christian community. The church has become universal and is not local like a Jewish synagogue. The presence of the Lord with his church replaces the Law and the temple as a unifying factor. Yet ultimate perfection has not been attained in the church. Need still exists to obey Jesus' teachings in light of future judgment that will issue in promised salvation.

In Matthew's scheme, then, Mark's exclusive attention to Christ's imminent return has been replaced by a joint emphasis on ecclesiology and eschatology. Late first-century Christian thought came to grips with the fact that the Messiah's return was not to be immediate and therefore originated the concept of a new institution, the church, to fill the interval before the return.

In Conzelmann's view, Luke, coming at about the time of Matthew or later (perhaps around A.D. 90 or after), delineates three distinct periods: the period of Israel, the period of Jesus' ministry, and the period since the ascension. The second and third periods are kept distinct by this writer. The former, when Jesus was alive ministering on earth, was the time of salvation, when Satan was far removed and temptation was nonexistent. Since his passion, however, Satan has returned and temptations are very real. The work of the Spirit in the church is presented as essentially fulfilling prophecies of the "last days." Hence Luke reflects a more general, weakened, eschatological expectation in the church of his time. The delay of Christ's return is, then, Luke's motif.

This means that Luke shifts from his predecessors' focus on a short time of waiting to deal with a Christian life of longer duration. This shift entails a development of ethical standards, among which perseverance is prominent. It also leads to development of a complete redemptive plan and the replacement of an imminent end by one that is "endlessly" remote.

Several additional observations will provide a better understanding of Redaction Criticism:

1. The following are examples of how the gospel writers allegedly incorporated their theological emphases:
   a. In the narrative connected with Caesarea Philippi (Mark 8:27–9:1), the writer reports questions and answers as from the lips of Jesus and Peter. In reality, Redaction Criticism alleges, the titles are from the Christological vocabulary of the early Christian community. Furthermore, though persons bear the names of individuals and groups connected with Jesus' ministry, the principal reference is to circumstances in the church of the late A.D. 60s. "Jesus" and his sayings represent the Lord from heaven and his message to this church. "Peter" pictures misled believers, who confess correctly but interpret their own confession erroneously. "The multitude" stands for the total church membership, for whom the teaching is intended. In other words, Redaction Criticism sees this story as bearing the form of a history about Jesus, but its actual purpose was the conveying of the risen Lord's message to his church, as con-

ceived by Mark. The historical impression is only a vehicle and is not to be equated with actual happenings.

b. Matthew took over the same incident at Caesarea Philippi and reworked it. Dominated by an ecclesiological interest, Matthew reshaped the Marcan narrative by inserting a formal blessing of Peter, on the basis of which Peter assumed full authority as founder and leader of the early church (Matt. 16:17–19). For Matthew the church was the sole medium of salvation. In fact, to the person within this church, salvation is assured. In effect, Matthew moved the "Son of Man" reference from 16:21 (cf. Mark 8:31) to 16:13, because, unlike Mark, he was not interested in generating a Christological discussion. Matthew's interest was in a formal proclamation by Jesus regarding the Christian church.

c. In the Lucan parallel (Luke 9:18–27) Luke removed the Marcan urgency based on an imminent return in favor of highlighting a consistent life of testimony over a considerable period of time. Such touches as the addition of "daily" to Luke 9:23 and the omission of "in this adulterous and sinful generation" and "come with power" from 9:26–27 changed the account's complexion drastically. This resulted when Luke rethought Mark's outlook regarding eschatology and introduced his own emphasis on delay. By attention to details such as these, the redaction critic purposes to capture this or that theological point being made by a gospel writer.

2. The preceding examples demonstrate in a small way how the redaction critic conceives the gospels writers' roles as that of theologians, but not historians. Mark supposedly was wholly dependent on the isolated units identified by Form Criticism. Matthew and Luke each had access to some special sources of their own, which they utilized along with Mark and Q. The task of these three consisted of adapting and connecting these units in ways that seemed best to them, so as to attribute to Jesus the viewpoints and emphases that they deemed most crucial for nurturing the faith of the church of their time. They were, then, theological editors, but not recorders of historical happenings. It was inconsequential to them that they falsely attributed to Jesus and his associates many things they never said or did. Their prime concern was to construct a theology that would meet the needs of the church, even if doing so successfully meant fabricating a life of Jesus in order to give the system more credibility.

3. The philosophical basis by which the redactionist attempts to grant respectability to this system of falsification is similar to that behind the neoorthodoxy of Karl Barth and the demythologizing of Rudolf Bultmann. Besides the obvious realm of reality where space, time,

and the physical senses prevail, another realm is visualized: the realm of faith. Anything that one is inwardly persuaded is true is taken to be real regardless of whether it is fact. For example, the postresurrection faith of early Christians was so strong that it became confused with space-time happenings to the point that many were fully convinced that the physical body of Jesus rose from death and departed, leaving an empty tomb. To the redaction critic, as to the form critic, this mental persuasion is not wrong, even though Jesus' resurrection cannot be advocated as a fact of history. To this person the resurrection is a fact of faith that proved to be health-giving for the early church, and this is enough. It need not coincide with history. Similarly, as a whole, the synoptic gospels need not portray the historical Jesus in toto. It is sufficient that they proved beneficial in the development of the early Christian community.

4. The preceding philosophical basis of Redaction Criticism eliminates the possibility of reconstructing a life of Jesus or of determining a theology of Jesus that is based on the gospels. Just as Form Criticism says that the events recorded in the gospels are fabrications of the early church, Redaction Criticism says that the theological teachings in the gospels are those of the individual writers, not of Jesus. Allegedly, early Christians were not guided by the modern concept of "historical" (that is, "factual"). Motivated by a strong religious experience, they had no qualms about imputing to the historical Jesus words that he never spoke. The gospels and the traditions behind them, therefore, are to the redaction critic primarily reflections of the early church's experience and theology. Only by stringent application of carefully contrived criteria for authenticity can one hope to derive accurate data about Jesus' life and teachings. And, says the redactionist, whatever is derived in this respect will be at best minimal.

EVALUATION

One who evaluates Redaction Criticism will note only a few "byproducts" in the way of benefits rendered to gospel study. As a corrective to Form Criticism, it has brought a recognition that the gospel writers were not mere compilers of tradition, but men who each wrote with a different purpose, which must be taken into account for an understanding of the differences in emphasis between the gospels. The rise of Redaction Criticism has also revived interest in a comparative study of the Synoptic Gospels, an interest that had lagged because of earlier efforts to merge the three into one strand of tradition. Furthermore, in its efforts to discover theological motivation it has induced scholars to pay closer attention to first-century Christianity. This is beneficial in that the more we know about the first century, the better we can understand the New Testament.

These "by-products," however, are of little value compared with the debilitating weaknesses of this method of study.

1. Redaction Criticism is based on the Two-Source Theory and on Form Criticism and therefore inherits their irresolvable problems (see essays 3 and 4). The redactionist methodology is vulnerable at the same points because of the foundational assumptions on which the discipline is built.

2. The period of time during which these theological and factual alterations were supposedly made and became universally accepted in Christendom is unbelievably short. For instance, to believe that the Christian community modified the factual data about Jesus' life and Mark contrived the theological data attributed to him and that these extensive alterations were accepted throughout first-century Christendom in only thirty to forty years is impossible. In these ancient times it took centuries for myths to be standardized and widely accepted.

3. The ethical question about this theory is also inevitable. Christianity in general and the gospel writers in particular have been noted for the high system of truthfulness for which they stand. Can the origin of such a system be traced to practitioners of extensive falsification regarding the life and teachings of Jesus, or can it be traced to Jesus himself, whose words and actions as found in the gospels were accurately transmitted by his early followers? The case for the latter alternative is by far the stronger.

4. Redaction critics utilize an approach to the gospels that is different from the way they handle other ancient writings. They initially assume the nonhistorical character of the bulk of gospel literature, as though some barrier separated the gospel writers from any interest in real happenings of the earlier portion of their century. They suppose that events and sayings were invented or reshaped for theological purposes. This is uncharacteristic of the way of handling other teachers in the ancient world, both Jewish and Greek. The unanswered evidence to the contrary says that early Christians did have considerable historical interest in Jesus of Nazareth. The writers' theological purposes, therefore, were not separate from, but rather anchored in, history.

5. The philosophical basis of Redaction Criticism is questionable. To grant recognition to a set of "faith realities" that stand in opposition to physically observable historical data must, after serious analysis, be rejected. Only the mind thoroughly conditioned by theories of modern rationalism can envisage two realms of reality in conflict with each other, and yet regard both as equally valid. The endorsing of such a state of affairs calls one's intuitive understanding of reality into serious question. Such a dualistic concept is quite artificial.

280

6. An unregulated subjectivism also characterizes Redaction Criticism. This is an outgrowth of the system's underlying philosophy. Redactors become their own norms, with the result that interpretations are often stretched. For example, Marxsen's explanation of "Peter" as Mark's representation of misled believers must be traced to Marxsen, not to Mark (cf. Mark 8:27–9:1). "Peter" in his confession could just as easily be taken by someone else to represent discerning believers. Only the factual data about who Peter was can rescue one from the dilemma of endlessly conflicting opinions about him. An objective control on these must be found. In other words, "faith realities" must be reduced to one "faith reality" by reaffirming the only reality to be the one that is historical. "Peter" was either a historical person or the figment of someone's imagination. He cannot be both.

Differences of opinion among redaction critics reflect this personal bias in their assumptions. That they have taken unjustified liberties in arguing for various emphases in each author could not be more clearly reflected than it is by their disagreements with one another. For example, theories of Mark's purpose variously hold his guideline to be typological fulfillment of Old Testament texts, the liturgical calendar, stages in the revelations of Messianic dignity, a geographical-theological outline, Pauline theology, and others. If redaction proponents cannot agree what theological theme Mark sought to inaugurate, it is probable he was not trying to inaugurate any such theme; the theological theme originates in the mind of the modern redactionist, not the gospel writer. Differing foundational assumptions by different modern scholars create different opinions, which are then read back into the gospel. This does a great injustice to the ancient record.

7. Redaction critics' method for recognizing "authentic Jesus material" is also subjective. Their three criteria, distinctiveness, multiple attestation, and consistency, stem from the presupposition that tradition about Jesus contains much that is unhistorical. If this is the foregone conclusion, it is impossible to examine historical sources without bias. The verdict is already passed before the beginning of the trial. It is not a question of whether the defendant will be found guilty, but how and when this person will be condemned. Thus Redaction Criticism has determined in advance what it will discover. The results of the process can therefore be nothing less than devastating to the synoptic gospels as historical records.

EVANGELICAL USE OF REDACTION CRITICISM

Some evangelical scholars have argued that there is a legitimate use of Redaction Criticism, pointing out that redact simply means "edit" and noting that evangelicals have long recognized editorial activity by the gospel writers. Redaction Criticism has observed four categories of editorial activity: selectivity, arrangement, modification, and creativity. "Selectivity" sees the gospel writers as not incorporating all the material available to them, but choosing what was best suited to accomplishing their purposes. "Arrangement" detects that they did not always put their material in chronological order, but sometimes arranged the material in a thematic sequence in order to emphasize some particular point about the life of Christ. "Modification" attributes to the writers the prerogative of changing material to accord with a writer's habits or purposes. Some of these modifications were minor, simply reflecting the individual styles of the writers, but others were more extensive, molding the accounts in accord with the theological interests of the evangelists and their communities rather than accurately portraying the situation in Jesus' day. "Creativity" allows that the writers creatively shaped their gospels by adding events to historical narratives and putting into his lips words that the historical Jesus did not utter. These creative additions maintain a continuity with the historical situations the accounts allege to describe.

These four categories represent the normative approach among evangelical practitioners of the redaction methodology. The methodology differs substantially from radical Redaction Criticism in the degree to which the historical validity of the Synoptic Gospels is questioned, but the tendency to dismiss historicity is still present.

In two and one half of the proposed categories the evangelical version is merely a continuation of long-standing evangelical methodology in gospel study. Well before the advent of Redaction Criticism, evangelicals advocated that the writers selected only part of the material available to them, but the selection was understood to be a truly representative and accurate portrayal of the historical happening. Matthew, a companion of Jesus, had to leave something out. "Selectivity" is not a discovery of Redaction Criticism.

The same is true of "arrangement." Evangelicals have always recognized that at times the writers put descriptions in a nonchronological sequence, understanding, of course, that nothing in the text specified chronological arrangement. In Matthew 8–9, for example, the grouping of Jesus' miracles emphasizes his authority. These miracles are not related in the order they occurred.

In the categories of "modification" and "creativity," however, evangelical redaction critics have veered toward radical procedures. Minor modifications of materials reflecting stylistic preferences of individual authors are in accord with the historic evangelical approach to biblical inspiration. When these modifications are alleged to be extensive enough to revise the substance of what was done or said on a given occasion, however, the long-standing evangelical commitment to the historical accuracy of Scripture has at least been undermined and more probably violated. Thus major modification and creativity move into the realm of radical Redaction Criticism by attributing to the gospel writers the recording of what was nonhistorical as though it were history.

The gospels must be interpreted according to the grammar of the Greek language and the historical background of their settings. To use questionable critical assumptions to override the latter is to open the historical basis of Christianity to serious question. Yet this is what Redaction Criticism, even the evangelical type, has done.

One must not allow whims arising from "discoveries" of redactional emphases to creep in and exclude the more obvious emphases of the gospels. "Redactional signals" in the text are usually inconsequential details that are blown out of proportion and given a far-reaching significance unintended by the author. Such a magnification of minor points is traceable to the imagination of the redaction critic, not to the text. Ignoring the meaning of larger units of thought in the text and dwelling upon minutiae is an example of tunnel vision exegesis. Advocates of verbal inspiration are often accused of focusing too strongly on individual words of the text and neglecting the broader message, but their fault is minuscule in comparison with how the redaction critic finds subtle but profound significance in the smallest elements of the text at the expense of the total meaning of the larger section. When one of these "redactional discoveries" raises questions about the gospels' historicity, to prefer the "discovery" over obvious historical import is extremely subjective on the part of the interpreter.

It is legitimate to endeavor to discover the theological emphases of the gospel writers, but it must be done without questioning the historical accuracy of what they record. Theological purpose and historical accuracy are compatible. Each writer has retained parts of Jesus' emphasis, so that when the emphases are combined, the theology of Jesus himself is the result. Redaction Criticism is an example of an approach that raises question about the reliability of gospel reports of Jesus' words and deeds, and as such is incompatible with a thoroughgoing commitment to the authority of Scripture.

Selected Reading List

Bornkamm, Günther. *The New Testament: A Guide to Its Writings.* Translated by Reginald H. Fuller and Ilse Fuller. Philadelphia: Fortress, 1973. Pp. 50–66.

Bornkamm, Günther, Gerhard Barth, and Heinz Joachim Held. *Tradition and Interpretation in Matthew.* Translated by Percy Scott. Philadelphia: Fortress, 1963.

Conzelmann, Hans. *The Theology of St. Luke.* Translated by Geoffrey Buswell. New York: Harper, 1960.

Feine, Paul, and Johannes Behm. *Introduction to the New Testament.* Reedited by Werner Georg Kummel. Translated by A. J. Mattill, Jr. Nashville: Abingdon, 1966. Pp. 62–68, 75–84, 91–102.

France, R. T. "The Authenticity of the Sayings of Jesus." In *History, Criticism and Faith*, edited by C. Brown, 101–43. Downers Grove, IL: InterVarsity, 1976.

Guelich, Robert A. "The Gospels: Portraits of Jesus and His Ministry," *Journal of the Evangelical Theological Society* 24 (1981): 117–25.

_____. *The Sermon on the Mount, a Foundation for Understanding*. Waco, TX: Word, 1982.

Gundry, Robert H. *Matthew, a Commentary on His Literary and Theological Art*. Grand Rapids: Eerdmans, 1982.

Guthrie, Donald. *New Testament Introduction*. Downers Grove, IL: InterVarsity, 1970. Pp. 214–19.

Hagner, Donald A. "Interpreting the Gospels: The Landscape and the Quest," *Journal of the Evangelical Theological Society* 24 (1981): 23–27.

Harrison, Everett F. "*Gemeindetheologie*: The Bane of Gospel Criticism." In *Jesus of Nazareth: Saviour and Lord*, edited by Carl F. H. Henry, 157–73. Grand Rapids: Eerdmans, 1966.

Hiebert, D. Edmond. *An Introduction to the New Testament. The Gospels and Acts*. Vol. 1. Chicago: Moody, 1975. Pp. 184–88.

Johnston, Wendell G., et al. "The Evangelical and Redaction Criticism in the Synoptic Gospels," *Talbot Review* 1:2 (Summer 1985): 6–13.

Kantzer, Kenneth S. "Redaction Criticism: Is It Worth the Risk?" *Christianity Today* 29:15 (Oct. 18, 1985): 1-I–12-I.

Lane, William L. *Commentary on the Gospel of Mark*. NIC. Grand Rapids: Eerdmans, 1974.

Marshall, I. Howard. *Luke: Historian and Theologian*. Grand Rapids: Zondervan, 1970.

_____. *Commentary on Luke*. NIGTC. Grand Rapids: Eerdmans, 1978.

Marxsen, Willi. *Introduction to the New Testament*. Translated by G. Buswell. Philadelphia: Fortress, 1964. Pp. 136–42, 147–52, 155–61.

_____. *Mark the Evangelist*. Translated by James Boyce, Donald Juel, and William Poehlmann with Roy A. Harrisville. Nashville: Abingdon, 1969.

Perrin, Norman. *What is Redaction Criticism?* Philadelphia: Fortress, 1969.

Stein, R. H. "The 'Criteria' for Authenticity," *Gospel Perspectives*. 2 vols., edited by R. T. France and D. Wenham. Sheffield, England: JSOT, 1980–1981. Pp. 1:225–63.

Silva, Moises. "Ned B. Stonehouse and Redaction Criticism," *Westminster Theological Journal* 40 (1977–1978): 77–88, 281–303.

Thomas, Robert L. "The Hermeneutics of Evangelical Redaction Criticism," *Journal of the Evangelical Theological Society* 29 (1986), 447–59.

_____. "The Rich Young Man in Matthew," *Grace Theological Journal* 3 (1982): 235–60.

_____. "Another View," *Christianity Today* 29:15 (Oct. 18, 1985): 8-I.

Criticism of the Gospel of John

The gospel of John and its historical integrity have long been objects of severe attack. Some believe that the gospel could not have been written by John the apostle, because no contemporary of Jesus could have held such a high view of his person. Past attitudes have at times bordered on skepticism about the value of a work that would picture the deity of Jesus Christ so clearly. Because of further research and discoveries, this near skepticism has largely disappeared. Nevertheless, many are still reluctant to endorse the gospel as completely reliable.

RECENT CHALLENGES OF HISTORICAL INTEGRITY

One frequently mentioned difficulty is related to the problems encountered by any theory of unified authorship. The differences in the gospel's Greek style, problems of sequence, and repetitions in discourse material have been cited as proving that more than one author was involved. So in modern times various attempts to explain the manner of composition have been made. One group of theories explains the alleged confusion in the gospel by suggesting that some of the sections were displaced accidentally; it seeks to correct the problem by rearranging the order. Another approach accounts for apparent stylistic differences and other problems by proposing that the gospel's compiler used a number of independent written sources in putting the work together. A third proposed solution has been to suggest that the gospel went through a number of editions before arriving at its present form.

Still another theory, called gradual composition, is perhaps the most prominent recent theory. It combines elements of the other theories and identifies five stages of growth and embellishment in the gospel's development. Stage one was the crystallizing of a body of traditional material pertaining to the words and works of Jesus. This was material that was similar to, but had origins independent of, material in the tradition of the synoptic gospels. The input of John the son of Zebedee was a major source of this historical tradition. Stage two saw this material creatively developed over a period of several decades into the form and style of the individual stories of the fourth gospel. The development was under the auspices of a close-knit school of thought and expression, which was led by a leader or master preacher (or evangelist). This same school is often theorized to have originated the Johannine epistles and

Revelation also. Stage three witnessed the organization of this material into a consecutive gospel, which was the first edition of the fourth gospel. The dominant figure from stage two, the evangelist, wrote this work in Greek, selecting from the much larger body of Johannine material developed at stage two. Stage four consisted of a second edition of this work issued by the evangelist to provide solutions to problems arising subsequent to stage three. This edition added material not previously incorporated into the work. Stage five was a final editing or redacting of the work by someone other than the evangelist. This redactor was probably a close friend or disciple of the evangelist. He was certainly a member of the school described at stage two. A main contribution of the redactor was to preserve from stage two all the available Johannine material not included in previous editions. Because it resulted from the preaching of the evangelist, it would not differ in style and vocabulary from the two previous editions. Chapter 21 was among the new material added by the redactor that had not come from the evangelist.

Thus the theory of gradual composition identifies three individuals in the process of the fourth gospel's development: John the apostle, who is called the author; the anonymous evangelist; and the anonymous redactor. It holds the process from beginning to end to have taken from about A.D. 40 to about A.D. 100, with stage three placed between A.D. 75 and A.D. 85. John the apostle is said to have survived until just before the gospel was put into its final form by the redactor.

Difficulties encountered by this theory are numerous. Unanswered is the question of how John the apostle, an eyewitness of gospel events, could have faded into the background while the evangelist rose to leadership in the school that derived its tradition from John himself. Also, would John have remained silent while unhistorical embellishments about Jesus' life were accumulating in his own circles? Furthermore, could three individuals, no matter how closely associated, have developed patterns of speech and writing almost identical to one another? Could such a tradition so tainted by exaggeration and myth have been developed and have been unanimously and universally accepted in six short decades? By no stretch of the imagination could this have happened. This and other challenges to the gospel's historical integrity fail to commend themselves as being the least bit probable.

RELATIONSHIP TO THE SYNOPTICS

Other issues pertaining to John's gospel are discussed with far more benefit because they relate to objective data that is available. At stake here also is the book's integrity.

The critical questions surrounding the fourth gospel are nearly all interrelated. Thus, discussion of any one area of critical questions necessarily presupposes matters relating to another area. This is true whether one discusses authorship, date, or the relationship existing between John's gospel and the synoptics. Choice of a starting point for the discussion is somewhat arbitrary, but the last of these issues may be the best way into the other two.

The first three gospels in the traditional order are commonly spoken of as the synoptic gospels, because they treat the life and ministry of Jesus from a similar perspective (*synoptic* means "seeing together"). Striking and extensive similarities of content, arrangement, and wording occur. One may readily see their similarity by examining the parallel columns of material in this *Harmony*.

But also evident is the fact that the gospel of John is in a class by itself. One notes more differences than similarities between John and the synoptics. Differences in material content are the most obvious. John does not record the virgin birth, the baptism, the temptation, the transfiguration, the institution of the Lord's Supper, the agony in the garden of Gethsemane, or the ascension. Synoptic-type parables and cures of demoniacs and lepers are notably absent. Many omissions of less significant material occur also.

Just as critical is the fact that John includes much material that is unique to it. John's prologue is without parallel (1:1–18). It is John that records the early Judean ministry (chaps. 2–3), including such notable events as the first miracle and the discussion with Nicodemus. It is John that details the journey through Samaria to Galilee, including the encounter with the Samaritan woman at Sychar. High points of the remaining material unique to John are the Sabbath healing of the lame man in Jerusalem, Jesus' failure in Capernaum to conform to popular Messianic ideas, the healing of the blind man in Jerusalem, the Good Shepherd discourse, the raising of Lazarus, the washing of the disciples' feet, the discourse in the upper room, Christ's intercessory prayer, and the miraculous catch of fish. In sum, there is an obvious difference in material content between the synoptics and John.

These, however, by no means exhaust the differences that set John apart. John's manner of presentation is different. The material content cited has already hinted at this. John has less narrative and more discourse, in contrast with the short aphorisms and parables characteristic of the synoptics. The book portrays Jesus more in the role of the rabbi. Jesus' manner of teaching in the synoptics would be more appropriate to the common people of Galilee, but in John to the more educated populace in and around Jerusalem.

Differences of chronology between John and the synoptics are also found. There is the question of whether there were one or two cleansings of the temple. The dating of the Last Supper is also a problem (see essay 10). Even more far-reaching in its implications is the duration of Christ's ministry. The synoptic accounts apparently require a ministry of only one year, although their chronological details are vague. But John's requires more than three years (see essay 11).

Our discussion of John's relationship to the synoptics must also embrace their similarities, although these are not so obvious. Indeed, because the differences do not necessarily involve contradiction or incompatibility, the similarities become especially significant. At least two of the synoptic gospels and John include material on John the Baptist, the feeding of the five thousand, the storm at sea, the triumphal entry into Jerusalem, Mary's anointing of Jesus, and parts of the Last Supper and passion narratives. In addition, similar material often occurs in the same order in John as in the synoptics. Little verbal similarity exists between John and the synoptics, however, except in some of the cases of words spoken by Jesus or others.

To identify these similarities and differences is not enough. What relationship between the synoptics and John do they evidence?

1. One solution offered is that John wrote with the intention of replacing the synoptic gospels. But taken by itself, John is an incomplete account of the life and ministry of Jesus. That any author would suppose that this account could replace one or all of the synoptics is stretching imagination too far.
2. A second proposal is that the book of John is an interpretation of Jesus and his teaching designed for Gentile readers. Those who hold this view, though, usually assume that John's intentions are not historical; if the assumption is wrong, the theory collapses. And if John is interpreting the other gospels, why is so little material held in common with them?
3. Closely akin are the views holding that John, having been written later, was dependent on one or more of the synoptics. John supposedly is a reworking of synoptic material. Attempts to identify sections of John that are dependent on written sources result in failure, however, because John is stylistically uniform. Furthermore, the similarities are not significant enough to justify the assumption of John's dependence on the synoptics. Variation is much more characteristic. John cites incidents not even in the synoptics, and its accounts of the same incidents differ in detail.
4. These considerations suggest a fourth view—that John is independent of the synoptics, that it was written neither to interpret nor to replace them, that it is in no sense dependent on them. This independence theory is preferable to the first three theories and has much more to commend it. It challenges the assumption of much gospel criticism that the gospels form a documentary series in literary dependence on one another.

Advocates of the independence view point out that in supposed instances of John's using synoptic or Marcan material, he so drastically alters it that either John's credibility is called into question or else the theory of literary dependence is itself in doubt. Yet nothing in John itself casts doubt on its credibility. As for the points of similarity and contact that do exist between John and the synoptic authors, these are precisely what would be expected from authors drawing upon an interlocking oral tradition about Christ. The tradition was stable and held great respect for the historical verities; John, as well as the synoptic authors, would have drawn on this and on his own recollections (assuming he was John the apostle).

Such a view of John's relationship to the synoptics has much to commend it and is a helpful corrective to those views already discussed. Some advocates of the independence theory, however, maintain that John either was unaware of the synoptics or that he wrote without any reference to their content and purpose. Because it is difficult to imagine a situation later in the first century in which the synoptics would be unknown, some have postulated an early date for John, perhaps earlier than any of the synoptics. But such an extreme view of John's independence is neither necessary nor the best accounting of the evidence.

It is preferable to combine the theory accepting John's essential literary independence with the supplemental view of its relationship to the synoptics. According to this view John did not use the synoptics as sources, but he did apparently write with a knowledge of their contents. He assumed his readers also knew their contents. Among his purposes seems to have been conscious supplementation of synoptic material; John filled in the gaps and avoided unnecessary duplication. Thus, John concentrated on the Judean, rather than on the Galilean, ministry of Jesus. By his mention of three Passovers and possible implication of a fourth, he made clear that Jesus' ministry lasted between three and four years. This is not clear from the synoptics. On the other hand, John's omission of so much important synoptic material, such as kingdom teaching and the institution of the ordinances, is difficult to explain unless we assume that he knew the synoptics and saw no need to repeat their content. Thus a view that accepts the literary independence of the gospel of John but that also sees its purpose as that of supplementing the synoptics best accounts for both the similarities on the one hand and the significant differences on the other. This seems to be the relationship of the fourth gospel to the first three.

Authorship of the Fourth Gospel

Traditionally, John the apostle has been thought to be the author of the fourth gospel. A recent variation of this view of apostolic authorship holds the apostle John to be the source of the gospel's historical data but suggests that a disciple or disciples of John actually wrote it. Under John's influence, it is said, they preached and developed John's reminiscences even further so as to meet the needs of the community to which they ministered. This viewpoint aligns itself with modern theories of composition connected with the synoptic gospels (see essays 4 and 5, "Form Criticism" and "Redaction Criticism," pp. 268–84, and the gradual composition theory described earlier in this essay). The proposal does injustice to the gospel of John itself, however, when it fails to recognize the gospel's own claim that the beloved disciple of Jesus wrote the book (John 21:20, 24).

Others have proposed that the John to whom early tradition ascribed authorship is John the Elder, referred to by Papias as quoted by Eusebius. Eusebius's interpretation of Papias's statement distinguishes between two persons in Ephesus by the name of John. Motivation for such a distinction is probably traceable to influential Christian leaders in Alexandria who questioned the millennial views of Revelation and therefore were seeking to dispense with the apostolic authorship of this last book of the Bible. By postulating another John in Ephesus at the time it was written, they thought they had grounds for doing this. It is not at all clear, however, that Papias intended to distinguish John the Elder from John the apostle in his quoted statement. A good argument can be advanced that the two were one and the same person, so that no confusion in the traditional ascription of authorship to John the apostle results.

Some theories of non-Johannine authorship discredit the external evidence for a John as author and argue that internal evidence makes apostolic authorship impossible. Actually, though, both external and internal evidence firmly support authorship by John the apostle.

Irenaeus is the first to say clearly (c. A.D. 180) that John the apostle wrote this gospel and that it was published by John at Ephesus, where he resided. Other late second-century evidence testifies to John the apostle's residence in Ephesus late in the first century. But Irenaeus's testimony is especially important; he was a disciple of Polycarp, and Polycarp had known the apostle John personally. Here then is a direct line between Irenaeus and John with only one connecting link—Polycarp. Writers after Irenaeus assume apostolic authorship of the fourth gospel without question.

At one time New Testament critics of the school following F. C. Baur argued that the fourth gospel was not written until about A.D. 160, so that John could not have been its author. The discovery of a papyrus fragment of this gospel in the collection of the John Rylands Library, however, demolished this view. Dated no later than A.D. 150 and perhaps as early as A.D. 130, the fragment (P^{52}) came from a community along the Nile in the hinterland of Egypt. When one calculates the time necessary for the processes of copying and circulation in order for this fragment to reach a remote Egyptian community, the origins of this gospel are easily pushed back into at least the late first century, when John was probably still alive.

Nowhere in the fourth gospel does the author identify himself by name, and the interpretation of internal evidence is subject to the preconceptions of the individual critic. Nevertheless this evidence fits well (many would say best) with apostolic and Johannine authorship. The writer claims to be an eyewitness (1:14; 19:35; 21:24–25). He has an accurate knowledge of Jewish customs and Palestinian topography before Jerusalem's destruction in A.D. 70. He employs the kind of vivid, incidental detail one would expect of an eyewitness (2:6; 6:19; 21:8). His writing style is Semitic. Even more specifically, the author seems to identify himself as the "disciple whom Jesus loved" (21:20, 24). James, John, and Peter formed the inner circle of disciples closest to Jesus (Mark 5:37; 9:2; Luke 22:8). James was martyred early in the history of the church (Acts 12:1–5), too early to have written the gospel. "The disciple whom Jesus loved" is distinguished from Peter in 13:23 and 21:7. By process of elimination, it must be John the son of Zebedee, one of the group from whom was singled out "the disciple whom Jesus loved" (John 21:2, 20). Although the beloved disciple is not identified by name, this very anonymity is best explained by John the apostle's authorship.

DATE OF THE FOURTH GOSPEL

Although it is impossible to date this gospel with certainty, most scholars today place it in the last ten or fifteen years of the first century or very early in the second. This view finds support from the early church Fathers. As already noted, the early dating of the P^{52} fragment hardly allows for a much later date. Critics who view this gospel as either corrective of or supplemental to the synoptics obviously must place its writing after one or more of the synoptics. Thus they usually prefer a later date, although it is difficult to place apostolic authorship after A.D. 100.

Scholars who maintain that the author either did not know or use the synoptics find it possible to place the writing very early, perhaps as the earliest of the gospels. In fact, those who maintain that John neither knew nor consciously supplemented the synoptics finds a pre-A.D. 70 date to be the easiest to maintain. There are no compelling reasons to insist on such an early date, however; those who see John as a conscious supplement to the synoptics usually date it between A.D. 85 and A.D. 100.

CONCLUSION

Because the gospel of John presents no insuperable problems in its relationship to the synoptic gospels and encounters no insurmountable difficulties as to its apostolic authorship and date, no valid reason exists for questioning its right to respect as another accurate report of the life of Christ. Jesus was recognized as God by his contemporaries even as John represents him to be.

Selected Reading List

Brown, Raymond E. *The Gospel According to John I–XII.* Vol. 29 of The Anchor Bible. Garden City, NY: Doubleday, 1966. Pp. xxxiv–cii.

Guthrie, Donald. *New Testament Introduction.* Downers Grove, IL: InterVarsity, 1970. Pp. 241–71, 282–87.

Harrison, Everett F. *Introduction to the New Testament.* Grand Rapids: Eerdmans, 1964. Pp. 204–14.

Hiebert, D. Edmond. *An Introduction to the New Testament. The Gospels and Acts.* Vol. 1. Chicago: Moody, 1975. Pp. 192–213, 222–26.

Morris, Leon. *Studies in the Fourth Gospel.* Grand Rapids: Eerdmans, 1969.

Morris, Leon. *The Gospel According to John.* Grand Rapids: Eerdmans, 1971. Pp. 8–35.

ESSAY 7

Problems and Principles of Harmonization

Distinct advantages accrue from studying the gospels in a harmony. All available information on the same or similar events, conversations, and discourses is put side by side on the same page. Narratives describing different occasions from all four gospels are integrated into probable chronological sequence so that one has an overview of the course of Jesus' life from his conception to his postresurrection ministry. For many readers this will be a new experience with great benefit.

But the first careful reading of a harmony can also be a disturbing experience, especially for the reader who accepts the inspiration and historical integrity of the gospels. Although readers recognize the obvious fact that there are *four* gospels and that they are not identical, many have never explored the implications of that fact. But when reading a harmony, one can hardly avoid noting the divergences. The reader begins to notice that the accounts of Christ's words sometimes differ. One evangelist's report of the same conversation, saying, or discourse may be more or less complete than another's. Differences may occur in grammatical construction. Synonyms may be substituted, verb voice or tense changed, or nouns replaced by pronouns. There may be differences in the order of discussion. Sometimes the differences in details reported even involve what appear to be contradictions. Occasionally the same or similar statements will be found in contexts that appear to reflect different situations. The Beatitudes as recorded by Matthew and Luke contain a number of typical variations. Which report is correct? Or are both correct? How are the variations to be accounted for?

Similarly, when reading of the activities of Jesus, one may notice that similar events occur in different situations. Are they different events, or are they the same events erroneously reported? To complicate matters, sometimes what appears to be the same event is reported in a different order in another gospel. Sometimes diverse descriptive details are given for what appears to be the same event, and sometimes these details may have the appearance of discrepancy. A few readers may be surprised to find that the gospel writers do not always report the same events.

The questions arising from these phenomena are as significant as they are obvious. Do these phenomena undermine the historical integrity of the gospels? Or are they fully consistent with historical integrity? Do they call in question the inspiration and inerrancy of the gospels? Or are

293

they consistent with the orthodox concept of inspiration? One thing seems certain: if the evangelists really are guilty of inaccuracies, misrepresentations, and contradictions, their reliability and the claim to inspiration are suspect.

It is neither possible nor necessary within these notes to give answers to all the harmonistic problems that might be raised in a comparative reading of the gospels. But the editors of this *Harmony* without equivocation hold to both the historical integrity and verbal plenary inspiration of the gospels. They also believe that most harmonistic problems can be resolved adequately when certain common-sense principles of reporting and writing are applied in the interpretation of the evidence. The remainder of the problems have reasonable explanations, though further information about them would help in reaching more clear-cut solutions.

Some general considerations especially apply to the manner in which Jesus' words are reported. Jesus most likely spoke three languages, as did many of his contemporaries (see essay 8). It must not be forgotten that in many cases the Greek text reporting what someone said is actually a translation of what was originally said in Aramaic or Hebrew. In translation a certain amount of variation is possible, even necessary; seldom, if ever, is there only one legitimate way to translate from one language into another. At times the evangelists may even have deemed it more suited to their purposes to depart from a strictly literal translation of what Jesus said. So long as what Jesus intended is faithfully represented in language that accurately and effectively communicates to the intended readership, they cannot properly be faulted for this. Sometimes a more free translation may have been employed in reporting what Jesus said, for occasionally free translation can communicate the impact of what was originally said with gestures, intonation, and expression better than a verbatim account.

Aside from the inevitable variations arising from literal and free translations of Jesus' words, there are other equally significant considerations. Modern writing style employs various devices to indicate direct and verbatim quotations. Words included within quotation marks are assumed to be the exact words of the speaker. Ellipses are used to indicate words left out of the original statement, and brackets indicate words added by the reporter to clarify the sense of the quotation even though they were not originally part of the quotation. Footnotes may be employed to distinguish quotations coming from different sources or made at different times. None of these devices was available to first-century writers, and it is wrong to impose upon them standards of writing that presuppose their availability.

Furthermore, the exacting rules for quotations in modern writing may presuppose the mechanical means by which oral speech can be exactly recorded. Obviously early writers had no tape recorders, but shorthand techniques were widely used in the first century. Matthew, a tax collector accustomed to keeping records, may have acquired this skill. It has even been suggested he may have kept records of Christ's words and deeds, thus creating a core of written tradition upon which early Christians, including the gospel writers, could draw. This would partially explain the remarkable similarities among the gospels. But it would not eliminate differences, because he was only one of a number who contributed to this core of tradition.

With these general considerations in mind, then, one should examine the theory that varying accounts of what Jesus or other individuals said are instances of unavoidable inaccuracy. Is this a necessary conclusion? By no means. The gospels should not be called inaccurate when there are at least two viable options for defending their accuracy.

1. One approach is to note that the writers were not necessarily bound to conform to standards of verbal exactitude that later times developed. This explanation does not see verbatim reproduction of Jesus' words as the real question always. Rather the issue is, Do the words of the evangelists that report what Jesus said faithfully represent what Jesus in fact said; and, apart from verbal differences, are the reports of what Jesus said as given by the different evangelists consistent with one another in meaning? If the answer is Yes, then their accuracy cannot be impugned.

Actually, in ordinary oral discourse this manner of reporting what others have said is still followed, and so long as it is done carefully, no one questions the integrity of what has been said. To repeat word for word the speech of another is not in every case the natural or even possible thing. It would sometimes be impossible to repeat every word and phrase. What one does expect to be reproduced from an ordinary discussion are the striking or important statements, the leading thoughts, the major divisions or topics, and the general drift of discussion, including transitions from one topic to another. Although different reports are expected to agree on these matters, it is also expected that there will be differences in details, reflecting the interests and purposes of the reporters. Modifications such as changes of person; substitutions of pronouns for nouns or vice versa; changes in tense, voice, or mood of the verbs; and substitutions of synonyms are too trivial to call into question a reporter's accuracy in ordinary discussion. Although wording is important, meaning can be conveyed in a variety of ways. Verbal inspiration does not imply that truth can be accurately communicated in only one way. Rather it means that what the Holy Spirit did speak through the human agents was inspired and hence accurate, word for word.

2. A second option for defending the gospels' accuracy despite differing parallel accounts of the same speech is based on the possibility that these accounts do in fact retain verbatim utterances of Jesus and others. These of course would be the occasions when the Greek language was used. It is certainly not inconceivable that those recording Jesus' teachings in shorthand did so in a manner so as to retain the very words spoken. In addition, sufficient allowance should be made for the highly trained memories among the Jewish people of this time. It is generally acknowledged that they were much more adept in remembering details than the average Western mind of the twentieth century.

Beyond the use of shorthand and memory, allowance must also be made for the activity of the Holy Spirit in calling to mind the words that Jesus had spoken. Jesus had promised such a helper when he said, "The Holy Spirit, whom the Father will send in my name, will teach you all things, and will remind you of everything I have said to you" (John 14:26). If the Spirit could provide for verbally inspired writings in the composition of other parts of Scripture, he could surely do the same in the gospels.

If one follows this approach, differences between parallel accounts of the same discourse or conversation are explained by noting that no single gospel records everything spoken on a single occasion. In fact, it is doubtful that any combination of parallel accounts records the entirety of a speech or dialogue. Christ undoubtedly repeated some of his teachings in slightly differing forms on different occasions. He most probably did so on the same occasion also. Thus parallel accounts reporting the same substance in slightly different forms may be examples of different but similar statements made on the same occasion, each writer selecting only a part of what was said for his account. A sample of this may be seen in the first Beatitude. Matthew relates, "Blessed are the poor in spirit, for theirs is the kingdom of heaven" (Matt. 5:3), and Luke writes, "Blessed are you who are poor, for yours is the kingdom of God" (Luke 6:20). Jesus probably repeated this Beatitude in at least two different forms on the occasion of his Sermon on the Mount. If so, he used the third person once, the second person another time, and referred to the kingdom by two different titles. Also, in one case he qualified the poverty with the addition "in spirit," and in the other he did not. Because we know that neither gospel records the whole sermon, this explanation is quite plausible.

The parable of the mustard tree (Matt. 13:32; Mark 4:32) may also illustrate how Jesus on the same occasion repeated something in a slightly different form. According to Matthew he said that the birds of the air perch "in its branches," but according to Mark they

296

perch "in its shade." Which did Jesus say? The chances are good that he said both. Again, according to Matthew Jesus in his Olivet discourse gives the claim of future imposters as "I am the Christ" (Matt. 24:5), but Mark and Luke quote him as saying, "I am he" (Mark 13:6; Luke 21:8) ("he" being supplied by the NIV translators). Minor variations of this type are numerous.

In other places the variations are not minor. The difference between "this is why" (Matt. 13:13) and "so that" (Mark 4:12) has far-reaching implications as to meaning. Did Jesus use parables because his rejectors were already spiritually blind, or did he do so as to produce their blindness? He probably said both. The alleged displacement of Matthew 13:12 in Mark (4:25) and Luke (8:18b) most likely has the same explanation: in Matthew's account the words speak of Jesus' enemies and in the other two, of his disciples. Again the difference in meaning is substantial. Differences of this magnitude are not infrequent and can well be resolved by postulating that Jesus often repeated the same essential meaning in more than one form on one occasion.

Either of the options, then, or a combination of the two is sufficient to show that inaccuracy is not an inevitable or even a likely means of accounting for differences in parallel accounts. Whether we have an accurate summary of what Jesus said or the very words he spoke is difficult for us to determine at this point. It may very well be that we have some cases of both. The important thing is to recognize the Holy Spirit's part in inspiring what was written so as to guarantee an accurate report. It is not difficult to see this in light of the many instances where the gospels confirm rather than differ from one another.

What is to be said of events that are put in different order by the evangelists? First, it is quite possible for two different occurrences, happening within the same sphere and under similar circumstances, to resemble each other in several respects. If the leading features of the accounts differ, however, they should not be understood to be reports of the same event. Thus apparent divergency of order may in fact indicate different events with differing details at certain crucial points. The fact that the gospels do not always give their material, whether of word or event, in the same order is a problem only if it is assumed that they must follow a strict and uniform chronological sequence, or if they categorically state that they will use only a chronological sequence and then proceed to violate it. The latter cannot be shown to be the case, and the former assumption is clearly inappropriate. Although a chronological arrangement might usually be expected to prevail, such is not a necessary condition of good writing. At their own discretion, authors are free to arrange materials according to subject rather than chronological sequence if that better serves their purposes. This freedom that authors may legitimately exercise creates many variations of order in the gospel. This, of course, causes problems for the harmonist, who is seeking to establish a chronological sequence. Which evangelist preserves that order? Sometimes indications of time or place give the necessary clue, but not always. This is, however, the problem of the harmonist, not the fault of the author.

Finally, the careful reader of a harmony will eventually notice cases of what appear to be discrepancies in the recounting of events by two or more gospel writers. The reader may discover that a few such instances may in fact be different events, so that no discrepancy, either real or apparent, exists. In most cases this is not the solution, but the solution is not hard to find. It is both possible and probable that when several writers narrate the same occurrence, they will differ at several points in their descriptions of what was said, what happened, and the attendant circumstances.

This fact is confirmed in daily experience. Referees are stationed at different positions on the court or playing field so that they can see different things. Equally calm and intelligent observers stationed on different corners of an intersection will report an automobile accident somewhat differently. Equally competent media reporters at a convention will differ in their accounts of what happened. Why? Each reports from the angle of his or her own vantage point or that of the sources used. Each chooses and narrates material in a manner that is consistent with his or her purposes. What one reports, another might pass over without falsity occurring in either account. In fact, reports that are too closely identical provide grounds for suspecting collusion.

Although gospel accounts might superficially *appear* to conflict with one another, the variety of perspectives and selectivity of reporting they exhibit are themselves marks of accuracy and reliability. In such instances the contradictions are *apparent*, not *real*. Careful analysis will generally resolve the apparent conflicts and harmonize the accounts. Even in those cases where clear or persuasive resolution of conflicting descriptions is lacking, one is not forced to the conclusion that the contradictions are real. Just as possibly, not enough information is available to bring to the surface the *real underlying harmony* between *apparently conflicting* accounts.

These considerations do not solve all the problems that comparative study of the gospels in a harmony may raise. They are valid principles, however, assumed to be true and operative in other areas, and they are equally apropos in a study of the gospels. They successfully resolve most of the problems of harmonization. For those matters that have no evident satisfactory solution, it is better to leave the matter unresolved than to resort to strained and artificial exegesis of the text. Textual corruption in copying manuscripts is a possibility, but this is a plea easily abused. The student believing in the inspiration of Scripture is not obligated to find a solution to every difficulty therein. In view of the repeatedly established integrity of the gospels, is it not presumptuous for anyone to claim sufficient knowledge to conclude that the gospels are in fact contradictory? Historical accounts of all kinds are selective in the material they include; such is an inescapable necessity. The gospel writers did not write with the idea in mind that one day someone would put together a harmony. Their purposes were much different, although we have no credible reason to doubt their reliability in reporting history. Had they wanted to produce accounts more easily harmonized, they could have done so and made the present task much easier. But that would have diverted them from the direction in which the Spirit led them and radically changed the literary character of the gospels. In the process their character as gospels, four independent accounts of the good news, would have been rendered ineffective.

Selected Reading List
Archer, Gleason. *Encyclopedia of Bible Difficulties.* Grand Rapids: Zondervan, 1982. Pp. 316–76.
Stein, Robert H. *Difficult Passages in the Gospels.* Grand Rapids: Baker, 1984.

ESSAY 8

The Languages Jesus Spoke

The language milieu of first-century Palestine has more than a passing interest for the reader of the gospels. It involves the question of what languages Jesus spoke and indirectly may have implications for one's view of the origin and integrity of the gospels as historical documents. For instance, on the assumption that the language exclusively, or at least primarily, spoken by Jesus was Aramaic, it has been commonplace to argue that the closer the language and style of the gospels to the language and style of Aramaic, the greater the presumption for authenticity. Conversely, it has often been argued that the absence of Semitisms creates a presumption against authenticity.

What has been the state of the debate? Almost certainly Latin was not in common use in Palestine, for conquest by the Roman armies had not involved conquest by the Latin language. Stemming from Alexander the Great's conquests in the fourth century B.C. and the subsequent Hellenistic movement, Greek had already been established as the *lingua franca*, and the conquests of Rome made no significant change. What was the use of Greek in Palestine in the time of Christ? Was it a language of culture and commerce for an elite few, or was it also used by the common people? And if it was used by more than the elite, how extensive was that use? Or was Aramaic the language of almost universal usage by the masses? A view commonly held since the Middle Ages is that beginning with the Babylonian exile, Hebrew gradually ceased to exist as a living language and that among Jewish people Aramaic became the language of everyday discourse. But did Hebrew really cease to be a living language; did it come to be only the religious vernacular of Jewish scholars? Advocates for the dominance of any of these three languages in Palestine have not been lacking, and cogent arguments have been made for the common usage of *all three* languages among Jews in first-century Palestine.

Perhaps this in itself should have alerted the advocates of the different viewpoints to the possibility that all three languages were in fact in common use. Robert H. Gundry has persuasively argued that this was the situation, and his work has been supplemented by that of Philip Edgcumbe Hughes.

Recently discovered archaeological data have done much to resolve the problem. Ossuaries, receptacles in which the bones of the dead were placed, often have writing on them. It is to be expected that in the presence of death the languages used would be those in which people customarily thought and spoke. Gundry briefly surveys ossuary finds in Palestine from the period in question and concludes that all three languages appear on them in roughly equal proportions.

This evidence for the currency of all three languages is further strengthened by discoveries coming from excavations in caves around the Dead Sea. In his two expeditions to the "Cave of Letters," Yigael Yadin and his associates unearthed some fifteen letters and more than forty other papyrus documents such as contracts and receipts. These date from the last years of the first century to the time of Bar Kokhba's revolt in A.D. 132–135. The cave appears to have been the hiding place of Bar Kokhba and his guerrilla band, and the documents are apparently representative of their routine correspondence on everyday and military matters. All three languages—Greek, Hebrew, and Aramaic—are represented in both the correspondence and miscellaneous documents. These men were not academicians. That they understood and used these languages strongly suggests their use among the people of Palestine generally. It appears that Hebrew was not confined to the scholars of Judea, and that Greek was not merely the language of commerce and culture. Apparently both were in common usage along with Aramaic, and therefore Jesus might easily have used any one of the three.

Impartial examination of the gospels seems to confirm that this was indeed the language environment of Jesus' day. Based on extensive research in Old Testament quotation material shared by Matthew and the other synoptic writers, Robert Gundry concludes that the modes of citation in these quotations reflects the trilingual situation evidenced in the archaeological data. The presence of Semitisms in the Greek of the gospels does not necessarily indicate that a Semitic language (Aramaic or Hebrew) was used exclusively in first-century Palestine. In polylingual areas, languages tend to interpenetrate one another in their vocabulary and manner of expression; the Septuagint, for example, is full of Semitic forms of expression. This widespread polylingualism would have influenced powerfully the type of Greek spoken in Palestine. The fact that Greek had been imported into an originally Semitic language milieu also gives reason to expect that the Greek spoken there reflected Semitic idiom and thought patterns.

But the gospels and Acts offer more positive evidence for the common currency of Greek in Christ's day and among those whom he taught. Two of the twelve disciples, Andrew and Philip, had Greek names. John 12:20–23 strongly suggest that Philip, Andrew, and Jesus understood and spoke Greek. Peter, the foremost among the twelve, bears not only Hebrew and Aramaic names (Simon and Cephas) but also is referred to by his Greek name (Peter). It is also likely that this same Peter spoke Greek to Cornelius's household in Acts 10 and wrote in Greek the two letters bearing his name. That a Galilean fisherman would have a Greek name and speak and write Greek testifies to the fact that those with little formal education were competent in that language as well. In the Greek text of John 21 Jesus uses two different Greek words for *love* and for *taking care of* the flock, and Peter uses two different words for *know*. None of these pairs, however, can be reproduced in Hebrew or Aramaic; this was apparently a conversation originally carried on in Greek. Also, the play on the Greek words *petra* and *petros* in Matthew 16:18 cannot be reproduced in Hebrew or Aramaic and is best explained as occurring in a discussion originally carried on in Greek. In all likelihood, Jesus' conversations with the Syrophoenician woman, the Roman centurion, and Pilate were in Greek. Stephen (Acts 7) and James (Acts 15) quote from the Septuagint, thus giving evidence of their facility in the Greek language.

That Aramaic was a language in popular usage in first-century Palestine is so clear from both biblical and extrabiblical sources that it is unnecessary to argue the point. Indeed, some have found the evidence so compelling they have argued that the language of the Jewish people in all districts of Palestine had become Aramaic long before the time of Christ. Semitic forms of expression and thought patterns in the gospels were cited as general evidence; more specific evidence was found in what were thought to be a large number of Aramaic terms and names in the gospels. Aramaic as the only language for common discourse was commonly held to be so firmly established that Josephus's references, the biblical references (John 19:20; Acts 21:40; 22:2; 26:14), and the patristic references to the Hebrew language were taken as really referring to Aramaic.

The obvious evidences of an Aramaic background for the gospels do not establish the exclusive use of Aramaic among the people of the land. In addition, much recent research has challenged the opinion that the transliterated Aramaic terms in the Greek text of the gospels are really Aramaic (see, for example, Matt. 27:46; Mark 5:41; 7:34; 14:36; 15:34). It is now argued that at least some of these transliterations are really Hebrew, and that when Josephus, the biblical writers, or the church Fathers refer to the Hebrew language, they do mean Hebrew. This is further confirmed by linguistic evidence that the Hebrew used by Jewish scholars was not a dead language. Instead it bears the earmarks of a typical vernacular language: new words are coined, it has a vocabulary that covers all of daily experience, and it is simple and direct. In rabbinic literature, Hebrew is used in conversations, and the subject matter is not confined to scholarly questions but includes matters of everyday life. Also, a number of Qumran documents are written in Hebrew. Again, subject matter is not confined to scholarly pursuits, and evidence suggests that the common person at Qumran understood it. Some have argued that one should not expect Aramaic to have so quickly and completely replaced Hebrew as the language of the common people. Aramaic initially was spoken in the commercial or governmental levels of Jewish society. Only gradually did it filter down to become the spoken and written language of the lower-class, ill-educated community. Hebrew long remained the language of the common people; the final blow to it as a spoken language came from the wars of A.D. 132–135, when the Jewish revolutionaries were crushingly defeated.

Apparently, then, Greek, Hebrew, and Aramaic were all commonly spoken and understood among the Palestinian Jews of Jesus' day. To determine precise proportions and use is not possible, and perhaps one language tended to predominate in one area more than the others. But it was a mixed language milieu. Almost certainly Jesus spoke in all three languages, and evidences for this exist in the gospels themselves.

Selected Reading List

Gundry, Robert H. "The Language Milieu of First-Century Palestine," *Journal of Biblical Literature* 83 (1964): 404–8.
Hughes, Philip Edgcumbe. "The Languages Spoken by Jesus." In *New Dimensions in New Testament Study*, edited by Richard N. Longenecker and Merrill C. Tenney, 125–43. Grand Rapids: Zondervan, 1974.

ESSAY 9

The Genealogies in Matthew and Luke
(Matt. 1:1–17; Luke 3:23b–38)

Both Matthew and Luke give a genealogical list for the descent of Jesus. When these are compared, differences and difficulties appear immediately. The most obvious difference is that Matthew's list begins with Abraham and descends to Jesus, whereas Luke's list begins with Jesus and ascends to Adam, the son of God. This in itself presents no difficulty; but when one of the lists is put in inverse order for convenience in comparing, it is quite another matter. Of course only Luke gives the generations from Adam to Abraham, and the lists of progenitors between Abraham and David as given by Matthew and Luke are nearly identical. No problem comes until we compare the two versions of the succession from David to Jesus:

Matthew's list	Luke's list (in inverse order)
David	David
Solomon	Nathan
Rehoboam	Mattatha
Abijah	Menna
Asa	Melea
Jehoshaphat	Eliakim
Jehoram	Jonam
Uzziah	Joseph
Jotham	Judah
Ahaz	Simeon
Hezekiah	Levi
Manasseh	Matthat
Amon	Jorim
Josiah	Eliezer
Jeconiah	Joshua
Shealtiel	Er
Zerubbabel	Elmadam
Abiud	Cosam
Eliakim	Addi
Azor	Melki
Zadok	Neri
Akim	Shealtiel
Eliud	Zerubbabel
Eleazar	Rhesa
Matthan	Joanan
Jacob	Joda

304

<pre>
Joseph (husband of Mary)   Josech
              Jesus   Semein
                                   Mattathias
                                   Maath
                                   Naggai
                                   Esli
                                   Nahum
                                   Amos
                                   Mattathias
                                   Joseph
                                   Jannai
                                   Melki
                                   Levi
                                   Matthat
                                   Heli
                                   Joseph
                                   Jesus ("the son, so it was
                                            thought, of Joseph")
</pre>

For students of a harmony of the gospels the above comparison presents two problems: the difference in the number of generations and the dissimilarity of names. How can the two genealogies be harmonized without sacrificing the historical integrity of either?

Recent critical studies have generally regarded past attempts at harmonization as just so much frustrated effort. Both H. C. Waetjen and M. D. Johnson summarily dismiss past efforts to preserve full historical authenticity as unconvincing, strained, and beside the point. In any event, it is said, historicity will not affect significantly the reader's existential response or understanding of New Testament theology. Instead, each genealogy must be understood individually and theologically in relation to the gospel in which it appears and the thought of the evangelist that it is intended to express. The content and structure of each supposedly is arbitrary to suit the evangelist's purpose. What those specific purposes were need not occupy our attention here, for the analyses of scholars such as Waetjen and Johnson follow the assumptions and methodology of much recent New Testament critical scholarship. Their analyses will be no better than their assumptions and methodology. And the fundamental question of the historical reliability of the genealogies cannot be bypassed in so cavalier a fashion. Consequently we turn our attention to the problems of harmonizing the two lists of Jesus' ancestral descent.

The first problem, the difference in the number of generations, is the easier to resolve. Although it is true that Matthew lists twenty-six progenitors between David and Jesus, compared with Luke's forty, two factors must be kept in mind. First, it is not uncommon for the generations in one line of descent to increase more rapidly than in another. Second, and more important, in Jewish thinking *son* might mean "grandson," or, even more generally, "descendant" (as "Jesus Christ, the son of David, the son of Abraham," Matt. 1:1). Similarly, *begat* (rendered by the pattern " 'X' [was] the father of 'Y' " in the New International Version, Matt. 1:2–16) does not necessarily mean "was the actual (that is, immediate) father of" but instead may simply indicate real descent. Just the fact that Matthew casts his list in the form of three groups of fourteen generations suggests this was a convenient though arbitrary arrangement from which some generations may have been omitted. In fact, it can be shown that Matthew's list has omissions (cf. 2 Kings 8:24; 1 Chron. 3:11; 2 Chron. 22:1, 11; 24:27; 2 Kings 23:34; 24:6). Omission of generations in biblical genealogies is not unique to this case, and Jews are known to have done this freely. The purpose of a genealogy was not to account for every generation, but to establish the fact of an undoubted succession, including especially the more prominent ancestors.

The second problem is more difficult to resolve. In the two lists of succession, between David and Joseph all the names are different except Shealtiel and Zerubbabel (connected in the list by dotted lines). How is this to be accounted for? Some exegetes unnecessarily despair of finding an adequate solution or even suggest the lists are in error. Others see them as redactional devices by which the writers sought to fulfill their theological purposes in writing (see essay 5). But among the attempts to harmonize the genealogies with each other, four proposals deserve consideration.

1. Julius Africanus (d. A.D. 240) suggested that Matthew gives the genealogy of Joseph through his actual father, Jacob, but Luke gives Joseph's genealogy through his legal father, Heli. In this view, Heli died childless. His half-brother, Jacob, who had the same mother but a different father, married Heli's widow and by her had Joseph. Known as levirate marriage, this action meant that physically Joseph was the son of Jacob and legally the son of Heli. Jacob was the descendant of David through David's son Solomon, and Heli was the descendant of David through David's son Nathan. Thus, by both legal and physical lineage Joseph had a rightful claim to the Davidic throne and so would his legal (but not physical) son Jesus. Matthew gives Joseph's physical lineage, Luke his legal lineage.

2. In his classic work, *The Virgin Birth of Christ*, J. Gresham Machen argued for the view that Matthew gives the legal descent of Joseph whereas for the most part (he does allow for levirate marriage or transfer of lineage to a collateral line in Joseph's physical line), Luke gives the physical descent. Although the physical and legal lines are reversed, the purpose is still to establish Joseph's rightful claim to the Davidic throne. This view holds that Solomon's line failed in Jeconiah (Jehoiachin) (Jer. 22:30). But when the kingly line through

Solomon became extinct, the living member of the collateral line of Nathan (Shealtiel, Matt. 1:12, cf. Luke 3:27) inherited the title to the throne. Thus, Machen asserts, Matthew is tracing the legal heirship to the throne from David, through Solomon, through Jeconiah, with transfer to a collateral line at that point. Luke traces the physical descent (with a possibility of jumps to a collateral line or levirate marriages) to David through Nathan. Matthew starts with the question, Who is the heir to David's throne? Luke starts with the question, Who is Joseph's father?

A large number of scholars have preferred some form of this view, including A. Hervey, Theodor Zahn, Vincent Taylor, and Brooke F. Westcott.

3. A third view suggests that the apparent conflict between the two genealogies of Joseph results from mistakenly assuming Luke is intending to give Joseph's genealogy. Instead it should be understood as Mary's genealogy. Joseph's name stands in for Mary's by virtue of the fact that he had become son or heir of Heli (Mary's father) by his marriage to her. This view holds that Heli died with no sons, and that Mary became his heiress (Num. 27:1–11; 36:1–12). The first of these passages seems to provide for the preservation of the name of the man who dies with daughters but no sons. In the case of Heli and his daughter, Mary, this could have been accomplished by Joseph's becoming identified with Mary's family. Joseph would be included in the family genealogy, although the genealogy is really Mary's. Thus the genealogies of Matthew and Luke diverge from David on because Matthew traces the Davidic descent of Joseph, and Luke the Davidic descent of Mary (with Joseph's name standing in).

Each of the three proposals discussed thus far would resolve the apparent conflict between the genealogies in Matthew and Luke. Each also appears to be within the realm of reasonable possibility. It must be pointed out that all three, however, rely upon conjecture that is possible but far from certain. In the first two views one must appeal to levirate marriages or collateral lines to resolve difficulties. The third view rests on the conjecture that Joseph takes Mary's place in the genealogy. In addition, the first must explain why Luke rather than Matthew is interested in the legal lineage of Joseph. Both the first and second views must explain why Luke, in light of his apparent interest in and close association with Mary, would be concerned with Joseph's genealogy at all. Interested as he was in Jesus' humanity, birth, and childhood, why would Luke give the genealogy of the man who was Jesus' legal but not physical father? These questions are not unanswerable, but they do leave the field open for a view less dependent on conjecture, one that does not raise these questions.

4. There is such a view. Like the third proposed solution, this fourth view understands the genealogy in Luke really to be Mary's, but for different reasons. Here Heli is understood to be the progenitor of Mary, not of Joseph. Joseph is not properly part of the genealogy, and is mentioned only parenthetically. Luke 3:23 should then read, "Jesus . . . was the son (so it was thought, of Joseph) of Heli." The support for this view is impressive.

   a. Placing the phrase "so it was thought, of Joseph" in parentheses, and thus in effect removing it from the genealogy, is grammatically justified. In the Greek text Joseph's name occurs without the Greek definite article prefixed; every other name in the series has the article. By this device Joseph's name is shown to be not properly a part of the genealogy. Jesus was only thought to be his son. This would make Jesus the son (that is, grandson or descendant) of Heli, Mary's progenitor, and is consistent with Luke's account of Jesus' conception, which makes clear that Joseph was not his physical father (Luke 1:26–38).

   b. This view allows the most natural meaning of *begat* to stand. In other words, *begat* refers to actual physical descent rather than to jumps to collateral lines.

   c. Matthew's interest in Jesus' relation to the Old Testament and the Messianic kingdom makes it appropriate that he give Joseph's real descent from David through Solomon—a descent that is also Jesus' legal descent—and thus gives him legal claim to the Davidic throne.

   d. Because Luke emphasizes the humanity of Jesus, his solidarity with the human race, and the universality of salvation, it is fitting that Luke show his humanity by recording his human descent through his human parent, Mary. His pedigree is then traced back to Adam.

   e. The objection that Mary's name is not in Luke's version needs only the reply that women were rarely included in Jewish genealogies; though giving her descent, Luke conforms to custom by not mentioning her by name. The objection that Jews never gave the genealogy of women is met by the answer that this is a unique case; Luke is talking about a virgin birth. How else could the physical descent of one who had no human father be traced? Furthermore, Luke has already shown a creative departure from customary genealogical lists by starting with Jesus and ascending up the list of ancestors rather than starting at some point in the past and descending to Jesus.

   f. This view allows easy resolution of the difficulties surrounding Jeconiah (Matt. 1:11), Joseph's ancestor and David's descendant through Solomon. In 2 Sam. 7:12–17 the perpetuity of the Davidic kingdom through Solomon (vv. 12–13) is unconditionally promised. Jeconiah (Jehoiachin) later was the royal representative of that line of descent for which eternal perpetuity had been promised. Yet for his gross sin (2 Chron. 24:8–9), Jeconiah was to be recorded as if childless, and no descendant of his would prosper on the Davidic throne (Jer. 22:30). This poses a dilemma. It is Jeconiah through whom the Solomonic descent and legal right to the throne properly should be traced. Solomon's throne had already been unconditionally promised eternal perpetuity. Yet Jeconiah will have no physical descendants who will prosper on that throne. How may both the divine promise and the curse be fulfilled?

First, notice that Jeremiah's account neither indicates Jeconiah would have no seed, nor does it say Jeconiah's line has had its legal claim to the throne removed by his sin. The legal claim to the throne remains with Jeconiah's line, and Matthew records that descent down to Joseph. In 1:16, Matthew preserves the virgin birth of Jesus and at the same time makes clear that Jesus does not come under the curse upon Jeconiah. He breaks the pattern and carefully avoids saying that Joseph (a descendant of Jeconiah) begat Jesus. Instead he refers to "Joseph, the husband of Mary, of whom was born Jesus." In the English translation the antecedent of "whom" is ambiguous. But in the Greek text, "whom" is feminine singular in form and can refer only to Mary who was not a descendant of Jeconiah. As to human parentage, Jesus was born of Mary alone, though Joseph was his legal father. As Jesus' legal father, Joseph's legal claim passed to Jesus. But because Jesus was not actually Jeconiah's seed, although of actual Davidic descent through Mary, descendant of Nathan, Jesus escaped the curse on Jeconiah's seed pronounced in Jeremiah 22:30. Thus the problem is resolved.

What we have then are two different genealogies of two people. Probably even the Shealtiel and Zerubbabel of Matthew and Luke are different persons. This view does not depend on conjecture, rests on evidence within the texts themselves, fits the purposes of the evangelists, and easily resolves the problem surrounding Jeconiah. Of this view L. M. Sweet appropriately wrote, "Its simplicity and felicitous adjustment to the whole complex situation is precisely its recommendation."

Although it is not, strictly speaking, a harmonistic problem, one other difficulty of lesser significance found in Matthew's record of Joseph's genealogy needs discussion here. In 1:17, Matthew divides the generations from Abraham to Christ into three groups of fourteen generations: from Abraham to David, from David to the deportation to Babylon, and from the deportation to Christ. In part, this was likely a device used by Matthew to aid memory; it does not imply that he mentioned every progenitor. At least five names are omitted: Ahaziah, Joash, Amaziah, Jehoiakim, and Eliakim. As previously stated, this procedure was not unusual and presents no real problem.

With three groups of fourteen generations, however, one does expect to find forty-two different names. But there are only forty-one. Although one set has only thirteen different names, the problem is only apparent. Matthew does not speak of forty-two different names but of three groups of fourteen generations, which he divides for himself. David's name concludes the first set and stands first in the second set (cf. 1:17). In other words, David is counted twice and is thus given special prominence in the genealogy that shows Jesus' Davidic throne rights through his legal father, Joseph. Another means used for increasing the focus on David is the title assigned to him in Matthew 1:6. He is called King David, and is the only person in the genealogy to whom a title is given. Possibly the Davidic emphasis is even further enhanced by the number 14. The sum of the numerical value of the Hebrew letters in the name *David* is 14. To the modern reader this might seem overly subtle, but it was not necessarily so in ancient Semitic thought. The numerical value of David's name, however, is not necessary to the resolution of this problem. Again, alleged discrepancies between and in the genealogical lists of Matthew and Luke are shown to be more apparent than real. Reasonable solutions to the problems exist and even throw further light on the text.

Selected Reading List

Johnson, Marshall D. *The Purpose of the Biblical Genealogies: With Special Reference to the Setting of the Genealogies of Jesus.* Cambridge: Cambridge University Press, 1969. Pp. 139–256.

Machen, J. Gresham. *The Virgin Birth of Christ.* New York: Harper, 1930.

The International Standard Bible Encyclopedia, s.v. "The Genealogy of Jesus Christ," by L. M. Sweet.

Waetjen, Herman C. "The Genealogy as the Key to the Gospel according to Matthew," *Journal of Biblical Literature* 95 (1976): 205–30.

The Day and Year of Christ's Crucifixion

Determining the day of the week, the date of the month, and the year of Christ's crucifixion is of greatest importance in settling upon a broad chronology of the life of Christ. For clarity's sake these three issues will be discussed in this article before proceeding to a study of other chronological aspects of the gospels that relate to the life of Christ. The three will be considered in the above order and discussed separately from each other insofar as is possible.

THE DAY OF THE WEEK

The Christian church has traditionally looked upon Friday as the day on which Jesus died. No strong reason has been advanced for abandoning this understanding. The most frequent objections to a Friday crucifixion arise from a misunderstanding that the "three days and three nights" found in Matthew 12:40 requires Jesus to have been in the tomb for three full, twenty-four-hour days. With this assumption, by counting backward from Sunday some settle upon Thursday or Wednesday as the day of crucifixion.

Such a conclusion, however, contradicts the explicit statement of all four gospels that Jesus was crucified on the day called preparation (*paraskeuē*) (Matt. 27:62; Mark 15:42; Luke 23:54; John 19:14, 31, 42), a technical designation among the Jews for the day of the week that corresponds to our Friday. Such a contradictory situation vanishes when it is observed that "three days and three nights," rightly understood, can encompass anything from just over twenty-four hours to up to seventy-two hours.

Jesus compared himself to Jonah in predicting a stay of "three days and three nights in the heart of the earth" (Matt. 12:40). In this statement he chose one of several possible ways to say the same thing. It was common practice among the Jews to refer to a fractional part of a day or a night as one day and one night (cf. Gen. 42:17–18; 1 Sam. 30:12–13; 1 Kings 20:29; 2 Chron. 10:5, 12; Esther 4:16; 5:1). Hence "three days and three nights" does not necessitate three twenty-four-hour days between Christ's crucifixion and resurrection but was just another way of saying he was raised on "the third day" (Matt. 16:21; 17:23; 20:19; 27:64; Luke 9:22; 18:33; 24:7, 21, 46; Acts 10:40; 1 Cor. 15:4) or after "three days"

(Matt. 26:61; 27:40, 63; Mark 8:31; 9:31; 10:34; 14:58; 15:29; John 2:19–20).

In light of the gospel accounts, then, it can be safely concluded that Jesus died at 3:00 P.M. on a Friday and was placed in the tomb later that same day (that is, before sundown). He remained there part of Friday (until sundown), all of the next day (from sundown Friday until sundown Saturday), and part of the third day (from sundown Saturday until early Sunday morning). The system of reckoning each day from sunset to sunset was followed by the Sadducees in Jerusalem. Another system of reckoning from sunrise to sunrise was also in vogue, but the sunset-to-sunset scheme was the more officially recognized of the two (cf. pp. 312–13 of this essay).

THE DATE OF THE MONTH

It is also of great moment to ascertain on which date of the Jewish calendar Christ was crucified. Was it on the fourteenth or the fifteenth of Nisan? The gospel of John gives an initial impression that it was the fourteenth, but the synoptic gospels appear to say the fifteenth. Stated another way, John seems to indicate that the Last Supper the night before the crucifixion was not a Passover meal, but the synoptic writers say it was.

John 13:1 says the supper the night preceding Jesus' crucifixion was "just before the Passover Feast." The gospel of John also says that Jesus' trial was on "the day of preparation of Passover week" (John 19:14). John 18:28 says that Jesus' Jewish accusers had not yet eaten the Passover. Also, in John 13:29 the misimpression of the other disciples about the nature of Judas' mission seems to be based on their anticipation of the Passover feast's coming on the next day. Because the Passover was normally eaten on the evening marking the end of the fourteenth and the beginning of the fifteenth (Lev. 23:5), it appears that John understands Jesus' death to have come on the fourteenth of Nisan.

On the other side of the question, Matthew, Mark, and Luke are specific in placing the Last Supper after sundown, ending the fourteenth and beginning the fifteenth of the month (Matt. 26:17–20; Mark 14:12–17; Luke 22:7–16). They refer to the sacrifice of the lambs, which occurred on the fourteenth, and the meal following it that same evening.

Different attempts have been made to resolve this apparent contradiction. Some have proposed that the synoptic gospels are right and John is wrong, and others have suggested the opposite. Another proposal has been to say both versions are correct and to strain the interpretation of one account to make it harmonize with the other.

The best approach to the issue is to accept the accuracy of both methods of dating the crucifixion. This can be done because the Jews of Jesus' day apparently recognized two methods of reckoning dates. In addition to the better-known system that regarded each new day as starting at sundown, the policy of some was to reckon from sunrise to sunrise. Each of these customs finds support from the Old Testament, the former in such places as Genesis 1:5 and Exodus 12:18 and the latter in Genesis 8:22 and 1 Samuel 19:11.

The system of reckoning used by Jesus and his disciples and described by Matthew, Mark, and Luke was from sunrise to sunrise. John describes the events from the perspective of a sunset-to-sunset reckoning because this system enjoyed more of an official recognition (see earlier discussion entitled "The Day of the Week" in this essay). Indications are that this difference in systems was also a point of disagreement between the Pharisees (sunrise to sunrise) and the Sadducees (sunset to sunset).

The synoptic accounts therefore see Jesus as eating a Passover meal the evening before his crucifixion. For those who followed the sunrise-to-sunrise reckoning, the Passover lambs had been slain a few hours earlier, in the afternoon. For them the slaughter took place on the fourteenth of Nisan, as did the Passover meal. The fifteenth did not begin until the next morning, Friday, at about six.

The Johannine description, however, views the events from the standpoint of the Sadducees, who controlled the temple. Jesus was crucified at the normal time of killing the Passover lambs, that is, the afternoon of Nisan 14. Nisan 14 had begun at sunset on Thursday and would not end until sunset on Friday. This was the normal time for the lambs to be slain, but the temple authorities had apparently compromised with those who followed the other calendar and allowed them to slay the lambs on Thursday afternoon. Otherwise, the facilities could not have accommodated the large number of people with their sacrifices who came to the Passover each year. This difference explains why Jesus' accusers had not yet eaten the Passover (John 18:28). They were about to do it Friday evening, Nisan 15, which began at sunset.

If the preceding solution is correct (and it is impossible to say dogmatically that it is, but it does seem to handle all the data more effectively than other proposals), then Jesus was crucified on Nisan 15 according to the sunrise-to-sunrise reckoning and on Nisan 14 according to the sunset-to-sunset method.

THE YEAR

The field of astronomy offers the most help in fixing the year of Christ's crucifixion. The Jewish calendar was based on lunar months. Hence by noting the dates of the new moons' appearances in the general period of Jesus' death, it is possible to determine in which years Nisan 14 (according to the sunset-to-sunset reckoning) fell between Thursday at sundown and Friday at sundown.

It is known that Jesus was crucified sometime between A.D. 26 and

A.D. 36, because this was the period of Pontius Pilate's governorship (cf. John 19:15–16). Complex astronomical calculations reveal that during this period Nisan 14 fell on Friday twice, in A.D. 30 and in A.D. 33.

Deciding between 30 and 33 is no easy matter. To a large degree the issue hinges upon chronological features related to the life of Christ as a whole. Such matters as the time of Christ's birth, what Luke means by "the fifteenth year of the reign of Tiberius Caesar" (Luke 3:1–2) and "about thirty years old" (Luke 3:23), what John means by "forty-six years to build this temple" (John 2:20), and other related matters must be analyzed before reaching a final decision as to the year of the crucifixion. The next essay will undertake this investigation.

Selected Reading List
Hoehner, Harold W. *Chronological Aspects of the Life of Christ.* Grand Rapids: Zondervan, 1977. Pp. 65–114.

Morris, Leon. *The Gospel According to John.* The New International Commentary on the New Testament. Grand Rapids: Eerdmans, 1971. Pp. 774–86.

Ogg, George. *The Chronology of the Public Ministry of Jesus.* Cambridge: Cambridge University Press, 1940. Pp. 203–85.

_____. "Chronology of the New Testament." In *Peake's Commentary on the Bible.* New York: Nelson, 1962. Pp. 729–30.

Chronology of the Life of Christ

Much uncertainty pervades a study of the chronology of Christ's life. It is generally assumed that he was born in about A.D. 1 and died in about A.D. 30. Yet these are only generalizations. Our Gregorian calendar, which sought to use his birth as its reference point, erred at that very point when it was initially established in A.D. 525. Anno Domini (A.D.) means "in the year of the Lord," but information that has come to light subsequently has shown that Jesus was born prior to A.D. 1.

Though complete certainty regarding dates is impossible, much light can be shed on the subject of when Jesus lived. Certain selected happenings and statements will be discussed to give more detailed data.

THE DEATH OF HEROD THE GREAT

According to Matthew 2:1 and Luke 1:5, Herod the Great was still reigning as king over the Jews at the time of Jesus' birth. It is now known from other sources that Herod's death came in 4 B.C., soon after Nisan 1 of that year. Jesus must have been born within the two years prior to that, because Herod after ascertaining the time of the star's appearance (Matt. 2:7) gave orders to execute all the male children who were two years old and younger (Matt. 2:16). Hence Jesus must have been born between 6 B.C. and 4 B.C.

THE CENSUS UNDER AUGUSTUS CAESAR

Luke 2:1–2 places the birth of Christ within the reign of the Roman emperor Augustus Caesar and also probably synchronizes it with Quirinius's governorship in Syria, though some understand Luke to say that the census came before this governorship. Augustus during his reign (30 B.C.–A.D. 14) established a system of census taking, and Luke refers to it in Luke 2:1. The particular census that brought Joseph and Mary to Bethlehem when Jesus was born was the first of these while Quirinius was governor (cf. Acts 5:37 for a reference to what was probably the second, which came in A.D. 6).

Evidence has surfaced to show that a census was taken every fourteen years. By counting back from those taken in neighboring Egypt, one discovers that a census must have been scheduled in 8 B.C. It is quite possible that turbulent conditions in Palestine and Syria at the time may have delayed the census for a couple of years.

Quirinius is known to have been governor of Syria in A.D. 6 at the time of a census, but this is about ten years too late for the birth of Jesus. Evidence from inscriptions, however, has shown the probability that Quirinius was involved in the Syrian government as joint ruler at an earlier time, about 8 B.C. His rule may well have extended until 6 B.C., when the governorship of Sentius Saturnius, alongside whom he ruled, ended.

The Fifteenth Year of Tiberius Caesar

In Luke 3:1 the fifteenth year of the reign of Tiberius Caesar is given as the date when John the Baptist began his public ministry. Because John's ministry began a short time before Jesus', this chronological note is helpful in setting time limits for Jesus' ministry.

Exact placement of this fifteenth year is attended with a great deal of difficulty, however, because Tiberius's rule had two beginnings. He became joint ruler with Augustus, his father, at some time before his father's death, but at Augustus's death in A.D. 14 he became sole ruler of the empire. If Luke is using an earlier date, John's prophetic ministry was probably initiated some time in A.D. 26 or A.D. 27. If the later date is meant, the fifteenth year was probably A.D. 28 or A.D. 29.

The latter of these two possibilities looks more probable when compared with the customary modes of dating practiced in ancient times, but the former finds more favor in light of biblical data yet to be discussed as this study proceeds. Specifically, A.D. 26 or A.D. 27 agrees better with the statement of Luke regarding Jesus' age at the outset of his ministry.

"About Thirty Years Old"

Luke says that Jesus at the beginning of his ministry was "about thirty years old" (Luke 3:23). Although this expression may denote an age anywhere from twenty-eight through thirty-two, customs of the times and other details of Jesus' life seem to indicate that Jesus was within one year of his thirtieth birthday when he began his ministry. Viewing this as a closer definition of Jesus' age also accords better with Luke's interest in furnishing precise chronological details (cf. Luke 1:5; 2:1–2; 3:1–2).

If his birth is placed in 6 B.C., he reached the age of thirty sometime in A.D. 25. If in 5 B.C., he was thirty years old sometime in the year A.D. 26. The latter date is more probable, because Jesus' crucifixion cannot be placed earlier than A.D. 30, as shown in the essay, "The Day and Year of Christ's Crucifixion" (pp. 311–14).

It is difficult to place the beginning of Jesus' ministry any later than A.D. 27, because this would put an intolerable strain on Luke's statement about his age. Furthermore, unless Jesus' ministry was only one or two years in duration, he could not have completed it by A.D. 30. Also, unless his ministry was more extensive than commonly thought—about four or five years—it could not have lasted until A.D. 33, the other possible date discussed in essay 10.

FORTY-SIX YEARS OF TEMPLE REMODELING

In John 2:20 Jesus' antagonists refer to a building project or, more correctly, remodeling project that had been initiated by Herod the Great forty-six years earlier. This consisted of the renovation of Zerubbabel's temple. According to secular history, Herod initiated the work sometime in 20 B.C. or 19 B.C. This statement was addressed to Jesus at the first Passover after he began his public ministry. The "forty-six years" therefore furnishes another means for identifying the year when his ministry began.

This extensive project had not been completed when Herod died in 4 B.C. In fact, it was still in progress when the Jews uttered the words of John 2:20. Completion of it did not come until A.D. 64.

Though some disagreement has arisen regarding the word translated *temple* and the tense of the verb for *build*, the more obvious meaning and the one that satisfies the context better is that the Jews were pointing to how long the project had taken up to that point in contrast with the three days in which Jesus said he could build the temple (John 2:19).

By counting forty-six years from 20 B.C. or 19 B.C., one arrives at A.D. 26 or A.D. 27. Hence the first Passover of Jesus' ministry must have been in the spring of A.D. 27.

THE LENGTH OF JESUS' MINISTRY

A date having been established for the beginning of Christ's ministry, the length of that ministry must be determined before a specific date for his crucifixion can be set.

Some have argued for a one-year ministry because the first three gospels mention only one Passover during his ministry, the one when he was crucified (Matt. 26:17–20; Mark 14:12–17; Luke 22:7–16). The gospel of John, however, contradicts this theory. John specifically names three Passovers in which Jesus was involved after he began public ministry (John 2:13; 6:4; 11:55).

Others favor a ministry of a little more than two years. They take the three Passovers in John's gospel as opening and closing each of the two years. This theory, however, is most often defended on the basis of transposing John 5 and 6. Because no manuscript evidence exists for this rearrangement, the two-year theory is weak.

Attempts to prove a ministry of a little more than four years have usually rested on the assumption of two Passovers not mentioned by John. One of these additional Passovers comes between John 4:35, which indicates the time is winter after the Passover of John 2:13, and John 5:1, which probably refers to the Feast of Tabernacles the following fall. To postulate this unmentioned Passover seems to be quite probable. The postulation of the other additional Passover, however, does not rest on good grounds. Some place it before the Passover of John 2:13, and others after the one mentioned in John 6:4. In neither case, however, has convincing evidence been adduced for concluding that there was a fifth Passover.

The most widely held viewpoint is that Jesus' ministry extended a little more than three years. The period of time from Jesus' baptism by John (Matt. 3:1–17; Mark 1:9–11; Luke 3:21–23a) until his first Passover (John 2:13) was several months, which found him in both Galilee and Judea. The first full year of ministry (between Passovers), also spent in Judea and Galilee, was terminated by a Passover, not mentioned in the biblical record, that came a few months after Jesus' statement of John 4:35 and six months before the Feast of Tabernacles mentioned in John 5:1. His second year, most of it spent in Galilee, ended with the Passover of John 6:4. The final year was spent in areas around Galilee, in Judea, and in Perea, and came to its conclusion with the Passover referred to in John 11:55.

The conclusion that Jesus had a ministry of a little more than three years is, then, the one supported by the strongest evidence and the one most free from difficulty.

THE CRUCIFIXION

As shown in the essay "The Day and Year of Christ's Crucifixion" (pp. 311–14), Nisan 14, the day of Passover, fell on Friday only twice between A.D. 26 and A.D. 36. This leaves two possible years for Christ's crucifixion, A.D. 30 or A.D. 33. If conclusions reached earlier in this essay are valid, the former possibility must be chosen as the year in which Jesus was crucified.

CONCLUSIONS

The conclusions of this essay may be summarized in a table into which more probable options from the preceding discussion are incorporated:

6 B.C. or	(late in year) or	birth of Christ
5 B.C.	(early in year)	
4 B.C.	(after Nisan 1)	death of Herod the Great
A.D. 12		beginning of Tiberius Caesar's rule
A.D. 26	(early in year)	beginning of John's ministry
A.D. 26	(middle or late in year)	beginning of Christ's ministry
A.D. 27	(Nisan 14)	first Passover in Christ's ministry

A.D. 28	(Nisan 14)	second Passover in Christ's ministry
A.D. 29	(Nisan 14)	third Passover in Christ's ministry
A.D. 30	(Nisan 14)	crucifixion of Christ

Although not completely free from difficulty, the preceding table of dates appears to provide a solution with stronger cumulative evidence than any other that has been proposed. It enables the student of the gospels to know more precisely when Jesus lived, ministered, and died.

Selected Reading List

Hoehner, Harold W. *Chronological Aspects of the Life of Christ.* Grand Rapids: Zondervan, 1977. Pp. 11–63.

Ogg, George. *The Chronology of the Public Ministry of Jesus.* Cambridge: Cambridge University Press, 1940. Pp. 3–201.

_____. "Chronology of the New Testament." In *Peake's Commentary on the Bible.* New York: Nelson, 1962. Pp. 728–29.

Thompson, W. A. "Chronology of the New Testament." In *The Zondervan Pictorial Encyclopedia of the Bible.* Grand Rapids: Zondervan, 1975. Vol. 1, pp. 816–21.

The Arrest and Trial of Jesus

When the evangelists came to the events that brought Jesus' earthly life to a close, they gave much more information than for the other periods of his life. When taken together, the gospels give a detailed description of Passion Week. Their accounts of Jesus' arrest and trial in particular have long fascinated both Jewish and Christian scholars.

If we assume the evangelists have given us reliable information, events leading up to Jesus' crucifixion apparently took the following course:

1. On Thursday evening of Passion Week, after the journey from the upper room to the Garden of Gethsemane, Judas, Jesus' betrayer, approached Jesus in the darkness of the garden. But Judas was not alone. What is described as a great multitude included representatives of the Sanhedrin, the temple police, and a company or cohort (probably about two hundred) of Roman soldiers. Although Jesus readily identified himself as the one whom they were seeking, Judas betrayed him to his captors with a kiss. With that they took Jesus and arrested him.

   Peter momentarily tried to thwart the arrest by drawing his sword and cutting off the right ear of the high priest's servant. But Jesus rebuked Peter and restored Malchus's ear. After being chastened for his bravado and misguided zeal, Peter, with all the disciples, left Jesus and fled. Peter did return to follow from a distance.
2. Jesus was then taken to Annas, the ex-high priest. In what constitutes the first phase of his Jewish trial, he was briefly questioned by Annas and then sent to Annas' son-in-law, the current high priest, Caiaphas.
3. In Caiaphas's house at least a quorum of the Sanhedrin had been brought together for a night session. This was to be the second Jewish phase of Jesus' trial. Witnesses were called to try to establish charges against Jesus, but no two witnesses could agree, and Jesus by his silence refused to confirm the charges. Finally, after badgering from Caiaphas, Jesus confessed he was the Messiah, the Son of God, the Son of Man. Caiaphas took this to be blasphemy and worthy of death. The assembled council concurred in this judgment, passed sentence upon him, and began to physically abuse him.

4. The third Jewish phase of the trial took place early the next morning. Although the earlier night session may have had only a quorum of the Sanhedrin, the entire council was clearly in attendance this time. The charge and sentence of the previous session were confirmed.
5. Now the trial of Jesus was to enter a new phase. Because the Jews did not have the general authority to administer a sentence of death, Jesus was taken before the Roman governor Pilate for the first Roman phase of the trial. The Sanhedrin presented a threefold charge against Jesus: "subverting our nation," opposing "payment of taxes to Caesar," and claiming "to be Christ, a king" (Luke 23:2).
6. Mention of Galilee led to the second Roman phase of the trial, for much of Jesus' activity had been in Galilee, the jurisdiction of Herod Antipas. Herod happened to be in Jerusalem at the time. Perhaps partly as a means of getting rid of a difficult case and perhaps partly as a means of gaining favor with Herod, Pilate sent Jesus to him. Herod was glad for the opportunity to question Jesus and make sport of him, but he did not adjudicate the matter, sending Jesus back to Pilate.
7. With the case back in Pilate's hands, the trial entered its third Roman phase. Pilate restated the charges that had been brought against Jesus and reaffirmed his own judgment of Jesus' innocence. He observed that Herod also had not found Jesus worthy of death. But Pilate was caught between his own conviction of Jesus' innocence and the rising clamor of the Jewish leadership for his death.

Then Pilate hit upon a scheme by which he thought he could solve the dilemma. He customarily released a prisoner to the Jews at Passover, and a crowd was gathering to demand the annual favor. Pilate decided to let them choose the release of either Jesus or an insurrectionist named Barabbas. Pilate knew that envy was behind the Jewish leadership's hatred for Jesus. Surely the multitudes would choose Jesus over Barabbas, and thus Pilate would be free of the case.

But Pilate had not taken into account the persuasiveness of the chief priests and elders who incited the crowd, or the popularity of Barabbas. Confronted with the choice, the crowd demanded the release of Barabbas and the crucifixion of Jesus. All Pilate's efforts to dissuade them only increased the uproar. When Pilate made a move to release Jesus anyway, the Jews charged that Pilate could not then be Caesar's friend. Such an accusation could have demolished Pilate's political standing. Putting career above conviction, he decided to accede to their demands. Hoping to absolve himself of responsibility for the death of an innocent man, Pilate washed his hands before the multitude and proclaimed his innocence of Jesus' blood. Barabbas was released. Jesus was scourged and delivered to what was the will of the Jews, a Roman crucifixion by Roman soldiers.

Such is the probable reconstruction of events surrounding the arrest and trial of Jesus. But there is a large body of contemporary literature that challenges this reconstruction by assuming the unreliability of the evangelists' accounts. The claim is often made that the tradition the evangelists drew upon was merely the creation of a Christian community having no biographical interest. This tradition, it is said, was adapted by the evangelists for their own purposes of propaganda. Thus from beginning to end the gospels are biased literature. Many of the recent attempts to rescue the "few bits of objective information" embedded in the passion story, and then to reconstruct what may have actually happened, follow the methodology laid down by source critical, form critical, and redaction critical assumptions (see essays 3, 4, and 5). Once the credibility of the gospel record is surrendered, that record becomes subject to the most arbitrary reinterpretation. To illustrate, we cite several recent theories of the arrest and trial.

Haim Cohn, a justice of the Supreme Court of Israel, argues that Jesus appeared before the Jewish authorities in a hearing, not a trial. Their purpose was not to find fault with and convict Jesus; rather, the high priest and court were attempting to find a way to save him.

Arguing that the gospel accounts of the arrest and trial contain incongruities and inconsistencies that prevent us from accepting them at face value, Cohn asserts that in fact the intention of the Jewish leaders was to prevent Jesus' execution by the Romans. Jesus enjoyed the love and affection of many of the people. The court tried to bring about his acquittal, or at least a suspension of sentence on condition of good behavior. But to achieve this, Jesus had to be persuaded not to plead guilty, and reliable witnesses to Jesus' innocence of the insurrection charge had to be found. Furthermore, they needed a commitment from Jesus not to participate in treasonable activities against Rome in the future. But reliable witnesses to his innocence were not to be found, and Jesus insisted on continuing to proclaim the teaching that Rome found seditious, and for which he was convicted and crucified. Thus, according to Cohn, Jesus was executed in spite of the efforts of the high priest and Sanhedrin to save him. Jesus had refused to cooperate and to bow to their authority, and nothing could be done to prevent a Roman trial from taking its course.

S. G. F. Brandon takes a different approach to the accounts of the arrest and trial. He claims Jesus was a nationalist patriot and either a member of, or a sympathizer with, the Zealots. His message reflected these concerns and, according to Brandon, Jesus' nationalistic concerns were well understood by both the Jews and Romans. As one espousing the cause of Israel's freedom from the yoke of heathen Rome, Jesus had many sympathizers and followers among the Jewish populace. But Jesus was obviously a threat to Rome and to those Jewish leaders who had compromised themselves with Rome. Jesus' appearances before the Sanhedrin were inquiries resulting in charges of sedition against Rome. The cooperation of Jewish leaders with Pilate led to Jesus' crucifixion as a rebel against the Roman government.

Obviously this is not how events are portrayed in the gospels. Nevertheless, following the assumptions and methodology of Source, Form, and Redaction Criticism, Brandon argues that the purpose of the gospels, of which the accounts of the arrest and trial are an integral part, was not to provide an objective, historical account of the career of Jesus. Instead, he claims, the evangelists consciously altered the facts to suit their apologetic purpose. The earliest Jewish followers of Jesus had not been troubled by the circumstances of Jesus' death. Indeed, in the tradition they developed they emphasized the Roman cross, for it enhanced the reputation of Jesus as the martyred Messiah of Israel.

According to Brandon the situation was different for later Gentile followers of Jesus. The Jewish revolt against Rome in A.D. 66, the initial atrocities against Gentiles, and the four years of bitter warfare that followed had inflamed an already existing anti-Semitism and had caused Jewish Messianism to be seen as a subversive force. The fact that Jesus had been executed by Pontius Pilate for sedition had become both embarrassing and a potential source of danger for Gentile followers of Jesus. The gospel accounts supposedly reflect this Gentile concern to shift the blame for Jesus' execution from Pilate to the Jews. Thus Mark, writing for Christians in Rome shortly after Flavian's triumph over rebel Judea in A.D. 71, initiated a different version of the trial of Jesus. Although not denying that Jesus had been put to death as a rebel against Rome, he tried to modify the tradition. Mark, Brandon asserts, presented Jesus as endorsing Jewish obligation to pay tribute to Rome, and he showed the Jewish leaders as condemning Jesus for blasphemy and then forcing Pilate to crucify him. This set the pattern, drawn upon and elaborated on by the later evangelists, of representing the Roman trial as a contest between Pilate, who was now represented as recognizing the innocence of Jesus and seeking to save him, and the Jews, who were intent upon his destruction.

Thus Mark's account of the arrest and trial is an apologetic, not history. Mark's record explained the scandal of a Roman cross; it showed the Jews to be criminally responsible; and it assured the Roman government that Christianity was not subversive. The later gospel writers, Brandon said, accepted this apologetic and further developed in their own ways the picture of the pacific Christ. Their common purpose was to make Pilate a witness to Jesus' innocence and the Jews solely responsible for his death. The fact that their purpose was apologetic rather than historical explains why the four accounts are (according to Brandon) full of contradictions, elusiveness, and absurdities.

Brandon's assessment of the gospels as biased and apologetic and the implications of this for the arrest and trial of Jesus are similar to the view of Paul Winter. He shares the opinion that Jesus was arrested, convicted, and executed as an insurrectionist against Rome, and that beginning with Mark the gospel writers were embarrassed by this fact. Because of this, the evangelists, writing in the post-A.D. 70 period, portray Pilate as convinced of Jesus' innocence and unwilling to pass the death sentence. They do this to ingratiate Christians with the Romans and to avoid persecution for Christians as subversives. But Winter is not convinced it can be shown that Jesus was closely aligned with the Zealots, or that the charge of insurrection was justified. The charge may have been concocted by his enemies, Jewish or Roman, but that would not necessarily indicate his own intentions. Winter feels it is impossible to make trustworthy, historical deductions from the gospels about Jesus' conflicts with other Jews before his last visit to Jerusalem.

Winter does argue, however, that Jesus stood close to Phariseeism, indeed, that he was a Pharisee, and that his teaching was Pharisaic in ethics and eschatology. He recognizes that Jesus probably had altercations with (other) Pharisees, but whatever quarrels he may have had with any Jewish individual or group prior to his last visit to Jerusalem had no determining influence on his fate. It was not the content of his teaching that led to his arrest and conviction; it was the effect his teaching had on certain sections of the populace that induced the authorities to take action against him. This would have been sufficient reason for Pilate to order his execution.

In widely read books and articles, Hugh Schonfield has popularized still another view that assumes the gospel accounts to be historically unreliable. He contends that from before his baptism by John, Jesus had carefully mapped out a program of events that would have to be fulfilled if he were to successfully carry out what he regarded as his Messianic task. This meant not only that he would have to do and say certain things necessary to the plan, but he would have to contrive situations in such a way as to produce certain reactions on the part of others. It was a conspiracy, a plot, that would produce a contrived fulfillment of the Scriptures. Moves and situations would have to be engineered so that others involved would perform their functions without their realizing they were being used. The road that Jesus mapped out was to culminate in the events of Passion Week. The arrest, trial, conviction, and crucifixion were the torturous conclusion of the contrived scenario.

If nothing else, one thing emerges from this survey of contemporary reinterpretations of the arrest and trial of Jesus. When one gives up on the historical reliability of the accounts, he or she cannot be assured of being any nearer the truth. Although he has no confidence in the trustworthiness of the gospels, Professor Samuel Sandmel is at least more consistent and realistic when he confesses that he does not know what happened historically, and that he sees no possibility of reconstructing a factual account of what really happened at the arrest and trial. Such would seem to be the inevitable conclusion if one surrenders the only accounts we have of the events to the whims of the reinterpreters.

But a significant segment of recent New Testament and historical scholarship has argued for at least the essential trustworthiness of the gospel accounts of the arrest and trial. Among these may be counted C. H. Dodd, A. N. Sherwin-White, Everett F. Harrison, and Josef Blinzler. Blinzler's work towers over that of all others. For the most part Blinzler accepts the essential historicity of the gospel accounts and the consequent traditional Christian understanding of the events as summarized in the opening part of this essay.

Many issues are raised by the radical reinterpretations of the arrest and trial. The most fundamental is that of the reliability of the gospel record. It is beyond the scope of this essay to argue the case for historical trustworthiness. But it should be noted that radical reinterpretations of the type previously mentioned proceed on the assumption of untrustworthiness. Evidence to give credibility to this assumption is either absent or of the most flimsy and subjective nature. The supposition argues from silence, assumes that the gospels are contradictory rather than allowing that they might be complementary, or is based on a prior assumption that the gospels cannot be accepted as credible by their own testimony and evidence because they are fundamentally apologetic pieces. The assumptions that are behind the allegedly objective methodology of the radical critics are themselves tendentious. For this reason it is difficult to find a common ground with them. The reliability of the evangelists' statements is dismissed when they do not happen to fit the critics' theories. Nevertheless, some of the more important issues should be mentioned.

Was Jesus really a Pharisee, as Winter argues? It must be granted that Jesus was often the guest of Pharisees, and that they held some things in common. The gospels, however, show the relationship, at least with the more legalistic branch of the Pharisees, to be fundamentally negative. There were many conflicts between Jesus and Pharisees. Jesus spoke against their understanding of Sabbath laws, external defilement, fastings, and divorce. Their hypocritical self-righteousness was the object of his most scorching denunciations.

Was Jesus closely aligned with the Zealot, as Brandon contends? A Zealot would never have advocated paying the taxes due the Roman emperor or loving one's enemies. A Zealot's message and concern were political; Jesus' was religious. To him membership in the kingdom depended on meeting moral and spiritual prerequisites.

One can make Jesus a Pharisee or a Zealot only by totally dismissing the portrayal of him in the gospels.

John's statement (18:3) that a detachment or cohort of Roman soldiers participated in the arrest is frequently said to be a fabrication. That Roman soldiers would participate in an arrest that involved Jewish concerns is considered inconceivable. But that they would be present to keep the peace at the request of Jewish authorities does not stretch the imagination. Again, a cohort at full strength consisted of six hundred men. Because it does seem strange that six hundred soldiers should be required for this mission in the middle of the night, some have taken this as another evidence of historical untrustworthiness. The term, however, can also be used of a detachment of two hundred men, which may well have been the situation.

One of the most serious claims is that there was no Sanhedrin trial. Grounds for this claim are various. It is pointed out that in the Jewish trial Jesus was convicted of blasphemy, which has no direct relation to the reason for conviction in the Roman trial, sedition. But there is no inconsistency in supposing that the Jews realized the difficulty of persuading Pilate to execute Jesus on religious gounds, so they assigned different charges when bringing him before Pilate. It is also pointed out that death by stoning was the usual Jewish method of execution. Crucifixion, however, does not becloud the credibility of a Jewish trial, for it is natural that an execution carried out by Roman soldiers would follow the Roman method, even if the original instigator were the Sanhedrin.

The most serious charge is that the Sanhedrin trial could not have taken place because it was so manifestly illegal. Instead the Sanhedrin trial is argued to be the creation of early Christians, primarily Mark, in order to try to shift the blame for a Roman crucifixion from Pilate to the Jews. Thus Christianity hoped to avoid the onus that its founder was an insurrectionist.

The Mishnah, in the Sanhedrin tractate, gives the procedures for the conduct of a trial in capital cases. It is true that the Sanhedrin trial, as recorded in the gospels, is in violation of these provisions at a number of crucial points. But that this indicates no such trial ever occurred does not follow. Possibly the Jewish leaders were so obsessed with quickly disposing of Jesus before the Sabbath and Passover Week that they knowingly violated their own procedures. This has been the traditional Christian explanation. More likely, however, the provisions of the Sanhedrin tractate were not operative in Jesus' time. The Mishnah was a collection of orally transmitted laws drawn up toward the close of the second century. By this time the ruling Sanhedrin, as it had existed historically, had ceased to exist and was only an academic institution having no authority. The regulations of the Sanhedrin tractate conflict with other Jewish sources closer to the first century, and its provisions are probably not a reflection of actual Sanhedrin procedures in the first third of the first century. Consequently it is probably wrong to accuse the Sanhedrin of illegal procedures, and definitely wrong to say such a trial could not have occurred.

Another focus for debate has been the statement attributed to the Jews in John 18:31, "We have no right to execute anyone." Critics assert that the Jews did have this authority and that this alleged statement was another device created to try to shift the blame for Jesus' execution from Pilate to the Jews. Everett F. Harrison, though, shows that, of the arguments given to establish that the Jews had general authority to execute, none is convincing. Alleged evidences were either exceptional cases or illegal acts.

A. N. Sherwin-White, renowned historian of Roman law, convincingly argues for the credibility of John 18:31. It was not Roman practice to grant the authority of capital punishment to local officials. Otherwise, anti-Roman groups might be able to eliminate pro-Roman groups by judicial action. Sherwin-White confidently asserts that turbulent Judea is the last place where one would expect such an extraordinary concession. Indeed, on the basis of his knowledge of Roman law and practice, he is willing to grant credibility not only to John 18:31 but to the basic gospel portrayal of events, moving from the Sanhedrin trial to the conviction for blasphemy to the alternative charge of sedition before Pilate.

Selected Reading List

Bammel, Ernst, ed. The Trial of Jesus: Cambridge Studies in Honour of C. F. D. Moule. Naperville, IL: Allenson, 1970.

Blinzler, Josef. The Trial of Jesus. Westminster, MD: Newman, 1959.

Brandon, S. G. F. The Trial of Jesus of Nazareth. New York: Stein and Day, 1968.

Catchpole, David R. The Trial of Jesus: A Study in the Gospels and Jewish Historiography from 1770 to the Present Day. Leiden, Netherlands: Brill, 1971.

Chandler, Walter M. The Trial of Jesus From a Lawyer's Standpoint. 2 vols. New York: Empire, 1908.

Danby, H. "The Bearing of the Rabbinical Criminal Code on the Jewish Trial Narratives in the Gospels," The Journal of Theological Studies 21 (1919): 51–76.

Dodd, C. H. More New Testament Studies. Manchester, England: Manchester University Press, 1968. Pp. 84–101.

Harrison, Everett F. A Short Life of Christ. Grand Rapids: Eerdmans, 1968. Pp. 198–216.

Maier, Paul L. Pontius Pilate. Wheaton, IL: Tyndale, 1970.

Merritt, Robert L. "Jesus, Barabbas and the Pascal Pardon," Journal of Biblical Literature 104 (March 1985): 57–68.

Montgomery, J. W. "Jesus Takes the Stand: An Argument to Support the Gospel Accounts," Christianity Today 26 (April 9, 1982): 26–27.

Overstreet, R. Larry. "Roman Law and the Trial of Christ," Bibliotheca Sacra 135 (1978): 323–32.

Rensberger, David. "The Politics of John: The Trial of Jesus in the Fourth Gospel (John 18)," Journal of Biblical Literature 103 (September 1984): 395–411.

Schonfield, Hugh J. The Passover Plot: New Light on the History of Jesus. New York: Random House, 1965. Pp. 45–47, 127–57.

Sherwin-White, A. N. *Roman Society and Roman Law in the New Testament*. Oxford: Oxford University Press, 1963. Pp. 24–47.

"The Trial of Jesus in the Light of History," *Judaism* 20 (1971): 6–74. This is a very helpful symposium of articles authored by Haim Cohn, Morton S. Enslin, David Flusser, Robert M. Grant, S. G. F. Brandon, Josef Blinzler, Gerard S. Sloyan, and Samuel Sandmel.

Winter, Paul. *On the Trial of Jesus*. Berlin: De Gruyter, 1961.

_____."The Trial of Jesus," *Commentary* (September 1964): 35–41.

TABLE OF SECTION CROSS-REFERENCES
(WITH POINT OF SIMILARITY)

Sec. No.	Cross-Referenced Sections and Point of Similarity
4	5, 9—foretelling a miraculous birth
5	4, 9—foretelling a miraculous birth
6	7, 8b, 13—song because of a miraculous birth
7	6, 8b, 13—song because of a miraculous birth
8b	6, 7, 13—song because of a miraculous birth
9	4, 5—foretelling a miraculous birth
13	6, 7, 8b—song because of a miraculous birth
21	26—a voice in the desert
23	26—preparatory nature of John's ministry
24	27—Spirit's descent on Jesus
	85—identification of the Son by the Father
26	21—a voice in the desert
	23—preparatory nature of John's ministry
27	24—Spirit's descent on Jesus
28	41, 47a—calling disciples
31	129b—cleansing the temple
34	71b—John's imprisonment
36	37, 39, 69—no honor at home
37	36, 39, 69—no honor at home
38	55—healing at a distance
39	36, 37, 69—no honor at home
41	28, 47a—calling disciples
47a	28, 41—calling disciples
49a–51	100c, 110, 114—Sabbath controversies
53	70b, Acts 1:13—twelve apostles listed
54c	64b, 106—lighting a lamp
	91, 115—salt of the earth
54d	117b—permanence of the Law
54e	91—loss of hand or eye
	108e—reconciliation
	117b, 122—divorce and remarriage
	137a—taking an oath
54f	105—the disciple's prayer
	121—unhypocritical prayer
	131—forgiveness of others and forgiveness by God
54g	64b—measuring out
	64b, 108b—anxieties of life
	70b, 145, 150b—followers not above the leader
	106—lamp of the body
	108a—value of birds
	108b—danger of riches
	117a—impossibility of being a slave to two masters
54h	61—recognition by fruit
	105—ask, seek, knock
	113a—narrow entrance
55	38—healing at a distance
58	102a—woes to cities

TABLES FOR FINDING PASSAGES IN THE *HARMONY*

MATTHEW

Chapter	Verse	Section	Page	Chapter	Verse	Section	Page
1	1–17	3	30	13	54–58	69	97
1	18–25	9	36	14	1–2	71a	100
2	1–12	14	38	14	3–12	71b	101
2	13–18	15	39	14	13–14	72b	103
2	19–23	16	39	14	15–21	72c	104
3	1–6	21	42	14	22–23	73	106
3	7–10	22	43	14	24–33	74	106
3	11–12	23	44	14	34–36	75	107
3	13–17	24	45	15	1–20	77	109
4	1–11	25	46	15	21–28	78	112
4	12	34	52	15	29–31	79a	113
4	13–16	40	56	15	32–38	79b	113
4	17	37	55	15	39–16:4	80	114
4	18–22	41	57	16	5–12	81a	115
4	23–25	44	60	16	13–20	82	116
5	1–2	54a	70	16	21–26	83	117
5	3–12	54b	71	16	27–28	84	118
5	13–16	54c	72	17	1–8	85	119
5	17–20	54d	72	17	9–13	86	120
5	21–48	54e	73	17	14–20	87	121
6	1–18	54f	74	17	22–23	88	122
6	19–7:6	54g	75	17	24–27	89	123
7	7–27	54h	76	18	1–5	90	123
7	28–28:1	54i	78	18	6–14	91	124
8	2–4	45	61	18	15–35	92	126
8	5–13	55	78	19	1–12	122	160
8	14–17	43	59	19	13–15	123	161
8	18	65	91	19	16–30	124a	161
8	19–22	93	127	20	1–16	124b	163
8	23–27	65	91	20	17–19	125a	164
8	28–34	66	92	20	20–28	125b	165
9	1–8	46	62	20	29–34	126	165
9	9	47a	63	21	1–11	128b	169
9	10–13	47b	63	21	12–13	129b	173
9	14–17	48	64	21	14–17	128b	169
9	18–26	67	94	21	18–19a	129a	173
9	27–34	68	96	21	19b–22	131	175
9	35–38	70a	97	21	23–27	132a	176
10	1–42	70b	98	21	28–22:14	132b	177
11	1	70c	100	22	15–22	133	180
11	2–19	57	79	22	23–33	134	181
11	20–30	58	81	22	34–40	135	182
12	1–8	50	67	22	41–46	136	183
12	9–14	51	68	23	1–36	137a	184
12	15–21	52	69	23	37–39	137b	185
12	22–37	61	83	24	1–3	139a	187
12	38–45	62	84	24	4–14	139b	187
12	46–50	63	85	24	15–28	139c	189
13	1–3a	64a	85	24	29–31	139d	190
13	3b–23	64b	86	24	32–41	139e	191
13	24–30	64d	88	24	42–25:30	139f	192
13	31–32	64e	89	25	31–46	139g	194
13	33–35	64f	89	26	1–5	140	195
13	36–43	64g	90	26	6–13	141	195
13	44	64h	90	26	14–16	142	196
13	45–46	64i	90	26	17–19	143	197
13	47–50	64j	90	26	20	144	198
13	51–53	64k	91	26	21–25	146	199

334

THE LIFE OF CHRIST

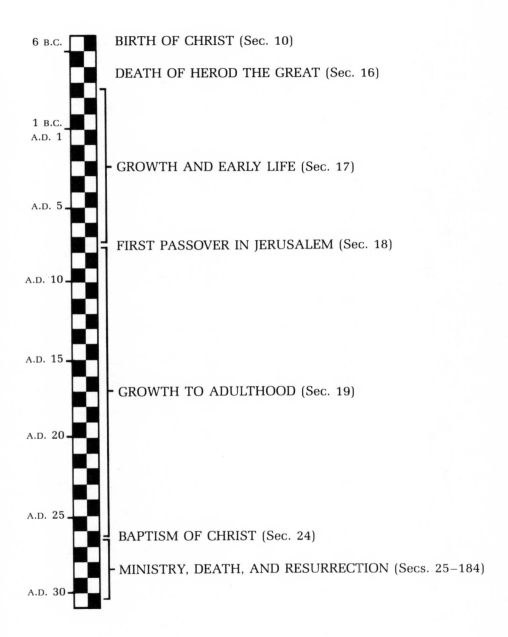

6 B.C. — BIRTH OF CHRIST (Sec. 10)

DEATH OF HEROD THE GREAT (Sec. 16)

1 B.C.
A.D. 1

GROWTH AND EARLY LIFE (Sec. 17)

A.D. 5

FIRST PASSOVER IN JERUSALEM (Sec. 18)

A.D. 10

A.D. 15

GROWTH TO ADULTHOOD (Sec. 19)

A.D. 20

A.D. 25

BAPTISM OF CHRIST (Sec. 24)

MINISTRY, DEATH, AND RESURRECTION (Secs. 25–184)

A.D. 30

THE MINISTRY OF CHRIST

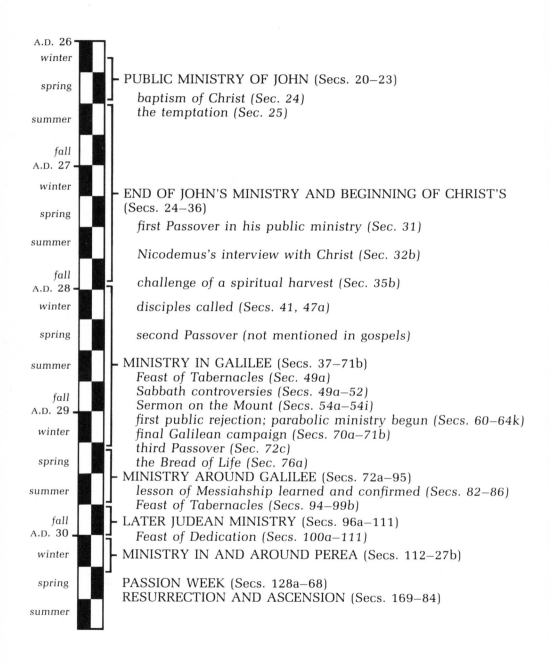

A.D. 26
winter

spring
PUBLIC MINISTRY OF JOHN (Secs. 20–23)
  baptism of Christ (Sec. 24)

summer
  the temptation (Sec. 25)

fall
A.D. 27

winter
END OF JOHN'S MINISTRY AND BEGINNING OF CHRIST'S
spring
(Secs. 24–36)
  first Passover in his public ministry (Sec. 31)

summer
  Nicodemus's interview with Christ (Sec. 32b)

fall
A.D. 28
  challenge of a spiritual harvest (Sec. 35b)

winter
  disciples called (Secs. 41, 47a)

spring
  second Passover (not mentioned in gospels)

summer
MINISTRY IN GALILEE (Secs. 37–71b)
  Feast of Tabernacles (Sec. 49a)
fall
  Sabbath controversies (Secs. 49a–52)
A.D. 29
  Sermon on the Mount (Secs. 54a–54i)
  first public rejection; parabolic ministry begun (Secs. 60–64k)
winter
  final Galilean campaign (Secs. 70a–71b)
  third Passover (Sec. 72c)
spring
  the Bread of Life (Sec. 76a)
MINISTRY AROUND GALILEE (Secs. 72a–95)
summer
  lesson of Messiahship learned and confirmed (Secs. 82–86)
  Feast of Tabernacles (Secs. 94–99b)
fall
LATER JUDEAN MINISTRY (Secs. 96a–111)
A.D. 30
  Feast of Dedication (Secs. 100a–111)
winter
MINISTRY IN AND AROUND PEREA (Secs. 112–27b)

spring
PASSION WEEK (Secs. 128a–68)
RESURRECTION AND ASCENSION (Secs. 169–84)
summer

PASSION WEEK

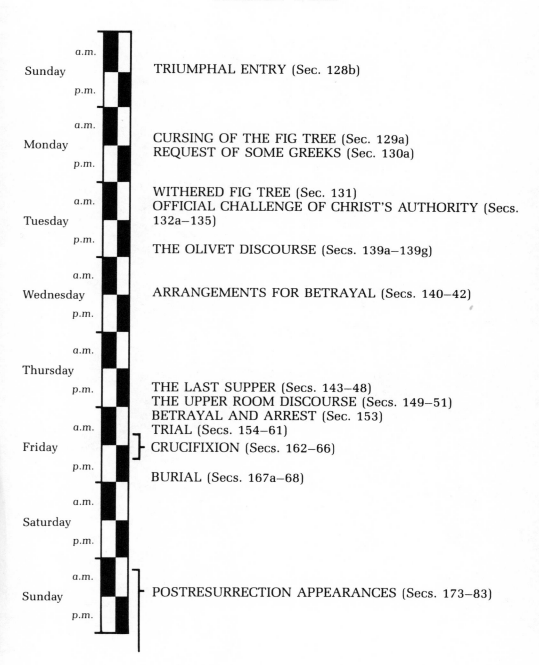

Sunday — TRIUMPHAL ENTRY (Sec. 128b)

Monday — CURSING OF THE FIG TREE (Sec. 129a)
REQUEST OF SOME GREEKS (Sec. 130a)

Tuesday — WITHERED FIG TREE (Sec. 131)
OFFICIAL CHALLENGE OF CHRIST'S AUTHORITY (Secs. 132a–135)
THE OLIVET DISCOURSE (Secs. 139a–139g)

Wednesday — ARRANGEMENTS FOR BETRAYAL (Secs. 140–42)

Thursday — THE LAST SUPPER (Secs. 143–48)
THE UPPER ROOM DISCOURSE (Secs. 149–51)
BETRAYAL AND ARREST (Sec. 153)

Friday — TRIAL (Secs. 154–61)
CRUCIFIXION (Secs. 162–66)
BURIAL (Secs. 167a–68)

Saturday

Sunday — POSTRESURRECTION APPEARANCES (Secs. 173–83)

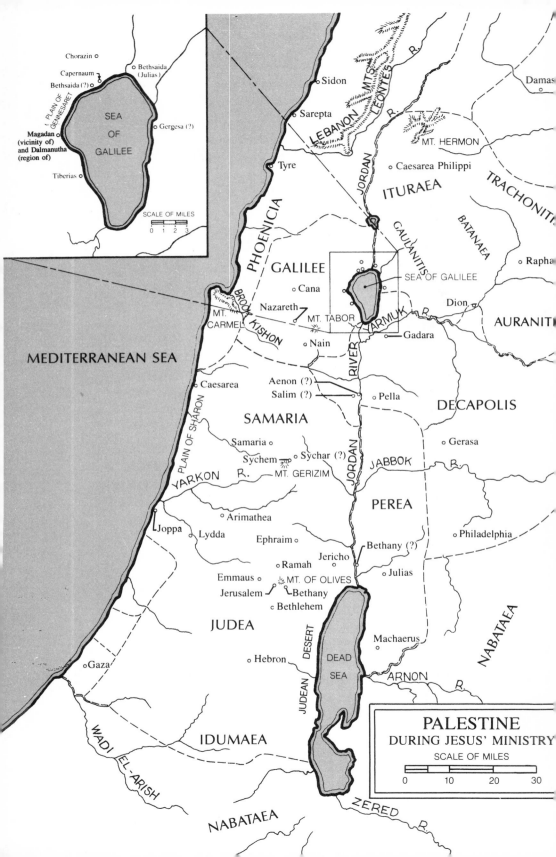

Chorazin

Capernaum
Bethsaida (?)

PLAIN OF GENNESARET

SEA
OF
GALILEE

Magadan
(vicinity of)
and Dalmanutha
(region of)

Tiberias

Bethsaida
(Julias)

Gergesa (?)

SCALE OF MILES
0 1 2 3

Sidon

Sarepta

LEBANON

MTS. LEONTES R.

MT. HERMON

Damas

Tyre

PHOENICIA

GALILEE

Cana

Nazareth

MT. TABOR

Nain

MT. CARMEL

BROOK KISHON

MEDITERRANEAN SEA

Caesarea

PLAIN OF SHARON

YARKON R.

JORDAN R.

GAULANITIS

Caesarea Philippi

ITURAEA

SEA OF GALILEE

RIVER YARMUK R.

Gadara

BATANAEA

Rapha

TRACHONITI

Dion

AURANITI

DECAPOLIS

Aenon (?)

Salim (?)

Pella

SAMARIA

Samaria

Sychem

Sychar (?)

MT. GERIZIM

Gerasa

JABBOK R.

PEREA

Arimathea

Joppa

Lydda

Ephraim

Emmaus

Jerusalem

Ramah

Jericho

MT. OF OLIVES

Bethany

Bethlehem

JUDEA

Philadelphia

Bethany (?)

Julias

JUDEAN DESERT

DEAD
SEA

Machaerus

Hebron

Gaza

ARNON R.

NABATAEA

WADI EL-ARISH

IDUMAEA

ZERED R.

NABATAEA

PALESTINE
DURING JESUS' MINISTRY

SCALE OF MILES

0   10   20   30

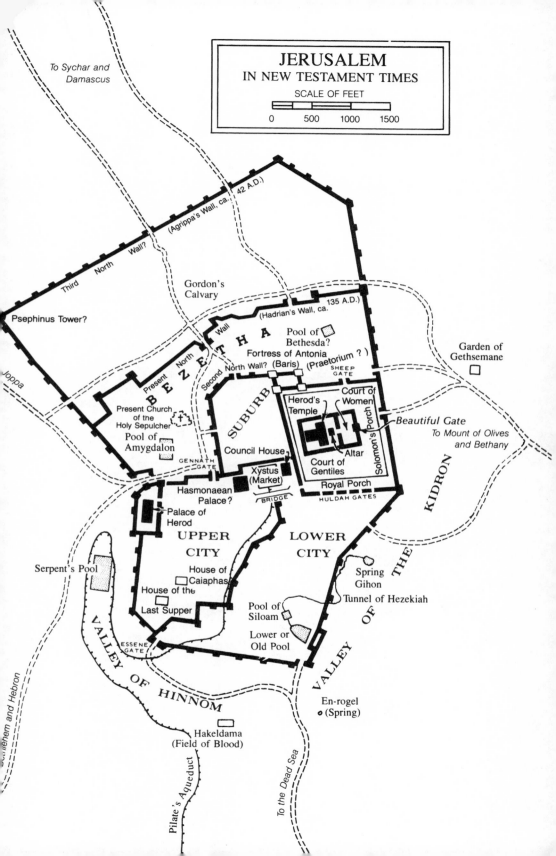

JERUSALEM
IN NEW TESTAMENT TIMES
SCALE OF FEET

0   500   1000   1500

To Sychar and
Damascus

(Agrippa's Wall, ca. 42 A.D.)

North Wall?

Third   North   Wall

Gordon's
Calvary

Psephinus Tower?

Joppa

(Hadrian's Wall, ca. 135 A.D.)

B E Z E T H A

Pool of
Bethesda?

Fortress of Antonia

North Wall? (Baris)   (Praetorium ?)

Present   North

Present Church
of the
Holy Sepulcher

SUBURB

Second   Wall

SHEEP
GATE

Garden of
Gethsemane

Herod's
Temple

Court of
Women

Beautiful Gate

To Mount of Olives
and Bethany

Pool of
Amygdalon

GENNATH
GATE

Council House

Xystus
(Market)

BRIDGE

Court of
Gentiles

Altar

Royal Porch

Solomon's Porch

HULDAH GATES

K I D R O N

V A L L E Y   O F   T H E

Hasmonaean
Palace?

Palace of
Herod

Serpent's Pool

UPPER
CITY

LOWER
CITY

House of
Caiaphas

House of the
Last Supper

ESSENE
GATE

Spring
Gihon

Tunnel of Hezekiah

Pool of
Siloam

Lower or
Old Pool

En-rogel
o (Spring)

V A L L E Y   O F   H I N N O M

To Bethlehem and Hebron

Hakeldama
(Field of Blood)

Pilate's Aqueduct

To the Dead Sea